T0314197

BANKING ON GROWTH MODELS

A volume in the series
Cornell Studies in Money
Edited by Eric Helleiner and Jonathan Kirshner

A list of titles in this series is available at
cornellpress.cornell.edu.

BANKING ON GROWTH MODELS

China's Troubled Pursuit of Financial Reform and Economic Rebalancing

Stephen Bell and Hui Feng

CORNELL UNIVERSITY PRESS   ITHACA AND LONDON

First published 2022 by Cornell University Press

Library of Congress Cataloging-in-Publication Data

Names: Bell, Stephen, 1954– author. | Feng, Hui, 1972– author.
Title: Banking on growth models : China's troubled pursuit of financial reform and economic rebalancing / Stephen Bell and Hui Feng.
Description: Ithaca [New York] : Cornell University Press, 2022. | Series: Cornell studies in money | Includes bibliographical references and index.
Identifiers: LCCN 2021034154 (print) | LCCN 2021034155 (ebook) | ISBN 9781501762529 (hardcover) | ISBN 9781501762536 (pdf) | ISBN 9781501762543 (epub)
Subjects: LCSH: Finance—China. | Finance—Government policy—China. | China—Economic policy—1976–2000. | Banks and banking—China. | Financial institutions—China. | China—Economic policy—2000–
Classification: LCC HG187.C6 B44 2022 (print) | LCC HG187.C6 (ebook) | DDC 332.0951—dc23
LC record available at https://lccn.loc.gov/2021034154
LC ebook record available at https://lccn.loc.gov/2021034155

Stephen Bell would like to dedicate this book to his new grandson, Leo,

and Hui Feng to his dear family, Qian and Ellie

Contents

Figures

Acknowledgments

This book follows our previous study on central banking in China, which examined the profound implications of China's transition to a more market-based economy in the context of an authoritarian state and the governance of its financial system (Bell and Feng 2013). Here, we extend the transition story to a much broader picture, exploring the mutual shaping mechanisms between China's financial system and its economic transition and how these have shaped the path of economic rebalancing.

This book builds on the work of a wide range of scholars of politics and political economy, and on our own theoretical and comparative work over the years. It also benefits from firsthand interview material and from contributions by a range of officials and practitioners in China and beyond, who graciously offered their time and views. Some of these matters are sensitive to the authorities and most of the interviewees requested anonymity, which we have honored. Many of the officials were willing to assist us in the hope that their contribution to this research could help the outside world to better understand the various ideas, debates, dilemmas, and challenges confronting the Chinese authorities. We hope that this book can live up to such expectations. We are also greatly indebted to those who have helped us arrange and coordinate the interviews.

Over the years we have benefited from discussions with colleagues at the University of Queensland (UQ) and Griffith University. Parts of the book's findings have been presented at a number of conferences and workshops. These include the Australian International Political Economy Network workshop at UQ in 2015, the workshop on shadow banking and alternative finance in China at the University of Sydney in 2016, and the workshop on institutions, governance, and economic performance in East Asia at the University of Auckland in 2017. The participants' comments and suggestions regarding our work have been helpful. Our special thanks also go to Michael Keating, who read and commented on earlier drafts of the manuscript. His critical reading and constructive suggestions are most appreciated. Two anonymous readers of the manuscript and the series editors at Cornell University Press (CUP) also provided valuable perspectives and comments that have been incorporated in the book. Any remaining errors in the book, however, are our own.

Chapter 7 of this book is derived in part from an article in the *Review of International Political Economy* 28 (1), 2021, copyright Taylor & Francis, available online at https://www.tandfonline.com/doi/full/10.1080/09692290.2019.1655083.

We would also like to thank Roger Haydon and Emily Andrew from CUP for their efforts in reviewing our manuscript and moving it forward during the trying time of the COVID-19 pandemic.

We should also like to thank the Australian Research Council for funding the bulk of the research on this book over the years. As usual, the School of Political Science and International Studies at UQ, the Griffith Asia Institute, and the Centre for Governance and Public Policy of Griffith University have provided an ideal base for our research activities. Michael Vaughan's meticulous assistance has also been indispensable.

Abbreviations

ABC	Agricultural Bank of China
AFC	Asian financial crisis
AMC	asset management company
BAT	Baidu, Alibaba, and Tencent
BOC	Bank of China
BOCOM	Bank of Communications
CBIRC	China Banking and Insurance Regulatory Commission
CBRC	China Banking Regulatory Commission
CCB	China Construction Bank
CCP	Chinese Communist Party
CD	certificate of deposit
CFWC	Central Finance Work Commission
CIC	China Investment Corporation
CIRC	China Insurance Regulatory Commission
CITIC	China International Trust Investment Corporation
CSRC	China Securities Regulatory Commission
FSDC	Financial Stability and Development Committee
GFC	global financial crisis
ICBC	Industrial and Commercial Bank of China
IMF	International Monetary Fund
IPO	initial public offering
LGB	local government bond
LGFV	local government financing vehicle
MOF	Ministry of Finance
NBFI	nonbank financial institution
NDRC	National Development and Reform Commission
NPL	nonperforming loan
PBC	People's Bank of China
PCBC	People's Construction Bank of China
P2P	peer-to-peer
RMB	renminbi
ROA	return on assets
ROE	return on equity
SAFE	State Administration of Foreign Exchange

SASAC	State Assets Supervision and Administration Commission
SME	small and medium-sized enterprise
SOB	state-owned bank
SOE	state-owned enterprise
TBR	trust beneficiary right
WMP	wealth management product
WTO	World Trade Organization

BANKING ON GROWTH MODELS

INTRODUCTION

Since China's economic reform and opening in 1979, a perplexing issue has been the achievement of rapid economic growth on the back of an often dysfunctional and increasingly fragile banking and financial system. This has led to recurrent prophecies of a potential banking or financial crisis in China, framed under a more general debt crisis amid an economy that is slowing and running into diminishing returns. Credit and finance act as the gasoline that helps drive consumption and investment processes, the engine room of the economy. In this book we examine the mutually shaping interactions between China's financial and banking system, on the one hand, and its economy and its prospects on the other, especially in terms of China's competing economic growth models and key questions about China's economic "rebalancing." The outcomes here are important, both for China's future and for the world economy.

There have been many studies of China's economic development and its banking and financial sector reforms since the late 1970s. Yet there have been no studies that have linked financial sector issues systematically to China's growth model dynamics and economic imbalances. This is what is new about this book.

Besides telling us much about the fate and direction of the Chinese economy and its financial system, a further payoff from our particular focus is that it provides key insights into two of the major issues in China's political economy. The first concerns the main political battle going on in contemporary China—namely, that between the contending liberal and conservative factions within the Chinese Communist Party (CCP) over the direction of the economy and the nature of the

Chinese state. The key battle is over what type of credit and banking system will drive what type of growth model. The second major issue is the extent to which market forces can or will be allowed to reshape Chinese political economy, or whether market forces will remain subject to tight and perhaps increasing control by the Chinese state.

Liberal factions within the leadership and wider Chinese state have favored a greater role for managed markets and a reduced role for the state in driving Chinese economic growth. This faction has been very influential in economic policymaking since the reform and opening up of the Chinese economy from the late 1970s. Liberal reform received a further, albeit indirect, boost in the wake of the global financial crisis (GFC) in 2008, when the Chinese economy was powered by a massive credit surge. This fostered the rapid growth of a more market-based shadow banking system that for a time challenged the main state-run banks and the prevailing state-led growth model.

At least up until 2015, this liberalizing change seemingly offered strong prospects of reforming and liberalizing the banking system and also of altering China's growth model in a more market-oriented and more rebalanced direction. The changes appeared to underline the gathering market momentum in the economy, further cementing the role of the private sector as the main engine of Chinese economic growth. Indeed, the growing private sector and higher levels of household credit and consumption promised a degree of much-needed economic rebalancing in China. However, from around 2015 these liberalizing changes elicited a powerful conservative counterreaction under the current Xi Jinping regime. Conservatives favor a state-directed banking system as a key vehicle for mobilizing and channeling national savings into state-based investment projects. The strength of the conservative counterreaction reminds us once again of the centrality of factional power and ideological struggles and of the centrality of the state in shaping China's future. The counterreaction has severely curtailed market-led reforms, curtailed the growth of shadow banking, constrained the private sector, and limited economic rebalancing. The financial system remains the servant of the prevailing statist growth model and those that benefit from it. The current situation thus reflects the power of the state over the market and the current power of conservative factions within the Chinese state. Thus far, the retardation of the private sector and domestic consumption, mounting debt, the accumulation of bad loans, inefficient investment, and faltering growth are the main outcomes of the continuance of the statist growth model.

As far back as 2007, in his famous "Four Uns" statement, Premier Wen Jiabao depicted China's economy as "unbalanced, unstable, uncoordinated, and unsustainable."[1] It is widely accepted, even by key elements within the Chinese leadership, that China's economy needs to be rebalanced. This means that the inefficient and increasingly debt-laden state sector of the economy needs to be rationalized and reformed to boost productivity and efficiency, and that seemingly endless debt-fueled investment going into the infrastructure sector needs to be curtailed. Instead, the market, the private sector, and the household consumption and services sectors need to further expand, largely because these sectors have proved to be far more dynamic and productive than the state sector (Naughton 1995; Lardy 2014).

However, the renewed statism under the current regime has frustrated liberal reformers and is posing major challenges to economic rebalancing and to the stability and growth of the Chinese economy. Fundamental reforms aimed at reducing savings and debt, together with recasting the financial system to better serve a revised growth model and economic rebalancing, are urgently needed.

China's Financial System and Growth Model Problems

There have been significant developments in China's financial system across various sectors, including banking, securities, and insurance. These developments also include China's financial opening to external investors in recent years in areas such as bonds and equity markets, albeit with ongoing efforts to maintain strong capital controls. In this book, however, we focus mainly on the banking and credit system, especially on the large state-owned banks and developments in shadow banking after the GFC. This key segment of the financial system is central to our account of the intermediation of China's high savings and of how these funds have been invested. This then leads to our analysis of the implications of such financial intermediation for China's economic structure and its prospects for growth model reform and economic rebalancing.

The Chinese financial system is contested and highly politicized, shaped primarily by competing interests within the CCP (Pei 1998; Shih 2008; Walter and Howie 2011). Some see China's high savings and its financial system as a means for the party to sustain corruption and special dealing in order to hold on to power, and as a key economic resource for the state (Walter and Howie 2011). Yet the politicization of finance and the leadership's existential quest for high growth as the basis for its political legitimacy have also seen a chronic accumulation of high debt levels in attempts to spur flagging growth (Pettis 2013; Magnus 2018; McMahon 2018).

Credit and financial intermediation are the lifeblood of the economy, supporting economic activity in key sectors. China's financial and banking system has long been linked to its state capitalist growth model, based partly on exports and overinvestment in the infrastructure sector, together with the inefficient and often loss-making state-owned enterprises (SOEs) that continue to dominate the commanding heights of the economy. China's "state-capitalist" growth model (Bremmer 2009; Aligica and Tarko 2012; *Economist* 2012) thus operates under a hierarchical system of state ownership and control. The state-owned banks (SOBs) that have long dominated the financial system have thus traditionally been embedded in a much wider system of state domination and control of the economy. Yet the system has also accommodated the rise of an alternative growth model based on markets and the private sector due to the latter's productivity.

The state controls important segments of the economy through its owner-ship of key sectors and through strategic planning and industrial policies using its administrative and regulatory bureaucracy. The state's huge SOEs in indus-try, infrastructure, energy, transport, communications, and other key sectors are central here. Of the 129 Chinese companies on the *Fortune* 500 list of the world's biggest firms in 2019, for example, more than 80 percent are state-owned (Zheng 2019).

China's main SOBs, especially the Big Four (the Industrial and Commercial Bank of China, the China Construction Bank, the Bank of China, and the Agri-cultural Bank of China), are the main players in the financial system and have long acted as a key fiscal agent within the state. These four SOBs are the largest banks in the world and dominate the bulk of China's bank balance sheets, now standing at 315 percent of GDP. This places China as having one of the largest banking sectors in the world, three times the emerging market average (IMF 2017, 19). Only France, the UK, and Japan have larger banking sectors compared to GDP. The Big Four banks occupy the top four places on the *Banker* (2020) magazine's list of the top one thousand global banks, as measured by Tier 1 capi-tal in 2020.

The state, as part of its growth strategy, has controlled the banking and finan-cial system, long employing administered interest rates, capital controls, and other measures that have constituted a system of "financial repression." This helps raise and mobilize savings, which are channeled into the main banks and the state sector. Bank profits have been boosted by this system, which has often administered fat interest rate margins to the banks. The banking system, in turn, shoulders the task of financing state-sector projects, especially the SOEs and local government infrastructure investment. Beijing allows the SOEs to oper-ate on "soft budgets," meaning that the SOEs lack financial discipline. The state requires the SOBs to fund the SOEs but does not necessarily force the latter to pay the money back, and instead steps in itself if needed, a game that simply moves money around the state system.[2] We argue that this system increases moral haz-ard.[3] And because of the inefficiencies and low returns on investment in the state sector, it also misallocates savings and capital on a grand scale at the expense of economic rebalancing and to the detriment of the economy.

Stuck between Two Growth Models

The system operates as follows. One side of China's financial system is driven by extraordinarily high national savings, which since 2003 have climbed to over 40 percent of GDP, peaking at over 50 percent in 2010. These savings have been generated by the household and corporate sectors in roughly equal measure. In the next chapter we explain the drivers and implications of these high savings, but of note here is that these savings patterns largely stem from the prevailing growth model and attendant political and sectoral income dynamics. China's savings of over twice the global average (of around 20 percent) need to be intermediated by the banking and financial system and then invested. The main state-owned banking system still dominates Chinese banking, but after the GFC, shadow banking grew rapidly,[4] at least until recently being reined in by the state. The main direction of lending has seen some offshore lending (especially sovereign credit to debtor countries like the United States and China-led development finance under the Belt and Road Initiative, as well as outward corporate investments), but primarily the big state banks have traditionally lent to the domestic state sector, which often displays low efficiency. This pattern was only reinforced by China's response to the GFC and the statist investment drive thereafter, and then reinforced again from 2012 by the new statism of the Xi regime. It is true that rapid economic development and the industrial and export drive from the 1990s required substantial investment at the expense of private consumption. But this has now continued for too long and is clearly running into diminishing returns. Rationalization and higher efficiency and productivity off a smaller investment base are now required. A further factor leading to inefficiency has been the scale of the credit and investment drive. At over twice the level of the global average of savings and investment, the challenge to funnel such high levels of investment productively was a huge one.

Nevertheless, some economic rebalancing has occurred, with a rising share of household income, more credit flows to the private sector and to households after the GFC, and a reduction of the external surplus. This was facilitated in part by the rising shadow banking system, although it is also true that the extra credit that helped increase household consumption also fueled a property boom. Approaches to encourage less household saving, such as increased income and welfare support, have also been pursued in recent years. Yet such measures have been incremental and have partly been offset by the fact that the investment levels of the government and corporate sectors remain compara-tively high, and that household debt level has been on a rapid rise. So, overall, some rebalancing has taken place, but this has been limited and more decisive moves are needed.

This juxtaposition of expanding statism and a degree of market liberalization underlines the fact that the Chinese economy is made up of two related systems: the state and the (managed) market. Lardy (2014) confidently argued that mar-kets and the private sector were successfully challenging the statist economic system, largely by outperforming it. For a time, much the same appeared to be happening in the banking and financial system as access to credit was relaxed and as markets and shadow banks offered more attractive options and put competi-tive pressure on the main state-owned banks.

Wright and Rosen (2018) argue that the changes just described have been pro-found in Chinese banking and credit. They contend that the initial credit stimu-lus after the GFC could have been wound back after several years but instead was continued at fever pitch thereafter as part of a new debt-fueled growth model, which has led to a "shift in the fundamentals of the financial system" (17). According to this account, this is marked by (1) the growth of shadow bank-ing and greater financial liberalization, (2) an increasing reliance on rising asset prices (especially property) as a source of rising incomes and wealth, and (3) the use of state support and guarantees for any troubles arising in financial markets, such as the government's salvation of the stock market crash in 2015–16, thus helping to perpetuate the credit boom and thus inducing a sharp rise in moral hazard.

China's high savings and the changes just noted have seen China encum-bered with extremely high debt levels. Indeed, Beijing's credit-fueled stimulus in response to the GFC, and the continued growth of credit thereafter, saw formal- and shadow-banking-sector assets grow from around $10 trillion just prior to the GFC to nearly $25 trillion by 2013. This added new financial assets equiva-lent to the entire US banking system (Anderlini 2014b). Since then, assets in the formal and shadow banking sectors have continued to expand rapidly. By the end of 2020, China's total banking assets stood at a whopping $49.5 trillion, roughly a fivefold increase since 2008 (*China Daily* 2021).[5] This figure is about the same value as US (20.6 trillion), Japanese (13.7 trillion), French (8.3 tril-lion), and British (7.2 trillion) banking assets combined. China's banking assets reached 315 percent of GDP by the end of 2020. This phenomenal growth tra-jectory in banking and credit is unmatched in global history. About two-thirds of the expansion of banking assets has come from traditional sources of credit, while about a third of the increase has come from the growth of shadow bank-ing. In more mature and more balanced economies, household incomes are used largely for consumption, but in China a high proportion of incomes are saved and channeled into the financial system, thus explaining China's outsized financial and banking system.

We agree with Wright and Rosen (2018) that the system has seen some significant changes. However, we do not agree that the growth of shadow banking and greater financial liberalization have altered the "fundamentals" of the system. True, for a time it looked as though the liberalizing tendencies in Chinese banking and finance might have developed a self-sustaining and increasingly market-based, path-dependent trajectory and that the genie had been let out of the bottle, so to speak. However, as we show, the rise of the Xi Jinping regime has seen a growing statist counterreaction that has reined in the earlier market push in banking and finance. The stock market meltdown in 2015–16, in which a third of the value of the Shanghai Stock Exchange was lost within one month, further reinforced this reaction against market liberalization and raised fears about financial stability. Both changes have helped curtail the key liberalizing changes and have seen a reassertion of state financial controls. Both the scale and growth of the shadow banking sector have been reined in through more comprehensive and aggressive regulation since around 2015, which has curtailed the earlier growth of credit to the private and market sectors. We agree with Wright and Rosen (2018) that there has been increasing reliance on rising asset prices to fuel a larger proportion of growth in wealth and incomes, as well as the use of state financial guarantees, and that both pose worrying trends and threaten stability. Nevertheless, we argue that the overall statist foundations of the financial system have persisted, suggesting that the system has not changed fundamentally.

As a result, China remains stuck between two faltering growth models. Current attempts by the Xi regime to rejuvenate the inefficient statist growth model, combined with extra doses of credit, do not look promising, as later chapters will argue. At the same time, the earlier successful surge of the market-based financial system and growth model are now being constrained. Despite several offsetting cushions, such as a large deposit base for the banks and relative insulation from dependence on foreign capital flows, the Chinese financial system remains heavily debt-laden and fragile, while the economy overall offers only limited signs of rebalancing.

Keynesian Rebalancing and the Banking System

These dynamics and the inefficiencies in the SOE-SOB nexus are also partly responsible for China's pattern of slowing economic growth. In contrast to mainstream neoclassical economics, which argues that economic growth is driven by the supply side of the economy, we instead adopt a Keynesian macroeconomic approach that argues that economic growth is largely driven by the main components of aggregate demand—investment, net exports, and consumption. These in turn are shaped by broader structural economic factors related to China's growth model, which include the distribution of income, labor market dynamics, consumption dynamics, savings and investment, and the size and competitiveness of the export sector. From this perspective, China's problem is that growth has largely been driven by investment and, until the GFC, by exports, with consumption, especially household consumption, remaining more or less constrained. In comparison, mature and more sustainable economies are largely driven by household consumption, with consumption-to-GDP ratios of around 60 to 65 percent found in many Western countries. In China, however, despite consumption growing in absolute terms, the share of household consumption in GDP has fallen from almost 50 percent in the 1980s to a low of only 35 percent by the 2000s, with a subsequent moderate rise to less than 38 percent in 2020.

Higher inequality and flatlining wages have slowed growth in many Western economies (Bell and Keating 2018), but in China there have been rising wages after the GFC, although labor's share in total output has been comparatively low and income inequality has been high and rising. In addition, Chinese households have used income growth less for consumption and more to sustain high household savings rates. As we show more fully in chapter 1, this stems mainly from the continuing pressure for high levels of precautionary saving, which in turn is driven in part by weaknesses in welfare systems and the high costs of health care and education in China. The high level of savings has had several consequences. First, there has been a strategy for the high level of savings to be supported by high levels of exports to help ensure sufficient aggregate demand and help boost employment. This reliance on high net exports as part of China's growth model was especially apparent in the decade or more prior to the GFC, but is now far less so. A second aspect of China's high savings level has been that the monetary resources that might have been used by households to help fund consumption have instead been funneled through the main banks and have then been used to fuel the credit needs of the statist growth model, pouring investment into the supply side of the economy. Hence the state system is central in shaping both the demand and supply sides of the economy. It sets the broader conditions that encourage or even force precautionary savings and that set the limits to household consumption growth.

The problems with the state mobilizing and channeling savings in this manner are twofold. First, given the consistently lower profitability of SOEs versus private enterprises, a directed credit regime favoring SOEs represents an inefficient misallocation of financial resources. Second, by distorting the price of money and capital in favor of statist borrowers at the expense of savers and depositors, it delays or inhibits economic rebalancing whereby household consumption could be taking on a much larger role in driving a more sustainable pattern of growth.

A further key aspect of the statist growth model, at least between the early 2000s and 2013, was that the state had used an administered exchange rate regime to spur export competitiveness. Again, an undervalued currency, by making exports cheaper and imports dearer, favored exports rather than (domestic) consumption. Moreover, this system relied largely on private and foreign direct investment to support China's export manufacturing sector while directing bank credit to SOE-dominated heavy industries. After the initial credit surge stemming from the GFC and the growth of the shadow credit system, the private sector for a time attracted stronger flows of credit from the banking and broader financial system, although this has more recently been reversed under the Xi administration.

China's state capitalism thus misallocates capital to often inefficient sectors and has long starved the private and household sectors of credit and investment returns, the key sectors that could sustain economic growth and drive economic rebalancing. The banks have also been subject to political and administrative direction, market distortions, and interest rate controls that subsidize profits, as well as high levels of nonperforming loans. The growth model has also run into diminishing returns in the export sector, especially now in increasingly tougher international markets amid the global slowdown in the wake of the GFC and the subsequent COVID-19 pandemic. The model is also distorting domestic monetary policy and currency markets as well as constraining the liberalization of financial markets domestically and yuan internationalization. Rising debt levels, on which the system increasingly depends, also pose systemic threats to the financial system as well as the wider economy.

The Chinese leadership has agreed that the economy needs to be rebalanced. The powerful National Development and Reform Commission has stated that "expanding domestic demand is the guiding long-term strategy of economic and social development" (Vermeiren 2013, 681). The Twelfth Five-Year Plan (2011–15) committed China to rebalancing the economy and boosting household income and consumption, a plan that was endorsed in the Thirteenth Five-Year Plan (2016–20) (Central Committee of the Chinese Communist Party 2011, 2016). This was followed up by Xi Jinping's economic reforms released in November 2013 in the Third Plenum of the Eighteenth Party Congress, which committed the government to a "decisive role" for market forces. Reflecting China's economic and political bifurcations, however, the same document also asserted that the state should play a "dominant role" in the economy (Central Committee of the Chinese Communist Party 2014a), and this was certainly reflected in the state-directed credit and investment surge in the GFC stimulus package and in statist moves since under the Xi regime (Jiang 2015).

A key challenge in rebalancing the economy is that it must involve a degree of income redistribution, the continuance of current wage increases, and especially social support measures to help reduce precautionary savings and support domestic consumption growth. At the same time, growth needs to be powered less by expansive investment and capital formation and more by productivity and efficiency gains through innovation. The services sector also needs further development. In addition, rebalancing should also involve creating a more level playing field for state, private, and foreign firms.

The Funnel of Causality

The Chinese economy and financial system can be seen as a "funnel of causality" (Simeon 1976, 553). At the top of the funnel in this structured system is the party-state that oversees the Chinese growth model and developments therein. For over two decades in its current guise, the system has been supported by a range of institutions, especially China's regime of financial repression built on capital controls as well as interest rate and exchange rate manipulation. Below this level, at the bottom of the funnel, are the main banks and other financial institutions, closely linked to institutions such as local governments and the SOEs. The party-state imposed this system in favor of the state sector and against savers and the household sector—a system that effectively channels household savings at low cost to the state sector. At all levels there are divergences within the state elite between liberal elements pushing for a greater role for markets and more leftist or conservative elements favoring statist controls. The role of banks and finance is conditioned by these debates and struggles and by the wider growth model and its supporting institutions and the type of savings and credit demands the system makes.

Despite institutional and regulatory reforms of the banking and financial system in the last four decades, the Chinese growth model and the distortions it produces still drive the manner in which the key sectors of the economy interact, including credit allocation and bank operations. This account suggests that no amount of incremental change or reform at the bottom of the funnel is going to have much impact higher up, and that fundamental institutional change and reform at the level of the banks can really stem only from a revised growth model and attendant change in all the intervening institutions that currently support this model. According to this view, changes in the growth model and attendant institutions must therefore *precede* banking reform.

Some are pessimistic on this front. In their account of the Chinese financial system in *Red Capitalism*, Walter and Howie (2011) see the system as an instrument of a corrupt political leadership with few prospects for reform. Others concur that the seemingly never-ending challenge of SOE reform is a prerequisite to banking reform (Lardy 1998).

We largely agree that financial reform will not occur without wider reforms. However, in later chapters that deal with the rapid growth of shadow banking in response to the credit surge during the GFC and thereafter, we argue that, for a time at least, the rising shadow banking sector did begin to have impacts on the wider banking system and even to some extent on the growth model. Indeed, the banking system was partly liberalized, and the growth model was altered somewhat as households and private businesses gained greater access to credit and investment returns. As we show, the growth of the shadow banking system has been tacitly and explicitly supported by the leadership, and promoted by key bureaucracies and the main banks, in part because the shadow banking sector has been instrumental in helping to spur economic growth and profits and, for liberal reformers, in slowly altering China's banking system and economic growth models. Under such developments, the Chinese banking and financial system thus supported the statist growth model and the contending market-based model, hence the title of this book. For a time after the GFC, the direction of change seemed likely to gradually favor further reforms and greater liberalization in the banking system as well as further economic rebalancing as more credit was made available to the private and household sectors. This promise, however, is now being disrupted by the statist ambitions of the Xi administration, which has renewed support for the state sector and reined in the earlier rapid growth of the shadow banks.

Banking Reform

Deng Xiaoping (1993a, 193) urged the CCP at the beginning of the reform era "to turn the banks into genuine banks." Four decades later, this goal is yet to be achieved. The stakes are high. Changes to finance and banking and China's growth models are an arena of political struggle over the nature and direction of China's economic and political future as well as the shape of the Chinese state. Banking reform has been pursued by the leadership and especially by authorities in the People's Bank of China (PBC), China's central bank. Gains have been made on the regulatory front and in making the banks more commercially oriented. Nevertheless, China's banking and financial systems remain fragile and conflicted, due largely to the continued impact of market distortions and politicization.

Heavily influenced by the political machinations and agendas of the party-state, they have financed dubious investments in the SOEs, in unsustainable local government debt, and in infrastructure, and have been plagued by inefficiency, poor corporate governance, and at times corruption and fraud (Pei 1998; Saez 2003; Walter and Howie 2011). The SOBs have piled up nonperforming loans and faced insolvency, only to be bailed out by emergency balance sheet repair and infusions of capital by the state.

Reforming the sector has been on the official agenda following the buildup of nonperforming loans (NPLs) from the late 1990s. Banking reform was given further impetus following the Asian financial crisis (AFC), which alerted the Chinese leadership to the potential dangers of financial exposures and calamities in neighboring countries. The ensuing reforms during the 2000s focused on cleaning up the bank's balance sheets through recapitalization, reducing the level of nonperforming loans, selling bank equities to foreign strategic investors, improving corporate governance, and introducing a somewhat greater reliance on market and commercial criteria in the credit system. The reforms to banking thus far, largely by liberal reformers in the party elite and in the PBC and relevant regulatory agencies, have been more meaningful than credited by critics such as Walter and Howie (2011). Nevertheless, if the leadership thought that China's growth model was working reasonably well in supporting strong economic growth, then the problems in banking and finance seemed tolerable, with little incentive for fundamental reform. Consequently, banking and financial reforms have lagged and have been largely ad hoc and needs driven. In any other system, the main challenge or risk would be a potential banking collapse based on credit misallocation and mounting NPLs. In China, however, there is a huge domestic deposit base and large foreign reserves (if needed) to support the banks. Domestic funding sources, as well as regulatory restrictions, have also meant that China's banks have not been exposed to the skittish international wholesale credit markets that did so much damage to Western banks during the crisis of 2008 (Bell and Hindmoor 2015). In the Chinese context, balance sheet problems and NPLs have seen bailouts by the state that have kept the banking system afloat. China's leaders therefore have consistently worried less about moral hazard in the banking system than they have about economic growth. Although the AFC was a concern for the leadership, there was no fundamental rethink. The main banks were given a clean balance sheet and seemingly triumphed with their public listings in the 2000s as international investors rallied.

Many Western observers have interpreted this episode of opening as part of a slow march toward a more market-based banking and financial system in China, an integral part of an emerging "regulatory state" that relies less on direct controls and increasingly on market regulation through administrative and institutional reforms (Yang 2004; Pearson 2005; Bach, Newman, and Weber 2006). Despite the establishment of a set of regulatory agencies, talk of a regulatory state in China is premature (Pearson 2005). Reformers have been pitted against the centrally orchestrated growth and credit models that have long structured the Chinese system. Reformers in China also had a setback when the luster of Western markets and banking models was tarnished following the GFC and again with the stock market meltdown in 2015–16. Moreover, the reforms during the 2000s were accompanied by a surge in state capitalism that saw only limited reforms to the SOEs. This was followed by a surge in SOE and wider state-sector credit and investment after 2008, with statism being further ramped up under the Xi Jinping regime. Hence, changes in the state sector and other contingencies have in many ways impeded rather than driven banking reform thus far.

Calomiris and Haber (2014) argue that banking systems are based on political conflicts and bargains among key players. Indeed, according to Heilman (2005, 11), "China's financial industry is a major battlefield for the most powerful political and economic actors who try to benefit from their control over state assets. . . . [T]he banking sector is a key political resource." Shih (2008) similarly sees Chinese banking and finance as providing key resources to the party-state and as a key arena of factional alignments and political struggles. Walter and Howie (2011) argue that corruption and leadership struggles have weakened the banking and financial sector and its reform. Pei (2012) points outs that "reforms would jeopardize probably close to ten million officials' sinecures." Moreover, fundamental financial reform has been constrained by the credit demands from the state sector and from local governments. Walter and Howie (2011, 52) thus point to the politicization of the banking and financial system and to the government's capacity to hide or restructure bad loans through creative accounting and other means, delaying the day of reckoning.[6] These authors also argue that the piecemeal banking reforms that have occurred have been a conspiracy by the party aimed at luring both domestic and international investors into funding a state-controlled financial system that continues to support state projects and the party elite's patronage system. For these reasons the Chinese leadership has been unwilling to hand over the "commanding heights" of the economy or financial system to the market, although market intermediation of credit and finance grew for a time after the GFC response and credit surge (Lardy 2014).

The Growth of Shadow Banking

For a number of years after the GFC, the growth of the more market-oriented shadow banking system offered hope of reform. Banking dysfunctions and poor returns to Chinese savers under financial repression, combined with the credit surge after 2008 and private- and household-sector credit demand, led to the rapid growth of alternative market-based credit arrangements in China's shadow banks (Li 2014; Armstrong-Taylor 2016; Collier 2017). The PBC and the banking regulator, the China Banking Regulatory Commission (CBRC), encouraged this form of financial innovation as part of an attempt to boost the role of markets, to provide funding to local governments and to households and businesses, and to aid in rebalancing the economy.

Developments in technology (such as internet banking) also propelled the credit surge and growth of shadow banking. There was also growing household and market demand for better returns and for a broader range of financial products and services. The credit surge was also driven by the use of state guarantees that supported distressed markets where needed, which reassured investors. The shadow banking system has also reflected and was spurred by regulatory arbitrage, which has impacted the formal banking system, especially through the loss of market share and growing competition confronting the main banks, together with growing incentives to move into off-balance-sheet shadow activities by the main banks themselves.

These growing market pressures have prompted change. Premier Li Keqiang, at the 2014 National People's Congress, announced moves to establish new private banks, reform the SOEs, and increase market access to services. Following this, in 2015, came the decision to liberalize the interest rate system by abolishing the last formal controls on deposit interest rates, thus formally ending the system of financial repression. This was a significant shift. Although the rapid growth of the shadow banking system has recently been reined in by the regulatory authorities, as we show in chapter 8, its effects in reshaping the broader banking system, pushing it in a more liberalized direction, and providing credit to the household and private sectors have been important.

These shifts reflect the work of liberal reformers. For these actors, in the PBC and elsewhere, this promised a path to "banking reform" in China. The GFC as a critical juncture provided a window of opportunity for change, or what Tsai (2006) refers to in the China setting as "adaptive informal institutional change," a classic Chinese workaround or reform response involving informal, experimental, and adaptive change in the shadow of the state. Such informal change has also spurred a degree of formal institutional change in the main banks and, for a time after the GFC, weakened the Chinese state's control over financial flows. The shadow banking sector and the opportunities it has offered to customers have put competitive pressure on the main or formal banking system, which has seen profits and market share fall. Further financial liberalization and regulatory arbitrage flowed from this when the main banks sought to respond and attempted to regain a competitive advantage.

In the wake of the GFC, there has thus, ironically, been a rise in credit-fueled state capitalism together with a more market-oriented shadow banking sector. Many analysts have emphasized China's "state capitalism," yet the market-led elements in the system should not be overlooked (Kroeber 2016, 89; Lardy 2014). Indeed, the impact of shadow banking on the formal banking system reflects the pattern of earlier developments in Western countries such as the United States (Krippner 2011) and Australia (Bell and Keating 2018), but also in many others. In these cases, post–World War II regulatory burdens on the main banking system encouraged regulatory arbitrage, with the shadow banking sector gaining market share. The growth of such markets in the China context, under the shadow of state hierarchy, is also closely aligned with the process described in Naughton's (1995) arguments about "growing out of the plan" in China.

Economic rebalancing in China must involve the transition from a low-wage, investment-led, and export-based economy to a higher-value-added, knowledge-based, and consumption- and services-led economy. An efficient financial system that can allocate credit and investment to its most productive uses is necessary to achieve this goal. A more market-oriented and efficient financial system is also necessary to support further international economic engagement and reduce reliance on the US dollar system, as well as promote a greater international role for the yuan. Reform of the growth model and reform of the financial and banking system are thus interdependent goals.

However, reform is turning out to be a fraught process and severe constraints on reform currently prevail. As we argue more fully in chapter 10 and in the conclusion, the state sector and links between the SOEs and the SOBs remain powerful. There are also myriad vested interests within the state, including within the CCP leadership at central and local levels, with large stakes in the current statist system. The leadership also remains ideologically committed to the state sector, a fact that has been reemphasized under the current Xi regime. Yet it was also the case that prior to the current regime, market forces and liberal reformers had long been ascendant, so it would appear that the direction of the top leadership may well be the decisive factor in shaping the Chinese political economy. If so, a major downturn in the economy and/or a leadership change could well tip the scales of change once again in a more liberal direction.

Change is indeed possible in this regard because the current economic trajectory looks problematic. With an ongoing reliance on debt to fuel growth, China is mimicking the recourse to debt that has fueled growth in the West prior to and since the GFC. As in the West, this is not a sustainable strategy and is fraught with dangers (Turner and Lund 2015; Bell and Keating 2018). Debt cannot continue to outpace GDP growth indefinitely, yet as Chinese growth has slowed in recent years, debt has increased and has also far surpassed the size of China's foreign reserves. Credit surges of this rapidity and magnitude are often associated with financial crises. Greater linkages across a more complex financial system also pose systemic risks.

Explanations: The Agents-in-Context Approach

As we have been arguing, in China, growth model dynamics interact strongly with the banking and financial system, reflecting complex processes of political and institutional change and also market pressures. The process works roughly as follows. The dynamics of contending growth models and associated credit demands largely reflect the role of powerful political actors driving policy and institutional change, in relation to both growth models and the dynamics of banking and finance. In such arenas, we are interested in the ideas, power, and actions of key actors, and with their mutually shaping interactions with the major contexts in which they operate. This approach starts with key agents (mainly, in this case, the party leadership, key bureaucrats, and those who control the major banks and the SOEs, as well as China's multitudes of household- and private-sector savers, borrowers, and investors) who propel institutional change (essentially changes in formal and informal rules, operating procedures, and norms) in banking and finance, as well as changes in broader growth model and economic dynamics. These changes are also influenced by changes in market dynamics, such as the rise of shadow banking markets. However, in a state-capitalist system such as China's, state actors play an important role in shaping markets. Yet market dynamics can also be driven by the choices of myriad private actors operating in markets. An example of the latter is the way in which credit consumers in China fueled the demand that helped drive the rise of shadow banking, together with the associated loss of market share by the main banks. Such market dynamics can be seen as structural forces driven by the myriad choices of market participants, although in China in particular, market dynamics are heavily influenced by the state.

To analyze and explain these dynamics, we use an "agents-in-context" approach, which is a broadened-out form of historical institutionalism, a major theory in political science and political economy used to explain both institutional and broader changes (Hall and Taylor 1996; Bell 2011; Bell and Feng 2013). We have previously used this approach in major studies of institutional and financial change (Bell and Feng 2013; Bell and Hindmoor 2015; Bell and Feng 2019).

Institutional theories like HI basically argue that institutional arrangements are produced by agents but in turn shape the "rules of the game" under which agents operate. Institutions matter because they shape actor identities, interpretations, and preferences, the norm- and rule-based scope of agents' discretion, and the resources and opportunities available to agents within institutions. Hence, Scharpf (1997, 41–42) argues that "once we know the institutional setting of interaction, we know a good deal about the actors involved, about their options, and about their perceptions and preferences." Institutions can be inertial and constraining. North (1990, 3) defines institutions as "the humanly devised constraints that shape human interaction." Yet institutions can also be enabling, conferring resources, authority, and power and creating and sustaining both vested interests and change agents.

The key, then, as a first step, is to study the interactions between agents and the institutional contexts in which they operate. Powerful agents are often able to shape institutional rules and arrangements to protect or further their interests (Koreh and Shalev 2009; Peters, Pierrea, and King 2005, 1278; Thelen 2004, 31; Mahoney and Thelen 2010). Moe (2015, 297) writes that "institutional change is power constrained," while North (1990, 16) argues that "institutions are not necessarily or even usually created to be socially efficient; rather they, or at least the formal rules, are created to serve the interests of those with the bargaining power to devise new rules."

The relationship between agents and the contexts in which they operate is mutually shaping, a two-way street. Agents may shape the contexts in which they operate, but these contexts, such as institutional imperatives or inertia or broader structural impacts, will also shape agents and their resources and options. The "agents-in-context" approach uses the basic model of HI regarding institutions but broadens this out to include a wider range of relevant contexts, including the context of political power, structural contexts, and ideational contexts, or the shaping power of prevailing mindsets and ideologies on actors.

An important structural context that we analyze at length as a "critical juncture" is the impact of the GFC. In such crisis contexts wrought by economic forces, existing arrangements can be called into question, often providing greater room for agency and change. Despite powerful forces of constraint and inertia in China, there have also been more pronounced episodes of change driven by several critical junctures (Bell and Feng 2019). While a degree of banking reform took place in the wake of the Asian financial crisis, the GFC was a more substantial critical juncture that saw a massive credit surge, the rapid rise of shadow banking, and more liberalized finance, which led to wider market impacts on the main banking system and growth model in China. We deal with this episode more fully in chapters 6, 7, and 8. We also probe the extent to which changes during and after the critical GFC juncture were challenged and later constrained by the rise of the statist Xi Jinping regime from 2012.

The Interviews

Apart from secondary sources and official data, this book also uses interview material sourced between 2010 and 2017. Due to the regime's secretive nature and the resultant lack of insiders' accounts regarding the political and institutional dynamics within the party-state, our account benefits from detailed interviews with key players in the government and financial sectors that help unveil the preferences of decision makers, as well as the political, institutional, and economic dynamics of change and the reform process. We have altogether recorded thirty-five structured and semistructured interviews, of which twenty-five are with Chinese officials in key ministries, such as the PBC, the China Banking Regulatory Commission, the National Development and Reform Commission, and the Ministry of Finance. We have also conducted interviews with management staff in the major banks and other financial institutions based both in their headquarters and at the provincial level. Our analysis has also benefited from a number of personal and professional communications with scholars and practitioners based in China and abroad. Access to potential interviews since 2018, however, has been very limited, given the Xi administration's heightened pressure and control over party and government officials, as well as the COVID-19 pandemic.

The Chapters

In chapter 1, we further detail the connections between the Chinese growth model and the broader financial and banking system. Although the financial system has largely served the needs of the party-state, informal change has played a role in altering the banking system, producing tensions between state-led and market-driven imperatives.

Chapter 2 considers the political interests and coalitions that shape growth models and the banking and financial system in China. The party-state has established and relies on financial hegemony, economic distortions, and income redistribution to the state sector via the banking system as part of the dominant statist growth model. This chapter shows how economic and financial policy and institutional change has been the result of an ongoing contest between conservative elements in the economy and in politics that favor state domination of the economy, versus more liberal elements that endorse a strong state but argue that markets and the private sector need to play a stronger role in China's economic development and in a reformed growth model.

In chapter 3, we start at the beginning of China's economic reform era in 1978 and explore how early experimentation with the Chinese growth model and the banking and financial sector evolved until the crucial reform changes of the early 1990s. Deng Xiaoping's reform approach during this era was epitomized as "grappling with the stones while crossing the river." The challenge was to gradually move beyond the failed central planning regime toward a new state-market nexus. These efforts to formulate a coherent growth model yielded mixed results. In the financial arena, there was the process of monetization of the economy, but financial repression, such as interest rate regulation, the rigid control of the capital account, and a managed exchange rate that suited the import substitution regime, remained in place from the old economy. There was a transition from the old mono-bank system to a two-tier system. The role of the SOBs in SOE financing was increased. Local governments tightened their control of local branches of the SOBs, but during this period, banking reform was not on the agenda. The financial system remained repressed and banking remained rudimentary.

In chapter 4 we examine how the growth model was consolidated from the early 1990s under the so-called second era of reform (Naughton 1995). This era was marked by a reformist leadership that emerged from the struggles after the Tiananmen crackdown in 1989. Under the new Jiang-Zhu regime there was an emphasis on coastal manufacturing development and the greater use of market-oriented reforms. The period from the 1990s to the early 2000s saw the first significant effort at banking reform with the introduction of national legislation further defining the role of the PBC and the SOBs. As the PBC became an exclusive central bank, the Big Four banks inherited the PBC's commercial business and continued to dominate the banking system, becoming key agents of financial repression. This period also saw the establishment of policy lending banks as well as the centralization of the banks' operations, aimed at reducing the influence of local governments on bank lending. However, limited SOE reform during this period saw NPLs pile up.

The AFC worried the leadership, and in its wake the period between 1997 and 2002 marked Beijing's first serious check on the banking system. However, the major policy responses, centering on bailouts by the state and the hiving off of bad loans to asset management companies, fell short of meaningful reform. Policymakers assumed that the problems of the banks could be addressed "internally," by recapitalization, strengthening industry self-regulation, and installing party discipline to deal with corruption. The reform agenda also included reforming the SOEs in order to avoid bailing out loss-making SOEs using bank funds. Reform was limited, however, because a politically hamstrung Premier Zhu Rongji had to trade the reform opportunity for a more politically convenient program of recapitalization amid resistance from party conservatives, the old planning apparatus, wary local governments, and a lukewarm banking industry. Hence, the policy package, initially developed in 1998, was more of a short-term rescue. In a typical case of moral hazard, the banks took the capital injection as a free lunch. In addition, they were also pushed to provide relaxed credit to state enterprises and the real estate sector in a bid to boost aggregate demand in the wake of the crisis-induced export slump. As a result, the NPLs piled up again by 2002.

In chapter 5 we further explore growth model dynamics and associated banking- and financial-sector changes as well as growing distortions in the banking system from the early 2000s. This era saw rapid economic growth, spurred by China's entry into the World Trade Organization (WTO) in 2001, which helped spur a phenomenal boom in foreign direct investment, industry development, and exports. This was also the era in which the exchange rate system was steered toward supporting manufactured exports, which led to major distortions in the interest rate system. From 2005, the Hu-Wen regime favored the SOEs as national champions, while local governments remained active in promoting growth, investment, and exports. Despite initial efforts in banking reform from the late 1990s as well as efforts to cleanse the balance sheets of the SOBs, the problem of mounting NPLs returned. Policymakers recognized that the previous strategy, which rested on the banks' internal checks, had failed, and that efforts must be made to prepare the banks for the looming competition against foreign giants as part of the WTO-mandated opening of the financial sector from 2006. The PBC took the lead in the subsequent banking reform and oversaw bank recapitalization, public listing of the SOBs, and efforts to improve corporate governance. The new reform strategy aimed to invite market mechanisms and external scrutiny without jeopardizing the state's control of the banking sector.

Parallel to these reforms was the restructuring of China's weak banking and financial regulatory system, once characterized by lax reserve requirements and weak legal infrastructure in terms of contracts, bankruptcy, property rights, and bank governance and organization. Banking supervision under the auspices of the PBC remained largely intact until the Asian financial crisis, when the Central Finance Work Commission was established by the party leadership in a bid to tackle rampant corruption in the banking sector. Given the commission's limited capacity, it was subsequently dissolved in 2002 and replaced by the new China Banking Regulatory Commission under the State Council, China's cabinet. A new regulatory framework emerged that saw the PBC responsible for overall financial stability (as a metaregulator), with the CBRC responsible for banking regulation as a sectoral supervisor. The replacement of a party supervisory organ with more professionalized and technocratic institutions thus manifested a new mode of governance in the most crucial part of the Chinese financial system (Feng 2007a). Although these institutions are not independent in Western terms and struggle for authority on various fronts (Pearson 2005), they herald at least some steps toward a more professionalized regulatory approach involving a degree of devolved authority to professionalized regulatory agencies. Nevertheless, as Pearson (2005) argues, the party remains unwilling to fully or formally devolve authority to regulatory agencies or to regulators such as the CBRC, which operates under the shadow of state hierarchy and confronts turf wars with other ministries and agencies.

Chapter 6 looks at the mounting problems of the prevailing growth model from 2008. The global financial crisis of 2008 and the large drop in external demand exposed how dependent the model had become on the export sector and on seemingly endless infrastructure investment at central and local levels. The stimulus response to the GFC by the government also highlighted the degree to which the model had become dependent on credit-fueled growth channeled through the SOBs and how credit had become focused on state-directed investment in local infrastructure and on the overheated property sector. The stimulus thus became a continuation of state capitalism under emergency conditions. The quality of the investments, however, will mean more NPLs in the future for the main banks. In this context, the PBC and the CBRC moved to emergency mode. They provided policy support for the leadership in stabilizing the economy but also became increasingly alarmed about the medium-term risks of the massive credit expansion and a new surge of NPLs in the banking system. The regulators started tightening lending to the property sector and to local governments. However, the large increase in the money supply amid the distorted system of interest rates prompted the explosive development of the unregulated shadow banking sector, which was channeling credit into the infrastructure and property sectors as well as to the private and household sectors. Meanwhile domestic consumption remained weak as a share of GDP.

The 2008 crisis strengthened the voices of the statist conservatives and nationalists in China, given the fate of the market economy in the West. Indeed, China's state-controlled banks emerged relatively unscathed amid the wider crisis, largely due to regulation and limited involvement in the toxic mortgage-backed securitization markets that hobbled many banks in the West (Bell and Hindmoor 2015).[7] Nevertheless, this was also a time when the full dimensions of the distorted and increasingly dysfunctional nature of China's growth model, and the unique dysfunctions of its financial system, became more widely recognized.

In chapter 7 we analyze China's confrontation with the global financial crisis and the stimulus package and credit surge after 2008, all of which marked a critical juncture that altered China's financial system with the rapid growth of the shadow banking system. The critical juncture saw a surge in largely informal institutional change in the form of a rapid rise in shadow banking activity and the main banks exploring new channels of off-balance-sheet activity in association with the rising shadow banks.

In chapter 8, we examine the empirical details of the rapid rise of the shadow banking sector during the post-2008 credit surge. The shock of the GFC saw the financial system and wider economy under pressure. Economic growth was threatened and exports weakened. There was also the legacy of the financial system that had disproportionally directed credit to inefficient SOEs and infrastructure rather than to the more dynamic and efficient private sector and to the domestic consumption sector. In this context, the rise of the shadow banking system as part of the post-2008 emergency stimulus and credit surge had significant impacts on the formal banking system. This form of informal market activity in finance was spurred by the relaxation of certain institutional settings, by pressures from the household and market sectors for more credit, and by the leadership's attempts to expand credit-fueled economic activity in the state sectors. In this way, market pressures partly weakened the hierarchy of the statist economic system, especially so with the growth of shadow credit and the relaxation of financial repression by 2015. This was focused on interest rate and capital account liberalization, greater commercialization in banking practices, and the freeing up of more credit for the private and household sectors. This chapter explains why and how shadow banking was fostered, using a light-touch approach, by central bank and regulatory authorities within a broader liberalization agenda. Finally, we use the example of internet finance to illustrate how this segment of the shadow banking industry has helped facilitate a degree of financial liberalization in China.

Chapter 9 explores the increasingly strident regulatory response by the authorities to the shadow banking sector from around 2015. Initially the leadership and the regulatory authorities tacitly and often explicitly supported the rise of shadow banking. However, since around 2015 there has been a regulatory clampdown on the shadow sector as concerns about risks have grown, especially after the stock market meltdown in 2015–16, and as the statist revival under the Xi regime has become more assertive. These controls have seen the previously rapid growth rate of the shadow sector halted.

Chapter 10 examines the buildup of risk in the emerging system. The problems of mounting corporate debt as well as rising aggregate debt levels in the Chinese economy are being increasingly seen as significant challenges to the statist growth model. This chapter deals with the risks in the shadow banking sector, risks in the real estate market, and risks in China's sharply rising level of aggregate debt. Systemic risks have increased. The Chinese leadership is increasingly aware of the risks and is responding in a range of ways, including with greater regulation. The leadership recognizes that reducing debt levels is crucial, yet progress here is constrained by the leadership's short-term economic growth imperative. We argue that there are particular features of the Chinese financial system that will hopefully mean that the risks are manageable, although, as we are learning from experiences with large and complex financial systems, there can be no guarantees when it comes to financial stability.

In chapter 11 we address the question of whether changes to the banking system have helped with economic rebalancing and growth model reform in China. The chapter also examines the politics of rebalancing and the current statist reaction by the Xi regime to earlier market developments. For a time, increased financial liberalization did help in providing more credit to the household and private sectors. Other positive changes saw slightly reduced savings rates and corporate debt levels, and moderate increases in household consumption. However, the statist ambitions and programs of the current Xi regime have become increasingly apparent and have challenged earlier market developments. As shown in chapter 9, increased regulation has reined in the earlier rapid growth of the shadow banking system. Although shadow banking and new forms of internet banking are important new developments, it is no longer as clear as it once seemed that China's banking and financial system is being altered through strong liberalizing forces. Indeed, the Xi regime has reasserted the dominant role of the state and the subservient role of the main banks in supporting statist ambitions. The earlier expansion of credit to the private sector has now gone into reverse, with the state sector now the dominant destination of new credit. Given the huge inefficiencies and poor performance of the state sector, plus doubts about reforming the sector, this shift looks to be a dangerous gamble on the part of the Xi regime. China therefore is now encumbered with two faltering growth models. The regime is banking on an attempted revamp of the state sector while the much more dynamic and productive private sector is once again being starved of credit. The prospects for fundamental reforms in banking and finance, and for a rebalanced economy, do not look bright.

Finally, in the conclusion, we summarize our argument and the book's empirical findings.

1

INTERACTIONS BETWEEN CHINA'S GROWTH MODEL AND THE FINANCIAL SYSTEM

Western descriptions of China's "market transition," or of China as an "emerging market economy," tend to overlook the fact that the economy and its market elements operate under the shadow of state hierarchy. This certainly applies to the financial and banking system, and this chapter outlines how this system has been constructed by the party-state to primarily serve the needs of the party's statist economic growth model. China's financial system is primarily one that collects together extraordinarily high levels of savings, primarily from the household and corporate sectors, and which then channels these savings through the banking system, which allocates credit and investments to a range of destinations. The distinctive characteristic of this system is that all of its components, including savings levels and credit allocations, are strongly influenced by the state and the credit requirements of its growth model.

The management of economies through a combination of statism and markets, as well as the contribution from the key economic sectors that power an economy, is now the focus of an emerging field of "growth model" analysis (Baccaro and Pontussen 2016; Hope and Soskice 2016). This chapter explores China's growth model dynamics, particularly its statist, investment-led growth, which has increasingly relied on debt funding and which has distorted the banking and financial system. It was once widely recognized, including by the Chinese leadership, that the prevailing growth model and the financial and banking system needed to change. As we have seen, Premier Wen outlined his dire "Four Uns" warning about the economy in 2007, and Premier Li Keqiang followed up in

2012, stating that "China has reached a crucial period in changing its economic model and [change] cannot be delayed." (Yao and Qing 2012). For a time after the credit surge associated with the GFC, liberalizing changes in the financial and banking system and the rise of shadow banks provided a greater flow of credit to the private and household sectors, long starved of credit under the statist credit system and growth model. An alternative growth model based on private-sector expansion and higher levels of domestic consumption appeared to be gaining ground. These changes for a time seemed to be highlighting the limits to state capitalism as a control mechanism. It has since transpired, however, that the Xi Jinping regime is now doubling down on the statist growth model, a move that will impede China's economic rebalancing and continue to distort the financial system.

Growth Model Analysis

Neoclassical economic theory assumes that economic growth is driven by supply-side factors, such as productivity, labor force participation, and population growth. Nevertheless, the structure or composition of economic growth also reflects the structure of aggregate demand in the economy and especially the major contributions from consumption (public and private), investment, and net exports. Baccaro and Pontussen (2016) have pointed to the way in which these different components of aggregate demand can define varying "national growth models" aimed at spurring economic growth and dealing with growing distributive tensions over income shares. These authors focus comparatively on an export-led growth model, an investment-led model, and a debt-consumption-led growth model. In the face of relatively weak domestic demand as a source of growth, countries such as Japan, South Korea, and Germany, as well as various Nordic countries to varying degrees, have emphasized an export-led growth and the associated accumulation of savings and current account surpluses. In the last two decades, as argued more fully below, China has combined varying degrees of an export-led model with an investment-led growth model, one that has repressed domestic demand and consumption and relied on high levels of domestic savings.

Baccaro and Pontussen (2016) argue that under export-led growth models, wages and domestic consumption are repressed to aid cost and export competitiveness and to also provide a large pool of savings. China's domestic consumption is comparatively low compared to GDP, with wages repressed, well below the level of productivity growth. China ran small trade surpluses or deficits until around 1996 when the surplus started growing. After China entered the WTO in late 2001, particularly since 2003, the trade surplus (net exports) surged to 10 percent of GDP. In 1990 investment was about 23 percent of GDP, but by 2011 it had soared to a whopping 47 percent of GDP. The current growth model was launched in the 1990s, but since the GFC in 2008 it has increasingly been driven by debt-fueled investment, with a post-GFC decline in the reliance on exports.

By contrast, and in order to deal with growing inequality and weakening domestic demand, the United States and other neoliberal market economies have relied more on a debt-fueled consumption model. In the United States, this formed the basis for a huge housing and consumption boom in the 2000s that eventually collapsed into the 2008 financial crisis (Stockhammer 2015; Bell and Hindmoor 2015).

Growth model analysis can be linked to the Varieties of Capitalism approach to comparative political economy, which focuses on the organization and management of production on the supply side of the economy (Hall and Soskice 2001). This approach differentiates between liberal market economies such as the United States, the UK, and Australia, which tend to rely mainly on markets to coordinate production relationships, and more coordinated market economies, as found in Germany, Japan, a number of European and Nordic countries, and indeed China. The liberal market economies are associated with relatively high consumption-to-GDP ratios, indicating a consumption-led growth path. Conversely, coordinated market economies have relied to a greater extent on an export-led growth model, featuring much higher net-exports-to-GDP ratios than found in the liberal market economies. In China's case, however, it has historically relied quite heavily as well on a domestic investment-led growth model.

These divergent growth models are strongly symbiotic. Consumption-led economies have depended on the flow of competitive exports and capital from the export-led economies, while the export-led economies have relied on the key export markets provided by the consumption-led economies—a dynamic that has featured perhaps most strongly in the China-US relationship over the last two decades. Yet these differing growth models are problematic, reflecting unstable current account imbalances in the world economy, destabilizing credit flows, distributional tensions between economic winners and losers within the countries concerned, and increasing efforts by governments to spur growth to help ameliorate such tensions (Stockhammer 2015). The latter is a central agenda in China as growth slows and inequality reaches new highs. More generally, current growth models also reveal the limits of both export-led and debt-based and consumption-led models as inequality increases, global growth slows, export markets weaken, and debt levels increase (Rajan 2010). The recourse to higher debt in a number of countries has also led to major problems of financial vulnerability and crises (Turner and Lund 2015). China is not immune to these threats, and as is widely recognized, there are clear limits to the current dominant growth model in China.

State Capitalism and the Statist Growth Model

China's growth model over recent decades has been managed under China's system of state capitalism. Neoliberals see state capitalism in largely negative terms, as a system of statist, market-manipulating political economy (Bremmer 2009). State-directed capitalism is of course not a new idea, with late industrializers and rising powers typically using the state to try and develop markets and kick-start growth through various means (Gerschenkron 1962). We employ "state capitalism" here to denote the Chinese state's dominant role in the economy, which has amounted to a more extreme version of the statist political culture and model found in other East Asian developmental states. The statist tradition from China's imperialist past was further reinforced under the planned economy model adopted from Soviet Russia following the 1949 seizure of power by the Chinese Communists, in which the state monopolizes and organizes the economy. In China, market expansion is an important goal, but so too has been the state's control and politicization of the economy. According to Bremmer (2009, 42), in China, "the state acts as the dominant economic player and uses markets primarily for political gain." State capitalism is alive and well in China, and there is no blind faith in Western models, especially since the market-led traumas of the AFC and the GFC and the installation of the Xi regime in 2012. State-directed credit will therefore remain important, especially as part of state efforts to drive or revitalize sectors of industry. It is also true, however, that private initiative and managed markets have also emerged over the last few decades as the main driver of economic growth in China (Lardy 2014).

Under state capitalism, which has been ramped up under the Xi regime, the state retains direct control of strategic assets in the economy in the form of state-owned enterprises (SOEs) and promotes its economic priorities through economic coordination and industrial policies. The party-state further retains control over the management of the SOEs and a wide range of other organizations through a *nomenklatura* system, which selects key personnel and administrative leaders. At the same time, the rest of the economy, such as light industry and export manufacturing, operates on market or at least managed-market principles influenced by the state. These sectors are largely subject to competition and are dominated by private small and medium-sized enterprises (SMEs) and foreign enterprises. This results in a dualist, hybrid political economy based on a nexus of state and market, where China's market elements operate under the hierarchy of the Chinese state. This is often referred to as state capitalism, but other labels include "centrally managed capitalism" (Lin 2011), "Sino-capitalism" (McNally 2012), and "Chinese market-liberal state capitalism" (Brink 2012). Amid this mix, the state has favored high levels of directed investment and the promotion of large SOEs, the key power base for the Communist Party. This system has also entailed the main banks playing a central role in serving the credit and investment needs of the statist growth model.

China's growth model has been evolving during the reform era. In the 1980s, in what Naughton (1995, 10–11) refers to as the first era of reform, the liberalization of agriculture and the rise of township and village enterprises were an important source of growth. From the early 1990s, however, factional struggles and the rise of new leadership within the party saw the shift to a second reform era that privileged state-led infrastructure investment and industrial growth, the latter based on the SOEs and on private-sector export-oriented manufacturers. Infrastructure investment and industrial growth have been dominant features of the growth model since the early 1990s and were further emphasized in the 2000s. Correspondingly, the credit and banking systems have been dominated by the credit needs of the state-led infrastructure and SOE sectors.

A central feature of China's state capitalism and the prevailing growth model is the SOE sector. SOEs and their subsidiaries often enjoy a range of benefits in the system, such as access to cheap credit from banks, operational funds and debt write-offs from banks or the state budget, and favorable tax treatment. The state also limits competition to favor national champions in the SOE sector and controls foreign ownership in the sector (Szamosszegi and Kyle 2011). This sector, including the state-owned banks (SOBs), is of critical importance to the Chinese party-state. The SOEs enable the Communist Party to directly control economic and financial resources in achieving its various goals and policies. In turn, the state uses SOEs as political and policy vehicles to boost employment and gain new technology and raw materials from overseas. The SOEs are also ideologically and politically important for the Communist Party and provide a training ground for party cadres, equipping them with management skills and experience. The SOEs also serve as a bulwark for the party against the rising private sector, and as the "white gloves" of the party, allocating economic and other benefits to followers and loyalists through a revolving door between the party, the government bureaucracy, and the corporate sector (Pearson 2005). As one government official commented, "Why are SOEs so important? The answer to this question lies in the question of what happens if there were no SOEs. Would that be called socialism? Can you imagine the Communist party surrounded by private entrepreneurs and capitalists?"[1]

Indeed, the party has been wary of the rise of private-sector business interests and has largely absorbed such interests into the party hierarchy since the late 1990s under Jiang and made them reliant on state support and privileges and, if necessary, sanctions (Tsai 2007; Dickson 2008). As Fewsmith (2013, 135) puts it, "The expansion of the party into the private realm reflects a continued refusal to acknowledge a legitimate line dividing state and society as well as continuing distrust of the private sector." The party-state's relation with foreign capital is also distinctive. China's penchant for foreign direct investment distinguishes it from the other East Asian developmental states that tended to insulate domestic producers from external capital (Hsueh 2011; Kroeber 2013). In China, by contrast, it appears that the party would rather accommodate foreign capital as a bulwark against the domestic private sector that could potentially challenge its dominance.

The state sector of the economy has three components. First, there are firms fully owned by all levels of government, central and local, which are usually administered by the State Assets Supervision and Administration Commission and its local agencies. Second, there are firms that are not formal SOEs but are controlled by SOEs as majority shareholders. Finally, a range of urban collective enterprises, local-government-owned township and village enterprises, and state-controlled firms linked to domestic and foreign affiliates can also been counted in the state sector. It is estimated that there are around 150,000 SOEs in China in the broad terms. The assets of the centrally controlled SOEs alone reached 72 trillion yuan ($10.4 trillion) in 2017, not far short of China's $14.2 trillion GDP in the same year. The SOEs also account for most of the Chinese companies that make it onto *Fortune*'s Global 500 list. The number of Chinese SOEs on the list grew from nine in 2000 to seventy-five in 2017 (Lin et al. 2020, 37).

Not only are the SOEs aimed at being the "national champions" that dominate China's domestic economy, but they are also major investors in foreign countries and are playing a leading role in China's Belt and Road Initiative, which aims to project the model of credit-fueled investment-led infrastructure growth offshore (Yu 2018).

The Guiding Opinion on Promoting the Adjustment of State-Owned Capital and the Reorganization of State-Owned Enterprises, released by the State Assets Supervision and Administration Commission in 2006, highlighted a major role for the SOEs. It stated that "the investment and operation of state-owned capital should serve national strategic goals and should be directed more toward the important industries and key sectors connected to national security and the lifelines of the national economy." The document defines defense, electric power and grid, telecommunications, petroleum, coal, civil aviation, and ship building as "strategic industries," and equipment manufacturing, auto, information technology, construction, iron and steel, nonferrous metals, chemicals, and surveying and design as "pillar industries." The party insists it will maintain "sole ownership and absolute control" over the strategic industries and "strong control" over the pillar industries (SASAC 2006).[2] At the Third Plenum of the Eighteenth Chinese Communist Party Central Committee in November 2013, the leadership also argued that state ownership is a "pillar" and "foundation" of China's distinctive "socialist market economy" (Central Committee of the Chinese Communist Party 2014).

Savings, Financial Repression, and the Banking System

The nature of the Chinese financial and banking system is shaped by its structured relationship with five key sectors of the economy and with the prevailing statist growth model more generally. Indeed, it is the operation and interactions of these sectors that constitute the Chinese growth model. The sectors include the household and corporate sector, which provides high levels of savings and acts as a key source of domestic consumption; the SOE sector; the state-led central and local infrastructure sector; the largely privately dominated export manufacturing sector; and the services sector, which has mixed ownership. The credit needs and credit and investment allocations of the Chinese growth model flow from these sectoral relationships. Different political and economic interests are associated with each of these sectors, but under the prevailing growth model, it has been the state-led sectors that have been its main beneficiaries, and that have shaped the way in which the savings and credit system and the banking system operate. Under this model, the household sector and nonfinancial institutions, in particular, provide around two-thirds of the total savings that are channeled into the formal banking and credit system.

Urban and rural households still contribute most of their savings to banks in China, in part because the state limits any alternative placements of funds. The trend of Chinese savings has been well above the global average for decades. The average ratio of savings to GDP across the world stands at around 20 percent, but the 2000s in China saw a dramatic increase in that ratio, from 38 percent in 2000 to a peak of 51.7 percent in 2010. This persistently high savings rate is indeed something of a puzzle that does not conform to conventional modeling of income and consumption (Modigliani and Cao 2004).

The national savings account consists of three components: government/public savings, corporate savings, and household savings, of which the latter two are roughly equal in contribution and by far the most important in terms of their contributions to national savings. The literature explaining the drivers of high savings in China has mostly focused on household savings (Chen and Kang 2018). The savings rate had increased across all demographic groups before the GFC, the highest being among the young and the old (Chamon and Prasad 2008). There were a number of pressures that boosted savings in the 2000s. First, demographic factors have been important, with the one-child policy, for example, resulting in less need to spend on children and a greater need to save for retirement. Second, as Nabar (2011) finds, Chinese households save with a target level in mind. Repressed and sluggish wage growth, together with declining real interest rates prior to the GFC, forced households to save a larger proportion of their income to meet their savings target. In addition, according to Chu and Wen (2017), interpersonal income inequality has been positively correlated with its marginal impact on household savings rates. In particular, the rising income inequality during this period, with the Gini coefficient peaking in 2008, has also contributed to the increase in savings. Third, economic reform has seen the government shift the burden of retirement incomes and public services from the public budget to households (Shimek and Wen 2008), which in turn has driven up the pressure for precautionary savings.

In particular, reforms since the 1990s have seen the dismantling of the generous welfare system that was formerly associated with *danwei* (welfare services provided by the public sector, including government agencies and SOEs). Concurrently, most employment growth since the 1990s has been in the private sector, which, beyond offering wages, does not offer welfare support to workers. The proposed new social safety net that is meant to replace the old welfare system has been slow in the making, and has been fragmented, inefficient, inflexible, and with poor accessibility and spotty coverage (Frazier 2014; Wills 2018). For example, according to Zhang et al. (2018), health care benefits for urban workers declined by 17 percentage points between the 1990s and 2000, while pension benefits declined by more than 30 percentage points. Consequentially, out-of-pocket expenditures for health care rose almost 40 percent between 1978 and 2000, and for education by more than 10 percent between 1990 and 2001. The marketization reform of the health care and education systems in the early 2000s under the Zhu Rongji administration further exacerbated the situation, as families were forced to spend more on such services. As a result, households have had to squeeze their consumption to save for potential unemployment as well as health care and education. Soaring property prices and high mortgages have further constrained consumer demand. Finally, poor interest rate returns due to financial repression (see below) have also played a role in repressing private consumption, thereby increasing savings. Indeed, the rigged interest rates under financial repression have punished private depositors and retail investors, while an undervalued exchange rate further reduced the purchasing power of domestic households.

More recent studies, especially by Chang et al. (2020), have argued that the high savings rate in China is also driven by a distributional imbalance of income between household and nonhousehold (public and corporate) sectors. This has been a direct consequence of China's regime of labor repression. Under this regime, trade unions became "an integral part of the party–state apparatus" whose main role has been to mobilize the urban workforce and maintain social stability rather than to protect labor rights and interests (Clarke and Pringle 2009, 85). As a result, trade unions do not play a significant role in affecting labor income in China (Zhang, Chen, and Wong 2011). Instead, the terms and conditions of employment have been determined administratively by the state. Economic reforms and the insatiable demand for business investment have delivered an entrepreneurial state (Zweig 1998), a China Inc. that drives probusiness policies in industrial relations, often with a heavy-handed approach to dealing with labor disputes and worker protests (O'Brien and Deng 2017). This has led to "a biased distribution of national income towards the [investing] non-household sector and away from the [consuming] household sector," with the high savings of the nonhousehold sector contributing substantially to aggregate saving (Chang et al. 2020, 2). Therefore, the decisions and behavior of both sectors matter in explaining excess savings in China.

Before the GFC, the share of disposable income of the nonhousehold sector had been rising at the expense of the household sector. For example, China's GDP grew at 10 percent a year on average between 1992 and 2011, while corporate income rose by almost 20 percent and government revenue by almost 17 percent per year, while household income rose well below the national average during this period. The declining share of household income prior to the GFC, from 67 percent of national income to 58 percent, was due to a big pool of surplus labor that repressed wages, caused by both supply (massive layoffs from SOEs and a huge population of rural migrant workers) and demand factors (lack of development in service industries and labor-intensive small businesses). At the same time, the corporate sector has been saving based on rising incomes and profits on the back of repressed wages as well as a series of state-induced price distortions in resources (such as interest rates) and subsidies that favored SOEs. Savings have also been boosted by large capital depreciation and retained earnings. Private firms' retained earnings have largely been used for self-financing, given their lack of access to the financial system (bank loans and equity finance), especially as regards the state financial sector. Public revenue also rose much faster than the national average due to strong economic growth, tax reforms, a huge inflow of land sale revenue on the part of local governments, and private and corporate co-contributions to the welfare funds with diminishing net transfers from the government.

These income trends and inequalities resulted in varying sectoral saving propensities. Public revenue was translated mainly into public savings used to finance infrastructure investment, while state corporate savings were largely ploughed back into further investment. A large proportion of SOE earnings, which otherwise would have been public income, were retained by the SOEs with no or heavily discounted dividend payouts to relevant governments. For instance, no dividends were paid by the SOEs to governments between 1993 and 2007 (Liu 2009). As a result, the nonhousehold sector was an important driver of the dramatic rise of China's savings rate in the 2000s, with the nonhousehold savings rate running higher than that of the household sector since 2000 (Chang et al. 2020, 6). Overall, the biased income distribution in favor of the nonhousehold sector (with a high propensity of investment) at the expense of the household sector (with repressed consumption) resulted in a spike in the savings rate in China leading up to the GFC.

Moreover, in the run-up to the GFC, this extraordinary pattern and volume of savings were deeply intertwined with the evolving dynamics of China's growth model, which was largely driven by domestic investment and external trade. During this period, as Chang et al. (2020, 10) argue,

> the redundant labor supply lowers real wages and depresses consumption demand, making it necessary to rely on export trade for economic growth. Trade expansion requires industrial development that in turn entails massive investment. Capital formation needs sustainable financing from sufficient saving that can be more effectively supplied by the non-household rather than the household sector. The non-household sector takes various measures to support preferred technological development, with high domestic saving maintained through low interest rates, favorable corporate taxes, and stagnant labor remuneration. The resultant rise in factor substitution leads to worsening income inequality that is bad for boosting consumption but good for stimulating profits and savings. A vicious circle thus created has continued for decades.

Despite these dynamics before the GFC, the savings situation has seen a degree of improvement since then. As we will discuss in more detail in chapter 11, China's national savings rate experienced a mild decline from its peak of 51.7 percent in 2010 to 45.7 percent in 2020 in the post-GFC era, although it still remains one of the highest in the world. This partly reflects a recent shift of incomes toward households and away from the nonhousehold sector. The share of household income in national income increased from 57.9 percent in 2008 to 59.9 percent in 2017. The rise in private income has been marked by strong growth in wages. In particular, nominal wages increased by 8.9 percent annually between 2013 and 2017 (International Labor Organization 2018, 113). Three factors are in play. The one-child policy and premature retirement have taken their toll on China's working population, whose growth turned negative in 2014 when the government started relaxing the one-child policy. This reduction in labor supply and the rapid development of labor-intensive service industries have also helped push up labor compensation in national income. Increased property ownership and increased investment returns due to financial liberalization (especially shadow banking) have also increased the asset income of households.

In addition, the government has also increased its net transfer to the household sector in the form of increased spending on social services (Huang and Lardy 2016). This saw government expenditures on social security increase from 5.2 to 7.3 percent of GDP between 2014 and 2018, thus partially disincentivizing precautionary savings. On the other hand, however, soaring property prices and the resultant dramatic increase in mortgages have again forced households to reduce consumption. The net result has been a rather mild increase in the share of household consumption in the GDP, from 35.6 percent in 2008 to 38.8 percent in 2019, while the share of household savings declined from 23.2 percent of GDP in 2008 to 21.7 percent in 2017.

Although China's corporate savings rate (savings-to-asset ratio) has been comparable to the global trend, the corporate savings share of GDP has been high due to the fact that China has a larger assets-to-GDP ratio given rapid investment over the last two decades (Zhang et al. 2018). This means corporate savings is an important component of the national savings account. Corporate income has declined moderately since the GFC, due to the continued slowdown of the economy and the exchange rate being more in line with market equilibrium (Zhang et al. 2018). In particular, the SOEs' savings rate has been lower than that of private enterprises, reflecting the former's relatively lower profitability and dividend payouts. However, the net savings rate (savings minus investment as a ratio of assets) of the SOEs is higher than that of the private sector, suggesting a lower investment ratio and dividend payout. Apart from industrial investment, another channel of SOE savings has been investing in the property and shadow banking sectors. Overall, corporate savings declined from 21.6 percent of GDP in 2008 to 19.6 percent in 2016, but this is still comparable to that of household savings, which stood at 21.7 percent in 2016 (official data available until 2016).

At the same time, the share of government savings in GDP has also declined, from 5.9 percent in 2008 to 4.7 percent in 2016. While revenue increased due to higher capital income, savings were reduced by an increase in government expenditures in boosting social security. As a result, government savings have been largely stabilized around 5 percent of GDP during this period. This rate is still higher than that of most countries in the world, which reflects lower consumption and higher investment by the Chinese government.

Overall, the savings rate of all three sectors—household, corporate, and government—has declined moderately since the GFC on the back of an increased share of household income and private consumption. However, the momentum of rebalancing has been dampened by housing expenditure pressures (especially on mortgages) and a sustained investment drive by the nonhousehold sector. In fact, China's excess savings helped finance an investment boom after the GFC compared with the trade boom before the GFC, representing a shift from external to internal imbalance. More problematically, what was meant to be a short-term anticrisis stimulus turned into a prolonged state-led investment boom based on the recycling of savings and a massive credit expansion through both formal and informal financial systems, with capital predominantly flowing into less efficient state sectors, including both SOEs and local governments. This whole mechanism has resulted in the rapid accumulation of debt and inefficient investments, producing slowing growth, the buildup of potential bad loans, and increased risks for the banks and the wider economy.

The banking system has been the key intermediator of Chinese savings. Under instruction from China's central leadership and from local governments, the banks channel credit into the giant SOEs while the public infrastructure sector is closely linked with the Communist Party at the central and local levels. The SOBs lend to the SOEs, partly under state direction and partly because lending to the private sector has long been seen as too uncertain and opaque because of poor accounting standards and information asymmetries. The SOBs also find the SOEs attractive because they assume that the loans they make to SOEs are backed by the state. Because of SOE inefficiency, however, lending to that sector has often generated mounting levels of nonperforming loans (NPLs). By the early 2000s, NPLs constituted around 40 percent of total bank assets, easily amounting to technical insolvency by international standards (Lardy 2001). The official agenda of "bank reform" that has been in place since the late 1990s and the Asian crisis scare has focused on trying to address this and other problems. As we will see in later chapters, several major injections of capital in the late 1990s and early 2000s and the hiving off of NPLs into asset management companies, along with efforts to improve bank governance and reform the SOEs, constituted the leadership's main response to this problem. However, limited SOE reform and associated NPL problems continue to be sources of systemic risk within the banking system. Although the NPLs were wound back during the 2000s, it is now widely expected that the state-dictated lending spree of 2009–10 in the wake of the GFC, and more recent commitments to state-led and credit-driven investment, will generate another wave of NPLs in the medium term.

Three institutional settings enabled this system, one featuring the dominance of state-owned banks in the financial system, along with capital controls and the state's regulation of interest rates and the exchange rate. First, as finance was identified as a "strategic industry," the degree of state ownership in the banking sector is close to the level found in China's strategic industries. The main banks in China are largely state controlled, and like the nonfinancial SOEs, the SOBs are run by party loyalists essentially as state bureaucracies under a system of directed credit, reflecting the agendas of the party leadership and traditions of central planning and the classic developmental state model. Despite market opening as part of market-based reforms, foreign investment has had little effect as a form of external market discipline. The Industrial and Commercial Bank of China, the China Construction Bank, the Agricultural Bank of China, and the Bank of China, collectively called the Big Four, are the main state-owned commercial banks. Together with the fifth- and sixth-largest state banks, the Bank of Communications and the Postal Savings Bank of China, they held almost 40 percent of banking assets by August 2020 (CBIRC 2021a). There are also thirteen major joint-stock commercial banks, with the state being the main shareholder. These hold about 18 percent of total banking assets. In addition, there are urban- and rural-based commercial banks and financial institutions that serve their localities, which have 13.1 percent and 13.3 percent of total assets, respectively. Other institutions, such as privately owned banks, credit unions, foreign banks, and other nonstate financial institutions, make up the rest of the system. Notably, these also include the so-called "policy banks," such as the Export-Import Bank of China, the China Development Bank, and the Agriculture Development Bank of China, which are fully state owned and act as instruments of state economic intervention.

Equity financing is underdeveloped in China, with around 70 percent of Chinese companies' financing coming from bank loans in 2017. Hence the banking sector plays a key role in Chinese finance, servicing the financial repression regime (see below) and structuring state capitalism and China's growth model.

The state assets in the SOBs are owned and managed by the Ministry of Finance and an SOE holding company, Central Huijin Investment Ltd. (hereafter referred to as Huijin). Huijin was created by the People's Bank of China (PBC) in 2003. Its main purpose is to invest capital in SOBs. Since 2007, Huijin has been owned by the China Investment Corporation, China's sovereign wealth fund working under the direction of the Ministry of Finance (Bell and Feng 2013). Although many of the major banks have been publicly listed since 2003, the state remains the dominant shareholder. This means that the banks under this system are the key hub for financial activities and key agents for the state in mobilizing domestic savings and directing credit flows.

Second, the state has imposed capital controls to restrict the flow of capital in and particularly out of China in a bid to hoard and constrain capital within the domestic financial system and to prevent capital flight. China's capital controls come in two forms: there are direct or administrative measures that control cross-border capital flows through what Ariyoshi et al. (2000, 33) call "outright prohibitions, explicit quantitative limits, or approval procedures," and indirect or market-based measures that disincentivize the flow of funds by raising transaction costs, including "explicit or implicit taxation of cross-border financial flows and dual or multiple exchange rate regimes" (34). China's leadership announced in 1994 that it planned to open up the capital account by 1996 (Laurenceson and Chai 2003, 110). However, the financial crisis in 1997 postponed the plan indefinitely, although there has been patchy progress since then in liberalizing the capital account. In China, restrictions on capital flows mainly take the form of direct controls, which commonly require official approval to transfer funds under certain limits, restricting foreign investment in strategic sectors (Lardy 2008). The state can also impose "minimum stay requirements" in regulating both direct and equity investment (Campion and Neumann 2003, 77). According to a study by Xiao and Kimball (2006), China has been one of the most effective countries at controlling cross-border capital flows, although in recent years these controls have been under greater stress as nervous investors and the rich elite seek safer havens offshore.

Third, and finally, given its control over financial institutions and capital flows, the Chinese state has long had leverage over domestic credit, enabling it to regulate interest rates in its own favor. Indeed, the interest rate regime has long included tightly administered interest rates, directed credit, and regular use of bank reserve requirements as policy tools (Huang and Wang 2011). Until greater liberalization in 2015, China had operated a system of formal financial repression. Financial repression includes measures such as close association between government and banks, state-directed lending and credit controls, interest rate regulation, and capital controls (Shaw 1973; Reinhart, Kirkegaard, and Sbrancia 2011). This system saw the central bank set a maximum rate for deposits and a lower rate for lending, thus granting the banks a safe and generous net margin (typically around 3 percent) compared with their international peers (Pei 1998; Okazaki 2007). At the same time, savers were punished with a low and often negative real return on deposits. This rigged interest rate regime became more pronounced from the late 1990s and especially the early 2000s.

China's financial repression system was used to draw savings from households and other sectors to support the state sector, the SOBs, and the party elite. Given

China's high savings, the administered interest rate regime provided the banks and the state sector with access to huge pools of low-cost funds. Lardy (2008) estimated that financial repression, in the form of an implicit tax, cost Chinese households about 255 billion yuan ($36 billion), or 4.1 percent of GDP, in the first quarter of 2008 alone. An important goal was to keep nominal interest rates lower than market levels so that the government interest payments could be reduced. For a given amount of debt, this can reduce official interest expenses and contribute to a reduced deficit. In more extreme circumstances of negative real interest rates, where nominal rates are lower than the inflation rate, financial repression is in essence a form of transfer from creditors to (state) borrowers, in that it helps reduce debt in both absolute and relative terms (Reinhart, Kirkegaard, and Sbrancia 2011). The main banks have benefited from this system. Financial repression guarantees a relatively wider margin for banks, which then provides cheap credit, especially to industry and investment in the state sector. Ferri and Liu (2010) find that the profits of the favored SOEs largely stem from the subsidized credit system.

At times, China has also managed its exchange rate system. This was especially so during China's export surge during the 2000s after China's accession to the WTO, with the yuan more or less undervalued through a managed exchange rate system that helped to keep exports competitive in international markets. This was done through a domestic capital control regime as well as routine intervention in the foreign exchange market by the central bank. The central bank absorbed most of the dollars earned in international transactions in the domestic foreign market at its desired level. Between 2000 and 2013, China ran a large surplus for both trade and capital inflow, and given the central bank's intervention in keeping the exchange rate below the market level, this resulted in a skyrocketing of China's foreign reserves and higher inflation. The bank had to "sterilize" such operations by withdrawing liquidity through issuing its own notes (Bell and Feng 2013, 211). The story after 2013 is different, however. As domestic real wages increased, the real exchange rate converged toward the market level, the scale of trade surplus was wound back, and foreign reserves were also reduced.

The arrangements described above, however, have led to major systemic financial distortions. The impact of the managed currency regime aimed at keeping the yuan low and competitive spilled over to the interest rate system. Moreover, incentives for main bank participation in foreign exchange sterilization have seen the above-noted rigging of interest rates to produce low deposit rates and often negative real returns for depositors. This may have helped sustain the profitability of the main state banks, but especially in recent years, as we explain in later chapters, the low deposit returns have seen the shadow banking sector expand rapidly as depositors have flocked to alternative savings vehicles with higher returns, which have become the funding source for shadow credits. Low returns from deposits and limited investment opportunities elsewhere have also seen household- and private-sector savings channeled into a booming property market. The shadow sector has also supplied credit to local government infrastructure investment. These sectors have become sources of systemic risk within the financial system, especially given the uncertain returns in infrastructure investment and the possibility of a major property market correction.

The closely associated use of a rigged interest rate system, financial repression, and the predominant use of quantitative monetary controls also create problems. The arrangements force the PBC to try and pursue an undervalued yuan and low inflation simultaneously. The PBC's currency intervention requires offsetting sterilization measures to avoid domestic inflation, meaning that the PBC requires the banks to purchase bonds and raise bank reserves to quarantine funds. This ties up funds in low-yielding government accounts and is costly to banks. To help offset this, the PBC kept deposit rates low, and also kept a lid on lending rates, thus providing the banks with a solid margin, as noted above. Lardy (2012b) dates this policy from about 2003, when the PBC was forced to deal with mounting foreign reserves stemming from its exchange rate interventions. From the PBC's perspective, according to Lardy (2012a), "the central bank had to pay interest on these bills and reserves, and the low-interest-rate policy made the cost of these operations less than it would have been had interest rates been market determined." The exchange rate system and capital controls, the export strategy, the resulting reserve accumulation, and the need for financial repression long constrained domestic financial liberalization (Vermeiren 2012).

A further associated problem with the managed currency regime is that it constrains the PBC's autonomy in monetary policy and forces the authorities to rely more heavily on quantitative measures, such as bank reserve ratio requirements and bank credit targets, to control inflation (Bell and Feng 2013). Murtaza and Shi (2012) argue that this system creates incentives for banks to venture into alternative finance, including informal lending, a typical scenario of regulatory arbitrage. The resultant rapid expansion of shadow banking has rendered the PBC's efforts in adjusting the money supply and enforcing its credit policy increasingly ineffective.

The Main Beneficiaries

The state sectors have been the main beneficiaries of China's administered banking and credit system, and the SOBs have become major financiers for the SOE sector. First, SOEs have privileged access to SOB loans at below-market interest rates. For example, the average monthly prime lending rate in China in December 2010 was 5.36 percent, but large petroleum SOEs, such as the Sinopec, could enjoy short-term loans from the banks at 2.7 percent, or almost half, during the same period. Indeed, China Southern, a state firm whose high debt levels risked an interest rate premium, reported an effective interest rate of 1.13 to 1.97 percent in 2010. Another benefit has been the way the SOBs deal with the SOEs' nonperforming or bad loans. The state banks simply write off the loans or continuously roll them over, a practice called "evergreening." In addition, the SOBs also issue loans to uncreditworthy SOEs just to keep the latter afloat, knowing that the bad loans will be underwritten by the central or local government. For instance, in 2010, SOBs were ordered to issue policy loans to the ailing SOEs in northeastern China as part of a "revitalization program." As a result, SOEs in declining sectors with growing NPLs continued to be kept afloat through bank loans. The Shenyang municipality, for example, was granted preferential loans from the China Development Bank, a state policy bank, totaling 148.9 billion yuan, in the decade up to 2018 (Tang 2018).

Local governments are also influential forces intervening in bank operations and have sought funds especially for infrastructure and real estate investment. China's large banks typically have thousands of local branches. Traditionally, and given their limited fiscal resources, local governments have had to tap into these local banks to help finance local investment and support local SOEs, in order to generate employment and public revenue (Pei 1998). This was made possible by the institutional structure of the state-bank nexus. According to the OECD (2005, 141), "The chief executives of the head offices of the SOCBs [state-owned commercial banks] are government appointed and the Party retains significant influence in their choice. Moreover, the traditionally close ties between government and bank officials at the local level have created a culture that has given local government officials substantial influence over bank lending decisions."

In contrast, and until the rise of shadow banks, private firms traditionally found it difficult to get credit from China's banks, while more recently, credit flows to the private sector have once again declined. The private export sector consists mainly of Chinese SMEs and foreign-owned companies. These entities have driven China's export manufacturing sector, especially since the late 1990s. In the early days of reform, many SMEs had to disguise their private ownership to get bank loans by registering as collective enterprises or being affiliated with SOEs. Overall, however, this sector has been starved of credit from the SOBs and has relied instead on self-financing and foreign direct investment, and more recently on informal financing or even illegal financing mechanisms (Tsai 2002, 2004, 2015).

The Growth Model and Financial Imbalances

In all economies, the national output is the combined sum of consumption, investment, and net exports. China's growth model has been based on consumption repression, and on investment and export-led growth, although the latter sector has declined since the global financial crisis in 2008. The institutional structure of state capitalism in China, especially the flow of state-directed capital to SOEs in priority and strategic industries at the expense of the private sector and household consumption, has led to another feature of China's growth model: an imbalance between consumption and investment in national output. In particular, this is a growth model that is centered on overinvestment, exports, and repressed consumption. It is an extreme version of the earlier East Asian development model and can generate strong growth for a period, though typically with growing imbalances and vulnerabilities. An IMF working paper argued in 2012 that in relation to China, "because its investment is predominantly financed by domestic savings, a crisis appears unlikely when assessed against the dependency on external funding. But this does not mean that the cost is absent. Rather, it is distributed to other sectors of the economy through a hidden transfer of resources [from households], estimated at an average of 4% of GDP per year" (Lee, Syed, and Liu 2012, 1).

Pettis (2013, 84) sees this subsidy as the reason behind the decline in the household share of China's GDP over the last few decades. He argues that "it has proven very difficult for China to raise the GDP share of consumption, largely because consumption-constraining policies are at the heart of China's growth model and indeed at the heart of the investment model more generally" (93). Therefore, rebalancing involving higher household income and consumption cannot be squared with maintaining high growth rates through the prevailing growth model. Increased domestic consumption requires a higher household share of national income and lower savings. However, instead of substantial moves to rebalance after 2008, and in the face of falling exports, state-led investment and debt continued to grow. In contrast, more liberal systems such as the United States, the UK, and Australia, among others, have relied on credit flows and exports from the surplus economies, and on wage-funded but increasingly on debt-funded domestic consumption to spur economic growth.

Although consumption has grown rapidly in absolute terms since 1978, its relative share of China's GDP has been on the decline, from over 50 percent in the 1980s, to 46 percent in the 1990s, and below 40 percent since the 2000s. China has the lowest household consumption share of any major economy in the world. In the United States and the United Kingdom, household consumption accounts for around 70 percent and 60 percent of GDP, respectively (Wong 2014, 3). Another useful comparison is with India. According to Lardy (2006, 4), "China's per capita GDP in 2004 was two and a half times that of India. But because household consumption as a share of GDP was so much lower in China, per capita consumption in China exceeded that in India by only two-thirds." This fall-off in domestic consumption was no accident; it has been integral to the growth model.

In recent decades, investment, particularly public investment, has driven much of the economic growth in China. The first decade of economic reform saw investment average around 36 percent of GDP. This is a high level by the standards of developing countries generally. Since the early 1990s the investment rate has risen well above the historic level of other East Asian countries, such as Japan and South Korea, during their periods of rapid growth (Lardy 2006, 5). As noted, the main investments are in the SOEs, infrastructure, and real estate. This type of investment-intensive and extensive pattern of growth has resulted in low efficiency in resource utilization. Indeed, investment growth has come with declining efficiency and productivity (Garnaut and Huang 2005). Hence, China has had to invest more and more at falling rates of return in order to keep growth going.

The period during the 2000s up to the GFC in 2008 saw net exports become an important driver of economic growth. For example, in 2005, at around the peak of the export boom, net exports accounted for about one-quarter of the growth of the economy. This was partly achieved with the help of the state undervaluing its currency, which further reduced the purchasing power of the renminbi and thus domestic consumption (Bell and Feng 2013, 208). Therefore, China's high trade surplus, according to Michael Pettis (2013, 22), is "simply a residual that is necessary to keep investment-driven growth manageable under conditions of repressed domestic consumption."

China's growth model over the years has thus led to an economy plagued by serious macroeconomic imbalances that are centered on chronic overinvestment and underconsumption. These in turn have led to overproduction and, for a time, high reliance on exports, with growing trade and current account surpluses, which have also contributed to global macroeconomic imbalances (Roach 2014).

The leadership in China operates under a key structural imperative: the need to pursue high growth in order to try and maintain legitimacy and ease social tensions. However, the old statist growth model is increasingly ineffective, marked by diminishing productivity, domestic imbalances, and slowing growth. As we will see in later chapters, China has increasingly resorted to debt to try and drive the economy, a pattern of growth that is not sustainable.

There are thus three basic, interrelated credit allocation problems: credit is still being overallocated to inefficient SOEs, too much credit is being allocated to inefficient local government investment, and too little credit is being allocated to the private business and household sector. Under the statist growth model, the credit system was increasingly becoming inefficient: between 1995 and 2015, the ratio of credit to GDP more than doubled amid the growing inefficiency in credit allocation and overcapacity and decreasing returns, with the prospect of mounting debt and NPLs. The last major investment surge in China in the 1990s ended in huge levels of NPLs in the banking system. Pettis (2013, 42) points to Germany in the 1930s, the USSR in the 1950s, Brazil in the 1960s and 1970s, and Japan in the 1980s as failed investment-led growth models that ended in high debt.

The Road to Reform?

As we will see in later chapters, despite these problems, the statist growth model was further ramped up in response to the GFC after 2008. Credit-fueled investment in industry and infrastructure was prioritized, sidelining moves to rebalance the economy. As Breslin (2011, 194) points out, "The crisis [i.e., the GFC] might have further undermined confidence in the existing growth model. The immediate solutions in some way meant a turn back to that growth model rather than a further move to a new paradigm." The most pressing reform issue therefore remains China's largely statist growth model that relies on uneconomic investment, its consequent impact on the banking and financial system, and its associated credit misallocation and inefficiencies, which all increasingly act as a dead weight on the economy. Under the prevailing model, the formal banking reforms that have occurred have not been systemic and have not been explicitly tied to a reoriented growth model. Devising and implementing a new growth model and reforming the banks and the financial system are thus key and interlinked challenges for the leadership.

In later chapters we will explore how financial repression and dysfunctions in the main banking system, together with the credit needs of the post-GFC stimulus, led to the rapid growth of the shadow banking sector in China. Low returns for China's myriad savers in the formal banking sector, as well as regulatory arbitrage by the banks, saw nontraditional lending and the shadow banking sector expand rapidly. China's main banking and financial regulators, the People's Bank of China and the China Banking Regulatory Commission, sanctioned this form of "financial innovation" and encouraged the growth of the shadow banking sector, as part of an attempt to boost the role of markets and to provide credit to local governments and to households and businesses. Indeed, regulators were sanguine when the main banks began to work with trust companies in the shadow sector to extend credit. The growth of shadow banking has thus acted as something of an informal escape route from financial repression. Former PBC governor Zhou Xiaochuan boldly announced at the National Party Congress in 2014 that by 2016 a key element of financial repression, the ceiling on bank-deposit rates, would be lifted. The change came sooner than expected, as rapidly mounting pressures on the formal system led to the formal liberalization of interest rates in 2015.

The new leadership under the Xi Jinping regime has, however, started to roll back these market reforms and instead has doubled down on support for the state sector. As we show in chapter 11, the Xi regime has imposed tighter regulation on shadow banks and has boosted the role of the state sector and SOEs in the economy. This is a significant illiberal turn, and the prospects for economic reform and rebalancing on the back of a more liberalized financial system have been dimmed.

According to Pettis (2013, 9), "Every country that has followed a consumption-repressing investment-driven growth model like China's has ended with an unsustainable debt burden caused by wasted debt-financed investment." Although it is true that a large part of China's debt burden amounts to state businesses owing money to state-owned banks, essentially moving money around within the state, it is certainly the case that China has produced much wasted debt-financed investment. China's growth model, with all its shortcomings, has been sustained by a set of institutions that ensure the state's continued control of economic activities through controls over the banking and credit system and through the SOEs and the state sector. Attempts to reform this system have therefore posed major political challenges, and in the next chapter we explore the agendas and interests of the main actors that have shaped China's banking system and growth model.

2

INTERESTS, IDEAS, INSTITUTIONS, AND THE POLITICS OF BANKING AND ECONOMIC REFORM IN CHINA

The fate of China's financial and banking system and that of its wider economy and growth model are intertwined and reflect complex political processes of institutional change shaped by changing power dynamics among key agents. In this chapter we focus on the interests and behavior of our key agents shaping change. The most powerful of these are within the party leadership, in the banking system, in the state sector, and in a range of government bureaucracies, including reformist agencies such as the People's Bank of China (PBC). Weaker actors include borrowers in the household and private sectors who succeeded, for a period, in gaining substantial flows of credit from the shadow banking sector after the GFC. For the most part, however, households and the private sector have been co-opted or repressed due to the authoritarian nature of the Chinese state and its controls over the economy and society (Dickson 2008). This chapter introduces the actors in our story, and their interests, motives, and relative powers, and outlines the nature of the institutional and political dynamics in which they operate.

Key Actors and Agendas within the Party-State

Our key agents are often able to exploit opportunities and institutional and political resources that enable them to effect political and institutional changes in the growth model. Given the hierarchical and authoritarian nature of China's political regime and its control over critical financial resources, the key actors involved have been policy elites, particularly political leaders and senior bureaucrats from the Communist Party and relevant institutions within the central government in Beijing and in local governments. Despite the predominance of the central state in China, local governments have also been significant players in growth-model and financial change.

In China's political economy there are several broadly defined groups and sets of institutions that have high stakes in growth-model dynamics and in the banking and financial sector. First there is the political state, involving the party as well as the government at both the central and local levels, including government agencies such as the Ministry of Finance (MOF), the National Development and Reform Commission (NDRC), and the PBC and financial regulatory agencies, such as the CBRC. There is also what might be called the economic state, especially the powerful SOEs and SOBs. Within the political state, the central leadership, the central bureaucracy, and local governments are important actors. Of these, the central leadership is the most powerful, and it is the policy preferences and decision-making dynamics of this core leadership group that, in negotiation with the wider party hierarchy, will shape China's future. Within the economic state, the interests of the SOEs and SOBs are often channeled through their connections with political leaders and the government bureaucracy, often involving a revolving door between senior party and government officials and senior management of the SOEs and SOBs.

Within the central political state, China's steep political hierarchy awards the top party leaders substantial power and personal authority in shaping policy and institutions to suit their agenda. Traditionally, the key institutional feature of the party leadership in the reform era has been collective leadership centered on the Politburo Standing Committee under the "core" of the secretary-general of the party (Fewsmith 1996). Collective leadership means the party recognizes the existence of factional interests, but the institutionalization of a "one-man core" is designed to support the party's overall strategic capacity and unity (Dittmer 1992; Shirk 1992; Zhao 1995). As Deng Xiaoping told the Politburo Standing Committee, "A leadership without a core is unreliable" (quoted in Fewsmith 1994, 8). The most powerful leader is the core (*hexin*) of the party, like Mao during the first-generation leadership, Deng Xiaoping in the second, Jiang Zemin the third, Hu Jintao in the fourth, and Xi Jinping in the fifth.

The dynamics of reform are strongly shaped by the ideological and policy preferences of the core leadership, yet because economic and financial affairs are often the portfolio of the premier rather than the secretary-general, we should extend the core to include both leaders, such as Jiang-Zhu, Hu-Wen, and Xi-Li.

It should be noted, however, that in the current era, the degree of centralized authority has increased under the leadership of Xi Jinping, to the point where Xi has taken over substantial authority in the economic policy arena, both formally and informally (Minzner 2018; Economy 2018; McGregor 2019).

The top leadership has substantial power and authority in pursuing change and in reshaping lower-level institutions by virtue of the position they hold within China's steeply hierarchical state. Although it is commonly the case that vested interests often block reform, another factor that can facilitate reform is that the top leadership does have the institutional capacity to drive change if needed. The model of "bureaucratic authoritarianism" (Hamrin and Zhao 1995) argues that "high politik" issues that have national ideological, political, and strategic significance remain largely the exclusive territory of the top leadership. The leadership retains the ultimate authority and leverage in arbitrating bureaucratic disputes and, with regard to certain critical issues or in crisis conditions, can resort to personal involvement and dictation, a mechanism Shirk (1992, 76; 1994, 32) calls "management by exception." This has been evident in action taken by the central party-state in several rounds of ruthless restructuring of the bureaucracy and in recentralizing authority. For example, when Mao felt increasingly marginalized after the fiasco of the Great Leap Forward, he uprooted the established bureaucracy in order to recapture power from the then nominal party boss, Liu Shaoqi, which then ignited the Cultural Revolution in the mid-1960s (MacFarquhar 1981).

In the post-Mao era, the personal authority of party leaders has been more institutionalized but remains a central focus for leadership ambitions (Dittmer 1995; Dittmer and Wu 1995; Fewsmith 2001a). Party leaders have pushed through major changes during this period. For example, in order to overcome a recalcitrant bureaucracy that stood to lose from China's accession to the World Trade Organization, Premier Zhu Rongji resorted to a major organizational streamlining that led to a power reshuffle within the bureaucracy (Feng 2006b). Under Zhu there was also substantial restructuring applied to the SOEs, involving millions of job losses. More recently, Xi Jinping has orchestrated a ruthless anticorruption purge that has shaken up the party from elite to grassroots. China's central leaders therefore have repeatedly displayed a capacity to force through major reforms if needed.

However, the top leadership, consisting of the secretary-general and the premier, cannot easily rule by dictate; a workable consensus among the senior figures in the party and in the Politburo is an important asset in supporting the top leadership's agenda. For example, Deng's consensus building in the early 1990s ensured a market-oriented direction in reforming the growth model, including banking reform. However, in the post-Deng era, Jiang Zemin had to strike a balance between the conservative Li Peng (number two in the party) and the reformist Zhu Rongji (number three in the party). This constrained Zhu in calling for more radical reforms of the banks in the wake of the Asian financial crisis, for example. Shih (2007) argues that Beijing's piecemeal banking reforms in this period, including the largely failed program of fiscal bailouts of the banks, were mostly due to Zhu's wariness amid conflicts between reformers and conservatives within the party. Zhu's position was also compromised during this period because of challenges over China's SOE reforms and China's WTO agenda, both of which were crucial to his political survival. The consensus-seeking style within the party leadership continued in the Hu Jintao–Wen Jiabao era that followed (between 2002 and 2012). Under the current leadership, Xi Jinping has, however, relied less on consensus and more on the brute assertion of leadership and power, in part using anticorruption campaigns to weaken opponents as well as managing to continue his tenure as head of the state beyond the period of two terms that was previously enshrined in the constitution (Minzner 2018).

Apart from power politics at the top, the largely fragmented institutional structures of the Chinese bureaucracy also give rise to institutional conflicts among key bureaucratic players in the central government. China's central bureaucracies play an important role in shaping policy, especially in crafting policy advice and in implementing policy. The highly fragmented organizational structure and the often ambiguous boundaries of bureaucratic turf in China (Lampton 1987; Lieberthal and Oksenberg 1988) have thus created ample room for agency and discretion, which Lampton (1987) refers to as the "implementation bias." For example, gaining or losing authority over the financial and banking sector has been a high-stakes game for traditionally powerful ministries, such as the MOF and the NDRC, both of which have increasingly contended with emerging regulatory agencies led by the PBC and the CBRC (which merged with the insurance regulator in 2018 to form the China Banking and Insurance Regulatory Commission). The arena of banking reform has also been shaped by the ebb and flow of influential party and government agencies, such as the Central Financial Work Commission (Heilmann 2005) and key corporate policy vehicles, such as Central Huijin (an initiative of the PBC that subsequently became a subsidiary of the MOF). Hence, bureaucratic turf wars have been a fixture in the policy process.

The relationship between the central and local governments has also been important; it is instrumental in propelling credit and investment surges in urban and regional China. Amid the recentralization of central state authority in the latter half of the 1990s, local governments became the targets of reforms aimed at strengthening central state administrative and fiscal capacity (Hu and Wang 1994; Jia and Lin 1994), leaving local governments with fewer resources (for similar obligations) and less influence than they had previously (Saich 2001).

Nonetheless, local governments remain important players in the constant wrangling with the center. Local leaders have formally defined growth-driven incentives, and these agendas have been particularly active in the investment and financial sector (Shih 2008). This has led to those leaders' interference with the operations of local bank branches, while the resultant maneuvers against the center have led to unique political business cycles in China (Huang 1996; Shih 2008). Moreover, in recent years, local governments have been increasingly relying on irregular financing vehicles that evade formal banking regulations, which, as we argue in later chapters, could pose systemic risks to the banking system and overall financial and economic stability.

Factions and vested interests also play a role. For example, although the SOBs have been strongly shaped by central state policies and the dynamics of growth models, nevertheless, the "revolving door" (Pearson 2005, 312) between top banking leaders and senior financial bureaucrats has meant that the concerns of the industry have been channeled into the policy processes. In fact, many if not most of the top-level financial bureaucrats, including those in the PBC and the CBRC, have worked in the SOBs during their careers.[1]

There have been a number of approaches to defining factions in Chinese politics. The narrowest approach is to look at the patron-client networks of individual leaders (for example, Li Peng's network in the electricity sector or Zhou Yongkang's network in the petroleum sector). Other wider definitions of factions look at political and family backgrounds (such as the "princelings") or at leadership in geographic terms (such as the "Shanghai Gang"). Such factions, however, are often fluid: some key leaders are often in more than one faction and the policy preferences of factions can change under different leaders (Unger 2002). A wider approach is Hung's (2008), which sees policy as strongly influenced by coastal-industrial elites (including members of the Shanghai Gang and the princelings). Hung argues that the coastal-industrial elite has largely dominated political and economic policymaking since the early 1990s, which has led to a general bias in favor of the urban, coastal, industrial, and export sectors. This view about unbridled dominance is questionable, however. First, the Tuanpai (Communist Youth League) faction, whose members are from families of an ordinary background and who have had work experience in inland regions, broke the monopoly of the so-called coastal elites in the 2000s when Hu Jintao, a former head of the Youth League, was elevated to become the party secretary-general. Political alignments within the CCP have therefore been complicated and fluid. Indeed, the so-called "coastal elites" drove China's strategy of developing the inland West from 1999. Tracing the sources of economic and financial policymaking from a factional perspective thus tends to be speculative. Also, when we look at economic sectors in broader terms, such as the SOEs, the boundary lines of factions are vague because although different factions have clout in various industrial sectors, they also have common interests in retaining or promoting the state sector as a whole and in driving rapid economic growth. This is also the case for the financial and banking sector. As finance has become more prominent, it has become an important arena of power and wealth for all factions. Therefore, issues such as financial and banking reform are not so much about faction versus faction, but are a contest between leaders who are pushing reform versus vested interests in this sector, such as the SOEs and SOBs, that have often resisted reform.

The Contest of Ideas and Interests

Ideas and ideological positions have helped shape the preferences of policy elites, and the clash between contending agendas has played an important role in shaping growth-model dynamics and the path of financial and banking reform. However, in contrast to prevailing Western views, China's trajectory cannot be judged against standard liberal criteria, which broadly insist that markets and the state operate according to distinctive logics, with more or less clear distinctions between public and private agendas. Instead, China is best seen through a statist lens, which highlights the politicization of the economy, insisting that markets and key economic institutions and agendas are politically constructed. The interests and agendas being served by such a system are focused on wider public or nation-building goals and on more particularistic, political goals, especially in relation to the ruling party elite (Nathan and Shi 1996). There has thus been a general statist consensus among policymakers in Beijing and in local governments that the state should play a dominant role in the economy and finance and retain the means of directed credit to establish state control in key strategic sectors through the creation of an oligarchy of giant state enterprises or "national champions" (OECD 2002; Thun 2004; Pearson 2007). This prevailing state-centric paradigm has also strongly shaped the direction of change in finance and banking.

Another dimension of elite consensus has been nationalism. The Century of Humiliation, marked by a series of losses to Western invasion and bullying, and the associated societal disintegration from the 1840s, runs deep in the national memory and popular discourse (Callahan 2004). The sense of "never again" and the aspiration for a rejuvenation of China as a great power has long been shared among Chinese elites and the public alike (Unger 1996; Gries 2001; Zhao 2002; Hughes 2006). With the slow decline of the Communist ideology and revolutionary fervor in China, the Communist Party has been increasingly outsourcing its legitimacy to nationalism, a strategy that so far appears effective (Zhao 2004; He and Guo 2018).

However, divisions over ideas and policy lines have emerged and developed from different positions along the spectrum of statism and nationalism, a contest in China that has primarily involved liberal reformers versus more conservative elements. These are referred to as "liberals" and "conservatives" in the discussions here, but it should be kept in mind that these terms typically have different connotations in China than they do in the West.

Both liberals and conservatives agree that sustaining the power of the party means maintaining a party-controlled economy, especially through the SOEs and SOBs. If the regime pursues market reforms too robustly and goes too far in relinquishing control over the economy, its capacity to allocate resources and buy crucial support through the patronage system will diminish, thus opening up new political vulnerabilities for the party. There is also the view that without maintaining key controls, the party would most likely be eventually challenged by capitalists and private interests in an increasingly marketized economy, which would jeopardize party rule. The key difference between liberal reformers on the one hand and the conservatives on the other is that the former believes that *party-controlled* SOEs and SOBs can potentially survive and thrive in a more market-oriented economy, especially if institutional reforms are undertaken to increase their efficiency.

Chinese liberals thus accept a more or less central role for the state in the economy but see reform as a process of introducing a greater focus on markets and commercial elements into economic life. Liberals, however, remain wedded to active state control over at least some credit allocation and investment as part of China's "socialist market" ideology and state-directed credit to key industry sectors and to infrastructure. Liberal party elites have been very important in driving reform in China, while important liberal institutions in banking and financial administration have included the PBC and the CBRC. In the liberal view, markets are an instrument of governance within a hierarchical system (Bell and Hindmoor 2009). This approach endorses the greater use of market elements, more accountability, and a revised credit, investment, and growth model, aimed at more efficient, competitive industries and a greater focus on domestic consumption. In this context, the key agenda for those who support a revised growth model and associated financial reform does not involve challenging the state ownership of the banks, but it does mean the increased transformation and marketization of the large SOBs from administrative units in the former planning system into risk-bearing and more competitive and commercially oriented enterprises less directly aligned with party dictates.

This approach is best demonstrated by various proclamations from key reformers, such as Deng, that the state and the market are not mutually exclusive strategies, but are complementary, with both seen as a means to achieve stability, growth, and development. Deng's doctrine of grafting the state and the market together has been broadly followed by successive leaderships, particularly Zhu Rongji, who initiated reforms and external integration but at the same time also recentralized power and administrative capacity with the central government. As we show in later chapters, liberal reformers have pushed through a range of reforms to China's growth model and to the banks and financial system since the 1990s, including market entry of foreign and domestic private banks, market listing of the major banks, the creation of bond markets, a new prudential regulator (the CBRC), formal liberalization of interest rates, some loosening of the exchange rate, the growth of shadow banking, and the promotion of new, internet-based finance (fintech).

The general aim for reformist leaders is to establish an essentially *state-managed* market economy, in which the state sector continues to play a leading role at the macro level, while at the micro level, market mechanisms and, if needed, administrative controls are utilized to address major problems with the state sector, such as lack of incentives, accountability, soft-budget constraints, and moral hazard. Moreover, foreign competition in a still developing economy is also a cause for concern among liberals. These reformers believe that, given a still developing private sector, the state is better equipped to compete with foreign players through the creation of large state enterprises and national champions in strategic sectors, including the banking and financial system. It is true that there are also liberals who believe that the aim of reform is to establish a less politicized market economy by shrinking the role of the state. Nevertheless, over the years, experimentation with such an agenda has suggested that Western market doctrines have needed to be bent and adapted to China's statist traditions and developmental needs. As a PBC official commented during an interview, "We are genuine students of Western lectures and doctrines. Over the years, some worked but many didn't. We came to realize that not all Western doctrines could explain issues in China because of the special and unique situation here—I mean the transition. We simply don't have the sort of fully fledged institutions of the advanced economies."[2] Many liberals are thus wary of any "naive" importation of market doctrines and tend to accommodate an active role for the state in the economy and in fine-tuning imported market-based policy elements to suit local conditions (Bell and Feng 2019).

Such ideational stances are also linked to institutional positions and incentives. For example, a key institutional promoter of banking reform has been the PBC. Like most bureaucracies in China, the PBC comprises both liberal reformers and more conservative elements, the latter of whom favor direct monetary control methods. Over the years, however, liberals have been more influential within the PBC, and part of the reason is that the PBC's capacity to boost the effectiveness of its core mission regarding monetary policy is partly linked to improving market-based policy instruments to better regulate the financial system and to fight inflation (Bell and Feng 2013, 155–76). This in turn has depended on the progress of other related reforms—for example, partial exchange rate liberalization and also banking reform, the latter of which is seen as essential in attempting to stabilize the financial system and in improving the transmission mechanisms of monetary policy. In this way, institutional incentives and agendas have been linked to the policy ideas and preferences of key senior technocrats.

Conservatives, meanwhile, are deeply suspicious of market mechanisms and maintain that the state should retain strong controls over the economy and the financial and banking sector through administrative commands and guidance (Brugger and Kelly 1991, 98; Chen 1999). Conservatives believe that a state-led developmental model is more compatible with Chinese traditions, culture, and political systems. They fear that liberal reforms could lead to chaos, volatility, and potentially a loss of party control. Developments both at home and abroad, especially the GFC in 2008 and the largely chaotic response to the COVID-19 crisis in the Western world, as well as the stock market meltdown in China in 2015–16, only further confirmed such views in the minds of conservatives. Conservatives are also shaped by personal experience, having often developed their careers within the statist economy, frequently with stakes in the traditional statist growth model.

This faction, then, is partly based on ideology and in many cases on strong economic interests or stakes in the SOEs and in the financial regime of directed credit. As Matacic (2014) argues, "Politically, although there appears to be broad consensus about the need for financial liberalization, there are powerful counterbalancing forces. In particular, demand for cheap credit from state-owned enterprises and local governments has blocked interest-rate liberalization for the past two decades, despite many promises of imminent reforms." Export-oriented manufacturers that favor a fixed and undervalued exchange regime have similarly resisted exchange rate liberalization. Support for such antimarket, antireform arguments waned somewhat from the early 1990s after Deng's renewed push for reform and increased recognition of the economic challenges confronting the leadership, including mounting NPLs within the banks (Feng 2006b). Li Peng was the key conservative exerting political influence during his premiership between 1987 and 1998. Li largely followed the conservative views of elder leaders, such as Chen Yun and Yao Yilin, calling for cautious economic opening and a minor or supplementary role for the market in relation to the central plan. Li's conservative wing was sidelined during the Jiang era, well before Zhu Rongji took over the premiership in 1998.

However, the 1990s saw the emergence of the New Left, a new generation of conservatives presenting an approach that differed from those of the Old Left (the ultraleft, conservative thinkers) and the liberals. The New Left recognizes the social problems and instability wrought by economic liberalization and opening up, and calls for a reorientation of the reforms to address social issues such as income inequality, unemployment, and social polarization (Yang 2001, 136). In addition, the New Leftists insist that the neoliberal international economic order only perpetuates international inequality and financial instability. Therefore, in order to overcome late-development disadvantages in countries such as China, they argue that the state should be in the driver's seat, mobilizing and deploying domestic resources. Under the leadership of Xi, policymakers have had to deal with populist pressures generated by the New Left in domestic policy debates, particularly as the New Left often resorts to nationalist sentiments at home. The global financial crisis in particular has partly substantiated some of the New Left's accusations regarding the instability generated by neoliberalism and global forces, and an ideational reorientation toward statist and nationalist agendas and administration has been apparent under the current Xi regime.

Institutional incentives have also shaped the approach of the conservatives. Key bureaucracies such as the NDRC and the MOF benefit institutionally from direct state controls over fiscal and financial allocations, largely because such controls mean that they retain considerable authority and access to resources within the state system. Any substantial move to marketize financial flows would give a greater role to banks as key financial intermediaries and would weaken the authority and role of these central agencies. For these reasons, the NDRC and the MOF have been broadly opposed to further marketization of the banking system. Local governments are also involved in credit allocation, have long influenced local banks and credit raising, and usually prefer administrative forms of credit allocation, although local governments have also favored more informal means of financing, such as the shadow banking system. The SOEs, one of the major beneficiaries of the growth model, also prefer administered finance and state-owned banking, largely because this system shifts risk from the SOEs (which often fail to repay loans) onto the banks and thence to the state.

Another major site of contest between liberals and conservatives has been economic and financial opening. Domestic reform and external opening since the late 1970s have been the twin pillars of the dynamics of economic growth. As discussed earlier, both the liberal and conservative camps share certain nationalist concerns that are centered on economic and financial sovereignty (Garrett 2001). Nevertheless, liberals believe that China should embrace the global market and foreign competition, and that financial opening is instrumental in improving domestic inefficiencies. Conservatives, on the other hand, are suspicious of and worry about potential foreign control of the economic and financial system and the instability this could entail (Han 2006). In other words, the liberals' view of economic openness is positive sum, and that of the conservatives is zero sum (Helleiner and Wang 2019).

As far as banking reform is concerned, the international approach of liberal reformers is seen as being bound to result in foreigners, one way or another, taking control of domestic financial resources, and eventually perhaps the entire economy. More specifically, the conservatives opposed the bank's initial public offerings in offshore markets, insisting that domestic investors should have the lion's share of China's economic growth, which is embodied in the growth potential of the banks. Nationalist sentiments also insist that the domestic banks need more protection from the foreign competition induced by WTO entry (Naughton 2006; Xie 2006). As nationalism has emerged as an influential force in domestic debates since the late 1990s, liberals find themselves increasingly compelled to frame their reform agenda under a nationalist banner. For instance, Zhou Xiaochuan managed to use nationalist sentiments in pushing forward the internationalization of the renminbi, which essentially required financial and capital account liberalization (Davis 2011b). On the other hand, given the growing economic prominence of the Chinese state in recent years, according to Helleiner and Wang (2019, 229), "the nature of financial nationalism has changed, from a largely inward and defensive orientation to an increasingly outward orientation," which is demonstrated by Beijing's active promotion of its currency, the overseas operations of the Chinese banks, and sovereign lending, along with the Belt and Road Initiative.

The ongoing battle over China's financial and economic resources and institutions has been fought out among a wide range of powerful actors within the party-state, in key central bureaucracies in the financial arena, in local governments, and within the banks and in key economic sectors. Broadly speaking, Chinese liberals have dominated economic policymaking during the reform era. For a time after the GFC they were also successful in pushing for greater financial liberalization and the growth of shadow banking. These changes were also supported by demand-pull factors in credit markets from the private and household sectors. More recently, however, the Xi Jinping regime appears intent on reasserting the role of the state and pushing economic governance in a more illiberal direction. This is a marked shift from the more liberal direction of previous decades and reflects the ultimate unwillingness of the current regime to relinquish its grip on state power over the economy and society—with largely negative effects, as we will see, for banking reform and economic rebalancing.

GROWTH MODEL REFORM AND THE BANKS AS THE STATE'S CASHIER, 1979–96

This chapter deals with the beginning of the reform era in post-Maoist China from 1979 and explores how early experimentation with China's growth model and the banking and financial sector evolved in the 1980s and 1990s, up until the Asian financial crisis in 1997. In this period, China could not learn from any successful precedents in its economic development path and had to chart a novel course. Party leader Deng Xiaoping's reform approach was cautious, epitomized by "grappling with the stones while crossing the river." The urgent challenge in terms of growth-model reform was to move beyond the failed central planning regime toward a new form of state activism combined with the increased use of private initiatives and markets. This period covers the so-called first reform era (Naughton 1995) until the early 1990s, when reforms gradually saw market elements added to the older planning regime, creating a hybrid "plan-market" system (Naughton 1995; Liew 2005, 333). This chapter also deals with the reform changes from the early 1990s that ushered in the so-called second reform era, which focused on industrial growth and a somewhat greater emphasis on market instruments in economic reform (Naughton 1995, 150).

China's growth model during the first era of reform featured attempts to liberalize the rural economy from the early 1980s and the urban sector, particularly the SOEs, through various forms of contracting systems. There were initiatives to promote exports and SOE reforms under Deng, but these were muddled amid ideological frictions with conservatives led by Chen Yun (Fewsmith 1998). The planning apparatus within the bureaucracy remained a formidable conservative force. Fiscal decentralization gave incentives to local activism through investment and taxation. These efforts to formulate a coherent growth model yielded mixed results.

Although banking and financial development were espoused as an aspect of Beijing's reform agenda, the financial system remained repressed and banking remained rudimentary. The economic and political sensitivities surrounding the financial sector and China's political gradualism put banking reforms on the back burner in the first decade of the reform era, with the banking sector experiencing few significant reforms during this period. During the 1980s, the leadership configuration and the nature of the growth model were the major forces that shaped the financial and banking landscape. The bank-centered financial system was exploited by the state to fulfill its immediate political and fiscal imperatives. The monobank system based on the domination of the People's Bank of China (PBC) in the planning era was split into a more modern structure, with a designated central bank and various large state-owned banks (SOBs). The role of the SOBs in SOE financing was also increased, and local governments tightened their control over local branches of the SOBs. The banking system also began to diversify, with the emergence of a range of financial institutions that started to compete with the SOBs.

While rapid expansion was initially recorded in the rural areas, urban reforms largely stalled and were not helped by growing macroeconomic instability and inflation or by ideological conflicts within the leadership, all of which led to the regime's crackdown on the mass protest at Tiananmen Square in 1989. The subsequent leadership turmoil and the final ushering in of the second reform era from the early 1990s under the new leadership was also the period of transition from import substitution under the previous planned economy to export-oriented manufacturing, as Beijing experimented with establishing special economic zones in selected coastal regions. There was also the process of monetization of the economy and the increased use of markets and the price mechanism. Household income increased in both urban and rural areas. Financial repression, such as interest rate regulation, rigid control of the capital account, and a managed exchange rate system that initially supported the import substitution regime and by the 1990s the export-led regime, remained in place from the old economy. Foreign investment, most of which was from overseas Chinese in East and Southeast Asia, was encouraged initially on a limited scale. Increasingly, as the new growth model gathered steam, foreign investment was encouraged. State-led investment, in the form of fixed-asset investment, remained a key driver of the economy, however.

The period that followed, during the second reform era, especially between 1992 and 1996, saw a renewed push for economic reform, but the scope and intensity of banking reform remained limited. But the earlier party leadership shake-up after Tiananmen, the macroeconomic economic turmoil of the early 1990s, and the institutional weaknesses of the banking sector prompted a new round of reforms. During this period, both the central bank and bank regulation were fortified, but the leadership was constrained from carrying out structural reforms to banking, especially in relation to bank-balance-sheet reform and SOE financing.

Initial Restructuring of the Banking Sector

Before 1979, the Chinese had a monobanking system following the Soviet style. After the Chinese Communist Party seized power from the Nationalists in 1949, it basically copied the Soviet model of political and economic governance—essentially a central planning and command system (Ward 1980). A feature of this was the exclusive concentration of credit in the state banking system (He 1998, 25–30). In China's case, most Chinese financial institutions had been either closed or merged with the PBC, making the latter the single state bank with a vast nationwide network of branches.[1]

Being at the center of the state banking system, the PBC had to perform both central-banking and retail-banking functions. However, this did not make it a powerful institution. Under the planning regime, the allocation of financial resources was dictated by the state's production plans based on material balance. Prices were largely irrelevant since they were set by government agencies rather than by market-based supply and demand. As a result, this severed the relationship between finance and the economy. Production and distribution were subject to the physical plan. The financial plan, dictating the flow of financial resources at official price levels, reflected but was subordinate to the physical plan. The major role of money and finance, therefore, was to supplement and facilitate the central planning process. The subordination of finance was also reflected in the marginalized institutional status of the PBC, acting as "an agent and cashier for the government rather than a bank" (Bell and Feng 2013, 32). At the same time, local branches of the banks were aligned with and controlled by local governments. The whole banking system merged with state treasuries at various levels during 1958–62, with "the PBC's head office," according to Jin (1994, 142–43), "becoming a department under the MOF with only eighty staff." Nevertheless, in the aftermath of the Cultural Revolution, the central government set out to restore financial order and establish a more modern financial system, albeit one controlled by the state. Hence, in March 1978, the State Council allowed an institutional separation of the PBC from the MOF, granting the PBC ministerial ranking (Tam 1986, 430).

The ambition to introduce market mechanisms into a state-dominated economy essentially required a more capable and efficient financial system that could provide vital support for the new economy. This was recognized by the party leadership at the time, particularly by Deng Xiaoping. According to Deng (1993c, 366), "Finance is vital as it is the core of the modern economy. Once we get finance right, the whole game [of economic management] is all right." He also stated, "We should take bolder steps in financial reforms, and turn the banks into genuine banks. The banks we have had in the past have been currency issuers and state treasuries, but not genuine banks" (1993a, 193). Indeed, the Chinese banking system was widely seen as rudimentary and incapable of providing efficient financial intermediation (Pei 1998; Guo 2002; Okazaki 2007). The lack of substantial development was mainly the result of the heavy politicization of finance during rural reforms in the early 1980s (Oi 1999), and during urban industrial reform focused on the SOEs from the mid-1980s (Shirk 1985).

The political distortion of finance also reflected what Shirk (1993) calls "the political logic of reform." According to Shirk (1993, 1994), the preeminent feature of China's economic reform has been its gradualist approach, especially compared with the big-bang approach prescribed for and adopted by Russia and the former Eastern European Communist countries in their reform push from the early 1990s. Decades of central planning had created conservative beliefs in state control of the economy, as well as powerful vested interests at elite and bureaucratic levels and in the state-owned sectors. To make reforms politically viable, reformers often had to maintain many older elements of the political and institutional system of central planning and gradually mix this with new, market dynamics in a dual-track mode. Over time, the reforms amounted to a process of slowly "growing out of the plan," with more efficient, market-oriented practices gradually outgrowing and generally outperforming the planning regime (Naughton 1995).

This dual-track approach was inevitably a result of intensive and extensive bargaining, consensus seeking, trade-offs, and compromises between the old and the new elements in the polity, primarily derived from divisions within the party elite. The Communist Party had just survived the disastrous impact of Mao's Cultural Revolution as the reformers within the party, led by Deng Xiaoping, pushed for change. Through a successful bloodless coup, the reformist faction managed to remove both the ultraleft ideologues (the Gang of Four) after Mao's death and Mao's designated successor, Hua Guofeng, in the early 1980s (Bucknall 1989, 25). Nevertheless, the subsequent years in the 1980s and early 1990s saw ongoing tensions between Deng Xiaoping and Chen Yun, who represented conservatives within the party. Chen's career had been in the central bureaucracy, especially in the planning system. For much of Deng's era, Chen was also the party's deputy chairman and a member of the Standing Committee of the Politburo.[2] These two were close allies at the beginning of the reforms, fighting off potential threats from loyal followers of Mao. However, their differences in economic management emerged in the 1980s, especially on urban reform (Dittmer and Wu 1995; Teiwes 1995). Thereafter there was a split between the reform and the conservative wings of the party. Chen insisted on limited reforms within the planning framework and on maintaining the leading positions of the SOEs. He and his supporters also had concerns about the potential negative impact of economic opening. On the other hand, Deng was more liberal and radical, advocating more extensive market-oriented reforms and the wider opening up of the economy (Feng 2006c). These conflicts shaped the first decade of reform, and despite them, according to Dittmer and Wu (1995, 473), "Chen never openly challenged Deng for power. Chen's strategy was to stage a side-protest to Deng's approach once the economy was overheated by radical reform programs and thereby force him to follow his own preferred policies."

This leadership cleavage significantly constrained the hands of the reformers and the path and pace of the banking reform. The contention at the very top meant that major reforms could be carried out only in areas of limited controversy and political convenience and of little threat to vested interests. Given the impasse at the top, grassroots experimentation was encouraged to help forge bottom-up momentum for reform (Shirk 1992). The power to allocate financial resources remained vital for the political leadership, both to help sustain one-party rule and to oil the systems of political patronage. Therefore, serious financial reforms were not on the agenda and the financial and banking system continued to serve the needs of the party-state.

The measures taken in the banking sector by the Chinese government during this period focused on organizational changes that dismantled the monobank system. To the reformers, administrative and fiscal decentralization put pressure on the old, centralized financial system (Guo 2002, 16–17). The emphasis on local development and the rural sector, which were a key part of the emerging growth model during the first reform era, required financial services that were more flexible and targeted than the rigid, centralized control of the monobank system. More importantly, the economic transition and China's expansion of international economic exchange demanded a more professional and sophisticated system of financial intermediation to finance production, investment, and consumption, which the PBC's universal system was unable to provide. Therefore, the aim of the institutional restructuring that subsequently took place was to functionally and institutionally separate the monobank system into a two-tiered system of banking, with the PBC acting as an exclusive central bank from 1984, while four SOBs, either reestablished or separated from the PBC, dealt with retail banking (Bell and Feng 2013, 41–67).

The focus on rural development in the 1980s placed an emphasis on rural credit. Accordingly, on March 13, 1979, the Agricultural Bank of China (ABC) was among the first to be split off from the PBC to facilitate rural reform. The Bank of China (BOC) was also split from the PBC, with foreign-exchange-related finance, investment, and clearance as its exclusive territory. The People's Construction Bank of China (PCBC), formerly an agent for the Ministry of Finance assisting state-led fixed-asset investment, was integrated into the banking system in January 1983 with similar functions. The major portion of the PBC's commercial operations in the urban and industrial sectors went to the Industrial and Commercial Bank of China (ICBC), which was created in January 1984 (Guo 2002, 69). The four SOBs—the ICBC, ABC, BOC, and PCBC (renamed the China Construction Bank in 1986)—collectively called the Big Four, became the backbone of China's banking and financial system.

The Big Four were also referred to as state-owned specialized banks because each had a designated business area. However, such restrictions began to fade in the mid-1980s, with a certain degree of competition emerging among the banks. This was described as follows: "The BOC is landing [from the supposedly higher end of overseas financing], the ABC is entering the cities, the ICBC is going to villages, and the PCBC is coming to enterprises" (quoted in Okazaki 2007, 8).[3] Despite the domination of the Big Four, small and regional banks, though much smaller in size, started to emerge. This included the establishment of several smaller banks, especially joint-stock banks, in the latter half of the 1980s that were owned by either joint stockholders or SOEs. Nine joint-stock banks had been established by 1992, the first being the Bank of Communications, established in 1986. Many of these banks started as regional banks but later expanded their business nationwide. Minsheng Bank, China's first private bank, was established in 1995 (Okazaki 2007, 9).

At the same time, nonbank financial institutions also emerged in the 1980s. According to Okazaki (2007, 10), "At the end of 1992, there were 12 insurance companies, 387 trust and investment companies, 87 securities companies, 29 finance companies, 11 leasing companies, 59,000 rural credit cooperatives, and 3,900 urban credit cooperatives in China." Moreover, foreign banks were given the green light to operate in China, and had established 98 branches and 302 representative offices by late 1992 (Shang 2000, 22). Nevertheless, until China's accession to the WTO in 2001, their business areas were highly restricted, mainly to financing an increasing number of foreign joint ventures and foreign-owned firms in China (Wang 2003).

The diversifications in the financial system have led to more competition and, importantly, created much-needed intermediation for the emerging non-state sector, which had not been favored by the SOBs. The impact was far reaching, particularly in terms of bank deposits. The share of deposits for major state banks declined, from 83 percent in 1986 to 72 percent by 1996. Correspondingly, the share for nonstate deposit-taking financial institutions increased considerably. On the lending side, the share for loans also saw a steady decline on the part of large state banks, from 90 percent to 78 percent between 1986 and 1996. Major challenges for the SOBs also stemmed from the rural credit cooperatives and from trust and investment companies, the latter gaining a market share of 15 percent during this period.

Apart from the increase in competitive pressures on deposits and lending, small and medium-sized banks, including rural and urban credit cooperatives, had also provided much-needed intermediation for China's dynamic private sector, with access to credit, as noted above. State banks dominated lending to the SOEs; such lending took up 84 percent of their loan portfolio, compared with just 5 percent for the nonstate sector. In contrast, the urban and rural credit cooperatives lent more than half of their loans to nonstate firms, at 64 percent and 53 percent, respectively.

SOEs and the Fiscalization of the Banking System

Another reason that the main banking system remained closely wedded to the needs of the state was the central state's fiscal needs. Fiscal decentralization in the early 1980s favored local governments, resulting in a steady decline in the central state's revenues and hence its budgetary power over funds distribution. One result was that the central government was increasingly not capable of providing new equity for the SOEs (Wong 1991; Ma 1997, 71). Instead there was a need to use bank loans in order to finance the SOEs through the government's administrative controls over the banks (*bo gai dai*). In essence, this meant a "fiscalization" of the banking system, in that the banks performed the duty of the state treasury in providing financing for the SOEs (Pei 1998, 332).

Hence, the banks assumed the responsibility of providing working capital for the SOEs as early as 1984, which was further extended to financing the SOEs' capital projects in 1986 (*Jingji cankaobao* 1996). This was made even clearer in the Eighth Five-Year Plan (1991–95) in 1991, which stated that "the specialized banks should carry out national industrial policy and economic adjustment functions." As a result, the credit holdings of Chinese banks increased almost twelve times between 1978 and 1992 (Lardy 1998, 80). By the mid-1990s, almost all of the SOEs' working capital (98 percent) was financed by banks gobbling up about 80 percent of bank credit (Pei 1998, 332). A World Bank (1996, 6) report suggests that SOE losses accounted for almost 9 percent of GDP, compared with a little over 2 percent of government budget deficits, between 1987 and 1995, resulting in public deficits of more than 11 percent of GDP. As the issuance of treasury bonds and external financing could cover only less than 3 percent of the deficits, the rest had to be financed by the banking system. This means that almost all SOE losses were financed by the banks during this period. Moreover, the heavy reliance on bank credit for SOE operations had further increased the SOEs' debt levels. For example, the debt-to-asset ratio reached 84 percent in 1994, more than double that in 1980. This had also diluted state holdings of SOE equities, which stood at only 20 percent in 1994.

Local Government Influence and Weak Central Regulation

The main banks' lack of independence from the state was further compounded by their institutional weakness. Bank staff, according to Pei (1998, 328), were "poorly trained and their equipment and use of modern technology backward." The organizational structure of the banks was aligned with the administrative order, rather than with modern corporate practices, and the state banks and their management and staff were simply another layer of the state bureaucracy.

Local influence over the SOBs was also important. Following the principle of "one level of local government, one level of bank branch" (Jin 1994, 149), banks' local branches were largely subject to the influence of local governments. Organizationally, the branches were subject to control from the bank's head office and local government, a typical feature of the Chinese bureaucratic system aimed at balancing functional and territorial interests (Halpern 1992; Naughton 1992). However, in practice, local governments were in charge of the local bank branch's personnel management and social welfare, which meant that local governments had a major influence on bank decision-making. As local officials' political careers and party standing were linked to the performance of the local economy, bank branches faced constant pressure for providing loans to local governments, even if this sometimes violated the banks' internal supervisory rules. Moreover, the head offices could not effectively control the branches due to information deficiencies and asymmetries owing to a lack of intra- and interbank settlement systems (Feng 2006a). As a result, credit expansion under local investment fetishism became a systemic issue, which directly contributed to the inflationary cycles in the 1980s and early 1990s (Huang 1996; Bell and Feng 2013, 68–88).

At the same time, the economic transition and the opportunities it created provided ample room for irregularities and corruption on the part of the banks. In the financial realm, the dual-track approach also led to a dual-track interest rate regime: the market rate and the administrative rate that was often below the market rate. The ensuing arbitrage would see those privileged few able to exploit the spread of the two rates by borrowing at the lower administrative rate and lending out at the higher market rate. This was a huge business because, as noted, the state banks around this time controlled about 80 percent of all lending. In addition, the state banks also sought revenue from the market sector, which was underregulated but offered higher returns. This was done mainly through setting up nonbank financial institutions, particularly trust and investment companies, despite the fact that these companies often violated government regulations (Tam 1986, 431; Pei 1998, 324).

These problems were further compounded by an institutionally weak PBC that was inexperienced at and incapable of regulating the emerging banking system and financial market. The PBC was turned into an exclusive central bank in 1984 after the Big Four took over its retail banking functions, as noted above, but the PBC retained the duty of banking supervision. However, the PBC and monetary policy remained sidelined in the 1980s and early 1990s under the legacies of the planning system, largely because centralized financial planning (in the form of the Credit Plan and the Cash Plan) continued to dominate China's monetary management (Bell and Feng 2013, 68–88). The PBC found it increasingly difficult to use traditional quantitative tools, such as credit quotas, as more and more financial institutions began operating outside of the Credit Plan. For example, regional banks and nonbank financial institutions (NBFIs) accounted for 22 percent of loans in 1995. By June 1996, the lending of the four SOBs accounted for only 62 percent of total credit issuance, which meant that almost 40 percent of the lending was beyond the control of the PBC (*Jingji daobao* 1996).

At the same time, the SOBs could also evade the credit controls of the PBC, particularly using avenues such as the interbank market. Before 1994, this market was poorly regulated, attracting both borrowers without access to bank credit and bank lenders lured by high interest rates (Pei 1998, 331). Thus, the interbank market became an alternative channel of funds outside the Credit Plan. Another way of circumventing the Credit Plan was to exploit repurchase agreements (repos), called "false repo," on the stock markets. Under this arrangement, bank loans were essentially transformed from short- to long-term loans, which were then used to speculate on the stock market. By 1995, such loans reached 70 billion yuan (Pei 1998, 331–32).

The PBC also faced technical barriers in the regulation of the market, particularly in relation to an outdated financial infrastructure. During most of the 1980s, the central bank largely inherited from the old planning era a manually based clearing system, which made cross-region, interbank settlements complicated and time consuming (Feng 2006a). The system also hampered the PBC's capacity in managing capital and liquidity and constrained the central bank's capability in monitoring banking performance and regulating bank practices.

Cautious Banking Reform, 1993–96

The political capital of the conservatives rose for a period after the crackdown in Tiananmen Square in 1989. There was a purge of the reformer Zhao Ziyang and the installment of Jiang Zemin as the new party secretary-general by party veterans. The subsequent economic retrenchment saw a number of reforms rolled back and a comeback by leftist ideologues. This setback led many to question the future of reform amid heated ideological debate over the compatibility between socialism and the market economy.

Subsequently, the largely conservative political climate in Beijing began to change in favor of the reformers. A key event was Deng Xiaoping's tour of southern China in 1992, during which he rallied local support for more radical reforms and called for an ideational shift aimed at rethinking the nature of socialism and the market economy (Fewsmith 2001a, 87). For Deng (1993b), the market and socialism were not necessarily incompatible, as the leftists had argued. Deng maintained that the two were complementary and that socialism could and should incorporate elements of a market economy. Deng's ideological breakthrough against the conservatives in the early 1990s further accelerated the pace and scale of economic reform, producing a more decisive reform momentum. Indeed, his call for a "socialist market economy" was accepted in 1992 by the Fourteenth Party Congress. Deng's renewed push for more radical reforms switched Chinese reform to the fast lane. Banking reforms during this period were subsequently shaped by a change in party leadership, the rising status and capacity of the PBC, and a new inflationary cycle during 1993 and 1994.

Deng's southern tour generated a renewed wave of economic expansion. The resulting inflationary surge and a banking crisis in the early 1990s led to calls for restructuring the banking system. Both capital investment and industrial growth reached a historical high by 1993. As a result, the consumer price index shot to 14.7 percent in 1993 and further climbed to a truly alarming 24.1 percent in 1994. The PBC's weak supervision of the largely distorted market and its weak credit controls were major factors that contributed to the economic chaos

(Bell and Feng 2013, 178–90). From the second half of 1992 and well into 1993, a flood of speculative funds, believed to be about 100 billion yuan, moved from the interbank market into real estate development, particularly in coastal regions. This led to monetary disruptions in the form of declining new banking deposits and a resultant liquidity shortage for the banks. For instance, in just six months, between the end of 1992 and June 1993, the payment reserve ratio at the state-owned banks declined from 8.3 percent to 5 percent (Pei 1998, 338).

China's top policymakers acted swiftly in reining in the economic overheating and the banking disruptions through the use of heavy-handed administrative measures. Although the banking system was saved from breakdown, this episode of economic and financial chaos rang alarm bells in Beijing. Hence, in May 1993, the leadership assigned a key advisory unit, the Commission on Economic System Reform, to come up with a comprehensive plan for deepening the reforms in areas such as finance, fiscal budgeting, and social security (Pei 1998, 340). Beijing adopted many of the suggestions proposed by the commission, which was staffed mainly by liberal reformers, and in November 1993, in a landmark party document titled "Decisions on Issues concerning the Establishment of a Socialist Market Economic Structure," distilled them into a number of broad principles for increased marketization of the economy.

The most important reform measures revolved around central banking, banking and financial markets, and foreign exchange reforms. According to the document, the party was to increase the authority of the central bank, especially in centralizing the PBC's decision-making structure against local government interventions, and in granting the PBC new tools of monetary policy (Bell and Feng 2013, 140–43). For the banking sector, the four SOBs were to be turned into commercial banks, and their state-directed policy lending functions were to be transferred to newly established policy banks. The state banks would have to increase their compliance with international standard practices. Urban and rural credit cooperatives were forced to be more competitive. In addition, the interest rate regime was to be more liberalized, with banks given more discretion in setting interest rates in relation to the PBC's benchmark rates. The nation's financial market was to be unified. Finally, China's foreign exchange system was to be reformed, with unified exchange rates and a more liberal regime for current account transactions.

As the party's blueprint for market reforms, the "Decisions on Issues" document delineated the strategic roadmap of the reforms as well as more specific policy measures in reforming the financial and banking sector. There had been a push by market-oriented reformers for a more comprehensive and radical program, but this had failed to win political support. More importantly, however, many of the policies that were rolled out failed to live up to expectations, partly due to tardy leadership and excessive caution, and partly to resistance on the reform and implementation front.

This to some extent reflected elite dynamics. As argued above, in the first era of reform, between 1979 and 1992, the lack of comprehensive reforms in the banking system reflected elite fragmentation, with power at the top dispersed across an array of contending revolutionary elders within the party-state. By contrast, the leadership in the second reform era after 1993 was more cohesive in pursuing market reforms and external integration. Nevertheless, the years between 1993 and 1996 marked a phase-in for the new reformist leadership headed by Jiang Zemin and Zhu Rongji, a period when their power was being consolidated. At the same time, the pressure from conservatives led by Li Peng was also a factor. Indeed, the evolving power dynamics between reformers and conservatives, particularly between Jiang, Li, and Zhu in the 1990s, largely determined China's political economy and the extent of market-based reform initiatives during this period. Replacing Zhao Ziyang, who was accused of sympathizing with and supporting the democratic movement, Jiang was promoted by Deng in 1989 to be the party's secretary-general after the Tiananmen crackdown.

Adopting his predecessor's lesson in not going too far in pushing for economic and political reforms against the will of the party elders, Jiang was cautious in clarifying his position on the nature and direction of reform in his early years as party boss. In the following eight years, however, Jiang rose within the party, military, and diplomatic arenas and rose further after Deng's death in February 1997. Yet Jiang's technocratic background meant that he lacked the legacy and charisma that Deng had derived from the revolutionary struggle. This saw him stop short of breaking with the Left and conservatives whose stocks rose for a time after 1989. True, Jiang, Zhu, and other reformers controlled the Politburo Standing Committee and thus the top leadership, but Jiang was not unfettered. The party was divided on economic reform and China's external engagement, and Jiang played the role of compromiser between the conservatives and the reformers, while distancing himself from disputes.

Premier Zhu Rongji also has a technocratic background, as an engineer, with an initial career in state planning. He was purged in 1958 and in 1970 for criticizing Mao's "irrational high growth." He was then brought back by Deng, who sought his economic experience (Naughton 2002). Deng argued, "We cannot promote cadres solely on political trustworthiness, but also on knowledge on economics. There aren't many senior cadres in our party who know about the economy. Zhu is one who really does" (Ling, Ma, and Deng 2003). Zhu was a liberal and got promoted to executive deputy premier in 1993. He achieved acclaim for reducing inflation in 1993 and for the "soft landing" of the economy in 1996 after tough measures. He built up his role in China's fiscal and banking system, especially with his appointment as the PBC governor between 1993 and 1995.

Jiang and Zhu both favored banking reform. The two leaders had also forged ties acting as party boss and mayor in Shanghai in the 1980s (Gao and He 1993, 72). But their stances were never fully united. Zhu was aware that reformers like Hu Yaobang and Zhao Ziyang had been scapegoats for Deng in times of economic and political difficulty. According to David Zweig (2001, 238), Zhu aimed to "patronize, not antagonize" Jiang, with Zhu holding less authority than Jiang. Nor did Zhu have broad support in the party. He was also unpopular with provincial leaders, having reduced provincial subsidies and reined in provincial control over local state banks. Therefore, on tough issues of political importance, Zhu needed Jiang's intervention, but when Jiang compromised, Zhu was likely do so as well.

Li Peng was Zhou Enlai's adopted son, a longtime party veteran and premier, and hence deeply embedded in the network of party elders. He was a high-profile conservative, influential in the Deng and Jiang eras. He held the premiership from 1987 to 1998 and then became the chairman of the National People's Congress. Li adopted the views of elders such as Chen Yun and Yao Yilin. He thought that central planning and careful economic opening should be supported, not replaced by the market. He had bureaucratic experience in heavy industry, a sector long favored under central planning. Although Li's conservative faction was somewhat on the outs during the Jiang era, they still had a degree of influence. Between 1993 and 1996, Li's position in the party and in the government had been higher than that of Zhu (number two in the party and premier). Despite the fact that Li relinquished his economic portfolio to Zhu back in 1993, he could maintain pressure on Jiang and Zhu (Gao and He 1993, 74).

This ideational configuration and delicate power balance between the reformers and conservatives meant that politically sensitive moves, such as banking reform, had to proceed with caution. Hence, the subsequent reforms proved to be piecemeal, featuring short-term solutions under a cautious, pragmatic leadership.

The Reform Package and Its Limitations

The actual reforms in the financial and banking sector during this period mainly included legislation, the establishment of policy banks, and enhanced competition and regulation in the financial system. Laws concerning the financial and banking sector were promulgated in 1995. These included the Law of the People's

Bank of China, the Law on Commercial Banks, the Insurance Law, the Law on Negotiable Instruments, and the Guarantee Law. In particular, the Commercial Bank Law established the legal framework for the banking sector. Reflecting the clear limits of the market reform agenda, however, the dominance of the state over the banking system was also enshrined in the new law. This meant that the banks were still required to provide credit to inefficient sectors, especially the debt-ridden SOEs.

New Policy Banks

Nevertheless, there was an attempt to reduce the exposure of the SOBs to inefficient state lending practices. Part of the reform program aimed to establish three "policy banks" in 1993. These banks were tasked to finance projects that were prioritized by the government but that were less commercially profitable. These include the China Development Bank in large capital project finance, the China Ex-Im Bank in the area of trade finance, and the Agricultural Development Bank for the rural sector. It was hoped that by handing over the function of policy lending, which amounted to about one-third of the total credit portfolio, to designated policy banks, the SOBs could be turned into state-owned commercial banks. Despite the fact that the policy banks were mandated to take over all policy loans from the state-owned commercial banks, this did not happen (Blanchard 1997, 17).

Indeed, the three new policy banks suffered from a number of problems. First, they were poorly capitalized. Given the weak fiscal position of the central government, the policy banks had to rely mainly on central bank loans. In fact, 95 percent of the PBC's loans to banks in 1994 and 1995 were allotted to policy banks (Pei 1998, 340). To access long-term capital, these banks had to turn to borrowing in the medium-term bond market. Without a reliable funding source from the government, the policy banks were laden with a highly leveraged capital structure that prevented them from generating incomes at sustainable levels.

In addition, the organizational structure of the policy banks was problematic, particularly given the fact that they could establish branches only in provincial capitals, having to delegate other local business to state banks. For example, the China Development Bank transferred its local business to the China Construction Bank, and the Bank of China has been in charge of the Ex-Im Bank's trade-related financing, as the Agricultural Bank of China has for the Agricultural Development Bank (Pei 1998, 346). This ran contrary to the original intention of establishing policy banks to insulate commercial banks from policy lending.

Regulation and Competition

Another important development in the financial system during this period was the rise of the PBC in Beijing's policy circle, as it increasingly became a more experienced and authoritative institution in China's macroeconomic management (Bell and Feng 2013). Given the fact that the lack of effective control by the central bank had largely resulted in the banking crisis in 1993, Zhu's tenure as governor at the PBC saw him tackle a runaway economy through a package of mostly administrative measures, which helped bring the economy to the above-noted soft landing in 1995–96. Not only was this experience a great personal victory in Zhu's political career, but it was also a huge credit for the central bank in the domestic polity, as it managed, for the first time, to rein in inflation. Moreover, Zhu's ruthless campaign against corruption and wrong dealings in the financial sector transformed the PBC from a relatively toothless regulator to one that was "frightening" for many bank officials and market practitioners (Bell and Feng 2013, 126). Under Zhu's leadership, the PBC's regulation over the banks was considerably strengthened.

A major banking issue was the close relationship between banks and a range of nonbank financial institutions (NBFIs) they operated. As we have discussed, credit leakage from banks to NBFIs largely contributed to the economic chaos in 1993. The comprehensive reforms in 1994 were designed to impose tighter regulatory controls over the banks in order to restrict risky investment activities. The first move was to end the banks' ownership of security firms and trust and investment companies. Following the Commercial Bank Law in March 1995, banks were separated from operating in securities and trust businesses by the end of 1996.

The Emergence of the Bad Loan Problem

As ideological concerns and leadership cleavages made extensive liberal reforms very difficult, the political imperative of containing unemployment by keeping loss-making SOEs afloat tended to build up a mountain of nonperforming loans, which became a key problem for the banking system.

To be sure, SOEs and SOBs shared one thing in common in the Chinese context: they both operated under soft-budget constraints. This implies that such organizations, according to Kornai (1986, 7), "expect that financial difficulties will lead to bail outs rather than liquidation or closure." Repaying bank loans was thus not considered essential by the SOEs, since the borrowers believed these loans were essentially fiscal funds. As one official described it, "They [the SOEs] think that, from the perspective of the government, loan repayments to the banks are like putting your money from your left pocket to your right pocket. It doesn't matter which pocket ends up with the money."[4] Under the same logic, the SOBs did not care much about recovering the loans from the SOEs since they believed the loan losses would at some stage be covered by the government, one way or another.

In effect, then, the banks were forced to operate according to the state's priorities rather than commercial considerations, including in their regional and local branches. According to a report by the PBC, 90 percent of loans issued by SOBs were subject to political pressures from government officials (Pei 1998, 332). To make things worse, the SOE sector had been losing steam and running in the red after the reforms, largely due to the inefficiencies exposed in an increasingly market-based economy. The share of SOEs' industrial output shrunk by more than half from the late 1970s to the mid-1990s (Sun 1996b, 8). Nonstate firms, on the other hand, had contributed 70 percent of the new growth of China's GDP in 1993 (Cong 1996, 22). Increasingly, the SOEs looked like industrial dinosaurs financed by directed state lending by the SOBs.

The result was that the deeply indebted SOEs were driving the increasing accumulation of NPLs in the banking sector. There were a number of estimates of the size of such loans. According to a government report, NPLs stood at around 1 trillion yuan, or a quarter of total outstanding loans, in early 1996. This NPL figure for the four SOBs stood at 532 billion yuan in 1994, or about 20 percent of their total loans. Moreover, NPLs held by NBFIs were also very large, with estimates of bad loans ranging "from 30 percent to 50 percent for trust and investment companies, 20 percent to 30 percent for UCCs [urban credit cooperatives], and 20 percent for RCCs [rural credit cooperatives]" (Pei 1998, 332).

The rising level of NPLs and the resultant decline in bank profitability led to a fall in capital adequacy ratios. Except for the Bank of China, the capital adequacy ratios of all banks declined from 2.7 percent to 2.1 percent by 1996, well below the 4 percent international average surveyed by the Bank of International Settlements.

All in all, the four SOBs were technically insolvent by the first half of the 1990s, with 530 billion yuan in NPLs, more than double the banks' total capital of 240.5 billion yuan in 1994. By 1996, the banks' capital could not cover their overdue and unrecoverable loans. According to Pei (1998, 342), "Even if state banks stopped lending to SOEs immediately, recover half of their current nonperforming loans, and write off all of their policy loans and deposit/loan interest subsidy losses, the total costs would be more than 20% of GDP and over four times the country's current bank capital."

For Chinese policymakers and state leaders, finance stands at the center of the quest for economic stability and has also provided key resources for political patronage. The continuing state dominance of the sector and the critical significance and political sensitivities surrounding the financial and banking system meant that banking reform was strategically delayed, postponed, or downgraded, compared with rural and industrial reforms, as part of growth-model reforms that topped the leadership's agenda. Despite some incremental changes introduced from the late 1970s, and despite Deng's urging to "turn the banks into genuine banks," the Chinese party-state had not created anything like an efficient, accountable, or commercially oriented banking system. The measures taken by the Chinese authorities in pursuing elements of bank reform during this period achieved only mixed results. The most noteworthy was the diversification of the financial and banking system in the 1980s and improved regulation and institution building of state banks in the early 1990s. However, the banking system continued to suffer from undercapitalization and the mounting problem of NPLs. There was also the continued reliance on the banking system, essentially as a fiscal arm of the state, to finance inefficient, loss-making SOEs. As a result, the banking sector was expected to carry the systemic costs of reforms in other sectors, thus becoming the weakest link in what was still a state-dominated economy and growth model.

QUICK-FIX BANKING REFORMS AFTER THE ASIAN CRISIS, 1997–2002

As we have seen, by the late 1990s, Beijing's exploitation of the big state banks had generated the buildup of huge amounts of NPLs originating in SOE lending. Radical reforms were ruled out in the 1980s and early 1990s due to elite cleavages and institutional constraints, as described in chapter 3. The party-state's main initial response was a largely failed program of bank recapitalization. However, the period after 1997 in the wake of the Asian financial crisis (AFC) saw somewhat more favorable political conditions for banking reform. Nevertheless, as we argue here, reformers remained constrained, largely because issues such as the dire condition of the SOEs and China's accession to the WTO were seen as more pressing. The leadership instead opted for a minimal-risk strategy that centered on further recapitalization, disposal of NPLs by manipulating institutional accounts, and measures aimed at improving banking supervision and regulation.

This chapter starts with a detailed examination of the political context surrounding Chinese banking reforms during this period, particularly leadership dynamics that were central in delaying major reforms yet again, despite the post-AFC context. We then look at various regulatory improvements that did occur during this period, including efforts to centralize the banking system and insulate it against local interference, the rising capacity and authority of the PBC in supervision, and improvements in the accounting systems of the banks. We then examine the bank bailout and recapitalization program and assess the implications of the NPL disposal programs centered on the establishment of asset management companies. Overall, despite the jolt of the AFC and the regional disturbances to economies and financial systems, this was a period of limited bank reform in China. True, various regulatory improvements were achieved, but the leadership was preoccupied with more pressing issues than the banking system. Moreover, the banking system, while problematic, did not appear to be posing a systemic risk to the wider economy and was certainly not appearing to act as a major drag on the economy or undermining the prevailing growth model. Indeed, despite the short-term scare of the Asian crisis, China's growth model, based increasingly on industrial production and exports in the state and private sector and on infrastructure investment, seemed to be working well. Therefore, more systemic or structural reforms aimed at dealing with soft-budget constraints on the SOEs and moral hazard on the part of the SOBs were not addressed. This meant that the SOBs were encouraged to continue to lend to SOEs because they believed any bad debt that ensued would be underwritten by the government. All of this may have served Zhu's strategy of minimal risk in the financial arena, but it created increasing problems of moral hazard, fiscal burdens, and financial instability for years to come.

A Missed Opportunity, Again

The death of Deng Xiaoping in February 1997 facilitated Jiang's consolidation of power at the top and paved the way for a more coherent and assertive leadership that was less influenced by conservative party veterans. The subsequent replacement of Li Peng by Zhu Rongji as the Chinese premier in March 1998 generated expectations of significant financial reform.

External shocks in the form of the AFC were also a catalyst for change. The crisis broke out in the autumn of 1997 in the economies neighboring China and further afield. China avoided an initial hit given its capital controls over hotmoney inflows and capital flight. However, the central leadership was alarmed by the situation in Indonesia, where economic hardship triggered political turmoil and regime change.

There was thus a sense of urgency generated by the perceived crisis, and momentum seemed to be growing for institutional and regulatory reforms in the financial and banking sector. Certainly, the leadership had become increasingly worried about the weakness of the financial system in China, and the crisis catapulted the NPL problem to the center of Beijing's attention. PBC governor Dai Xianglong (2001) used the opportunity and weighed in by emphasizing how the crisis had been partly driven in affected countries by fragile financial systems, inadequate corporate governance, weak risk management and supervisory frameworks, and a rigid foreign-exchange-rate management regime, all of which also reflected the realities in China.

Nevertheless, despite this heightened saliency, political considerations, institutional constraints, and vested interests continued to limit the reform push. A key issue was that banking reform was seen as hinging on SOE reform. The problem here was that the SOEs, with their vast fixed assets and huge urban employment share, were a major yet unwieldy sector of the economy.

From 1996, SOE losses exceeded profits. And for the greater part of the 1990s, the SOEs continued to fall deeper into debt. As a result, the government had to provide hundreds of millions of yuan to the loss-making SOEs as subsidies. The bottomless pit of "soft budgets" thus put fiscal pressure on the state budget in the form of ongoing SOE subsidies. As discussed in chapter 3, the state banks were obliged to provide the majority of their lending to the SOEs, often with little chance of loan repayment, resulting in a pile-up of NPLs and associated financial risks to the economy.

Hence, the banks were essentially being pressured to lend to the bankrupt SOEs, suggesting that banking system reform was strongly tied to SOE reform. The Chinese leadership therefore did not favor financial system reform without first reforming the SOEs. After several decades of creeping economic liberalization, the SOEs had become a burden and a key weakness in China's economy and growth model. The reformist leaders were increasingly confronted by this issue, one that was also the focus of Lardy's (1998) *China's Unfinished Economic Revolution*. As Premier Zhu Rongji argued, "China's economy has reached the point where it cannot further develop without [SOEs] being restructured" (quoted in Fewsmith 2001b, 574).

Another priority of the Jiang-Zhu leadership had been China's external integration, particularly its accession to the WTO, where negotiations were well underway by the mid-1990s (Feng 2006a). It was widely understood that WTO membership would partly remove the shield behind which domestic banks had so far been protected from foreign competition, which meant that Beijing should undertake forced reforms to the banking sector. To be sure, the reformers changed their perception of WTO membership. The enthusiasm in the 1980s evolved into a more circumspect stance in the 1990s, especially after 1997 and the AFC. Nevertheless, the reformers concluded that China would join the WTO, allowing it to further integrate into the international economy on the back of its low-cost labor force and a relatively liberal foreign direct investment regime. But WTO membership meant exposure of the SOEs and domestic banks to foreign competition. The reformers realized that this would provide additional leverage in the form of an "external" imperative that would help the push to reform the state sector of the economy. Zhu became Chinese premier in 1998 and his focus was more on SOE reform than on the WTO question. Mounting pressure erupted after the AFC, however, and Zhu came to see that external pressures, especially WTO accession, would help trump vested interests in the state sector. The significance of WTO accession for domestic SOE reforms thus intensified. As opening up, embodied in WTO membership, became a form of political correctness, domestic resistance to reforms was increasingly weakened. Indeed, Zhu could offload the reform pressure to the WTO instead of his own policy initiatives.

Nevertheless, reform of the state sector and WTO accession seemed politically risky to the top leadership. Zhu adopted a largely neoliberal approach to SOE reform, focused on economic efficiency. He formulated and implemented the so-called strategy of "grasping the big and letting go the small" (*zhua da fang xiao*), and an ambitious program to get SOEs "out of difficulties" in three years. This gave rise to a new economic structure in which the state monopolized the key and often the most profitable sectors, which were regarded as strategically significant. Large enterprise groups (the "national champions") were formed in order to increase China's international competitiveness (Pearson 2007). At the same time, small and medium-sized SOEs were privatized through various means with massive layoffs. In fact, some 25 percent of workers, or 27.8 million, were laid off from the SOE workforce (Hurst 2004, 101). Furthermore, Zhu implemented a reorganization of the economic bureaucracy in 1998 with the aim of ceasing the micromanagement of enterprises to instead focus on macroeconomic management and industrial development (Worthley and Tsao 1999, 580). As a result, twenty-six of the forty ministries and departments were eliminated or merged, and thirty-two thousand central government officials were transferred or discharged (Pearson 2007, 721). Not surprisingly, these reforms adversely affected a wide array of interests and vital constituencies of the party and were attacked by leftists and conservatives. When Sichuan, Shaanxi, and Henan Provinces promulgated laws privatizing the small and medium-sized enterprises, they were attacked by Song Ping and conservatives sponsored by Li Peng. Zhu was thus on the defensive given the political and social backlash against massive layoffs in the state sector (Zweig 2001, 240).

This backlash did not make Zhu's push in WTO negotiations any easier. Nevertheless, the leadership's eagerness to conclude the WTO talks in the late 1990s saw some radical concessions put on the table, but China failed to strike a deal with the United States in talks in early 1999. At the same time, the diplomatic crisis of NATO's air assault on the Chinese embassy in Belgrade in May 1999 saw a rise in Chinese nationalist sentiment. Criticisms of Zhu's deals with the

United States also arose, from the party, government ministries, and the public, and he was seen as a "traitor" on the internet for trading off Chinese sovereignty and economic rights to please "American imperialism" (Gries 2001, 36). Consequently, Zhu faced fierce attacks by conservatives led by Li for his handling of the WTO negotiations and the "radical programs" of restructuring that had allegedly trapped bureaucrats and common people in financial hardship (Fewsmith 1999, 31).

Zhu's push on the SOE and WTO fronts clearly threatened his political survival. Jiang defended Zhu in general terms but found himself in a difficult position with little room to manipulate the situation, other than to balance his stance against conservative criticisms and occasionally act at Zhu's expense. Zhu tendered his resignation three times in 1999, but Jiang refused his requests (Fewsmith 1999, 32). Given such pressures, the last thing Zhu intended to do was to set off another political land mine by aggressively restructuring the banking and financial system. Hence, instead of radical surgery, Zhu's strategy on banking reform was a Band-Aid, a temporary fix for the pressing need for recapitalization and NPL disposal, together with minor regulatory reforms with minimal risks. In addition, the leadership was also confronting fiscal constraints in the face of likely massive capital injections and a full write-off of the banks' NPLs. Given the persistent deflation in the aftermath of the AFC, Zhu instead resorted to fiscal stimulus to prop up the economy. Together with the SOE subsidies discussed earlier, these short-term budget commitments further limited Zhu's options on the banking issue. Therefore, given the political position of key reformers and short-term budget constraints, serious banking reforms were again delayed.

Regulatory Improvements

One positive impact of the AFC on Chinese banking, though, was the fact that the latter had prompted supervision and regulatory reforms in the financial sector, led by the PBC. Given the political and institutional constraints outlined above, this was the main area in which reformers were able to make at least some progress. Beijing rolled out a series of measures as the leadership and the PBC became increasingly worried about the largely ineffective supervisory system in China, which would not have coped with a crisis scenario such as that of the AFC. This led to policies aimed at insulating the banking sector from local intervention, beefing up the PBC's supervisory capacity, and improving the accounting systems of the banks.

Centralization of the Banking System

As we saw in chapter 3, both the PBC and the state banks suffered from capture by local governments under a dual-control system, which had been one of the major drivers of local economic overheating in China in the 1980s and early 1990s. The traumatic experience of the banking crisis and economic turmoil in 1993 and the subsequent painstaking anti-inflation campaign made it a priority of the leadership to reclaim direct control over the banking and credit system. In the wake of the Asian financial crisis, there had also been various financial scandals and a number of bankruptcies in the banking industry involving local governments, most notably the collapse of the Guangdong International Trust Investment Corporation, China's second-largest financial trust company, which triggered a standoff between the central government and the international lending community (Laris 1999). These incidents made the leadership more determined to stem territorial control of the banking system and centralize control in the central government's hands, leading to a restructure of the regional branch system of the PBC in 1998 to help insulate the bank from local interference (Bell and Feng 2013, 143–45).

As for the banking sector, the Central Financial Work Commission was established to insulate the PBC's and SOBs' local branches from local governments (Heilmann 2005). This was a mechanism designed to establish a vertical line of command by the party within the financial system in order to insulate the center from local interventions, thus exerting greater central authority over China's banking, securities, and insurance sectors. The reforms also aimed at attacking special insider dealing within the financial sector. The main focus was on the PBC, state regulatory bodies, and twenty-seven key financial firms. The commission operated between 1997 and 2003 and primarily asserted the party's control over the *nomenklatura* process so as to institute a system of recruitment, dismissal, and surveillance of executive personnel. In top-down fashion, the commission thus implemented a one-off purge of certain key officials in order to stem insider dealing and collusion and also to reduce the influence of local governments on the branches of the SOBs.

In addition to centralizing the SOBs' internal decision-making structures, their local branches' lending discretion, according to Okazaki (2007, 22), was also reduced from "billions of RMB to hundreds of millions of RMB." With the help of an improved payment and settlement system, the head offices of the banks became better at gathering information from local branches and dealing with risk management issues (Feng 2006a, 20). At the same time, major banks also undertook a restructuring campaign that reduced their workforce by over half a million and closed forty thousand of their branches, thus improving efficiency in terms of business operations (Borst 2013, 4).

The PBC's Strengthened Capacity

In chapter 3 we saw how the PBC had been largely sidelined in Beijing's macro-economic policymaking in the 1980s and early 1990s. However, Zhu's governorship of the PBC and his attempts to quell the banking and inflationary crisis of 1993 marked the turning point for the bank, significantly elevating its capacity and authority, including its banking supervisory capacity, from the latter half of the 1990s (Bell and Feng 2013, 140–54).

This began with increased access to external expertise. The PBC's relationship with the Bank for International Settlements started in 1984; the PBC began as an observer and then became a full member in 1996. The engagement with the bank enabled the PBC to discuss with other central bankers broader issues of interest, including bank regulation (*Jinron shibao* 2006; Bell and Feng 2019, 921). In addition, the PBC had also pledged full compliance with the Basel Capital Accord, a global banking regulatory standard regime whose Core Principles for Effective Banking Supervision were rolled out in 1997. This strengthened the PBC's capacity in regulating the banking sector.

Perhaps more important were changes in the way the PBC managed the monetary and financial system, which had been based on older legacy measures of financial planning, particularly the centralized Credit Plan. As discussed in chapter 3, with the diversification of financial institutions and the deepening of financial markets, the Credit Plan had been increasingly dilapidated and unfit for the support of market-oriented reforms. The PBC therefore scrapped the Credit Plan in January 1998, marking a new, more market-oriented era in China's financial and monetary management. This move would also promote commercial lending by state banks, propelling them to improve their assets-and-liabilities management practices. The state banks, at least formally, also gained more discretion in choosing their customers and projects, although the PBC continued to maintain quantitative aggregates for credit through administrative channels (Tong and Ding 2001, 27).

The PBC also pressured financial institutions to align themselves more consistently with national needs, especially in relation to controlling inflation (Geiger 2008, 6). This approach, called window guidance, used moral suasion and a degree of coercion to help encourage the banks to stick to official guidelines. To be sure, such practices were not invented by the PBC. The Bank of Japan had controlled bank lending during its economic takeoff in the 1960s, but this was formally abolished in 1991. The PBC started to adopt the policy, also known as "jawboning," in 1998. The usual form of window guidance is for the PBC to convene monthly or unscheduled meetings (in special or urgent circumstances) with representatives of selected financial institutions (mainly banks).

Sometimes the head of the PBC's relevant branch is also present in these meetings.[1] Officially, the process serves to impart general guidance on the sectors to which banks are encouraged or discouraged to lend; however, in practice, this often includes lending-volume guidelines (Green 2005). In commenting on the effectiveness of this traditional administrative lever, a PBC official offered the following example: "If the PBC had not held exclusive meetings with the Big Four, the increase of credit in 2003 would have skyrocketed to 3.6 trillion yuan. What does this mean? It means this could lead to five hundred to one thousand million nonperforming loans within the next five years."[2]

Improvements in the Accounting System

At the same time, efforts were also made by the Ministry of Finance to modernize bank accounting systems in terms of transparency and loan classification. A good example is interest accrual on bad loans. Before 1998, interest had to accrue on loans regardless of their healthiness. Between 1998 and 2001, the interest on loans 180 or more days overdue was stipulated not to accrue on bank books. This was further reduced to 90 days, which was the international standard.

At the same time, the government also brought the loan classification system into line with international standards. The old four-category system was centered on the status of payments, which is essentially backward looking and thus could represent risks to the banks. This was addressed by a new forward-looking system that reflected the prospect of loan repayment on a timely basis. The new system consisted of various categories of loan risk, including "special mention" loans, "doubtful" loans, and loans deemed as loss making. Therefore, the new classification system would help both banks and their regulators to identify actual credit risks in a more transparent way.

Banks are usually required to set aside loss provisions to cover potential bad loans, but this had not been the case for Chinese banks before the early 1990s. Loans that otherwise should have been regarded as nonperforming were classified as "performing," as long as the loan did not mature; therefore banks did not need to allocate provisions for these loans. This practice changed after 1993, when banks were required to allocate 0.6 percent of outstanding loans as provisions, rising by 0.1 percent every year until the figure reached 1 percent. After the new loan classification system was implemented, banks were required to make more aggressive provisioning against NPLs.

In 2002, the PBC further modified the previsioning regime into one that comprised both "general reserves" and "special reserves." While the banks are required to allocate 1 percent or more of total loans as general reserves, special reserves are required on top of this to cover potential losses from loans other than "pass." In particular, rates of special reserves are differentiated according to categories of loans: 2 percent for "special mention," 25 percent for "substandard," 50 percent for "doubtful," and 100 percent for "loss" loans.

A "Magical" Touch

Apart from strengthening financial regulation, the AFC also prompted Beijing to deal with the issue of mounting NPLs sitting on the banks' balance sheets. In November 1997 it initiated the first National Financial Work Conference, which was focused on emergency recapitalization of the SOBs. The latter were the major creditors for the economy and were regarded as too big and too important to fail. A series of measures aimed at mounting NPLs and SOB recapitalization were thus rolled out in the aftermath of the conference.

Recapitalization

The seriousness of a potential banking crisis due to mounting NPLs helped Premier Zhu convince the leadership to address the problem. This was dealt with in two dimensions. The first was to deal with the existing stocks of NPLs and the resultant erosion of bank balance sheets. The solution was to transfer existing NPLs into "bad banks," or asset management companies (AMCs), and to recapitalize the banks to give them a clean start. Second, more risk-based regulatory regimes were established to try and avoid the creation of new NPLs.

The first task of bringing down the stock NPLs was more urgent and important for the government. The eventual plan adopted by the State Council in March 1998 was a rather complicated operation. First, the PBC lowered banks' reserve ratio by 5 percentage points, effectively releasing liquidities of RMB 270 billion for SOBs and RMB 107 billion for other banks. The SOBs then used the additional liquidities of RMB 270 billion to purchase the same amount of special bonds issued by the MOF. As the institutional owner of the SOBs, the MOF then used the proceeds from the bond sales as its capital injection into the SOBs. Overall, the whole process was essentially an accounting maneuver. This was done through the manipulation of the balance sheets between the MOF and the SOBs, as the latter got capital injections in the form of government bonds while the MOF did not need to commit any hard cash.

Disposal of NPLs

The amount of capital that Beijing could afford to inject into the state banks, however, was far less than what was required to write off the bad loans. Therefore, an inseparable part of Zhu's recapitalization campaign involved the establishment of four AMCs to take over part of the NPLs from the SOBs.

The four AMCs—Huangrong, Great Wall, Orient, and Cinda—were established in 1999, soon after the start of Zhu's premiership in 1998, with each receiving initial capital of RMB 10 billion from the MOF. Each of the four AMCs was assigned to one of the Big Four to absorb its NPLs (with the exception that Cinda was designated to the China Construction Bank and the China Development Bank). In essence, the SOBs acquired AMC bonds and transferred the same amount of bad loans (at book value) to the AMCs. These bonds were guaranteed by the MOF, so this meant that the SOBs replaced their bad debt with treasury-backed capital. The AMCs were given ten years to dispose of the NPLs through debt-to-equity swap programs and auctions. The MOF would buy back the remaining NPLs with fiscal funds at the end of the ten-year term.

In total, the AMCs purchased almost RMB 1.4 trillion worth of NPLs from the Big Four and the China Development Bank at book value, which amounted to 21 percent of the loan balance of the Big Four at the end of 1998. To fund the purchase, the AMCs received RMB 548 billion in refinancing from the PBC, and issued RMB 846 billion in bonds, which were purchased by the Big Four at a fixed interest rate underwritten by the MOF with the same amount of NPLs. In accounting terms, the scheme entailed the SOBs shedding their NPLs by RMB 1,394 billion while increasing holdings of RMB 846 billion in AMC bonds on their asset side, while the banks' loans from the PBC were reduced by RMB 548 billion on their liability side.

After the AMCs took over the NPLs from the SOBs, Beijing introduced a debt-for-equity swap system to avoid SOE bankruptcy. Five hundred eighty SOEs were chosen to participate in the program. The arrangement meant that, instead of being transferred to the AMCs, the bad debt was converted to equities. The indebted SOEs would have to pay dividends (when they made a profit) rather than paying interest on debt. These SOEs were thus given short-term relief on debt repayment and expected to buy back their equities from the AMCs within ten years.

It is apparent that this round of bank recapitalization and NPL disposal was centered on using the AMCs as policy vehicles as well as manipulating the balance sheets of the related parties. Under this approach, AMCs essentially became the government's "bad banks" that enabled the government and the state banks to offload bad debt from their balance sheets. By doing so, the SOBs converted RMB

1.4 trillion of NPLs into MOF-backed AMC bonds. Meanwhile, these bonds would not appear on the MOF's formal budget, as the latter acted only as a guarantor for the AMCs in issuing the bonds. The AMCs, on the other hand, took over RMB 1.4 trillion in NPLs that were later transferred into the same value of corporate equities. According to this debt-to-equity plan, the AMCs were scheduled to purchase the NPLs at face value. The AMCs were reluctant on this score until the MOF clarified that the latter would underwrite any undisposed NPLs at the end of ten years.

Back to the Future

From the perspective of long-term financial stability, this round of bank bailouts and NPL disposals, centering on state-sponsored recapitalization and balance sheet manipulation, was merely a form of temporary relief from a chronic disease. It failed to address the deeper structural deficiencies in the banking sector, such as soft-budget constraints and forms of state intervention aimed at propping up the SOEs despite the mounting levels of moral hazard that this implied for the banking system.

The NPL disposal plan served the interests of the major bureaucratic players. The state banks replaced NPLs with capital, but the MOF avoided making a massive fiscal commitment as the AMCs shared part of the burden. Although the MOF promised to buy back the undisposed NPLs in ten years, postponing the day of reckoning, MOF officials were not concerned about this, given their career interests in short-term performance. The PBC, however, had grave concerns over the possible moral hazard induced by the one-way injection of capital into the SOBs without major complementary reforms of the banks, but it was not in a position to provide a politically better alternative for Zhu. At the time, the bank was more concerned with strengthening overall financial stability. Since a majority of the costs were borne by the MOF, the PBC did not oppose the package. The State Economic and Trade Commission, a supraministerial body revitalized by Zhu and under his personal control (Feng 2006c, 102), gained enormous power, as it was in charge of choosing participating SOEs in the debt-to-equity program (Shih 2004, 931).

All in all, the 1998 episode of bank recapitalization and NPL disposal was impressive only in accounting terms and was done without significantly challenging Beijing's fiscal position. However, Zhu's strategy essentially meant kicking the can down the road by disguising fiscal liability on the AMC's books and leaving the NPLs for the future. This was indeed a politically convenient move, so much so that Beijing later increased the NPL transfer to the AMCs from RMB

400 billion to RMB 1.4 trillion (Chang 2002, 5). Instead of a fiscal injection of capital that could have wiped off the NPLs in one clean stroke, this set of complicated capital maneuvers between different institutional accounts did not remove the NPLs from the banks' balance sheets, but simply hid them within the AMC bonds that the banks held (Walter and Howie 2011, 166).

Institutionally, the AMCs were supposed to be independent from the banks, with the MOF being their sole shareholder. However, the AMCs and the banks were intricately linked, as the AMCs were staffed mainly from the banks whose NPLs the AMCs were expected to dispose of.

The AMCs "bought" the NPLs at their face value, and their actual cash recovery rate was far lower than the 30 to 50 percent official figure (Gilley 2000, 25). As it turned out, the recovery rate has been dismal at best. For example, as of the end of 2005, AMCs had disposed of more than RMB 400 billion in NPLs, but only RMB 154 billion was recovered in cash, or 11 percent of the total transferred NPLs (Wang 2005). By 2011, the average recovery rate stood at a mere 20 percent (CBRC 2012, 8).

The bailout model also created enormous moral hazard on the part of the banks. It simply confirmed the long-held common wisdom among bank officials that the bad debts of the state sector would eventually be written off by the government, one way or another. As one PBC official recalled, "The government reiterated its warnings to the banks that this round of capital injection was 'the last supper.' Not clear about Beijing's strategic intentions, the banks did not disclose their NPLs in full at the beginning. The banks eventually realized that this [the recapitalization] was actually a free lunch; therefore the deeply concealed figure [of NPLs] subsequently popped up to the surface."[3]

Despite shedding the existing pile of NPLs to the AMCs and certain progress on regulation, this round of bank recapitalization failed to address the underlying structural problems involving soft budgets for the SOEs and the acceptance of moral hazard for the SOBs. Instead the banks were pushed by political pressures for more relaxed credit to state enterprises and the real estate sector in a bid to boost aggregate demand in the wake of an export slump in the post-AFC period. There were two major components of Beijing's SOE rescue plan, both of which came at the expense of the banking system. First was the debt-to-equity swaps, which converted SOE debt into equities held by banks and AMCs. Given the continuation of soft-budget constraints, this program further ensnared the banking system within the indebted SOE sector. This program was handled mainly by the Zhu-favored State Economic and Trade Commission, which greatly enhanced the latter's power, as noted. Second, the government also provided discounted loans, through the state banks, to major commission-approved projects handled by SOEs, amounting to RMB 200 billion in 1998. As these loans were essentially guaranteed by the central government, they represented severe moral hazard for both the SOEs and the SOBs. Through these programs, the state ensured its control over finance, particularly directed credit to the SOEs, crowding out the nonstate sector. Indeed, the share of credit to the private sector remained largely stagnant, increasing only modestly by less than 3 percent between 1997 and 2003, whereas credit to the SOEs increased almost 15 percent during the same period.

The continuation of soft-budget constraints meant that the balance sheets of the SOBs continued to be plagued by newly created NPLs. In fact, improvements to accounting practices showed further accumulations of NPLs by the banks despite the write-offs. According to Dai Xianglong (2002), then the PBC governor, this round of capital injection had reduced the overall level of NPLs from 35 percent to 25 percent of GDP by the end of 2000. However, according to Lardy (2001), the figure of RMB 2 trillion in NPLs on the state banks' balance sheets could actually be as high as RMB 5 trillion as measured by international accounting standards, which would amount to a whopping 40–75 percent of GDP in 2000. Another independent estimate placed China's NPL ratio by 2001 between 40 percent and 45 percent of all loans outstanding, or some 44 percent to 55 percent of China's GDP (Berger, Nast, and Raubach 2002, 141).

For the Big Four, the NPLs piled up again, to an average of 17.8 percent of total portfolios by 2002, according to the CBRC's Wang (2004, 17), while the average capital adequacy ratio of the Big Four fell to 4.61 percent at the end of 2002, well below the 8 percent requirement of the Basel Accord (Ye 2009). Liu Mingkang (2004), the chairman of the CBRC, later admitted that the government had been focused in the 1998 program on addressing the banks' short-term financial weakness rather than their structural problems. In short, the bailout program failed to defuse the NPL time bomb in the banking system and instead shuffled funds between different state accounts. It was a costly business for the government: with RMB 270 billion in special treasury bonds and RMB 1.4 trillion in guaranteed AMC bonds, Beijing assumed a total bill of RMB 1.71 trillion for the entire package during 1998–99. To put the figure in perspective, the bailout accounted for a staggering 25 percent of the total state revenue in the fifty years since the People's Republic was founded in 1949 (Ye 2009).

Despite some improvements in the area of banking regulation, the policy measures for the banking system during this period can hardly be seen as serious reforms aimed at the key structural problems of moral hazard in the banking system and soft budgets in the SEOs, all of which had produced the mounting problem of NPLs and SOB fragility. Instead, fiscal responsibility in recapitalizing the SOBs was deferred to the future through the use of vehicles such as the

AMCs. Premier Zhu should be credited for helping both the central bank and the SOBs fight off local government interventions by centralizing their internal decision-making structure. On the other hand, the SOBs continued to dominate the banking and financial system and continued to funnel credit to the SOE sector. In other words, the existing pile of NPLs was still hidden in the balance sheets of the banks in the form of AMC bonds, while continued lending to the state sector created new piles of NPLs. Zhu's patch-up job failed, at least as a means of fixing the banks while the systemic risks of the NPLs remained. By such means, the state's domination of the banking sector was simply storing up mounting problems for the future.

5

FURTHER BANKING
REFORMS, 2003-8

We have shown in previous chapters how the Chinese banks had been amassing huge amounts of nonperforming loans due to politicization and their dysfunctional relations with the state sector based on the prevailing statist growth model. Not surprisingly, an important issue, especially for reformers, had become how to wind back the level of NPLs and prevent the creation of new NPLs, as well as to try and make the banks operate on sounder commercial principles. As we have seen, Beijing's earlier strategy of blind capital injection and reliance on industry self-discipline and party supervision (through the Central Financial Work Commission) turned out to be a major failure. Hence, the key issue for reformist policymakers was focused on attempting to discipline and reform the banks. This was difficult under the prevailing growth model, but for reformers there were nevertheless attempts to step beyond the earlier fiscal balance-sheet injections and a shift toward more market-oriented structural reforms, of the type advocated by the PBC.

In this chapter, we will first discuss the external momentum for a renewed push for banking reform—namely, China's accession to the World Trade Organization in 2001 and the associated commitment to financial opening thereafter. This is followed by a detailed discussion and assessment of the institutional context of policymaking and the actual reform process during the 2000s, prior to the GFC. We argue that, while reformers were active, they were nevertheless constrained by various political and institutional imperatives, particularly the state's dominance in the banking sector, as well as bureaucratic rivalry between the PBC and the MOF. Therefore, banking reform during this period was shaped by both reformist agency activism and prevailing institutional constraints. The push for reform by the PBC, as well as a more favorable external context related to WTO entry, supported a degree of institutional change and reform. Nevertheless, the fundamental politicization of Chinese banking and finance was not overcome and became far more pronounced as the leadership confronted the GFC in 2008 and thereafter, as we show in the next chapter.

The Wolf Is Coming

As we have seen, China's banking reform was largely sidelined and downgraded despite alarm calls following the Asian financial crisis. There was, however, renewed momentum for reform after China acceded to the World Trade Organization in late 2001. By any standards this was a significant institutional and structural shift in the economic transition process and in the dynamics of banking reform. For the Chinese leadership, the apparent benefit of WTO membership was to ensure better access for Chinese exports to global markets by securing most-favored-nation treatment from its major trading partners, particularly the United States. But more importantly, elements of the leadership hoped that more integration in the world market would foster the deepening of domestic reforms, especially the SOE reform that had been more or less stalled amid fierce resistance. Many in the leadership also wanted to foster anticorruption campaigns through the WTO's binding requirements for administrative transparency. Therefore, the negotiation processes saw the leadership, mainly under Premier Zhu Rongji, forcefully run over the largely recalcitrant bureaucracy, making major concessions on a number of fronts, including in the services sector (Feng 2006c, 98–110). In fact, according to Mattoo (2004, 125), Beijing made "relatively deep and wider" commitments, compared to many other acceding nations, in terms of market access and national treatment.

Yet Beijing faced a difficult challenge in its negotiations over financial-sector opening. On the one hand, Western countries were eager to crack open China's financial market, which had been kept largely closed for decades. On the other hand, the Chinese government acknowledged the benefits China may have gained from opening-induced reforms but remained concerned about the fragility of domestic institutions and businesses. As a result, Zhu adopted a selective approach with regard to WTO-induced financial opening. China agreed to grant foreign access to banking and to non-life-insurance sectors within five years after accession but kept the life insurance and stock markets off limits to foreign interests (Mattoo 2004, 124; Feng 2006c, 108). For the banking sector in particular, a major commitment was that Beijing would allow foreign banks full access (both in foreign and local currencies) to the Chinese market (both residents and enterprises) by December 2006, a five-year phase-in period after the WTO accession. This meant that Beijing was effectively given a brief period of time to prepare the moribund banking sector for the looming showdown with global financial giants before the latter were to be granted apparently unfettered access to the domestic market.

Zhu's Legacy

As discussed in chapter 4, reformers in the government, including Zhu, knew all too well about the problems plaguing the banking sector and the need for reform. However, the lack of a broad political support base had seen Zhu struggling with higher-priority issues, such as SOE reform and WTO accession, in a hotly contested internal and external environment. As a result, banking reform became an ad hoc program of recapitalization and NPL disposal based largely on political convenience. Nevertheless, Zhu's achievement regarding WTO membership ensured that the reform and opening-up process was locked in and made irreversible. The associated commitment to financial opening, in particular, thus formed a powerful external dynamic in support of banking reforms. Apart from inviting external pressures, Zhu also ensured that the momentum of reform was maintained by installing like-minded successors to the leadership and to key bureaucratic positions.

The Sixteenth Party Congress in November 2002 marked a leadership transition from Jiang Zemin and Zhu Rongji to Hu Jintao and Wen Jiabao. While Zhu stepped down from the premiership and was succeeded by Wen in March 2003, Hu became the party boss and president after the congress, while Jiang remained the chairman of the powerful Central Military Committee until March 2005. The change of leadership led to a shift in emphasis between the two administrations. While the Jiang administration was adamant about China's external integration into the global economy, the Hu administration was more concerned with what Liew and Wu (2007, 116) call "the externalities of liberal reforms," in particular mounting poverty and income inequality (Naughton 2004). A staple in the Chinese press was the ascription to the new leadership the terms "scientific development" or "putting people first" (*yiren weiben*), implying a much broader approach than the previous growth-at-any-cost strategy. The approach also advocated the establishment of a "Harmonious Society," which saw tackling social inequalities and polarization as the foundation for comprehensive, coordinated, and sustainable development (Naughton 2005a). The shift in focus from reform and external integration to domestic inequality did not necessarily represent a U-turn or a rollback in the general direction of the reforms. Rather, it represented a more cautious approach toward the liberalist and internationalist themes of the Jiang-Zhu reforms.

Hu essentially opted out of the leadership in economic and financial affairs, leaving Wen as the major decision-maker in this area (Liew and Wu 2007, 117). Prior to his premiership, Wen had been assisting Zhu in financial affairs as vice premier and head of the Central Financial Work Commission (restructured into the China Banking Regulatory Commission by 2003). The vice premier with a finance portfolio under Wen's leadership was Huang Ju, who, upon his death, was replaced by Wang Qishan in 2008. Huang was associated with Jiang's power base in Shanghai. Wang, once a vice governor of the PBC (1993–94) under then PBC governor Zhu, was considered a Zhu protégé and an entrusted firefighter who was used to being assigned to tough jobs, such as mopping up the mess after the collapse of the Guangdong International Trust and Investment Company. Henry Paulson (2009), the former US treasury secretary, thought Wang was "the man China's leaders look to for an understanding of the markets and the global economy," and the one who "managed the largest bankruptcy restructuring in China's history in 1998 and thereby prevented a banking crisis that could have crippled the country's growth."

Zhu also handpicked reformers and elevated them to head key economic and financial ministries, particularly in his appointment of Zhou Xiaochuan as the new governor of the PBC in December 2002. Zhou was widely seen as "the brightest financial star in government" (Murphy 2003). Trained as an engineer, Zhou later became an economist. Alan Greenspan (2007, 298) described him as a Chinese technocrat with "fluency in English and international finance." Zhou was also a staunch promoter of market initiatives, with comprehensive experience as a central banker, commercial banker, and financial regulator. His long career at the top of the financial sector included serving as vice governor of the PBC, chief director of the State Administration of Foreign Exchange (SAFE), governor of the China Construction Bank (one of the Big Four), and chief regulator of China's securities market, the China Securities Regulatory Commission (CSRC).

More importantly, Zhou maintained considerable political clout during both the Jiang and Hu administrations. He had served in a key reform think tank in the 1980s, and he not only survived the purge of former reformist premier Zhao after the 1989 turmoil but flourished. This is less surprising given his family connections. Jiang was supported and mentored by Zhou during important moments in his early career. Zhou also had the respect of Zhu Rongji, who was instrumental in promoting him to head the central bank (Murphy 2003). Within the new administration, Zhou forged a strong relationship with Wen, so much so that Wen "effectively delegated authority and decisive action to Zhou," according to Naughton (2004, 5). In addition, Huang Ju, the vice premier with the finance portfolio, had been very supportive of Zhou and the PBC in the State Council (Walter and Howie 2011, 166). Zhou's governorship at the PBC also ensured that, on top of the bank's growing formal and informal authority following Zhu's premiership in the 1990s, the PBC would continue its pioneering efforts in bringing a more market-oriented approach to central banking and financial reforms (Bell and Feng 2013, 155–77).

Hence, the lineup of pro-reform leaders in key positions during the post-Zhu financial decision-making era meant that Zhu's legacy would be largely kept intact under the Hu-Wen regime. This was particularly so in the finance sector, since only by pushing ahead with reforms, particularly in the banking system, could Beijing establish a sound foundation for sustainable development and social stability.

A New Approach

As we saw in chapter 4, Beijing's earlier strategy of blind capital injection and reliance on industry self-discipline and party supervision (through the Central Financial Work Commission) had turned out to be a major failure. Accordingly, the new crop of political and financial elites actively sought new ideas and new ways of rejuvenating the banking sector in the face of the looming WTO-mandated financial opening. In February 2002, right after China's WTO accession, a national financial work conference was held to discuss a follow-up strategy in the WTO era. According to Zhou (2010, 6), a number of existing problems were identified and considered, including issues relating to the burgeoning NPLs, misfunctioning financial markets, and incompetent financial regulation.

For banking system reform in particular, the government finally acknowledged that the vested interests, nested in ambiguous ownership structures, omnipresent political connections, and lack of disclosure, were major hurdles in reform. Therefore, it proposed to recast the state banks as joint stock banks, which, once conditions had improved, could be listed. This was in fact based on long-established arguments by various PBC governors for a major shareholding reform of the banking system. Back in the 1990s, PBC leaders, such as Zhou Xiaochuan (Wu and Zhou 1999; Zhou 1999) and Wu Xiaoling (1992), PBC vice governor from 2000 to 2007, had explored various options of realigning the banks' incentives in an increasingly marketized economy. Based on his theoretical understanding and past experience, Zhou formed the view that, given the institutional settings in China's political and financial sector, structural reforms would not be driven by the corporate insiders. The way out, he argued, was to adopt a more market-oriented approach by subjecting the banking industry to more effective market and shareholder discipline and international scrutiny.

Under Zhou's leadership, the PBC thus designed a new roadmap for banking reform. The first aim was to increase bank capital levels to internationally endorsed levels and set them up as listed enterprises subject to enhanced market discipline. After cleaning their balance sheets through a further round of NPL disposals, the banks would then engage in attracting foreign strategic investors so that the banks could garner greater management expertise and market endorsement. The next step would be to have the banks listed in an overseas stock market.

A New Compromise

There are starkly differing interpretations of the role of the party-state in relation to enterprise and banking reforms. For Walter and Howie (2011, 76–81), Zhou and the PBC's strategy was yet another plot of the party-state in manipulating the market in order to recapitalize China's state banks through what they describe as "accounting legerdemain." On the other hand, Pearson (2007, 725) insists that the state has been "very active" in structuring the markets, and that "the call to increase market competition in order to help firms become more efficient, profitable, and competitive against foreign firms has been *genuine* and has emanated from the highest levels of government and the party" (emphasis in the original). These polarized assessments are not surprising given a lack of nuanced study in this arena. We argue that the eventual path chosen was neither a conspiracy on the part of the state nor a wholehearted embrace of the market and competition. Rather, the policy approach is best seen as a compromise established between the overarching concerns of the leadership, an emerging approach for SOE reform, and pressure from advocates of liberal reform.

For liberals, state ownership implied soft-budget constraints, moral hazard, and continuous state intervention, which are interpreted as key institutional sources of low efficiency and mounting NPLs. In this view, the ownership structure needed to be diversified in order to try and separate commercial banking from politics. The party leadership held a different view. As discussed in chapter 2, reformist leaders of the party are not necessarily "liberal" in the Western sense, but they do believe in inviting market mechanisms to help revive the state sector, particularly since that sector is a key constituency. The critical significance of the banking system further entrenched the view among the leadership that the sector should be under the tight control of the party-state; hence a true privatization was never on the agenda. Thus, the leadership's insistence on the dominance of state ownership set the perimeters of the reform.

At the same time, the contemplation of a new approach to banking reform was in fact more in line with Beijing's broader strategy in tackling SOE reforms, not least because state banks are essentially state-owned enterprises. As the fiscal burden of bailing out loss-making SOEs became increasingly onerous, Beijing adopted a selective approach to SOE reform through a strategy of "grasping the big and letting go the small" (*zhua da fang xiao*). The purpose was to ensure more effective control of state assets and more efficiency in the statist economy. Accordingly, the central government would retain its control of large state enterprises and attempt to turn them into "national champions" in strategic sectors. By contrast, small and medium-sized enterprises would be merged or privatized. At the same time, major state firms would be "decoupled" from the line ministries, their traditional managers under the old central planning system, and listed in domestic or overseas stock markets, especially Hong Kong (Green 2003; Walter and Howie 2003, 148).

Indeed, the intention to corporatize large SOEs would involve a state-owned holding corporation retaining a majority of the shares, with public investors holding noncontrolling shares, so that the SOEs would be able to make decisions but be subject to a degree of external scrutiny. A report by the Organisation for Economic Cooperation and Development found that as of 2002, "the state directly or indirectly controls almost 70 percent of every single Chinese listed company" (OECD 2002, 431). According to Walter and Howie (2011, 153) and Clarke (2003, 27), this "corporatization without privatization" is geared primarily toward raising capital rather than an overhaul of the system of state control. Clarke (2003, 28) argues that "the apparent dilution of state ownership through sale of shares in listed companies, which leads some observers to assume the inevitability of eventual privatization, is in fact a mechanism for *expanding* the state's economic empire" (emphasis in the original).

The Big Four state banks had already been national champions in the banking sector in terms of their dominant role in deposit and lending markets, but they appeared vulnerable in the pending clash with foreign giants storming in under the WTO. From the outset, Zhou's approach to banking reform resembled the key feature of the "grasping the big" strategy in terms of corporatization and public listing. However, a notable difference existed in terms of supervision. The national industrial firms are supervised by the State Assets Supervision and Administration Commission (SASAC), which was established in 2003. SASAC reports to the State Council and functions as the "owner" of the state assets in large SOE firms (Naughton 2005b). Therefore, according to Pearson (2007, 722), there is "inherent tension between corporatization to enhance managerial autonomy, compared to greater supervision by a comprehensive state body reporting to the highest reaches of the government." As will be discussed in more detail in the following sections, Zhou's approach substituted a SASAC-like institution with a policy vehicle that was under the control of the PBC. In other words, Zhou's ideas for more market-driven corporate governance reforms would be undertaken under the leadership of Zhou and the PBC.

Hence, the strategy of banking reform was in fact a grafting together of statist hierarchical control and complementary market measures. While this strategy incorporated the core ideas of liberal reformers by inviting market scrutiny and a degree of external discipline, it was nevertheless a compromise that fulfilled a limited but important reform agenda within a system of wider political constraints. As the clock was ticking on the brief window of opportunity for substantial institutional change, a consensus was finally reached within the political elite to undertake reforms of the banks based on Zhou's approach. As a result, a broad consensus within the party was reached in October 2003 to undertake reforms to the ownership structure of the major banks, including the Big Four and the Bank of Communications (BOCOM).[1]

The PBC as a New Lead Agency

A far-reaching event in terms of financial regulation was the dissolution of the Central Finance Work Commission (CFWC), which was replaced by the China Banking Regulatory Commission (CBRC) in 2003. As discussed in chapter 4, the CFWC was essentially a party organ that served a role for the central leadership to regain its control of the financial sector, which was plagued by rampant corruption, local capture, and informal dealings. Nevertheless, top-down political control and intervention had been increasingly out of line with the increasingly marketized economy and the need for more nuanced forms of state intervention. As one PBC official stated, "The CFWC warrants its own historical status, but let's admit that it was an extraordinary arrangement for an extraordinary time in the wake of the [Asian] crisis. It's more of a knee-jerk reaction in a traditional [Leninist] way. Once the crisis was over, it [the CFWC] was over."[2]

At the same time, there had been a debate on the configuration of an institutional structure for the post-CFWC era, which gradually favored separating banking regulation from the PBC and giving this role to a separate designated body. An argument often made in the literature suggests a potential conflict of interest between the implementation of monetary policy and banking regulation—hence the argument that it is desirable to have the latter function designated to a specialized agency, a move often practiced in more advanced economies (Courtis 2006, 24; Arnone and Gambini 2007, 97). The move to a new regulatory model also reflected an attempt to insulate the PBC from the direct influence of the large state banks (Heilmann 2005). Moreover, although the supervisory duty was assigned to the PBC at the beginning of the reform era, the institutional capacity of the bank's regulatory arm had been more underdeveloped than that of monetary policy (Liang 2006).[3] The establishment of a designated watchdog was thus seen as more likely to encourage more professional practices in financial supervision (Xia 2003).

A 2003 amendment to the 1995 Central Bank Law formally ratified this institutional restructure, removing the responsibility for banking supervision from the PBC and giving it to the CBRC, which officially began operations in April 2003. This was the final part of a wider process of building a two-tier system of financial regulation, with the central bank overseeing national financial stability, and three prudential regulators—the China Securities Regulatory Commission (CSRC, established in 1992), the China Insurance Regulatory Commission (CIRC, established in 1998), and the CBRC (established in 2003)— in charge of the securities, insurance, and banking businesses, respectively (Feng 2007a, 45). This one-plus-three framework, following the classic specialized model,[4] was aimed at catering to the increasing specialization of various branches of the economy, particularly the diversification of financial markets and the associated imperative for rational and professional industrial regulation (Tang 2003).

An important dynamic of this round of banking reform thus saw the PBC taking the lead as reform champion. Although it lost the supervision function to the CBRC, the PBC emerged as essentially a metagovernor of the new regulatory framework, with a mandate to ensure national financial stability (Miao and Li 2008; State Council 2008; Bell and Feng 2013, 148). Institutionally, the CBRC could have been a major player, but being a new agency, it lacked the experience and clout to steer banking reform (Sun 1996a). Indeed, the PBC proved itself as the big brother by often circumventing the sectoral agencies in directly engaging with the agencies' jurisdiction under its discretion. As will be discussed later, the PBC effectively bypassed the CBRC and the CSRC and directly controlled the banking and securities institutions through its recapitalization program.

In chapter 4, we saw that the PBC had increasingly gained authority in the financial arena in the 1990s in both formal (institutional) and informal (political) terms. On the other hand, government intervention and irregular practices significantly distorted the banking sector and the PBC's monetary policy transmission mechanisms. With its growing prominence in the monetary arena, an increasingly authoritative and ambitious PBC spearheaded a series of reforms of the Chinese financial system after 2003 under the governorship of Zhou Xiaochuan, particularly in the banking sector. A PBC official summarized the reason for the PBC's leadership role succinctly: "We have the mandate, we have the ideas, and we have the funds."[5] Given the short notice of Beijing's WTO commitment, the PBC took it as an urgent renewed mandate for radical therapy on the banks. In addition, the PBC was now equipped with both expertise and experience to devise a reform strategy that was politically viable and that also seemed technically sound. Through banking reform, the PBC's aim was to reduce market distortions, thereby increasing the effectiveness of its monetary policy and, in the long term, establishing a sustainable foundation for China's financial and economic stability.

The 2003 reform campaign was conducted under the general oversight of the new premier, Wen Jiabao, and Vice Premier Huang Ju, but the actual stewardship went to the PBC and Zhou Xiaochuan. Institutionally speaking, banking reform since 2003 has been led by an ad hoc cross-ministerial State Council Leading Group on Shareholding Reforms of State Banks. This was chaired by Huang, who was essentially in charge of the nation's financial affairs. But in effect the group was directed by Zhou, who was trusted and supported by Huang (Davis 2011a). In addition, the secretariat office of the group also operated within the Financial Stability Bureau of the PBC.[6] In the Chinese bureaucratic setting, this meant that in practice, the PBC was the central coordinating body (*qiantou*) on this issue and therefore the leading and the most influential institution in this arena. As Naughton (2004, 5) observed, "Zhou is the technocrat with lead authority in this area. The fact that the program went ahead in December 2003 demonstrates that Wen Jiabao has accepted Zhou Xiaochuan's overall blueprint for financial reforms and has assembled a workable political consensus around the proposals."

Crucially, the PBC's ambitious reforms of the state banks and wider financial restructuring were carried out by the establishment of the PBC-sponsored Central Huijin Investment Company (also named the SAFE Investment Company, "Huijin" hereafter) in December 2003. Huijin's capital was drawn from China's foreign reserves, which were managed by the State Administration of Foreign Exchange (SAFE), which was in turn subordinated to the PBC. As we will show below, the PBC conducted bank recapitalization through Huijin, a special policy vehicle and effectively a proxy of the PBC. The institutional design and daily operation of the company operates under the instruction of the Financial Stability Bureau of the PBC. Although the personnel are from various ministries, the executives and the backbone staff came from the PBC and SAFE. Moreover, Huijin's first general manager, Xie Ping, a liberal reformer, was a former chief of the Research Bureau, director of the Financial Stability Bureau, and the right-hand man of Zhou Xiaochuan.

A Balance Sheet Cleanup

Under these arrangements, the government adopted a combination of three measures to clean up the balance sheet of the banks: straightforward recapitalization, the issuing of bonds to replenish capital, and the removal of NPLs off the banks' books through asset management companies (AMCs).

Any structural reform package, however, needed first to deal with the "historical burdens" of the banking sector—namely, the existing stocks of NPLs that had piled up over the last three decades. Given a resurgence of NPLs after the 1998 bailout and mounting international attention to the solvency of the Chinese banks, the idea of a second-round capitalization had been floated after 2000. But there was a lack of viable plans on the table, and the agenda stalled over the following two years. The MOF lacked both the financial capacity and the incentive to be once again entangled with the risky business of banking recapitalization and reform.[7] The PBC also easily defeated proposals for a second fiscal injection. As a PBC official stated, "Recapitalization using fiscal capital had been totally discredited [since 1998]. Look what happened last time. Everyone in our circle knew that such a proposal stood no chance of passing in the People's Congress this time."[8]

Crucially, however, this time the central bank had access to a critical institutional resource: the capital to deliver its strategy. The PBC "innovatively" proposed to tap into China's foreign reserves, which it administered, to recapitalize the banks.[9] Like other Asian countries, China had started to build large amounts of foreign reserves after the 1997 Asian financial crisis for the "rainy days," and also to better shield itself from international financial pressures. This was made possible through the rapid increase in savings in the 2000s, along with the exponential expansion of trade and investment as a result of China's accession to the WTO, all of which translated into ballooning external surpluses in China's current and capital accounts. China's foreign reserves reached $403.25 billion at the end of 2003, triple that of the 1997 figure of $139.89 billion, and for years thereafter grew at a phenomenal pace of around $200 billion a year after 2003 (Feng 2007b, 30). Therefore, the PBC argued convincingly that it was well placed to use part of the excess reserves to recapitalize the SOBs without affecting fiscal healthiness. Moreover, this allocation of capital from a PBC-managed fund did

TABLE 5.1 Reform arrangements of the five largest SOBs, 2003–8

BANK	CAPITAL INJECTION			DISPOSAL OF NPLS (RMB BILLION)	FOREIGN STRATEGIC INVESTMENT		INITIAL PUBLIC OFFERINGS		
	INSTITUTION	AMOUNT (RMB BILLION)	DATE		INVESTMENT (RMB BILLION)	INITIAL SHARE IN CAPITAL (%)	LOCATION	DATE	AMOUNT (RMB BILLION)
ABC	Hujin[a]	130.0	Nov. 2008	815.6[c]			Hong Kong	July 2010	12.2 (HKD)
							Shanghai	July 2010	68.5
ICBC	Hujin[b]	124.0	Apr. 2005	705.0[d]	30.5	10	Hong Kong	Oct. 2006	126.6
BOC	Hujin	186.4	Dec. 2003	308.1	43.0	17	Hong Kong	Jun. 2006	90.0
							Shanghai	July 2006	20.0
CCB	Hujin	186.2	Dec. 2003	185.8	32.8	14.2	Hong Kong	Oct. 2005	74.6
BOCOM	MOF	5.0	June 2004	53.0	14.5	19.9	Hong Kong	June 2005	18.0
	Hujin	3.0	June 2004				Shanghai	May 2007	25.2
	Social Security Fund	10.0	June 2004						
Totals		644.6		2067.5	120.8				601.0

Sources: Okazaki 2011, the CBRC, and the PBC.

Notes: [a] The MOF keeps its original invested capital of RMB 124.0 billion.

[b] The MOF keeps its original invested capital of RMB 130.0 billion.

[c] This amount of NPLs was transferred to a comanaged account between the MOF and Hujin. The receivables are expected to be offset in fifteen years against a refund of income tax, the bank's future dividends to the MOF, and/or the MOF selling part of its equities in the bank.

[d] The bank transferred the loss of NPLs worth 246 billion yuan to the Huarong Asset Management Company in June 2005 at book value. Huarong then set up a comanaged account with the MOF, with the latter giving receivables to the bank.

not need formal approval by the People's Congress. This move thus saved time and a potentially sensitive debate in the legislature. The State Council's eventual approval of the plan effectively awarded the PBC the institutional leadership of the reform campaign. Institutionally, the roles of the PBC and the MOF had been reversed this time, as the latter was sidelined in this round of reform (Walter and Howie 2011, 74).

Between 2003 and 2005, Huijin had finalized the recapitalization of the CCB, the BOC, the ICBC, and BOCOM, using China's official foreign exchange reserves (see table 5.1). In doing so, all of the preexisting capital of the banks "owned" by the MOF was written off, so that Huijin became the dominant force in the ownership structure of the banks.

To put the scale of such a capital injection into perspective, it accounted for 10 percent of the central government's revenue between 1998 and 2005. This more than doubled a similar campaign by the Japanese government in recapitalizing its banks, which cost 4 percent of Tokyo's fiscal revenue (Okazaki 2007, 34).

The PBC's targets were not limited to the state banks, however, but were extended to the entire financial system, including the existing shareholding commercial banks, policy banks, stock brokerage, and insurance companies. Indeed, the reform plans for the individual policy banks were initially designed by the research bureau of the PBC under the personal supervision of Zhou Xiaochuan (Li 2006). At the same time, the PBC sought to reform and revitalize the stock market by copying its capitalize-and-reform approach in the banking sector through Huijin. The PBC's strategy has been to recapitalize and take control of those large national brokerages through Huijin, and the medium-sized brokerages through the Construction Investment Company, also owned by Huijin. In 2005, Huijin finalized its recapitalization of the Galaxy Securities, Southern Securities, Shenyin Wanguo Securities, and Guotai Jun'an Securities. By the end of 2005, the State Council had approved thirteen brokerages to receive $37.5 billion of capital injections from Huijin. It is estimated that the overall recapitalization ended up at double that amount, reaching $75 billion (Liu 2006). Huijin's majority control of the securities companies also enabled the PBC to regain some of the supervising authority from the CSRC.

Disposal of NPLs Using Market Mechanisms

Given the return of high levels of NPLs, the banks that were intended to go public needed, again, to shed their NPLs to the "bad banks," the AMCs. The NPLs transferred to the AMCs were mostly in the "loss" and "doubtful" categories. RMB 778 billion out of RMB 814 billion "doubtfuls" at the end of 2002, and RMB

456 billion out of RMB 633 billion of "losses," totaling RMB 1.2 trillion, were transferred to the AMCs in this way (Okazaki 2007, 35; CBRC 2012, 5).

It is notable that the funds that the AMCs used in purchasing the NPLs from the banks were from paid-in capital from the MOF and/or loans from the PBC. This manner of NPL disposal—using fiscal and monetary funds in granting the banks a clean start—suggested that the central government recognized that the source of such NPLs was mostly its SOE-centered industrial policies. In other words, these were policy-derived NPLs, rather than problematic decisions by the banks.

However, the government also intended to introduce market mechanisms in this round of NPL disposals. As we discussed in chapter 4, the AMCs had purchased the NPLs at their face value in the last round of disposal in 1998. This time, the authorities introduced an auction system and severed the designated ties between the banks and the AMCs at the same time. Under the new arrangement, the AMCs were allowed to purchase doubtful NPLs in the primary market and then sell them in the secondary market at more market-oriented values.

The Introduction of Foreign Strategic Investors

Introducing foreign strategic investors was also a key feature of the 2003 reforms. The Chinese government had long restricted foreign investment in its banking system until December 2003, when the CBRC allowed foreign investors to increase their equity holdings in Chinese financial institutions from 15 percent to 20 percent. The allowable level of foreign investors' shares in any bank was also raised to 25 percent (CBRC 2003).[10]

To be sure, Beijing was seeking to diversify the capital sources of recapitalization, but the options available were limited. China's high savings and private-sector growth in the 1990s meant that inviting in domestic private capital was financially viable. Yet this could be risky for the party leadership, as it potentially meant weakening controls over key financial resources—resources that had been central to its operations, including those used to fund the patronage system. The PBC and Huijin also approached some of the key industrial SOEs with the financial capacity, but none of them showed confidence in their banking counterparts.[11] This meant that supervised foreign investment in domestic institutions was instead put on the table.

To be sure, foreign financial institutions were interested in forming joint ventures with Chinese banks, given China's regulatory restrictions, the lack of local expertise, and their need to prime and prepare for future enlarged operations in China once such restrictions were relaxed. On the Chinese side, however, more emphasis was placed on the "strategicness" of foreign involvement, meaning that such foreign investments were expected to be long term, that there would be knowledge transfer from overseas partners, and that this would improve the corporate governance of domestic banks. Although there were concerns about the actual impact of foreign players, participation on the China bandwagon proved to be attractive. According to the CBRC, thirty foreign financial institutions had acquired shares in twenty-one Chinese banks by the end of 2006, with a total investment of $19 billion.

Public Listing and Corporate Governance Reforms

A further step in this round of reforms was the public listing of banks, largely in stock markets outside mainland China, such as Hong Kong. This was in part due to the fact that China's domestic stock market had been sluggish. But more importantly, the PBC intended to subject the banks to more scrutiny in overseas markets with higher qualification and disclosure standards, which would hopefully in turn force the banks to carry out necessary reforms at home. The first two initial public offerings (IPOs), for BOCOM and the CCB, were set up in Hong Kong. However, growing criticism that this would deprive domestic investors of a "fair share" in some of the largest banks in China saw the authorities list the BOC and ICBC dually, in both Hong Kong and Shanghai. The IPOs were mostly successful, with higher-than-expected selling prices, resulting in an increase in the capital of the Big Four ranging between 30 and 80 percent (Okazaki 2007, 45).

Huijin and the PBC also played a role in attracting external interest in Chinese banks. The fact that various banking reforms were underwritten by the Chinese central bank, an institution that increasingly had substantial credibility and professionalism in the emerging market economy and one dominated by liberal reformers (Bell and Feng 2013, 263–97), appealed to hesitant international investors in lessening suspicion and doubt about Beijing's banking revamp. In this manner, the PBC founded its authority and credibility on bank reform. Huijin was also directly involved in negotiations with foreign institutions for strategic shareholdings before the banks' IPOs (Li 2005, 23). According to Bergera, Hasan, and Zhou (2009), it was hoped that foreign investors would help improve the efficiency and performance of the Chinese banks, with foreign investors taking up over 15 percent of total equity in Chinese banking. According to Yang (2009), there has been extensive cooperation between Chinese banks and a number of foreign strategic investors. For example, the CCB cooperated with the Bank of America over corporate governance, risk management, human resource management, and liquidity management, while the ICBC dealt with Goldman Sachs and Alliance on investment banking and corporate governance.

Other improvements occurred in public disclosure. It has been a standard practice that the Big Four, as listed companies, invite major international accounting firms to review their books and draft their reports to the market. This practice has further spread to most of the joint stock banks.

There were also attempts to enhance domestic scrutiny of the banks. Like the SOEs, the SOBs suffered from the problem of "virtual" state ownership, which meant that a number of government bureaucracies shared authority over the administration and management of the banks, which effectively meant the banks were accountable to no one. With its predominance in the share structure of the banks, Huijin became a "visible hand" in promoting banking reform, with a mandate to take proactive measures to ensure the safety of the state's capital injection and to obtain a reasonable return on investment. As a state investment company, Huijin's injections are not fiscal allocations, but capital investment, and therefore a return was expected.

Both PBC and Huijin officials stressed that the bank's public listing was not an end, but a means to address chronic problems of poor credit analysis and risk management, rampant insider controls, and most importantly, poor corporate governance. Wang Jianxi, vice chairman of Huijin, made it clear that "we are their [the banks'] shareholders and they need to report to us. One of our important tasks is to help them restructure" (quoted in Shi 2005, 4). First, the PBC and Huijin, being the majority shareholders, regained the authority from the Communist Party's Central Organization Department to appoint desirable senior management of the Big Four. This was an attempt to weaken overt political intervention in the financial sector. For instance, Guo Shuqing, chairman of Huijin, was sent to chair the board of the CCB when Zhang Enzhao, then the board chairman, was allegedly involved in financial mishandlings. The size of the CCB's board of directors was drastically cut from sixty to fifteen, making it more efficient in overseeing management and operations. In addition, Huijin introduced independent directors to the boards of the CCB and the BOC, assigning four directors to the former and six to the latter (*Jingji guancha bao* 2004). The directors assigned by Huijin were no longer government officials but employees of Huijin, who were awarded higher salaries and more flexible incentives to look after state investment in the banks. Foreign expertise was also invited into the board, with the Bank of America's head of corporate planning and strategy taking up a directorship on the board of the CCB (*Jingji guancha bao* 2004).

At the same time, supervisory boards were installed in the CCB and BOC to ensure better compliance with the principles of international best practice in the financial sphere. In terms of income and promotion, banking personnel were increasingly linked to their performance rather than their years of service. Xie Ping declared, "The board must provide me with written reports on the performances of all the senior managers and board directors, and I will decide how much they will get paid" (quoted in Shi 2005, 4).

Other notable progress was the establishment of high-level committees charged with prudential risk management on a commercial basis, thus consolidating the authority of loan approvals to the committee. The long-term problem of overstaffing was also a target of internal restructuring. For the CCB alone, one-third of its branches were scrapped and the number of its employees was reduced by nearly a quarter in 2004 (Thomas and Li 2006, 113). Other measures designed to increase efficiency were also put in place, such as favoring short-term rather than long-term staff contracts.

A Setback amid Bureaucratic Tussles

The major dynamic of the banking and financial reforms after 2003 was that an increasingly authoritative central bank had begun to flex its muscles, not just in the traditional monetary policy arena but also in its reach to other sectors, notably banking and finance. This inevitably challenged and encroached on the jurisdictions of other institutional players. For example, the PBC's often unilateral actions through window guidance annoyed the banking regulator, the CBRC; Huijin's dominance of some of the major securities companies alerted the CSRC (Feng 2007a, 46); and the PBC's initiative on the corporate bond market was at loggerheads with the NDRC and the CSRC (Wheatley 2008). Most serious, however, was the MOF's concern over the PBC's wresting of the Big Four from its control, which sparked a turf war between the two institutions.

Under the auspices of a vague corporate law, the MOF had become used to being seen as the owner of the banking system, including the Big Four. In particular, the MOF's Finance Department was directly in charge of the operation of the banks, albeit often with lax supervision. However, as the CCB and BOC were recapitalized by Huijin under the PBC, the MOF found itself instantly deprived of its privilege over the banks. As we have shown, since the two banks were allowed to allocate all of their initial capital (the existing net equity held by the MOF) to a special fund in writing off their bad loans, the MOF's equity in these banks was effectively wiped out and therefore it lost its control of the banks to Huijin.

A fierce debate in China as the CCB and BOC were publicly listed on the stock exchanges helped the MOF in regaining part of its lost territory. Skeptics of the reform saw potential strategic damage to China's future development through foreign participation, pointing to the allegedly limited transfer of banking expertise to domestic banks, the marginalization of domestic investors, and the prospect of eventual foreign control of China's financial system, on top of a cheap share price for foreign strategic investors in what some saw as a "garage sale" (Naughton 2006; *Zhongguo zhengquan bao* 2005). The criticisms of the reform were largely framed within a wider debate between liberals, nationalists, and the New Left on the orientation of economic policy and the trajectory of the Chinese state. This, combined with and exploited by opposition from the MOF and other institutions that had been reluctantly under the shadow of the PBC, created strain on the PBC and particularly on the newly installed Hu-Wen regime, which felt under pressure to restore the power balance to placate the major bureaucratic players.

As the PBC was put on the defensive, the MOF recovered and sought to strengthen its position. It had been wary about the fact that the PBC had effectively been in control of the major state-owned banks through Huijin. Therefore, when Huijin initiated the recapitalization of BOCOM in June 2004, the MOF managed to increase its investment in the bank by RMB 5 billion (compared with Huijin's RMB 3 billion) so that its share in the bank would not be diluted. As a result, the MOF managed to retain its control of the bank with a 26 percent equity, compared with Huijin's 8 percent share. The MOF further managed to retain its half equity in the recapitalization of the ICBC with a $15 billion investment equal to that of Huijin in April 2005. By doing so, the MOF avoided losing all of its preexisting equity. Instead, the existing bad loans worth 240 billion yuan were to be gradually written off from the bank's income tax, equity returns, and potential sales of the ICBC shares by the MOF (Liu 2005). This equally-split-ownership model between the MOF and Huijin was copied for the recapitalization of the last of the Big Four, the ABC, in November 2008, as Huijin injected 190 billion US-dollar-equivalent yuan into the bank.

On another front, the MOF had long been aiming to secure some control over the foreign reserves that had been managed by the PBC-supervised SAFE. In late 2007, the MOF convinced the State Council to establish and place under its control a sovereign wealth fund, the China Investment Corporation (CIC). A more profound development was announced at the same time: namely, that Huijin would be merged into the CIC as the latter's wholly owned subsidiary. This was done by the MOF issuing RMB 1.55 trillion ($208 billion) of special treasury bonds to buy the foreign reserves from the PBC in order to capitalize the

CIC and acquire Huijin.[12] This was a major win for the MOF, and losing Huijin to the CIC meant the PBC had lost a key vehicle in its financial restructuring plan.

A U-Turn?

In *Red Capitalism*, Walter and Howie (2011, 19–21) argue that the year 2005 marked something of a retreat for financial reform under the leadership of Zhu Rongji and Zhou Xiaochuan. According to them, this was mostly due to the fact that Zhou's key ally at the top, Jiang Zemin, eventually stepped down from his supreme position, as did his key supporter in the State Council, then vice premier Huang Ju, who had been in charge of financial affairs but who became terminally ill during the year. Certain pieces of empirical evidence seem to support this argument, particularly a subsequent rebalancing of power within the bureaucracy against the PBC's "radicalism."

However, despite the setbacks on the part of the PBC during this period, we argue that 2005 was not the end of financial reforms in China but instead marked a new phase of reform, one in which the PBC remained central but in which it deliberated through a more consensus-seeking process, compared with its previous unilateralism. Importantly, and contrary to the argument by Walter and Howie (2011), the PBC and Zhou still found support from the top leadership. As discussed earlier, the Hu-Wen administration maintained a general reformist line, despite a professed change in priority toward social and equitable development. Moreover, Premier Wen Jiabao, who was in charge of overall economic and financial affairs, had been a veteran reformer and a major supporter of Zhou and the PBC. Zhou's reappointment as the PBC governor in 2008 reflected confidence and trust by the top leadership. At the same time, a number of important PBC-initiated reforms after 2005, such as banking and exchange rate reforms, would not have proceeded without support from above. It is also the case that the inclusiveness of the new policy process also helped with better coordination and less conflict during policy implementation.

More importantly, the trajectory of financial policies after 2005 followed the track of Zhu's legacy and Zhou's rationale. The PBC had made concrete progress in promoting a domestic bond market (Cookson 2010; Wheatley 2008). It also played a major role in pushing for a switch back to a more market-oriented exchange rate regime in 2010 (Bell and Feng 2013, 209), in an ambitious campaign of lifting the RMB's international profile (Feng 2011), and in its "active coordination" with the CSRC in introducing an international board to China's stock market in 2011 (Li 2011). In addition, the PBC's argument for structural reforms, such as capital account liberalization and interest rate marketization, appeared to be gaining traction after early 2012 (Feng 2012; Su 2012).

In the banking sector in particular, despite the MOF acquiring Huijin from the PBC, it could not provide a credible alternative to the PBC's approach, which had proven successful in the CCB's and the BOC's IPOs. Therefore, the restructure of the remaining ICBC and the ABC also followed the PBC's model. In particular, the ICBC was listed in Hong Kong and Shanghai in October 2006, raising $19.1 billion. The ABC's public listing was regarded as a challenge for the government because of its high NPL ratio and historical debt burdens. In 2007, Zhou managed to have Xiang Junbo, vice governor of the PBC since 2004, appointed as the president of the ABC, where he was instrumental in the reforms to the bank. The ABC eventually went public in July 2010. Listed on the exchanges in both Shanghai and Hong Kong, the bank raised a total capital of $22.1 billion (with both overallotment options exercised), smashing the ICBC's former record of the world's largest IPO in history (Tudor 2010).

Assessing the Reforms

The PBC's approach to banking and financial reform after 2003 represented something of a departure from the traditional state socialist model adopted in 1998. It was a proactive strategy to tackle institutional deficiencies in the financial system, rather than the former ex post, passive reaction to bank insolvency. It centered on the idea of market discipline, upgrading expertise, institutional innovation, and improved financial intermediation, rather than the traditional approach of lax supervision and ad hoc fiscal bailouts offered by the old regime. In describing the PBC's strategy, one of its officials used a Chinese saying: "It's more desirable to teach one fishing rather than to offer one fish."[13] The PBC-led banking restructuring thus represented a systemic effort in tackling difficult challenges in the financial sector. Despite the loss of Huijin, the reform campaign saw a number of improvements. Hence, the recapitalized banks saw return on assets improve from 0.15 percent to 1.37 percent between 2003 and 2008. Over the same period, capital adequacy improved from minus 3 percent to 8.19 percent, while the NPL ratio dropped from 17.8 percent to 2.4 percent. The cost-to-income ratio also improved, from 54 percent to 32 percent (*Almanac of China's Finance and Banking* 2004, 32–33; 2009, 19).

To some observers, Chinese banks had been transformed into what Anderlini (2010) calls "the world's most valuable and profitable lenders in terms of market capitalization and absolute profits." The organizational streamlining both before and after the restructuring helped increase operational efficiency and reduce cost-to-income ratios. The PBC's recapitalization of the banks and the subsequent IPOs helped increase the banks' capital, improve their capital adequacy ratio, and reduce their NPLs to internationally acceptable standards (*Zhongguo zhengquan bao* 2005). In particular, according to the CBRC (2009, 6), the average NPL ratio of Chinese banking institutions stood at 2.42 percent by the end of 2008, well under the Basel standards. Under the CBRC's tightened regulation, the banks had also increased their risk affordability by raising their NPL provision coverage ratios. These changes made the major Chinese banks better equipped for the looming global financial crisis of 2008. By 2011, 101 Chinese banks made it into the *Banker*'s "Top 1000 World Banks 2011" ranking, and 3 of them were in the top 10 in terms of capital strength (the ICBC, CCB, and BOC, measured by Tier 1 capital). Chinese banks (the ICBC and the CCB) were also the top two largest banks by market capitalization. In contrast, many of their Western counterparts were exposed to "toxic" mortgage-backed securities and saw a large-scale shrinkage of capitalization, profits, and share prices.

Despite these achievements in terms of improved financial capacity, corporate governance, and risk aversion capability, there were a number of issues that remained to be addressed. The average return on asset (ROA) ratio (showing how profitable a bank's assets are in generating revenue) and average return on equity ratio (ROE) (measuring a bank's efficiency at generating profit) of the Chinese banks might have been higher than those of some of the major Western banks, but this was based on a rudimentary business model of relying on a generous interest rate spread set by the central bank under the system of financial repression. As a result, any growth in profitability was due mainly to the increase in the size of interest-bearing assets instead of the efficiency and quality of the financial intermediation on the part of the banks.

More importantly, the PBC-led reforms did not address the fundamental issue of state intervention in banking, given that the state remained the largest shareholder of the listed banks and was not averse to politicized intervention. The state's shares in these banks are parked in Huijin's accounts, which are usually shielded from market transactions (buying or selling). For normal investors, these shares appear "hidden," as they are not circulated in the market, leaving a back door for the state to control the banks. All of this aids banking politicization, which became even more pronounced amid Beijing's response to the GFC.

Compared with the government's ad hoc and emergency support efforts in 1998 and 1999, banking reform after 2003 and before the GFC in 2008 became more comprehensive, transparent, and market oriented under the influence of the PBC. Despite various setbacks and deficiencies, the PBC's efforts represented a serious first step in establishing more efficient and effective financial intermediation in

China. Walter and Howie's (2011) account runs the risk of obscuring the reach and complexity of market reforms in China's transition context, in which progress has been subject to drawn-out battles on two fronts. In ideational terms, as discussed earlier, liberal reformers have had to accommodate the leadership's state-centric political imperative and defend their rationale against conservatives and economic nationalists. The fate of the reforms has also depended on the competition between divergent agendas within the state, between the old planning, administrative allocation agenda, such as the MOF's, and the more liberal agenda that tried to forge ahead with market reforms and commercial banking practices, driven by the PBC and the emerging CBRC. These dynamics largely prescribe the dynamics of institutional change and banking reform in China, often marked by progress and then partial retreat. Indeed, gradualism is not just a politically convenient strategy, but also often a result of the ongoing conflicts and compromises within the party and bureaucratic elite. As we shall see in the next chapter, however, these dynamics were altered again by the critical juncture of the GFC, in which politicization of the main banks reached new heights and where avenues of banking reform were pursued mainly in the rapidly growing informal or shadow banking sector.

6

THE GFC AND STATE CAPITALISM ON STEROIDS

Despite the reforms and institutional improvements to the banks after 2003, which were aimed in part at a greater commercial focus, this kind of liberal reform momentum received a major setback as the state-directed credit system was put into overdrive as part of Beijing's massive stimulus program in response to the global financial crisis after 2008. Due to the central government's limited fiscal capacity, the banking sector was called on to shoulder the burden of financing the stimulus package, which mainly funded infrastructure investments and statist industrial policies on a massive scale. This not only led to an explosive expansion of bank credit, but also facilitated and indeed relied on the growth of the shadow banking system, which often involved complex relations with the main banks, including the increased use of off-balance-sheet activities by the main banks. The growth of the banking and credit system could have been slowed after the initial challenge of the GFC, but the system continued to rapidly expand thereafter. This was because the leadership became increasingly hooked on using financial means and credit expansion to drive a further continuance of its statist economic growth model. This path has ramped up risks for the financial system and growth model ever since, a move that has increasingly been questioned amid regulatory efforts to rein in shadow banking and on-and-off-again attempts to reduce the pace of credit growth.

This chapter first outlines the domestic debate on macroeconomic policies amid the GFC, and how this helped shape a massive government stimulus package. It then examines in detail how the formal and then the rapidly rising shadow banking sector facilitated a national campaign of credit expansion that saw funds flow largely to key designated sectors in the stimulus program, especially local governments engaged in infrastructure investment and the state-owned enterprises. Finally, we explore the continuation of this credit-and-spending binge after the GFC and its implications for China's growth model.

The GFC's Repercussions in China

The leadership as well as officials in Beijing were shocked when what they believed to be a local infection in the US financial system quickly spiraled into a global financial pandemic. Economies were hard hit and world trade declined sharply, dropping 10.7 percent in 2009, the sharpest annual contraction since the 1930s. Although the Chinese banks were not involved in the leveraged securitization crash that brought down many Western banks, the external crisis nevertheless translated into a dire situation for the Chinese economy. GDP growth decreased from around 15 percent in 2007 to 10 percent in 2008 and 8 percent in 2009. China's exports, which had supported its phenomenal growth in the previous two decades, also dropped sharply. Prior to the GFC, goods exports were growing at a rate of about 20 percent per annum. However, by 2009, in the immediate wake of the GFC, exports declined by minus 18 percent. They grew again thereafter, but goods exports slowed between 2012 and 2014, to grow at about 7 percent per annum, and by 2015–16 by minus 2 percent (Shih 2019, 65). China's export boom was essentially ended by the GFC, reflected in a slump in the current account surplus, from a peak of almost 10 percent of GDP prior to the crisis to just 1 percent of GDP by 2019. GDP growth also dropped sharply, to under 8 percent in the first half of 2009, a worrying decline by Chinese standards.

According to data from the Ministry of Human Resources and Social Security (2010), twenty million workers lost their jobs due to the financial crisis. Roach (2011) observes that for policymakers, "China was in the throes of the functional equivalent of a full-blown recession." The Chinese leadership saw that they needed to quickly spur domestic demand in order to try and sustain economic growth, recognized by the leadership as the primary source of the regime's legitimacy and their own political survival. Domestic demand has two main components: investment spending and domestic consumption, the latter especially in terms of household consumption. Spurring the latter may have been on the leadership's medium-term agenda for rebalancing the economy, but this could not be done quickly, as changes in consumption patterns tend to occur only slowly (Kroeber 2016, 217). The main alternative was to spur investment spending, which is what happened on a grand scale.

A key feature of Beijing's anticrisis measures was thus essentially a Keynesian stimulus approach (Jiang 2015), which also paved the way for a further surge in state capitalism. Beijing's response to the previous shock, the Asian financial crisis of 1997–98, contained both a fiscal stimulus featuring deficit spending and a range of liberal reforms in the sectors such as state-owned enterprises, health, and education (Zhang 2003). The stimulus policies adopted at that time were considered successful with regard to short-term stabilization and in aiding recovery (Stiglitz 2010, 301; Mei 2010). In the immediate aftermath of the GFC, Beijing adopted a similar Keynesian stimulus approach, but on a much larger scale than that after the AFC (Xing 2009; Mei 2010; He 2013). This was due to the severity of the GFC and its more devastating impact on the Chinese economy, which created greater urgency for state action.

The turn to Keynesianism and the heavy statist-style stimulus also reflected an ideational change on the part of the political elite. From the start, the conservative statists saw their arguments against Western neoliberalism vindicated, offering a great opportunity to further legitimize China's state-capitalist development model. For their part, liberals accepted the need for stimulus, but also saw the crisis as an opportunity to rebalance the economy away from an emphasis on external demand and toward a more balanced and sustainable domestic-consumption-led model. Notable figures in this camp included Professors Wu Jinglian (2009b) and Zhang Weiying (2010). For them, although the GFC was indicative of a crash in unfettered Western markets, China's key problem was market distortion by the state rather than market failure (see also Li 2009; Fan 2009).

According to the *Wall Street Journal*, the PBC had concerns about the inflationary impact of the stimulus program (Davis 2011a), but in fact insiders suggest that the bank was actually more worried about deflation in the short term since employment was believed to be well under the equilibrium level due to massive layoffs in the wake of the crisis. In addition, there were ample signs of excess capacity in the economy. When asked which industrial sector had excess capacity, Fan Gang, then a member of the PBC's Monetary Policy Committee, reportedly answered "each and every" (Feng 2009, 40). On the other hand, many liberals tended to treat the stimulus package in a more pragmatic manner: as an extraordinary measure for extraordinary times. The PBC's governor at the time, Zhou, said during the National People's Congress in March 2009, "If we act slowly and less decisively, we are likely to see what happened in other countries, [which is] a slide in confidence. . . . We would rather be faster and heavy-handed if it can prevent confidence slumping during the financial crisis, and spur fast recovery of the economy amid the crisis" (Zhang 2009). Therefore, liberal reformers arguing for rebalancing were largely on the defensive in the domestic debate, with the dominant concern, at least until 2012, being the need for the state to come to the rescue via a credit and investment surge in crisis mode.

Meanwhile, Beijing had deployed various means and resources in steering public debate in favor of its Keynesian responses in the wake of the GFC—responses that were a textbook combination of fiscal, monetary, and credit policies. Indeed, there was general agreement within the leadership on the "necessities" of "special policies" on a gargantuan scale (Fan 2010). In the end, the leadership managed to steer the debate to such a degree that "everyone was Keynesian now" (Zou 2009). However, it was not long until the state largesse took its toll, in the form of mounting inflation (especially capital goods), out-of-control money supply and credit creation, and dubious public projects given the green light without proper scrutiny. This led to renewed criticism of state intervention from liberals. However, given the long-term nature of infrastructure investment, both the central and local governments had to follow up with the essential policy support for the initial expansionist policies. Overall, Beijing gained wide support in the teeth of the crisis.

Shock-and-Awe Stimulus

The immediate stimulus began on the monetary front as the PBC reduced interest rates and lowered banks' reserve ratio requirements in September 2008 (Lardy 2012b, 8–11; Han 2012, 370). The State Council then approved railway construction worth 2 trillion yuan in October 2008. This led to an announcement by the leadership, in November, of a 4 trillion yuan ($586 billion) stimulus package. This was about 15 percent of China's GDP in 2007. The stimulus program of the Obama administration in the United States, passed in February 2009, represented less than 6 percent of GDP. The party hierarchy also held an emergency meeting and issued an internal document with ten policies to further expand domestic demand. Between January and February 2009, the State Council convened intensive executive meetings and approved restructuring and upgrading for ten industries: automobiles, iron and steel, textiles, equipment manufacturing, shipbuilding, electronics and information technology, petrochemicals, light industries, nonferrous metals, and logistics (*People's Daily* 2009).

It is notable that the implementation of the stimulus was carried out under a nationwide mobilization of both the party and the executive branch of the government. It helped add what Naughton (2009b, 1) calls "the sense of urgency" that dictated bypassing routine procedures of project scrutiny and approvals. For example, the National Development and Reform Commission held an emergency meeting, during which it stated that "the absolutely most important economic work is to urgently implement the center's increased investment and other measures to increase domestic demand," and that "agencies must 'make every second count' [*zhengfen duomiao*]" (NDRC 2008).

However, a major feature of the stimulus was that the central government did not have sufficient financial capacity to support it. If we examine China's consolidated fiscal balance as a proportion of GDP, involving both central and local governments, we find that between 1995 and 2020, it has mostly been negative. Briefly, in 2007, governments had recovered fiscal balance slightly into positive territory in the wake of the post-AFC stimulus. But by 2020, consolidated fiscal balance had dropped almost continuously to minus 5.8 percent of GDP. Moreover, as figure 6.1 shows, if we consider central government debt, this grew rapidly after 2006, almost doubling by 2008. In such circumstances, it was not surprising that the Ministry of Finance was reluctant to commit to a bigger deficit. Li Yizhong (2013), then the minister for industry and information technology, recalls that during a consultation between Premier Wen Jiabao and NDRC and MOF officials in December 2008, the minister of finance, Xie Xuren, suggested to Li that the ministry had insufficient funds to support the announced scale of the stimulus. This explains the earlier clarification from the MOF in November that the central government would contribute less than 1.2 trillion yuan to the 4 trillion yuan program. Even with this limited post-GFC fiscal commitment, the central government's budget deficit deteriorated drastically between 2008 and

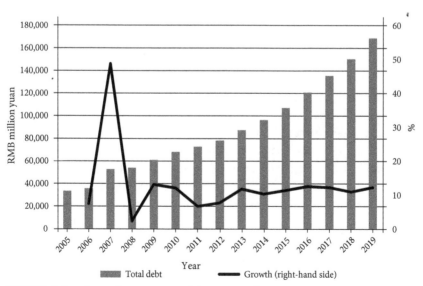

FIGURE 6.1. Central government debt outstanding and debt growth.

Source: National Bureau of Statistics of China.

2009, while its debt grew thereafter (see figure 6.1). These were testaments to the limits of Beijing's fiscal capacity before and after the GFC.

In any event, local governments and enterprises would have to come up with the bulk of the funding, which would be largely based on credit expansion. In response, Premier Wen approved the massive expansion of bank credit to help finance the stimulus (Jiang 2015). Between 2009 and 2011, banking assets in China expanded by $7.6 trillion, a figure 77 percent higher than the 2008 level, while bank credit and new loans expanded by $4.2 trillion during these three years (Wright and Rosen 2018, 20). Even after the initial needs for the stimulus, credit growth continued. Chinese banks were ordered to contribute to a lending spree, first as part of a state-directed stimulus package after the GFC, and second as part of an ongoing credit-fueled growth strategy.

State Capitalism on Steroids

State capitalism in China, with its investment and export-driven growth model, had experienced a golden era after China's accession to the WTO in 2001. The state had utilized different combinations of fiscal, monetary, financial, and exchange rate policies to promote exports and infrastructural investment. This led to booms in the private sector due to trade expansion, as well as a partial increase in efficiency and gradual deleveraging of debt in the public sector due to structural reforms of the SOEs in the late 1990s. Nevertheless, the GFC disrupted the growth model in terms of the above-noted decline in external demand for Chinese exports as well as a decline in corporate earnings that forced the corporate sector to increase leverage in order to maintain growth. This, and the regime's increasing use of credit more widely to spur growth, even after the GFC, would help embed the new credit-fueled growth model thereafter.

As we have seen, Premier Wen Jiabao had already admitted even before the GFC that under the surface of China's rapid growth lay an economy that was increasingly unstable, unbalanced, uncoordinated, and ultimately unsustainable. In light of the strong growth China had experienced in the years prior to this, it was an extraordinarily frank admission from the leadership about China's underlying structural problems. China's external vulnerability and growing weaknesses in the state sector in the wake of the GFC clearly suggested that China could have used the opportunity to address the Four Uns and to carry out structural reforms to tackle the distortions and imbalances in the domestic economy. Instead, the response was conditioned by the short-term growth imperative and an acceleration of the statist growth model. Beijing's approach was thus largely dominated by boosting aggregate demand through public and state-sector investment rather than by boosting potentially more efficient forms of private investment and household demand. In the years after 2008, investment surged as GDP growth slowed. As Song and Xiong (2017, 273) argue, the statist economic stimulus turned around the resource flows between the state and private sectors: "Local government financing vehicles and state-owned enterprises increased their investment but crowded out the more efficient private investment . . . worsening misallocation." As noted above, key state-sector industries were targeted, as were large infrastructure investments and real estate development (especially at local levels), which saw a sudden jump in fixed capital formation after 2008 (see figure 6.2). The PBC governor, Zhou Xiaochuan (2013a), acknowledged that the state's "policy guidance will be strengthened," but in effect this produced a situation where credit was allocated disproportionately to low productivity and inefficient state firms and sectors. After the GFC, deteriorating resource allocation efficiency saw the aggregate return to capital drop from an average of 10 percent before 2008 to a low of only 4 percent by 2013 (Song and Xiong 2017, 275).

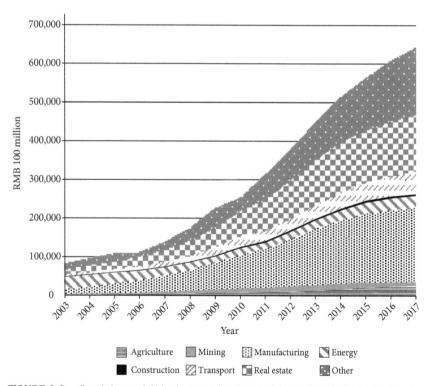

FIGURE 6.2.   Breakdown of China's gross fixed capital formation (RMB 100 million).

Source: National Bureau of Statistics of China. The NBS ceased to update the sectoral breakdown data since 2018.

Much of the stimulus was driven through credit and investment by local governments. Because of their limited fiscal capacity, local governments came to rely largely on debt financing. Key elements of the statist growth model—namely, local governments and the SOEs—became major beneficiaries of the stimulus package and were thus further empowered.

The performance of local government officials has traditionally been evaluated by the party hierarchy on a short-term basis, and has primarily focused on local economic growth measured by GDP. An empirical study by Li and Shen (2014) suggest that the average duration of local official posts (on the municipal and provincial levels) is less than two years. Therefore, the short time horizon on the part of local officials tends to result in the discounting of long-term local development. Local officials thus not only are short termist in orientation, but often tend to resort to radical, irregular measures to boost growth.

In response to the GFC, Beijing granted a great deal of discretion to provincial and sublevel governments. The lack of fiscal capacity at the center meant that provincial and local governments had to come up with almost three-quarters of the 4 trillion yuan in stimulus funds, one way or another, to develop their local projects. Local officials saw this as a great opportunity to accumulate their political capital for promotion through expanded investment. One deputy mayor argued, "Now is a special time that requires special methods. If we are not fast enough, we will be in disadvantage, falling far behind others. . . . This is a serious political problem" (quoted in Jiang 2015). Local governments were quick in responding to the call from the party. For example, according to Naughton (2009a, 2), Shandong officials were encouraged to "seize the favorable opportunity created by expansionary fiscal policy and the 'appropriately loose' monetary policy." In another instance, the head of Wugong County in Shaanxi Province insisted on the need to seize "an extremely rare and precious opportunity. . . . [W]e must concentrate our forces and act quickly, strengthen our links with the provincial and municipal authorities, and make sure that more key-point investment projects come to our county. . . . Getting more project funding is our top current task" (2).

The proposal and approval of local projects was a two-way process. The center would give signals on the scale of investment and the type of projects, and lower-level governments would come up with corresponding proposals, which would then be subject to the NDRC's checking and approval procedures. Provincial governments were quick to jump on the bandwagon, and within the first month after Beijing's announcement of the stimulus package, eighteen out of thirty-one provinces had submitted proposals worth 25 trillion yuan, over 80 percent of China's annual GDP (Huo, Wang, and Wang, 2009).

However, even if the projects were approved, local governments still needed to provide funding for them, given the limited fiscal commitment from the central government. The tax reform in 1994 redistributed revenues in favor of the center, while the spending obligations of local governments remained and usually increased over time (Jin and Zou 2003, 311). In addition, Beijing also prohibited local governments from borrowing through its Budget Law from 1993 (Clarke and Lu 2017). Hence, the funding for the extra stimulus spending was drawn mainly from an expansion of land-related revenue and borrowing from banks and increasingly shadow banks. First, local governments had come to rely heavily on extrabudgetary income to pay for their obligations after 1994, especially income from land sales (Han 2010). Land is owned by the state in China, which gives local government the capacity to raise income from land sales by manipulating land supply and the rental price of land-use rights. This has led to high land prices, particularly for residential land, and a flow-on effect on property prices. As a result, land financing increased rapidly to 1.6 trillion yuan, or 5 percent of GDP, in 2009 (Xing 2009). At the same time, the government also encouraged developers, especially local state-owned developers, to increase their leverage. This then resulted in high property prices, banks' high exposure to the property sector (in lending to both developers and households), and the increasingly high leverage of households in the form of mortgages. As local governments became key stakeholders in the real estate industry through land sales, they also became recalcitrant obstacles to Beijing's recurrent attempts to fight asset price inflation.

In addition, the 1993 Budget Law's borrowing ban on the local governments was relaxed somewhat in 2009, after which the central government would allow qualified provincial-level governments to issue bonds, which were to be issued by the Ministry of Finance and subject to the center's approval and annual quota allocation. The center eventually removed the ban altogether in 2014 by revising the Budget Law, allowing local governments to issue bonds by themselves but subject to the center's approval and annual quota system (Sheng and Ng 2016, 53). Nevertheless, both local bond and land sale revenues fell far short of meeting local demand for infrastructure investment. This prompted local governments to adopt an alternative financing strategy, through which, without violating the regulation and laws, they were able to raise funds by way of vehicles disguised as corporate investments, which were to be supported by cash flows from the infrastructure to be built.

Local governments thus established various types of credit and investment vehicles, especially local government financing vehicles, to borrow from the banks and increasingly from shadow or nonbank financial institutions using future cash flows from the projects as guarantees. This is represented in the "self-raising funds," which took the lion's share of total fixed capital investment compared with formal bank credit and government budget allocations. Consequently, local government debt skyrocketed after the GFC (figure 6.3).

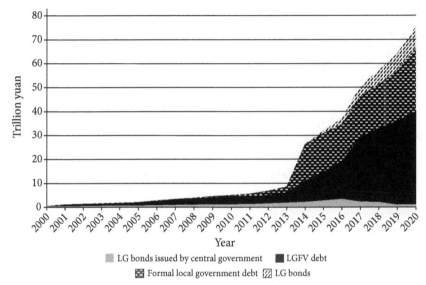

FIGURE 6.3. Local government debt (trillion yuan). The sudden increase in formal local government debt since 2014 was due to the inclusion of local government financing vehicle (LGFV) debt recognized by the Ministry of Finance as local government debt after the survey by the National Audit Office in 2013.

Sources: Central and local government bond issuances are from the Ministry of Finance; local government financial vehicle loans are from IMF 2021.

Not surprisingly, the lack of state-based checks and balances on vital resources such as land led to rent seeking, economic inefficiency, and rampant corruption. Funds were used to construct entire cities that were never populated, as well as often questionable roads, bridges, and other infrastructure projects. A study by Ang, Bai, and Zhou (2015) suggests a close correlation between corruption indices and local governments' involvement in the real estate sector. For the IMF (2013, 1), the "renewed run-up in China's property prices followed by the sharp correction in property markets, and financial stress related to credit exposures on local government financing vehicles, are two major domestic risks." These risks will be further explored in chapter 10.

The Advance of the SOEs

The credit and investment surge during this era also propelled the SOEs. In the midst of this era, Lardy (2014) published a book—*Markets over Mao*—which pointed to the superior performance of the private sector in China, as overwhelmingly *the* major creator of growth, jobs, and exports, and for a time the major recipient of bank credit. Accordingly, Lardy saw the private sector and market economy in China advancing at the expense of the state. Even at the time, however, this argument understated the continued importance of the state and the state sector in China's political economy, especially so amid the surge in statism in the wake of the GFC and also since the installation of the highly statist Xi Jinping regime in late 2012. In fact, it was the state that was at the time, and continues to be, in the passing lane, with China's post-GFC era featuring "an advance of the state and the retreat of the private" (*guojin mintui*). Lardy (2019) has more recently acknowledged the rise of the statist Xi regime in *The State Strikes Back*, and now concedes this point, a major issue in terms of economic rebalancing that we explore further in chapter 11.

As noted, a large portion of the stimulus spending was targeted at infrastructure and the SOEs. A majority of the ten industries Beijing set out to promote were strategic and heavy industries, dominated by SOEs, which are political heavyweights in China's political economy. They have long been the main vehicles to implement government policies and to achieve the government's economic and political goals. They deliver fiscal revenues to the government and create employment. There is also the "revolving door" between senior SOE management and the political elite and government bureaucracy, which further ensures the integration of interests between the SOE sector and the state. SOEs had wielded increased power during the Hu-Wen administration, when Beijing expanded the scale of support for the SOEs compared to the previous Jiang-Zhu era. Supported by industrial policies aimed at creating "national champions," industrial oligarchs were expected to fight against the "invasion" of foreign competition after China's WTO accession in 2001. According to a study by the China Investment Association, SOEs were allowed to enter seventy-two out of eighty "key economic sectors," compared with sixty-two for foreign companies and a mere forty-one for private firms (Liu 2010).

At the same time, the way industrial policy is formulated in China also carries a heavy bias in favor of the SOEs. Institutionally, there are two key agencies involved in the policy process: the National Development and Reform Commission and the Ministry of Industry and Information Technology, both of which have intimate relationships with the SOE sector and are powerful advocates for its interests. The industrial rejuvenation policies in the wake of the GFC were no exception. These policies were put together by the NDRC, based on input from the Ministry of Industry and Information Technology, business associations, and the SOEs (Huang 2009). The support measures included various forms of fiscal and monetary subsidies, favored treatment in government procurement, and various forms of protectionism and transfers of technology from foreign companies (Jiang 2015). The implementation of the plans was also monitored and supervised by the two agencies. In addition, the State Assets Supervision and Administration Commission is mandated to manage the state assets of the SOEs. It was given the task before the GFC to address the issue of excessive expansion and overcapacity in the SOEs. But after the GFC, its main task was to propose policies to rescue or strengthen the SOEs. According to Xu (2010), the level of concentration for central SOEs reached 88 percent in their respective sectors by the end of 2009, while in the key sectors of telecommunications and electricity, this figure was 96 percent and 94 percent, respectively. Such comprehensive support from the government, as well as high levels of concentration in industry sectors, has consolidated the dominance of the SOEs across the commanding heights of the domestic economy and boosted revenues (Meng 2011). For example, SOE revenues increased by 23 percent between 2010 and 2011. By contrast, the income for urban residents during the same period rose by less than 8 percent (*Southern Weekend* 2011).

Bank Credit: The Great Leap Forward

The credit- and investment-led GFC stimulus was not abandoned after the immediacy of the crisis but was maintained, becoming a credit-fueled adjunct to the statist growth model, essentially a riskier but expedient "new normal." Between 2012 and 2017, for example, Chinese banks added almost $21 trillion in new assets. This was the result of choices by the leadership. According to Wright and Rosen (2018, 21), "China's financial system kept growing because the authorities chose to allow financial risks to accumulate rather than risk the political fallout from slower growth and financial losses."

Figure 6.4 shows the dramatic credit expansion from 2008 and thereafter. The monetary and credit stimulus saw the central bank undertake significant monetary easing, especially in the interbank market. Prior to the GFC, the PBC had been selling central bank bills to absorb the excess liquidity due to its sterilization operations caused by its ongoing intervention in the foreign exchange market (Bell and Feng 2013, 229). However, this operation was halted in late 2008, only to see a dramatic increase of liquidity in the interbank market, a deliberate move by the central bank to incentivize bank lending.

The leadership's endorsement, as well as a series of moves from central institutions, gave a strong impetus to the financial system, and particularly the banks, for this massive credit surge. Initially, China's foreign reserves had been bulging and the banks were flushed with liquidity due to China's high trade and current account surpluses prior to the GFC. By around 2012, however, as the credit

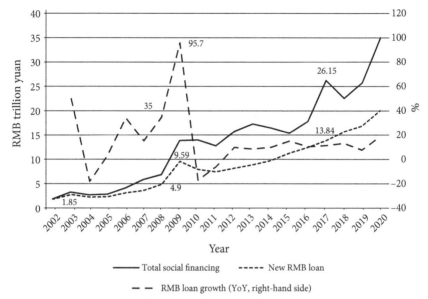

FIGURE 6.4.   China's credit levels.

Source: *Monetary Policy Reports*, PBC, various years.

surge continued, these inflows had slowed to a trickle. Instead of printing yuan to exchange for dollars and other foreign currency as part of sterilization arrangements during the trade and current-account-surpluses boom prior to the GFC, the PBC was forced instead to print a rapidly increasing supply of yuan to expand the credit supply to help fuel the stimulus. In this manner, PBC loans to domestic banks and financial institutions rose from 4 trillion yuan at the end of 2010 to almost 14 trillion yuan at the end of 2020, a three-and-a-half-fold increase.

At the micro level, bank loan officers realized that they were off the hook for any scrutiny of their lending under the stimulus and subsequent lending frenzy. The Guangxi governor put it straightforwardly in early 2009: "Government and budgetary authorities of every city and county should strengthen their links with their local banks, build stronger government credit platforms, realize the budget's ability to provide seed capital, and fully bring into play local banks' *enthusiasm for disbursing loan funds*" (*Guangxi Daily* 2009; emphasis added).

As a senior member of the Risk Committee of one of the Big Four's provincial branches recalls, he used to review eight loan application packages a week, but during the post-GFC great leap forward, he was examining more than forty a week, which, he says, was "unmanageable and crazy."[1] Given this urgency and intensity, it was not surprising to see a surge in lending quantity combined with a deterioration in loan quality. Bank loans increased by 4.7 trillion yuan in 2009, almost double that of 2008. Overall, between 2009 and 2017, post-GFC new bank credit in terms of new RMB loans more than tripled compared to pre-GFC levels between 2002 and 2008.

Banking's SOE Bias

The new credit surge largely missed the household sector, which saw only 9 percent of the incremental lending growth. Instead, around 90 percent of the total stimulus lending went to nonfinancial businesses in financing infrastructure, various public projects, and mergers among SOEs (Sun and Xi 2009). Indeed, most of the increased lending went to the SOE sector, which is demonstrated by the divergence in debt levels between the SOE and private sectors after 2008. Leverage for the industrial private sector, as measured by the liability/equity ratio, continued to decline steadily from its peak at 158 percent in 2004 to 112 percent in 2017. On the other hand, the liability/equity ratio for the state industrial sector bottomed out at 117 percent in 2007 and then rose steeply to 167 percent in 2012. Although it has declined since then, falling to 116 percent in 2017, the leverage of SOEs has been growing as a share of GDP. Moreover, the ratio of SOE liabilities to the total liabilities of nonfinancial enterprises has risen more sharply since 2014 (see figure 6.5).

We return to the question of the bank lending bias against the private sector under the Xi Jinping regime from 2012 in chapter 11, but for now we can say that this bias was largely based on both political and commercial grounds. It is true, as we saw in chapter 5, that the banks had made some progress in modernizing and commercializing their lending decisions in the years leading up to the GFC. The banks had begun to restructure their loan portfolios according to a set of more commercial standards using improved risk assessment methods. As we have seen, Chinese banks started adopting a five-tier risk-based classification system that gave greater emphasis to NPLs, and loan officials were made personally accountable for new NPLs. At the same time, a "5Cs" criterion for loan assessment was also adopted: namely, character (the reputation of the applicant in terms of credit records), capital (the leverage or liability of the applicant), capacity (to repay the loans on time), collateral, and cycle (macroeconomic cycle) (CBRC 2012, 3). The loan approval procedures within the banks were also centralized somewhat to reduce the influence of local governments on the banks' regional branches.

However, as Yeung's (2009) study and interviews reveal, despite the existence of such formal mechanisms, it is the *informal* criteria that often matter in loan approvals, especially the ownership and size of the borrowers. In such processes, SOEs are favored for a variety of reasons. Indeed, in the context facing banks,

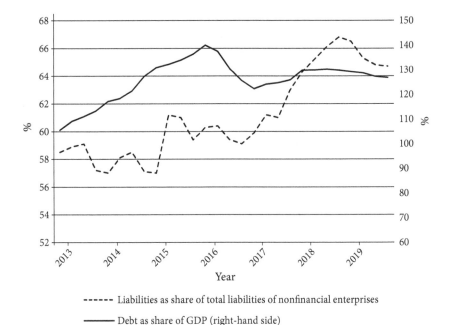

FIGURE 6.5.   SOE debt (%).

Source: Adapted from IMF 2019, 2021.

lending to the SOE sector appears both safer and more attractive, given state support and encouragement; the long legacy and experience of such lending by the banks; the fact that lending to the SEOs is seen as riskless, given state guarantees on such lending; and internal reward systems that mean bankers earn a higher commission on large SOE loans than they do on smaller loans to private companies. As one CBRC official commented in an interview, "Bank employees tell you the same story. If I lend to an SOE and it defaults, I can tell my boss, 'Sorry, this was a commercial mistake.' . . . But if I lend to a private company, I need to do a lot of explaining and the investigation is much tougher."[2] Liu Yonghao (2016), cofounder of Minsheng Bank, admitted in a forum speech that "the banking sector isn't fit for the age we live in. . . . Our banks and financial institutions serve the state-owned sector and the government. . . . From the time they were founded, they lacked the objective of providing funding for private enterprises."

Although a bias against the private sector is apparent, it should be noted that corporate loans in China are also shaped by variations in sectors and ownership types. According to Ma and Laurenceson (2019), the total liabilities for the real estate sector doubled between 2008 and 2015, compared with a 7 percent increase in the construction sector. Within the real estate sector, however, it had been the private developers that had leveraged up while most of the SOEs had deleveraged. These large private developers gained access to bank credit by presenting land as collateral, which is acquired from local governments, often through intimate and irregular dealings. As a result, although the private sector overall has been deleveraging in the post-GFC era, the large private developers have been increasing their leverage. This has further crowded out credit for small private enterprises. The fact that large private developers could enjoy expanded access to bank credit reflects their unique function under state capitalism. On the one hand, local officials gained from their intimate relationships with the developers. On the other hand, local governments were able to gain fiscally from increased land sale prices and volumes, which have become a key part of local government revenue. In other words, real estate developers have been a favorite of the banks due to their functional role within state capitalism.

Thanks to the stimulus package, in the years between 2008 and 2011, the growth of China's GDP remained above the leadership's goal of 8 percent, ranging from 9.2 to 10.4 percent. However, the financing arrangements that have emerged from the crisis have left dangerous debt dependence and mounting debt, while bad loans and systemic risks have increased (see chapter 10). In essence, the economic model that had been successful in driving growth in China before the GFC continued after the crisis, though increasingly on a supercharged debt path. This entrenched the economy's broader structural problems in terms of a distorted consumption-investment structure through a regime of directed credit. Nevertheless, as argued in the next two chapters, developments in the shadow banking sector appeared for a time to offer a silver lining for banking reform. Many liberals hoped that the growth of the shadow banking sector, if properly managed, could stimulate consumption and innovation and even put competitive pressure on the state sector and the main banking system.

7

THE GFC CRITICAL JUNCTURE AND THE RISE OF SHADOW BANKING

China's confrontation with the global financial crisis and its post-2008 stimulus package and credit surge marked a "critical juncture" that helped alter China's banking and financial system, putting competitive pressure on the main state-directed banking system. The key development was the rapid growth of shadow banking, which was broadly supported as part of an emergency response by the party leadership. It was also supported by liberal reformers, mostly housed within the People's Bank of China and the main banking regulator, the China Banking Regulatory Commission. Reformers saw the growth of shadow banking and the associated degree of financial liberalization as a positive move and as their version of "banking reform." The growth of shadow banking as an institutional shift was not a direct confrontation with the main banks, but instead was more marked by incremental "informal institutional adaptation," which also involved the main banks exploring new channels of off-balance-sheet activity in association with the shadow banks.

In this chapter, we employ insights from historical institutionalist theory, especially its analysis of critical junctures, to help frame and explain these developments. Some versions of historical institutionalism emphasize the hard-to-change, inertial role of institutions and posit change as occurring mainly during crises or critical junctures (Capoccia and Kelemen 2007). As Krasner (1984, 234) argues, critical junctures are central to change processes: "Change is difficult. . . . Institutional change is episodic and dramatic rather than continuous and incremental. Crises are of central importance" (see also Ikenberry 1988, 223–24).

In contrast, we adopt our more flexible "agents-in-context" approach, which we outlined at the start of this book. This argues that critical junctures can be important. The shocks of the AFC and GFC in China were both critical junctures that saw key agents exploit the available opportunities in these moments of crisis. However, our approach also argues that institutions are often changing in an evolutionary mode, where small progressive changes can end up producing substantial changes over time (see Thelen 2004; Campbell 2004; Streeck and Thelen 2005; and Mahoney and Thelen 2010). This approach thus argues that important changes can occur both prior to and after critical junctures. Prior circumstances and change will condition what happens during a critical juncture, and changes afterward can tell us whether the changes during the critical juncture were sustained, reshaped, or abandoned. Here we show, on the one hand, how increasing returns and better deals in expanding credit markets helped sustain shadow banking and financial liberalization for a period after China's credit-fueled response to the GFC. On the other hand, as we explore more fully in chapters 9 and 11, the statist reaction of the post-2012 Xi Jinping regime has increasingly wound back or constrained many of the elements of financial liberalization stemming from the critical juncture of the GFC.

Prior to the GFC

Critical junctures like the GFC in China do not arise from a blank slate. Slater and Simmons (2010, 889) point out that "antecedent conditions" are often important in shaping what happens during critical junctures. Relevant agents and developments during the GFC were influenced by three antecedent conditions: (1) the existence of liberal reformers within key institutions and a broader leadership sympathetic to their critique of the financial system, which led to incremental banking reforms after the AFC from the late 1990s; (2) the incremental though constrained growth of shadow banking prior to the GFC; and (3) growing doubts within the leadership about the Chinese growth model.

The Asian Financial Crisis can be defined as a mild critical juncture that prompted a degree of banking reform. Nevertheless, compared to the GFC, the AFC was a more limited regional disruption. Although the AFC saw a slump in external demand, this was due mainly to China's decision not to devalue the RMB. China's capital account was relatively closed compared to the Southeast Asian countries, so that volatilities in markets could not be translated into a disruptive capital flight out of the country. Further, during the AFC, Beijing was able to achieve stability and recovery through fiscal measures between

1997 and 2000 without resorting to financial stimulus, due to the relatively smaller scale of the AFC's economic disruption. The fact that China did not devalue its currency suggests the confidence of the Chinese leadership in seeing this through. Overall, however, although the AFC did not pose a challenge to the Chinese growth model, it did nevertheless prompt at least some efforts with banking reform.

Above all, the AFC alerted the leadership and the authorities to the dangers of a weak banking system and regional financial contagion. The monetary and banking authorities were strengthened institutionally during the period following the AFC, and, just as importantly, they developed a policy framework and regulatory discourse centered on banking reform (Bell and Feng 2013, 263). In this view, the main problem stemmed from the fact that the Big Four state-owned banks operated within a state-directed credit system where low-cost funds, thanks to the system of financial repression, were channeled mainly to the state sector and especially to the giant SOEs (Pei 1998). As we have seen, inefficiencies in the state sector and limited commercial discipline in the banks had produced a huge problem of nonperforming loans within the banks that had grown ever worse during the 1990s, especially with the concurrent shift in the Chinese growth model and its growing emphasis on the state sector and industrial expansion (Lardy 1998). As outlined in previous chapters, moves to reform the financial sector were initiated in several phases from the mid-1990s, including passing national legislation on central banking and commercial banking, separating policy lending from retail banking, recapitalizing major state banks, removing a large proportion of their NPLs to newly established asset management companies, and listing major banks in the stock market, which was designed to invite market scrutiny over the banks (Shih 2007; Okazaki 2011). Despite these changes, there was a greater focus on SOE reform than on thoroughgoing banking reform during this period (Feng 2006c, 92). There were important institutional and political constraints that protected financial repression and placed a limit on financial liberalization and reform, especially since the prevailing financial arrangements did not appear to be threatening economic growth. Fundamental change was also resisted because the prevailing banking and growth models were supported by a dense network of political and economic interests that benefited directly from the growth model and its financial arrangements (Shih 2007, 2008, 2011; Bell and Feng 2013).

The second key antecedent condition was the (limited) development of a shadow banking sector. This was in part due to unmet credit needs that could not be fulfilled by the formal credit system and through regulatory arbitrage and funds leakage from the main banks. The Financial Stability Board (2013, 5) defines shadow banking as "the system of credit intermediation that involves entities and activities fully or partially outside the regular banking system, or non-bank credit intermediation in short." In China, as we detail in the next chapter, the shadow sector involves a range of practices, from various forms of "back alley banking" and internet financing (such as online peer-to-peer lending) to more formal arrangements such as the operation of trust companies and their links to the formal banks through off-balance-sheet activities (Tsai 2002; Zhang 2013; Sheng and Soon 2016; Collier 2017). Institutional space existed for the development of the shadow banking sector, which initially emerged from what Tsai (2006, 135) refers to as a "regulatory void." Although officials had ruled out exotic financial trading of the type that infected Wall Street and London prior to the GFC, in the banking sector they did not rule out shadow banking, reflecting China's capacity to support incremental institutional change. Nevertheless, the authorities did impose limits. As Shih (2011) argues, periods of economic stress, such as periods of higher inflation or slowing growth, would normally see the suppression of the informal financial sector in China. According to him, the shadow banking sector and moves toward interest rate liberalization have ebbed and flowed in recent decades. Periods of low inflation and strong growth have tended to support some liberalization, while economic shocks have curtailed liberalization: "High inflation repeatedly led to spontaneous interest rate liberalization as depositors withdrew money from the state banks, which paid negative interest rates in favor of underground banks paying market rates. To maintain the state bank's oligopoly, central technocrats time and again suppressed these unregulated financial institutions. . . . [C]entral technocrats demanded strict control over interest rates in order to maintain the system of credit rationing to priority industries and investment projects" (Shih 2011, 438).

The third key antecedent condition was that just prior to the shock of the GFC, the Chinese leadership and authorities were becoming increasingly concerned about the Chinese growth model and its links to the financial system. Despite reasonable rates of economic growth, in 2007, just prior to the GFC, Premier Wen nevertheless described China's economy as "unbalanced, unstable, uncoordinated, and unsustainable." Increasingly, the marginal costs of running the state-capitalist system were highlighted, and explicit links were being made between problems in the banking system and problems of balance and stability within the growth model. Among reformers based in the PBC and the financial regulatory authorities, the view formed that banking reform was fundamental to sustaining economic growth and a revised growth model, as the current model was increasingly seen as dysfunctional and as misallocating credit and capital. Although long constrained, the system was ripe for greater liberalization, with the explosive growth of shadow banking after the critical juncture of the GFC supporting this view.

The Critical Juncture

In relation to the critical juncture itself, Soifer (2012, 1592, 1574) argues that "all critical junctures are bounded by permissive conditions," which are defined as "those factors or conditions that change the underlying context to increase the causal power of agency." A better definition might be that permissive conditions during a critical juncture are those that change the context to *potentially* increase the role of agency and change. Whether such opportunities are acted on or realized by agents is another matter. Indeed, it might arise that conditions are conducive to the possibility of change but that change doesn't occur, perhaps due to inactive or constrained agents.

The permissive conditions in this case were (1) the economic shock of the GFC, and (2) the leadership's decision to respond to this with a large stimulus. As we saw in the previous chapter, the GFC generated a major shock to the growth model, especially in terms of slowing global growth and producing a sharp decline in external demand for Chinese exports. The GFC thus highlighted mounting problems with China's overreliance on external demand. It seemed as if China could no longer afford to treat Premier Wen's Four Uns as a theoretical conjecture. The second important permissive condition was that, as we also saw in the previous chapter, the leadership decided that a massive fiscal and monetary stimulus package was to be the main response to the crisis (Naughton 2009b; Jiang 2015).

Soifer (2012, 1575) argues that "in the presence of permissive conditions, a set of productive conditions *determine* the outcome that emerges from the critical juncture" (emphasis added). It is unwise, however, to think that outcomes can be determined simply by productive conditions. It is better to see permissive conditions as opening up "windows of opportunity" (Cortell and Peterson 1999, 191) or the *possibilities* for change, while productive conditions are those that might encourage or facilitate actors within relevant institutions in forging processes of institutional change *during* a critical juncture.

The leadership had long thought that so long as China's growth model worked tolerably well and delivered high rates of economic growth, then the problems in banking and finance seemed manageable, with few incentives for fundamental reform. But the shock of the GFC, growing dysfunctions in the growth model, and the secular slowing of economic growth raised growing concerns. The productive results of this critical juncture were two sets of decisions by policymakers.

The first decision was to respond to the crisis with a mainly debt-fueled investment surge, driven by both short-term political and economic imperatives as well as the earlier dead weight of institutional legacies, especially the existing growth model and its financial regime and entrenched interest groups. The second was to allow the growth of shadow banking as a supplement to the perceived limits of the main banks in expanding credit.

The crisis could have provided a window of opportunity for Beijing to turn to internal demand and finally tackle key structural issues and move toward rebalancing the economy. Instead the response was more expedient, with the leadership choosing the short-term growth imperative over fundamental reform. As we have seen, the leadership put the traditional growth model on steroids by ramping up credit and state-sector investment given an already stretched fiscal budget at that time. In this manner, a huge credit surge emerged as a key feature of China's GFC response.

Furthermore, unlike earlier periods where the shadow sector was suppressed during times of economic stress, the expansion of the shadow banks was instead sanctioned by the authorities in the context of the huge GFC stimulus package. Hence, institutional constraints in the main banking system opened up scope for change in the informal banking sector.

Our approach thus highlights the role of informal institutions as well as the mutually shaping interaction between formal and informal institutions. Tsai (2006, 120) argues that institutional theory has traditionally focused on formal institutions but that informal institutional arrangements can also be important. Indeed, informal institutions can be empowering, used by institutions and perhaps by weaker agents to bypass or work around more formal existing arrangements. These agents include households, private businesses, rural borrowers, and local governments starved of funds, as well as the shadow banks and the main banks through expanding off-balance-sheet activities in the shadow sector.[1]

As we argue more fully in chapter 9, the expansion of shadow banking also fitted the reform agenda of liberal elements within the Chinese state, represented in particular by the PBC and CBRC in the financial area. For liberal reformers, the expansion of shadow banking was seen as helping to fuel economic growth by making finance cheaper and more widely available, as well as by offering a wider range of financial services. The growth of the shadow sector in the context of the GFC critical juncture was also supported tacitly by the wider leadership, who recognized that the shadow banks would play an important role in expanding credit and in funding and developing lending platforms for local governments. Shadow banking, then, did not arise from deregulation but was instead spurred by crisis exigencies and state leaders' attempts to rapidly expand credit after 2008; by pressures from the household, market, and state sectors for more credit; and by liberal reformers in the state who were eager to capitalize on events by expanding the shadow sector as a form of informal financial deregulation that would hopefully lead to wider changes. Under these productive conditions, the shadow sector grew rapidly. So successful was this as a workaround that it eventually altered the main system, as we show in chapter 8.

Post-critical-juncture Conditions

Permissive and productive conditions operate *during* a critical juncture in the context of antecedent conditions. But what happens afterward also matters, particularly in terms of whether the changes that occurred during the critical juncture are sustained. In the case at hand, the post-critical-juncture conditions for a time sustained the rapid expansion of the shadow banking sector. The leadership continued the credit expansion after the GFC as part of an increasingly credit-fueled growth model. For their part, as argued in chapter 9, liberal reformers saw shadow banking as a means to help further liberalize the financial system and to assist with economic rebalancing. The rapidly expanding shadow banks reached out to new customers in the household and private sectors long starved of credit, shaping a self-reinforcing market path of increasing returns through better credit deals and new financial services. Streeck and Thelen (2005, 6) argue that "increasing returns and positive feedback are more helpful in understanding institutional resiliency than institutional change." Yet the increasing returns in this case drove change for a period, with a multitude of actors voting with their feet in credit markets. Mahoney and Thelen (2010, 16) thus argue that in China, the new market context "pits a new institutional system against an older one. As more and more actors defect to the market institutions they may erode and slowly overtake the previous state-controlled arrangements."

Collier (2017, 8) has a different view, asserting that the growth of shadow banking "allowed the Communist Party to allow a market economy to flourish without directly challenging state control." The problem with Collier's argument is that the growth of market opportunities in finance did challenge the statist system, at least for a time. And Mahoney and Thelen go too far in suggesting that the new arrangements would "overtake the previous state-controlled arrangements." For a period, the rapid growth of the shadow sector did reflect a lessening of control by the Chinese state over the credit system. This did not reflect overt conflict or an attempt to use power to try and attack the citadel of the main banking system head-on. Instead it involved subtler processes, whereby reformers within the state and agents in the broader market partially sidestepped existing arrangements, thus weakening them. Thereafter, however, as we see below and in later chapters, the Xi Jinping regime reasserted state controls over the credit system.

During its rapid growth phase, shadow banking was facilitated by a convergence of the interests of multiple agents from both public and private sectors. On the credit-supply side, shadow banking products benefited retail/household and institutional/corporate savers by enabling higher returns than those offered from bank deposits. Struggling with overcapacity, low efficiency, and an overall slowdown in economic growth, but with continued access to credit from the formal banking system, the SOEs have also sought higher returns in the shadow banking industry, mainly in the form of entrusted loans. In addition, as we show in the next chapter, given the increasing diversion of deposits and low lending rates administered by the authorities, profit-seeking banks jumped on the bandwagon of shadow banking, employing off-balance-sheet activities in cooperation with nonbank financial institutions (NBFIs).

As we elaborate further in chapter 9, liberal reformers, especially in the PBC, accepted the necessity of China's state-led stimulus as an emergency measure. But they also insisted that such measures could be used only in extraordinary times, that in the long run the debt-driven growth model was not sustainable, and that there was no alternative way to sustain growth other than rebalancing the economy away from public investment and toward private consumption (Zhou 2013a; Zhang 2014). Moreover, regulatory arbitrage or even malpractice is often associated with shadow banking, yet this form of banking can also have positive implications in a statist economy such as China's. Elliott, Kroeber, and Yu (2015, 5) suggest that "in an over-regulated economy with too large a state role, there can be societal benefits from such regulatory arbitrage. It can diminish the deadweight costs of inappropriate or excessive regulation, and it can help force the pace of more comprehensive reforms." It can also foster competition and cooperation between formal and informal institutions.

Therefore, the attitude of the regulatory authorities toward shadow banking has been quite strategic. They have recognized the need for a more liberalized shadow banking sector but have sought to avoid the worst excesses of overseas experiences as displayed in the run-up to the GFC in core Western financial markets. In response to perceived risk, government officials have increased monitoring and regulation and complied with the Financial Stability Board's monitoring framework, as we detail in chapter 9. In China's political context, the acceptance of shadow banking by reformers was essentially seen as a Trojan horse in the sense that, as an agent of change, shadow banking was expected to be able to compete with and eventually challenge and change the formal banking system over time.

The rise of shadow banking can be likened to what Tsai (2006, 123) refers to as "adaptive informal institutional change," which is a classic Chinese reform response involving informal, experimental, and adaptive change in the shadow of state hierarchy. Tsai (2006, 124) uses this formulation to describe "the way in which business interests in China initially evaded formal institutional constraints," which eventually led to more "formal institutional change and facilitation of their activities." She further argues that the "etiology of formal institutional change lies in the informal coping strategies devised by local actors to evade the restrictions of formal institutions" (2006, 125). This has been the strategy used both by private agents seeking profit and credit and by supportive liberal reformers. Tsai (2006, 140) points to a number of "contextual conditions that foster adaptive informal institutional change," particularly when "formal and informal agents' interests converge," and when there are "cross-cutting institutions" and "multi-layered institutional environments" that "create greater space for agency and institutional innovation." As we have seen, this, too, has been the pattern in China in relation to the expansion of shadow banking, whereby private and official agents' interests have converged and where complex, multilayered institutional environments have created space and scope for innovation. These mechanisms of incremental institutional change reflect both "layering," in which "proponents of change work around institutions that have powerful vested interests" (Hacker 2005, 48), and "displacement," where "new models emerge and diffuse which call into question previously taken-for-granted organizational forms and practices" (Streeck and Thelen 2005, 19).

The pattern of informal institutional change in encouraging more formal change in financial systems has also been experienced in the Western economies, including in the United States and Australia (Krippner 2011; Bell and Keating 2018). In the West, the main driver was the constraints on finance imposed by the postwar regulatory system. The growth of the unregulated shadow banking sector was essentially a market-led informal escape route, especially as the regulatory structure became increasingly unworkable in the 1970s as the costs of compliance and inflation rose (Krippner 2011). Similarly, in China, an important driver of change has been growing market pressures, but liberal reformers have also exploited the opportunity to push their own deregulatory agenda. This has essentially been a gradualist approach that has allowed a new, more market-oriented system to grow alongside and for a time challenge the old statist system. Indeed, this is another example of "growing out of the plan," the venerable Chinese pattern of gradualist, market-oriented change in the shadow of the state (Naughton 1995). A key difference, however, between China's experience and that of the West is that while shadow banking in the United States, for example, takes the form of a full-fledged and relatively independent set of NBFIs, in China shadow banking is strongly linked to the main banks. Although there had initially been active NBFIs in China, shadow banking has increasingly become something that occurs in association with the main banks through off-balance-sheet activity.

Having boosted the old statist growth model under the emergency conditions of the GFC, the growth of the shadow banking sector was seen, especially by reformers, as a way of potentially shifting and rebalancing the banking system and the growth model over time. Naughton (2018a, 505) argues that "regulators could have squelched this emerging sector" but were aware that shadow banks "often provide funds to private and small-scale businesses . . . and that shadow banking can contribute to the diversification and restructuring of the economy that policymakers would like to see." A more open, efficient, and market-oriented financial system was also seen as useful in achieving Beijing's goal of greater international economic integration, reducing exposure to the US dollar system, and supporting a greater international role for the yuan. Shadow banking also created increasing returns in more open credit markets, which helped shift the main banking sector itself in a more liberalized direction via loss of market share, pressure on interest rates, and arbitrage and greater involvement with the shadow sector. There was thus a parallel rise of state capitalism on steroids amid the credit surge and the growth of a more market-oriented shadow banking sector, suggesting both a state-led *and* a market-led political economy in finance. For a time, growing market momentum empowered key agents and looked set to help change the system.

Indeed, the main banks were increasingly losing profits and market share, as we show in chapter 8. Other changes included the rapid growth of internet banking and e-commerce in China. During his visit to WeBank, an online bank operated by the internet giant Tencent, Premier Li acknowledged that internet banking "will lower costs for and deliver practical benefits to small clients, while forcing traditional financial institutions to accelerate reforms" (quoted in Wildau 2015). These pressures saw the PBC liberalizing the interest rate system from 2012. By late 2015, the PBC had finally removed the ceiling on bank-deposit rates, which was the last major, direct interest-rate-control measure. Despite the continuance of informal benchmark interest rate guidance by the authorities, these changes marked an important step in moderating the financial repression regime and in putting pressure on the main banks to offer better deals. During the 2014 National People's Congress, Li announced measures to reform the SOEs, increase market access to services, and establish new private banks. The regime thus appeared to be supporting the old growth model and a new emergent one, with apparent momentum behind the latter.

The liberal and market momentum unleashed after the critical juncture was sustained for a period. However, these incremental changes helped set the stage for a conservative reaction in the form of a revitalized statism under the Xi Jin-ping regime, which came to power in 2012. The Xi regime constitutes a constraint on earlier financial market liberalization based on the rise of shadow banking. As we will see in later chapters, the new regime has challenged and partly rolled back the liberalizing and market-oriented momentum stemming from the GFC critical juncture and its aftermath. Long-held expectations about China's market transition (Lardy 2014) are now being challenged by Xi's state "striking back" (Lardy 2019). At a time when private firms were accounting for around 70 per-cent of China's output, the party declared during its congress in 2013 that it would "let the market play a more decisive role in resource allocation." However, the congress also declared that the party would give "full play to the leading role of the state sector, continuously increasing its vitality, controlling force, and influ-ence" (*China Daily* 2013). This latter approach reflects the more conservative, statist vision that has taken hold under the Xi regime.

This chapter has used the lens of historical institutionalist theory and critical juncture analysis to help explain the rise and subsequent curtailment of the shadow banking sector. As we have seen, the GFC was an important critical juncture that provided the opportunity for key agents to support the rise of the shadow banking system and for reforms to the financial system. We have also emphasized that institutional and market-driven change during critical junctures is important, but that what happens before and after a critical juncture is also important. There were important preconditions prior to the critical juncture of the GFC that facilitated the rise of shadow banking. There has also been ongoing change after the GFC, first with the consolidation and growth of shadow banks, and then by a statist reaction under the Xi regime that is now curtailing the growth of shadow banking and reasserting the state's economic role.

SHADOW BANKING AFTER THE GFC

In this chapter we examine the empirical details of the rapid rise of the shadow banking sector in China amid the credit surge in 2008 and thereafter. We show how various agents, such as households, the private sector, banks, and nonbank financial institutions, and the SOEs and local governments, embraced informal finance, with a convergence of interests in seeking both more access to credit and higher returns awarded by market-based opportunities. The chapter assesses the size of the shadow banking sector and outlines various drivers that caused the sector to expand. The rise of this sector increased the role of competitive pressures and commercial criteria within the formal banking system and saw strong connections develop between the main state-owned banks and the shadow banks. We use the example of internet finance to illustrate how this segment and wider shadow banking changes have helped facilitate a degree of financial liberalization in China in recent years, albeit under the shadow of state hierarchy.

The Shadow Banking System

As we saw in chapter 6, the credit expansion and investment drive in the wake of the GFC tended to reinforce state capitalism. The less efficient state sector received a disproportionally large share of credit from the formal banking system. The state sector was also stimulated through a surge in local government investment in infrastructure. Yet the very momentum that fortified the state sector after the GFC also fostered the rapid development of an informal, market-oriented shadow banking sector. China's leadership and the authorities found it convenient to allow the shadow banking sector to expand, as it helped to satisfy liquidity and credit demand in the post-GFC stimulus era. This was especially the case for local governments. As discussed in chapter 6, the stimulus spending that went to the infrastructure sector was carried out mainly by local governments using borrowed funds. Although the ban on local government borrowing was relaxed in 2009 and again in 2014 as part of the credit drive, the center had been wary of the explosion of local government borrowing in 2009 and 2010 and subsequently restricted bank lending. In such a context, local governments found it hard to obtain loans from the formal financial system, which gave them strong incentives to turn to informal or shadow financing.

In China, "shadow banking" and "informal finance" are rather loosely used terms, referring to a range of financing vehicles that traditionally have been only lightly regulated by the authorities—the PBC and the CBRC. To be sure, informal or shadow finance is not new in China and can be dated back thousands of years. Since the early years of the reform era, private businesses and households have relied on a variety of informal financing mechanisms (Tsai 2015).

The first attempt at conceptualizing shadow banking in China was in a paper by the Investigation and Statistics Department of the PBC in 2012, in which the term is defined as "entities and semi-entities that engage in financial intermediation, perform similar functions in credit, term and liquidity conversion as traditional banks but are not subject to Basel III regulations or its equivalent" (PBC 2012, 53). The official definition of shadow banking appears in a State Council document, in which it is split into three categories of institutions: credit intermediation institutions that have no financial licenses and are under no regulation, such as internet-based finance and third-party wealth management institutions; institutions that do not have financial licenses and are under limited regulation, such as microcredit and finance guarantee companies; and institutions that have financial licenses but are under inadequate regulation or conduct businesses that evade regulation, such as asset securitization, money market funds, and certain types of wealth management operations (Elliot, Kroeber, and Yu 2015). In a similar vein to the definition used by the Financial Stability Board (2013, 5), perhaps the most succinct definition is by the PBC (2013, 8), which defines shadow banking as "credit intermediation involving entities and activities outside the regular banking system that serves to provide liquidity and credit transformation" and "which could potentially be a source of systemic risk or regulatory arbitrage."

The PBC's *Report on Financial Regulation in China 2014* categorizes shadow banking according to three gauges. The narrow measure is based on whether the operation is under the regulatory radar; these operations include nonlicensed businesses, such as microcredit, financing guarantee, peer-to-peer (P2P) lending, third-party wealth management, and private lending. The intermediate gauge includes the narrow gauge as well as those licensed operations outside banking intermediation, such as trust, wealth management, and bond finance. The broad gauge includes the intermediate gauge as well as on-sheet money market funds, asset management, asset securitization, equity nontraditional credit businesses (such as standard and nonstandard investment, interbank business, deposits at the central bank, etc.), and off-sheet nontraditional credit (such as bankers' acceptance bills, credit certificates, payables, and lines of credit).

We argue, however, that a more comprehensive and realistic measure of shadow banking in China should extend the PBC's broad gauge to include asset management by nonbank financial institutions (NBFIs) and financing businesses by other institutions, which best captures the distinct nature of shadow banking in China's business and regulatory contexts. This measuring model would include nontraditional credit from banks in the form of entrusted loans and undiscounted bankers' acceptance bills, a wide range of asset management operations by NBFIs, and other financing operations such as P2P loans, financing guarantees, and microcredit loans. The evolution of the relative share of each subsector of shadow banking according to our broad measure is illustrated in figure 8.1.

Figure 8.2 depicts the main elements and linkages of the shadow banking sector in China. On the supply side, a key source of funds for shadow banking has been wealth management products (WMPs), which are "investment products that provide a return based on the performance of a pool of underlying assets" (Elliot, Kroeber, and Qiao 2015, 2). WMPs can be issued by banks, trust companies, and securities firms, with returns frequently higher than retail deposit rates. On the receiver's end, shadow banking products in China are mainly in the form of trust and entrusted loans, bankers' acceptance bills, corporate bonds, and internet finance (Hsu 2015; Collier 2017, 22). Another major arena of shadow banking is the interbank market, in which banks and NBFIs lend to each other in deposit-like deals designed to circumvent regulatory imposts, such as the cap on deposit ratios and required reserve ratios (Elliot, Kroeber, and Qiao 2015, 3). Finally, as we will elaborate in more detail in a later section, internet finance has become an increasingly popular channel of shadow credit through new digital technologies dubbed "fintech." Such online-based intermediation mainly takes the form of P2P lending and crowdfunding.

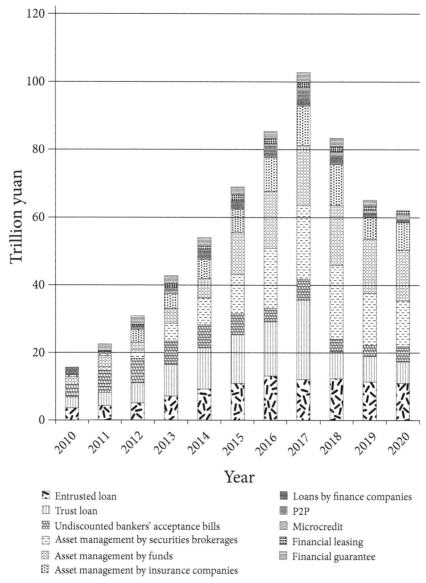

Year

FIGURE 8.1. The composition of China's shadow banking by business sector (trillion yuan).

Sources: Data for "Financial leasing" are from the *Almanac of China's Finance and Banking*, various years; the rest of the data are from the PBC, the CBRC, the CSRC, and the China Securities Depository and Clearing Corporation.

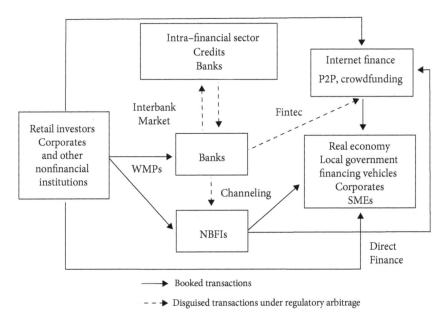

FIGURE 8.2. Main players and businesses of shadow banking in China.

Sizing Shadow Banking in China

Estimates of the relative size of the shadow banking sector in China vary widely, depending on the metrics used. The international regulatory supervisor, the Financial Stability Board (2018, 3), for example, finds that the size of global shadow banking stood at $45 trillion, $99 trillion, and $160 trillion in 2016 according to its narrow, intermediate, and broad measures, accounting for 13 percent, 30 percent, and 48 percent of total global financial assets, respectively. However, all three measures used by the board focus on nonbank financial intermediation. This tends to underestimate China's shadow banking sector, which has featured substantial off-balance-sheet activity by the main banks.

A more common method of calculating the size of shadow banking in China is to look at the size of the core, or traditional shadow banking businesses within the data category of "total social financing," published quarterly by the PBC since 2011, which includes trust loans, entrusted loans, corporate bonds, and undiscounted bankers' acceptance bills (hereafter the "PBC framework") (Zhu 2017). Some studies tend not to include corporate bonds in their measurement of the shadow banking activities in China. However, as Lin and Milhaupt (2017, 38) argue, "If shadow banking is broadly defined as non-bank intermediated finance,

China's corporate bond market is *an integral part* of the shadow banking system" (emphasis in the original). This is due to the fact that various kinds of off-balance-sheet assets, such as WMPs, are often invested in the corporate bond market, forming what Barnett and Roach (2014) call "the largest component of shadow banking" in China.

Another gauge is used by Moody's and adds asset management and other NBFI-initiated intermediations to the PBC method. Both the PBC's and Moody's approaches are indicative of the core components of shadow banking in China and therefore are helpful in accounting for the scale of off-balance-sheet activities. Nevertheless, the scope covered by these gauges is not adequate in estimating the broader risks entailed, given the opaqueness, interconnectedness, and complexity of financial products that have been increasingly popular in China. In addition, as we will discuss in the next chapter, the regulatory tightening, particularly since 2015, has spurred off-balance-sheet activities that are more complicated and beyond the radar of the two approaches above. Therefore, we see the need to construct a broader gauge with a more comprehensive account of de facto credit intermediations by banks and NBFIs in China, which we have detailed at the beginning of this chapter. It should be noted that these three gauges are not mutually exclusive. Rather, they serve different purposes. A look at the broader range of financial intermediations is bound to involve a degree of repetitive calculations and therefore an overestimation of the actual size of the sector, just as the PBC's and Moody's tend to underestimate it. But our approach provides a more dynamic insight into the true magnitude of the shadow banking system in terms of its risk profile to the wider economic and financial system.

According to our model and relevant official data, we therefore estimate that the size of the shadow sector had been under RMB 8 trillion before 2010 but grew rapidly between 2010 and 2016, peaking at RMB 103 trillion (or $15.3 trillion) at the end of 2017, or almost 125 percent of GDP, substantially larger than the estimates by the PBC (2017) and Moody's (2017), which stood at RMB 45.3 trillion and RMB 65.6 trillion, respectively.

As figure 8.3 indicates, comparatively, if measured against the Financial Stability Board's narrower gauge without considering equity and self-securitization, which have a bigger share in advanced economies, China's shadow banking sector was the third-largest in the world by the end of 2016, after Canada and the United States. The solid black bar in figure 8.3 represents the Chinese figure calculated in our own broad measure. Although it is based on a different benchmark and is thus not comparable with the other measures in the figure, it is nonetheless indicative of the magnitude and potential risk of a spillover effect of shadow banking in China.

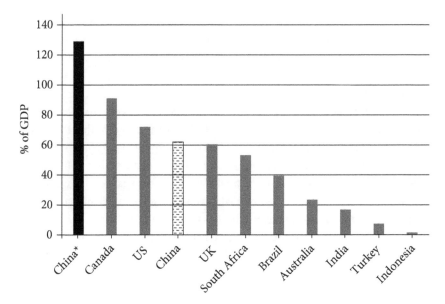

FIGURE 8.3. Comparative view of shadow banking activity by countries (% of GDP as of December 2016). China* refers to our broad measure of shadow banking at the end of 2017.

Sources: FSB 2017; IMF 2017; author's calculation of data from the PBC, the CBRC, the CSRC, and the CIRC.

Key Drivers of Shadow Banking

Here we will outline the role played by the growth of credit pressures, financial liberalization, and state guarantees as major promoters of the growth of shadow banking in China, while in chapter 9 we will examine the role and agendas of the leadership and regulatory authorities in supporting the growth of shadow banking during its boom phase.

Credit Demands

As we have argued, the stimulus and credit surge in response to the GFC and the decision to continue this thereafter as a credit-fueled growth model placed huge demands for credit on the financial system. This saw the distorted, regulated, and repressed financial system unable to cope with such pressure, especially with the bias of lending mainly to the SOEs. As Sheng and Soon (2016, 8) put it, the rise of shadow banking was thus a "roundabout market response to real sector funding needs arising from the bank-dominated system that tended to lend more to the SOE sector."

As we have seen, the statist and credit-fueled growth model that was ramped up after the GFC saw a sharp rise on the demand side for credit, especially from SOEs and local governments. On the one hand, banks were given the green light in expanding their loan profile, knowing that any bad debt ensuing from Beijing-approved projects would eventually be underwritten by the government. On the other hand, local governments, in particular, worked around the formal restrictions of bank finance by borrowing through specially purposed invest-ment vehicles controlled by local governments. A large part of such borrowings took the form of shadow credits packaged by NBFIs and sold by banks to retail and corporate investors as investment products rather than deposits, a standard practice of shadow banking.

At the same time, pressures for more credit also emanated from the society at large. Rapid economic growth in previous decades drove a rising stock of income and wealth within Chinese society, especially the increasingly bulging urban middle class. In this context, households and investors were seeking better returns than the repressed financial system could offer. This and the high level of Chinese savings led to rising demand for retail investments promising higher returns. In this context, wealth management products, for example, by offering substantially higher returns than bank deposits to retail investors, formed a key source of funding for the expanding shadow banking sector.

Furthermore, the statist bias in the credit system had seen the credit needs of small and medium-sized enterprises largely ignored. This led to a financing gap for SMEs, which also sought help from the shadow credit system. The scale of such a gap can be calculated from the equation (Financing Gap = Total Social Financing – New RMB Credit – New Credit in Foreign Currencies – Domestic Corporate Bonds – Domestic Equity Finance by Nonfinancial Enterprises). According to Ren (2017), the annual average of the gap stood at over RMB 2,000 billion between 2009 and 2015, encouraging recourse to the shadow sector.

China's system of prudential banking regulation and attempts to evade it through regulatory arbitrage also drove shadow banking. As we will elaborate further in chapter 9, China has been a champion in adopting key global regula-tory standards such as the Basel III capital regulations, which involve the banks holding capital on their balance sheets to increase their resilience to shocks or market downturns (Knaack 2017). China not only has applied stricter rules than Basel III requires, but has also implemented them well before the agreed-on global rollout schedule. As a result, China's banking regulatory regime has been quite stringent with regulatory restrictions, including substantial reserve require-ments, capital adequacy requirements of no less than 8 percent, a ratio of liquid assets to total liabilities of no less than 25 percent, caps on lending volumes, a loan-to-deposit ratio of 75 percent, and sectoral lending guidelines. By contrast, nonbanks have traditionally had lower capital and liquidity requirements, can avoid PBC reserve requirements, and have not traditionally been subjected to lending restrictions. The relatively tight controls over the main banking system, especially in the context of the stimulus and credit surge after 2008, "forced the banks to look for new ways to generate income and feed the insatiable demand for credit," according to Collier (2017, 6).

More recently, the general slowdown of the economy has led to a decline in returns from the real economy and, with lax monetary policy coupled with a constant narrowing of interest rate differentials on various terms, has created a shortage of investable assets in the real economy. As a result, the "redundant" funds tend to shift away from the real economy and instead circulate within the overall financial system, thus increasing the leverage of financial institutions and the riskier exuberance of the shadow banking sector.

Interest Rate Liberalization

An important part of the shifting boundaries of the banking bargain between the state and the economy and society in China has been the relaxation of financial repression and greater financial liberalization, especially in relation to interest rates. This shift helped spur shadow banking. As we have seen, interest rate regulation had formed a key part of China's financial repression that had distorted the entire financial system, subsidizing the state sector and guaranteeing fat margins in the main banking sector at the expense of depositors and investors. Shih (2011, 437) earlier argued that the leadership "has held onto control of interest rates because of their need to maintain state banks' dominance and to mobilize bank funds. . . . [F]ull liberalization of interest rates remains out of reach." On the other hand, interest rate liberalization had been an announced goal of financial reforms by the authorities for decades, though progress had been tardy. However, the post-GFC credit surge and the growth of shadow banking are an illustration of how informal changes in the shadow sector had a knock-on effect on the formal sector through mounting pressure for the liberalization of interest rates, which formally occurred in 2015.

The motive behind interest rate deregulation came from the fact that the rate distortions based on administrative decrees from the central bank (in the form of benchmark interest rates set by the PBC) have inevitably reduced efficiency in the allocation of financial resources. This has led to overcapacity and debt reliance in the state sector and an unmet hunger for credit in the more efficient and productive private sector, increasingly the key to economic growth and employment in China (Lardy 2014). These distortions have led to the growth of shadow banking, and for their part, banks sought to evade the directed credit system and engage in more lucrative lending to the parties that were largely shut off from formal finance. Given the banks' long-term experience as the monopoly in a statist and protective context, the increasing participation and, indeed, increasing domination in shadow lending by the banks in recent years has helped the latter to "internalize" and digest business pressures in an increasingly marketized environment. The expansion of this practice, in turn, set the scene for the central bank to formally liberalize interest rates, with the PBC increasingly less concerned about the prospect that the banks would not survive in the postderegulation era.[1] In this sense, the shadow banking system acted, as has happened elsewhere in the world, as a catalyst of wider financial liberalization.

Public officials tend to be somewhat coy about the shadow sector due to political sensitivities. As one PBC official put it in an interview, "People tend to be uncomfortable with anything that is called 'shadow.'" Many in the government have also been uneasy, as the sector is seen as risky. "But from the perspective of us regulators," the official continued, "it might not be that bad at all. It is something we can call on to fight against vested interests in our financial reforms."[2] Another PBC official said, "We all love sunshine and hate shadow. But if we can bring the shadow under the sunshine, we will have a more beautiful scene. So don't be afraid of the shadow, because it will be the last shadow before we see the sunshine."[3]

Indeed, the sunshine came earlier than expected, with interest rates being gradually deregulated. First the authorities allowed for greater room to set lending rates, leading to the abolition of controls over lending rates in 2013. PBC governor Zhou Xiaochuan then announced at the National Party Congress in 2014 that by 2016 the final major regulation, the ceiling on bank-deposit rates, would be lifted. This occurred earlier than expected—in October 2015. The deregulation of interest rates is a key reform: the formal ceiling on deposit yields was the final remaining direct interest rate control.

These moves represent a significant shift from a state-controlled quantitative credit system to one with a greater focus on supply and demand in the market. This reform and the move away from earlier financial repression have also been supported by the banks that once benefited from the interest rate controls and the fat margins and profits that financial repression provided. As Armstrong-Taylor (2016, 84) puts it, "Instead of opposing reforms, they [the banks] now have an incentive to support them." The reason for this shift in the attitudes of the banks is that interest rate liberalization now offers them a means to enter the market and compete more effectively with the shadow banks and indeed colonize this arena themselves, increasingly operating in tandem with shadow banking entities and practices.

However, it should be noted that these deregulatory moves are still short of full liberalization in practice. It is true that Chinese banks are able to set lending and deposit rates, but these rates still have to be more or less in line with the PBC's window guidance and "benchmark rates," especially in relation to the preferential rates at which SOEs and local governments borrow. Moreover, the fact that the (lower-than-market-level) benchmark lending rates are still having an influence means the continuation of the directed credit system that favors the state sector (Bisio 2020, 7). Relatedly, this also means that the interest rate regime is still not reflecting the level of risk in the credit system, especially given the ever-growing levels of credit that are being extended.

In essence, then, de facto interest rate liberalization may still be somewhere down the road. Nevertheless, the formal liberalization of interest rates has been a substantial achievement for the PBC and liberal reformers and a critical step in a drawn-out process, one that has already had significant impact on the banks and that has also encouraged the growth of shadow banking.

State Guarantees

A further important part of the changing banking bargain in China has been the explicit and implicit rise of state support and guarantees for financial markets and assets in China, extending even into the shadow banking sector and helping to propel its growth. Indeed, China's high debt and weak credit efficiency, as well as various distortions in the financial system, can be traced to perceptions of implicit government guarantees by all parties in the system. Depositors and investors assume that their lending and savings are implicitly guaranteed by the state, a view further cemented by the introduction of deposit insurance by the government in 2014. Investors also believe that the state is responsible for underwriting debt issued by SOEs and local government financing vehicles, and that the state or government will, as has been the case, come to the rescue of distressed banks and stabilize stock and bond markets in times of volatility, such as Beijing's rescue of the stock market in 2015.

A good example for the banking industry is Beijing's takeover of the failed Baoshang Bank and Jinzhou Bank in 2019. Baoshang Bank was a state-guaranteed liquidation, while in the case of Jinzhou Bank, the government orchestrated an investor consortium to take over the failed bank, with the ICBC (one of the Big Four) as the lead investor. As the Reserve Bank of Australia (2018, 10) argues, "Implicit guarantees of loans and other financial products in China are also likely to have resulted in weaker lending standards. Low credit spreads on debt securities issued by SOEs and local governments suggest that investors assume they are effectively guaranteed by the central government. Similarly, many investors in the wide range of asset management products (AMPs) sold by banks and non-bank financial institutions (NBFIs) reportedly believe they are implicitly guaranteed by the issuer."

Impacts on and Responses from the Main Banks

The main banks have also been willing allies in the growth of shadow banking. The imposts of formal prudential regulation, as well as growing competitiveness challenges and the impact of interest rate liberalization, have impacted and squeezed the main banks. These pressures saw the growth rate of formal bank loans fall increasingly after 2008, accelerating a longer-term trend. Although the volume of deposits in the main banks has been rising, increased competition from shadow banks has left the main banks with less of the share of the new growth in deposits. This has been a major challenge for the banks, reflected in the general decline since 2011 of the growth rate of main bank deposits, which has dropped from around nearly 14 percent in 2011 to only 8 percent in 2018 (except between 2014 and 2015).

In recent years, increased competition has also resulted in a decline in large commercial banks and policy banks' share of total banking assets in China. As figure 8.4 shows, the proportion of formal credit in total social financing has declined, moving from 92 percent in 2002 to only 51 percent in 2013, sitting at 57.5 percent by 2020. Figure 8.4 also shows the corresponding decline in shadow credit as a proportion of total social financing. This has been largely due to growing risk concerns and increased regulatory measures, which we explore in chapter 9.

As for the Big Four banks, their proportion in total banking assets fell from over 84 percent in 1993 to 30 percent in 2020, with growing competition from other types of finance (Kwong 2011, 163; PBC 2021). As a result, deposit and loan pricing have been increasingly competitive, with the main banks' net interest margins falling to record-low levels in recent years. Furthermore, as figure 8.5 illustrates, the fall in net interest rate margins has had negative impacts on the return on equity and the profits of the Big Four banks, which previously flowed from the favorable interest rate settings under financial repression.

Before the regulatory crackdown from around 2015, which we detail in the next chapter, and before the renewed statist surge under the Xi Jinping regime, which we detail in chapter 11, these growing competitive pressures were placing considerable stress on the main banks to offer more credit and become more competitive. This strongly incentivized a shift on their part into shadow banking.

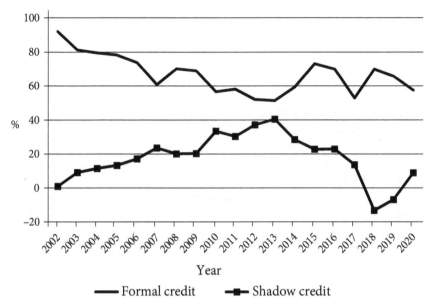

FIGURE 8.4. Share of formal credit (RMB loan) and shadow credit in total social financing (%).

Source: Monetary Policy Implementation Reports, PBC, various years.

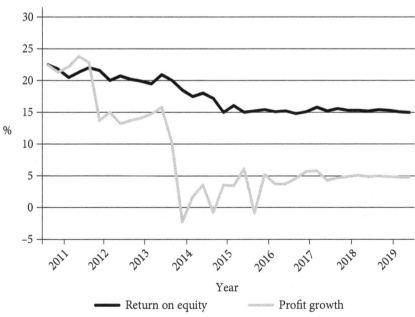

FIGURE 8.5. ROE and annual profit growth of the Big Four (%).

Source: CBIRC 2021b.

As Naughton (2018, 506) argues, "Marketization of bank interest rates is a cru-cial step in shrinking the big difference between banks and shadow banks and moving toward a more uniform financial system." Indeed, Naughton writes, "financial market reforms are creating powerful forces that are eroding financial repression and displacing the banking system from its heretofore overwhelming dominance of the financial system" (507). The main banks have responded by becoming more commercially oriented and by offering better terms and service to a wider range of customers. Importantly, they have also responded through regulatory arbitrage and by engaging in shadow banking activities themselves. As Liao, Sun, and Zhang (2016, 4) report, competitiveness and bottom-line pres-sures have "imposed a significant burden on banks' balance sheets, driving banks to expand off-balance sheet business, both to circumvent stringent regulation on capital and liquidity, and to tap into new clients and asset classes." Pressures to expand credit and competitiveness as well as arbitrage dynamics are the usual suspects that drive shadow banking worldwide, as regulated firms exploit regula-tory loopholes to circumvent unfavorable regulation through financial innova-tion. China is no exception.

Through regulatory arbitrage and supported by the initial tacit liberalization agenda of key regulatory authorities, particularly the PBC, a flurry of NBFIs experienced rapid development, including trust companies, mutual funds, wealth management companies within security brokerages, and more modern insurance companies. These NBFIs have served the economy with diversified financial products, such as WMPs, universal insurance, and interbank deposit certificates, which has further encouraged interbank entrusted loans, struc-tured finance, and embedded transactions. Demand from SMEs also resulted in the emergence and rapid development of NBFIs in the shadow sector, such as microcredit companies, financial guarantee companies, pawnshops, and online P2P platforms. It has further resulted in the rapid increase in entrusted loans between enterprises and other private lending. Figure 8.6 depicts the growth rate of shadow banking compared to credit growth in the financial system. Compared with formal credit's free fall in 2010 and lukewarm growth thereaf-ter, the growth of shadow credit has been largely cyclical. As we discuss further in chapter 9, this has reflected the stop-and-go style of approach by various sectoral regulators.

The banks themselves have thus taken on new risks and rewards through transacting loans and financial products through various channels—namely, NBFIs—to avoid or reduce regulatory imposts. Here, the NBFIs help assemble loans into wealth management products with better returns than those available under official deposit rates. These WMPs are then sold to a range of investors through the banks. There are therefore strong links between the main banks and

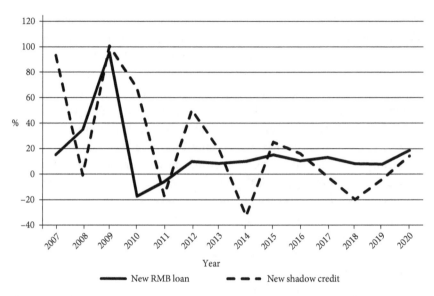

FIGURE 8.6. Growth of new shadow credit compared with new RMB credit in the financial system (%, YoY). "Shadow credit" refers to the PBC's narrow gauge of shadow banking, which includes entrusted loans, trust loans, undiscounted bills, and corporate bonds.

Source: Monetary Policy Implementation Reports, PBC, various years.

shadow banking through various funding channels, lines of credit, and implicit interbank guarantees (Bowman, Hack, and Waring 2018, 59). Elliot, Kroeber, and Qiao (2015, 1) argue that around 66 percent of shadow banking is "bank loans in disguise," whereas the remainder is due to the competitive advantage that nonbanks enjoy because of weaker regulation of the shadow sector as well as a willingness to reach out to nontraditional, smaller customers. In other words, the banks have increasingly become the major player in the shadow banking system, in cooperation with the nonbank institutions. As Collier (2017, 145) puts it, shadow banking has increasingly become "the stepchild of the mainstream banking system."

Jumping on the bandwagon of shadow banking has also provided a profit incentive for the main banks, whose profits have been limited in particular areas through low returns in lending to the SOEs and in the required purchasing of PBC bills. In essence, shadow banking, according to (Sheng and Soon 2016, 27), has "allowed banks to entice depositors with whatever returns they deem attractive yet prudent, and to lend to whichever borrower they wished."

Shadow banking has also fostered competition within the wider financial system on two fronts. First, it has encouraged the emergence and rapid

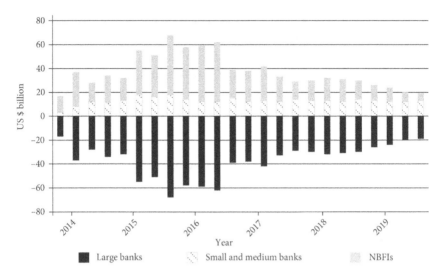

FIGURE 8.7. Large banks funding small banks and NBFIs in the interbank market (quarterly data, US $ billion). "Large banks" include the Big Four and the Bank of Communications.

Sources: IMF 2017 and CBIRC website.

development of new types of NBFIs, such as wealth management companies under stock brokerages, microcredit companies, and P2P platforms. The increasing diversification of financial institutions thus boasts innovation and entrepreneurship amid competition with the financial establishment. Second, within the banking sector, shadow banking businesses have helped smaller, regional banks boost leverage and profits. Since 2013, as figure 8.7 shows, these banks have utilized opportunities in the interbank wholesale market by borrowing from the big state banks via intra-financial-sector credit and in turn lending out to areas of higher return (see also Chen and Kang 2018). Although the practices are risky, they nonetheless provide an opportunity to enlarge assets in catching up with the big players.

Internet Finance: Digital Disruption in the Shadow Sector

The growth of internet finance in China is a good example of how shadow banking has helped spur greater financial liberalization. That rapid growth has been propelled not by the established financial institutions or the main banks, but by nonfinancial companies, most notably newly emerging e-commerce and other tech firms. Internet-based financial services have been growing explosively since 2013, reflecting changed regulatory and market conditions and technological innovation. Indeed, based on the latest internet technologies, China's private internet firms are venturing into the financial sector as so-called fintech firms, posing challenges to the established banking system and regulatory framework.

The Disruption

"Internet finance" is a loosely used catch-all term for financial activities and services conducted over the internet, including online payment, credit, and wealth management tools. By moving financial intermediation online, internet finance has been able to cut into traditional banking by offering more convenient payment solutions and investment channels with higher returns to consumers and investors.

In China, in particular, there has been a perfect storm of conditions for the meteoric rise of internet finance. The popularity of cell phones in China, thanks to ever-lower production costs, provides the hardware for internet services, especially e-commerce and associated online payments. Under a regime of financial repression, online WMPs generate returns as much as twice as high as traditional bank returns for the emerging middle class with increasing liquidity, while online credit systems channel funds to individual borrowers and small businesses that have been kept out of the formal realm of finance. There are three main components of the booming industry: online payment platforms, WMPs, and online credit, especially peer-to-peer lending, or P2P.

Internet-based financial platforms, especially those handled by mobile devices, have grown rapidly in China. As figure 8.8 shows, the annual transaction value of mobile payments in China has exploded from less than 10 trillion yuan in 2013 to 432 trillion yuan in 2020.

These forms of finance in China largely originated from digital payment systems, which have in turn benefited from the rise of e-commerce as a result of rising household disposable income. For example, Alibaba, the largest e-commerce company in China, recorded a huge $38 billion in sales during its Singles Day (November 11) promotion in 2019, China's version of Cyber Monday (*Forbes* 2019). Accordingly, by the end of 2019, Alibaba had over 900 million Chinese users (1.2 billion globally) of its online payment platform, Alipay. It also had 230 million daily active users of Alipay Wallet, the mobile version of Alipay based on quick response (QR) codes (Liao 2019). Compare that to PayPal, a major international player in this business, which had only 305 million users by 2019. By eliminating the intermediation of banks, these third-party payment systems are encroaching on the main banks' bottom lines.[4]

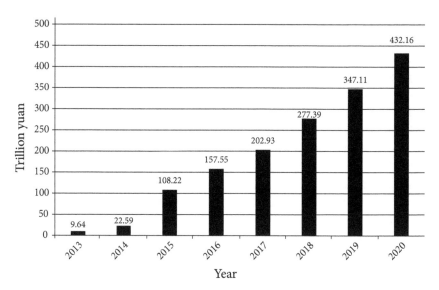

FIGURE 8.8. Annual transaction value of mobile payments in China (trillion yuan).

Source: PBC.

For their part, WMPs provided on the internet are essentially money market funds that channel retail investments into interbank markets. By issuing online WMPs, these internet companies have effectively become fund managers. For example, Alibaba's Yu'ebao has been the most popular online WMP, an instant success that attracted 124 million clients in the year after its launch in June 2013. By the end of 2015, Yu'ebao had over 260 million users and assets worth RMB 627 billion, making Tianhong, the asset management firm for Yu'ebao, China's largest mutual fund (*Shenzhen tequ bao* 2016).

The online WMPs have been extremely popular in China for several reasons. First, they offer comparatively high annual yields by making demand deposit accounts payable at market interest rates that Chinese depositors cannot get from banks. By lowering the minimum investment of publicly offered funds from 1,000 yuan to only 1 yuan, these online WMPs have made money market funds more accessible to the masses, particularly to younger generations who are the most active users of the internet and arguably the most active consumers in China (Jingu 2014). These online WMPs are also attractive due to their liquidity. Many of these products can be redeemed on the day of request, compared with two to three days for traditional money market funds and a few weeks for those issued by banks (PricewaterhouseCoopers 2015, 3). Although the total volume of retail deposits at the banks has continued to rise over the years, its year-on-year growth rate has been declining in general since it peaked in May 2012 (Bloomberg 2014). Finally, while online WMPs attract more risk-averse conservative investors, web-based peer-to-peer lending appeals to more tech-savvy and wealthier investors who have driven rapid growth in this sector prior to a fall-off in 2018.

To the Chinese authorities, internet finance emerged fortuitously at a time when they sought to advance digitalization to help spur the slowing economy. The consensus in Beijing, at least among financial regulators of a liberal stance, is that internet finance can play a role in facilitating economic rebalancing by boosting consumption. On March 5, 2015, Premier Li Keqiang announced the national strategy of "Internet Plus," which calls for the utilization of digital and internet technologies to achieve industrial upgrade and catch-up. This approach aims in particular "to integrate mobile internet, cloud computing, big data, and the Internet of Things with modern manufacturing, to encourage the healthy development of e-commerce, industrial networks, and internet banking, as well as to get internet-based companies to increase their presence in the international market" (State Council 2015). Internet finance occupies a unique position in the Internet Plus strategy. The web-based finance industry has been benefiting from the advancement of internet technologies, which in turn has fueled a wave of innovation, entrepreneurship, and development in the service sector in China that has helped mitigate the general slowdown of the economy and build a booming—indeed, world-leading—e-commerce sector (PricewaterhouseCoopers 2017). According to a report by the McKinsey Global Institute (2017), China's share in global e-commerce transactions skyrocketed from less than 1 percent in 2007 to more than 40 percent in 2016. China has a larger e-commerce sector than France, Germany, Japan, the United Kingdom, and the United States combined.

Internet financing also serves as an important vehicle for the central bank's agenda in liberalizing the banking and financial sector with increased market competition. As Ma Weihua, a former president of China Merchant Bank, candidly admitted, "Why is all the money going into Yu'ebao? Because banks fail to pay what savers deserve. You can't fool them. . . . Yu'ebao is forcing banks to face up to the challenges of interest-rate deregulation" (Bloomberg 2014). At the same time, the online credit sector can also help channel funds to individuals and particularly small and medium-sized enterprises. Premier Li, during a visit to an online bank operated by Tencent, said that internet banking "will lower costs for and deliver practical benefits to small clients, while forcing traditional financial institutions to accelerate reforms" (PricewaterhouseCoopers 2015, 38).

Coping Strategies of the Established Banks

Conducting financial business online has caused a degree of disruption to the traditional banks by providing a more convenient platform for payment and more lucrative alternatives for savings and investment. What is interesting is how the banks have coped with the disruption from the shadow sector, and how new (informal) institutions have elicited adaptive institutional transformation on the part of the established (formal) institutions.

The main banking and financial sectors have responded with a combination of strategies. The initial strategy was a defensive, knee-jerk reaction. Internet funds, such as Yu'ebao, were accused of being "a vampire sucking blood out of the banks and a typical financial parasite" that "didn't create value" (Bloomberg 2014). Verbal allegations were accompanied by action. Some banks blocked deposits from the online funds, and some set up quotas for their customers' daily transfer to the funds. At the same time, the banks pressed the regulators to slow the rapid expansion of the new sector, demanding a "level playing field" with internet companies alleged to have benefited from the absence of regulation for capital, liquidity, and provision requirements. In particular, the banks have ignited a nationwide debate on whether online funds should be subject to reserve requirements, a regulatory requirement that sets the minimum fraction of customer deposits that the banks must park in the central bank as reserves (rather than lend out). The banks argue that the "investments" collected by online WMPs are essentially "deposits," and so the online money market funds should be subject to the same capital restraint as the banks. According to an estimate by a PBC official, the annualized return of Yu'ebao would be reduced by one percentage point if, like the banks, it were subject to the reserve ratio requirement (*Wall Street Journal* 2015). Eventually the PBC came up with a compromise: the deposits by financial institutions (including online funds) at the banks would be subject to reserve requirements from the beginning of 2015, but thus far the ratio has been kept at zero. All of this helped the banks let off steam but at the same time avoided a heavy-handed approach to online banking. Over time, the return from bank-issued WMPs has increasingly converged with that offered by their internet rivals, which means internet finance has helped achieve interest rate liberalization in this particular segment of the financial market.

Another response from the banks, as outlined earlier, is that they have been active in funding the burgeoning shadow sector. In fact, the banks have increasingly been a major actor in the shadow credit system by either using trust companies as sales channels or packaging and selling WMPs directly to their customers. For the banks, this represents their version of "adaptive informal institutional change" (Tsai 2006), as they have sought to navigate a path between the constraints imposed by financial repression and regulation and new market opportunities in the shadow sector. The decline of financial repression has already seen the main banks move more boldly into the market and attempt to win back market share by offering more attractive deals and products to customers (Kroeber 2016, 129). In terms of the rapid growth of the online sector, China's banks have come to realize that they could not nip the online business in the bud, and that they must adapt to the new world of the internet. Hence, the banking sector adopted a bandwagon strategy by setting up "direct banks" that offer competitive services over the internet or by telephone instead of through brick-and-mortar branches. As early as 2014, for instance, as many as fifteen banks launched such "direct banks" online (PricewaterhouseCoopers 2015, 32). There is great potential for direct banking in China, given the increasingly extensive penetration of the internet and mobile phones. According to a survey from Accenture, more than 21 percent of Chinese customers have completely switched to direct banking, with substantial potential for further growth. Indeed, more than 60 percent of the Chinese population looks to shift to more direct banking methods (quoted in Laudermilk 2019).

The third strategy of the banks in competing against internet companies has been that of "divide and rule," which involves either teaming up with external partners or cooperating with China's biggest internet conglomerates. A good example of the first approach has been the introduction of Apple Pay by China UnionPay (CUP) in February 2016. China UnionPay is essentially a state-backed payment monopoly based on an association of domestic banks. As discussed earlier, the online third-party payment platforms, such as Alipay, have been cutting into banks' margin in the payment industry, particularly in the mobile payment market, where they have a market share of almost 70 percent. The partnership between China UnionPay and Apple will help the latter crack open potentially the largest mobile market in the world. For China UnionPay, this is also a good deal. Apple charges Chinese banks only 0.07 percent of each transaction, compared with the 0.15 percent it charges banks in the United States (Zhang 2016). This will increase the banks' margin in handling payments and will help defend the market that has been lost to Alibaba and Tencent, thus redrawing the strategic landscape in this market segment.

At the same time, the banks have also sought to play into the competitive game between the three internet giants in China. In recent years, China's internet world has been increasingly dominated by three internet companies: Baidu, Alibaba, and Tencent (collectively known as the BAT). While each entity holds a commanding market share in its core business (Baidu in search engines, Alibaba in e-commerce, and Tencent in social media), the BAT has been branching out into other business areas, particularly internet finance, and has become the dominant player in virtually all subsections of the internet finance market.

Among the BAT, Baidu has been a relative latecomer in the online financial market compared with Alibaba and Tencent, and it has been eager to penetrate this strategic sector. The banks, in playing the catch-up game, have seized this opportunity and sought to forge business partnerships with Baidu in various areas. For example, in June 2015, China's biggest bank, the Industrial and Commercial Bank of China (ICBC), teamed up with Baidu in a strategic partnership that will enable both sides to cooperate in areas such as internet finance, map services, online marketing, business financing, and life services. In November of the same year, China's CITIC (China International Trust Investment Corporation) bank and Baidu also set up a direct bank, dubbed Baixin Bank, in which CITIC has a controlling stake. Such a partnership is expected to present a more credible challenge to MyBank and WeBank, owned by Alibaba and Tencent, respectively.

The Liberals' Delicate Balance

The Chinese government, and especially the central bank, has been taking a more tolerant if not supportive role in online banking given the PBC's reform agenda. Yet as the new industry has grown quickly, risks have emerged and caused concerns for regulators and the public.

Although we cover emerging risks in detail in chapter 10, we note here that risks have arisen in the online WMP market. Some funds offer rates of return well above the market level, and some are alleged to have engaged in irregular if not unlawful sales (Jingu 2014). So far, the major risks have been in the P2P lending area, where borrowers and lenders meet online without intermediation by traditional banks. The explosive development in the P2P sector has been due to low interest rates from the banks, a sluggish real estate market, and an increasingly volatile stock market. As a result, almost 3,500 P2P platforms had been established at the sector's peak at the end of 2015, compared with fewer than 200 in the United States.

However, an absence of regulation in this area, with almost no entry barriers, has made it the online equivalent of the Wild West. P2P platforms that were supposed to funnel micro loans to small businesses instead sometimes featured investment products channeling money into risky areas, such as real estate and the stock market. In particular, part of the P2P industry became a platform for investors using borrowed money to trade stocks, which helped fuel a surge in Chinese stock markets that peaked in June 2015. The subsequent tumble in the market wiped some $3 trillion from China's stock market. The malpractice in the P2P industry ultimately morphed into the Ezubao scandal in early 2016, a Ponzi scheme that involved $7.6 billion from almost one million investors (Rauhala 2016).

The spike in online investor fraud raised concerns on the part of the PBC and CBRC as segments of the fast-growing internet business, without proper regulation, increasingly jeopardized financial (and, further, social) stability. The crash in the stock market in June 2015 led to enormous pressure on Premier Li, who prompted the central bank to try and fend off further financial crises in the wake of the blow-up. This marked the end of the PBC's largely hands-off approach toward internet finance, but the new regulatory framework (see chapter 9) reflects the bank's delicate balance between containing risks and nurturing reforms.

In summary, internet finance has been utilized to fulfill the liberal agenda of breaking into and reforming the main banking system. The traditional banking sector's response to the rise of internet finance has evolved from the early defensive reactions to a more proactive approach that has transformed bank operations both online and offline. It has made the banks more competitive, flexible, and efficient in providing better financial services for retail customers. This in turn will translate into further momentum in boosting consumption and service industries that are increasingly reliant on the Internet of Things. These industries are still at the technology-driven stage, which gives the internet companies an edge in competing against the banks. However, as the banks ramp up the pace of adaptation, the online finance sector will develop into a more competitive market and become further entrenched as a catalyst of wider banking reforms.

The shadow banking sector existed in an embryonic form for decades during the earlier part of the reform era. Increasingly, however, and especially from 2008, its growth has been supported by the rapid growth in the demand for credit during and after the post-GFC stimulus, as well as through efforts by liberal reformers within the state. More and more, it has come to challenge the formal banking system, eventually spurring formal deregulation and forcing the banks to confront increasingly intense market and competitive pressures.

The rise of the shadow banks reflects the relatively flexible institutional conditions in China's mixed economy, as well as its capacity to benefit from incremental institutional change. Flexibility and incrementalism, based on "growing out of plan," are hallmarks of China's economic transition and development. However, shadow banking by its very nature is often risky, which calls for wider financial reforms that should reduce some of the impetus for shadow banking and see closer alignment between the shadow and formal sectors, as is already happening.

Although these wider reforms will further help dismantle the regime of financial repression that has long been central to the statist economic agenda, the changes in shadow banking have also seen a parallel movement by the state to pursue a directed credit system and the ramping up of investment in the SOEs and the state sector under the Xi Jinping regime. Although the increased competitive pressures in financial markets outlined above will likely stay, the broader reality is that the financial system in China still operates under the shadow of state hierarchy.

THE POLITICS OF BANKING
REGULATION AND REFORM

In this chapter, we examine key agents that have shaped banking reform over the last decade or more, especially within the leadership and the bureaucracy. We first analyze the leadership's preferences and trade-offs, which tend to set the scene for the bureaucracy in relation to the regulation of both formal and shadow finance. We then look at how key bureaucrats exploited the external shock of the GFC in achieving their agenda of greater liberalization. The chapter will also examine the institutional politics between key institutions, providing a more nuanced view of how bureaucratic turf wars between major regulatory agencies have helped shape banking dynamics and reform. We also explore key shifts in the regulatory dynamics of shadow banking, from earlier implicit fostering and liberalization to the more recent and explicit reining in of the shadow banking sector as statist ambitions and risk perceptions have increased. Although aggregate credit continues to grow, the result of this regulatory clampdown is that the shadow sector's rate of growth stalled after 2017, while the size of the sector shrunk from 2018. The shadow sector nevertheless remains important, though its earlier forward rush has clearly been halted. Whether the sector will grow again is unclear, although regulatory arbitrage is still occurring and regulators appear to be caught in an ongoing game of cat and mouse, as they attempt to catch up with new market developments.

The Matrix of Political Players and Imperatives

The style and dynamics of financial regulation in China, as with most of the other aspects of economic management, were inherited largely from the old Soviet model of top-down, direct, administrative supervision dictated by the central planning authorities. Despite a degree of relaxation in the reform era, the Chinese regulatory state still bears a considerable resemblance to the planning state in both normative and institutional terms (Pearson 2005). Compared with the arms-length and more rules-based approach in modern Western regulatory states, the Chinese regulatory approach remains state-centered and highly politicized.

The stability and reform agendas of Chinese leaders and key bureaucrats shape banking and financial reform. Leadership matters in any polity, and more so in authoritarian regimes such as China, where a steeply hierarchic political system ensures that the elite leadership has a direct impact on both national strategy and specific policies. It is also ironic that, for a regime renowned for a lack of transparency, the policy priorities of its leaders have been quite public. These priorities are distilled in "the relationship between reform, development, and stability," first revealed in CCP secretary-general Jiang Zemin's report to the Fifteenth Party Congress in 2002. They have been further elaborated in subsequent reports by successive leaders Hu Jintao (2007, 2012) and Xi Jinping (2017) in a fairly consistent manner. For the party leaders, "*development* is the fundamental principle" (Jiang 2002; emphasis added). After rounds of political purges and the mass chaos of the Cultural Revolution, the legitimacy of the party as a revolutionary force for the working class had broken down. Leaders since Deng Xiaoping know all too well that they have to resort to economic development, rather than to political commandments, to reestablish legitimacy and sustain the rule of the party. As Xi (2017) puts it, "Development is the underpinning and the key for solving all our country's problems."

At the same time, *reform* is seen as vital to ensure development. In China's context, reform means a structural shift away from the old, closed, planned economy and toward a more market-oriented economy, albeit one operating under the shadow of state hierarchy. Hence, for Jiang (2002), "development requires that we uphold and deepen the reform." According to Hu (2007), "Reform and opening up are the path to a stronger China and the source of vitality for the Party and the nation in development and progress. . . . [R]eform and opening up are the only way of . . . rejuvenating the Chinese nation. . . . To stop or reverse reform and opening up would only lead to a blind alley." Finally, *stability* is taken as "a principle of overriding importance" (Jiang 2002) and "an important prerequisite for reform and development" (Jiang 2002; Hu 2007, 2012). In this view, any major instability would lead to the erosion of the party's legitimacy and political authority, which could lead to further political instability that could threaten the political regime.

The party leadership has been promoting "a *holistic* approach" to reform, development, and stability (Hu 2012; emphasis added). For Jiang (2002), the party "should take into full consideration the momentum of reform, the speed of development and the sustainability of the general public. . . . We should press ahead with reform and development amid social stability and promote social stability through reform and development." On the one hand, reforms help spur economic growth by tackling what Hu (2007) describes as "structural and institutional obstacles slowing down development." On the other hand, reforms, in certain scenarios, could jeopardize stability and development. Reforms that are poorly designed, or those implemented too radically without support from other parts of the system, tend to threaten social and political stability. For instance, the radical price reforms under Deng in 1987–88 at least partially led to the student protests in Tiananmen Square in 1989, arguably the most severe challenge to the party-state since 1949. In addition, reforms tend to "break through the blockades of vested interests" (Xi 2017), and "further reform in difficult areas is confronted with deep-seated problems" (Hu 2007), both of which could result in clashes between winners and losers, which, if poorly managed, could create undesirable chaos for the regime.

Therefore, reform, development, and stability form a triangular set of priorities for the party leadership that shapes the latter's strategic and policy preferences. Development is about legitimacy, and reform is the critical means to that end. But stability remains the bottom line for the leadership. Accordingly, this tripartite matrix also shapes the bureaucracy and financial regulation. Development, in terms of the growth of the financial system, is seen as vital in supporting the real economy. Reform is desirable and essential in that it leads to efficiency gains in the financial system, while (financial) stability is paramount in that it is the prerequisite for sustainable development and viable reforms. These elements form the perimeters of the overall financial regulatory framework to which institutions and actors typically conform.

According to the large body of literature on bureaucratic authoritarianism in China, political strategies from the leadership typically rely on the technocratic bureaucracy to follow up with concrete policies and their implementation (O'Donnell 1979; Hamrin and Zhao 1995; Huber and Shipan 2002). This form of reliance on bureaucratic advice and implementation can create expertise and information disequilibria, one of the key features of the principal-agent problem, and this can often award government institutions a degree of leverage in influencing policymaking as well as discretion during implementation. This relationship has influenced how the bureaucracy plays its role in the politics of regulation in China.

Overall, we thus see two key variables in shaping the politics of regulation in China: strategic political imperatives on the part of the leadership, and the policy agendas, institutional mandates, and turf wars between the key regulatory agencies. While strategic considerations by the political leadership dictate the overall framework of regulation, the agenda and mandates of regulatory institutions and senior bureaucrats also play an important role in shaping the more specific dynamics of regulation, including financial regulation.

Formal Banking Regulation: China and Basel III

China has been active in recent years in ramping up banking regulation at various levels as the high costs of financial mishaps in the wake of the GFC have become ever more apparent and as China's financial system grows in size and complexity. International financial regulation has increased since the GFC, led by the Basel banking standards. This is one area where international cooperation has been supported, unlike a range of other areas, including trade (Walter 2019).

One key aspect of China's response on the regulatory front has been its rapid embrace of the post-GFC Basel III prudential regulations. Basel III is the third installment of a set of global regulatory banking standards promulgated by the Basel Committee on Banking Supervision, which is institutionally nested in the Bank for International Settlements. It is essentially a voluntary regulatory framework covering key regulatory concerns of banking, such as bank capital adequacy and liquidity risk. Basel III was agreed on and issued by members of the committee between 2010 and 2011 in response to the clear deficiencies of the financial system in the lead-up to the GFC. Basel III was also introduced due to the significant deficiencies in the Basel II framework, which encouraged self-risk assessment by banks as well as off-balance-sheet activities, both of which helped drive the GFC. In response, Basel III broadly aims to tighten regulation, especially by strengthening bank capital requirements and decreasing bank leverage (BCBS 2010).

Although Basel I was promulgated in 1988, China did not engage with the process until 2003 due to tardy domestic legislation and institutional reforms during that era, as well as limited engagement with the international regulatory regime. When the CBRC was established in 2003, one of its inaugural decrees was to implement Basel I standards (Rana 2012, 220). China's attitude toward Basel II, released in 2007, was also cautious, suggesting that the banks meet the requirements "in a phased, well-sequenced manner" (CBRC 2007; Walter 2008, 76). However, after China became a member of the Basel Committee in 2009, the general tone shifted significantly with Basel III, from a gradualist to a more fulsome approach. Indeed, China has been overcompliant ("gold-plating") in terms of both regulatory standards and its implementation schedule (Knaack 2017).

Indeed, Chinese rules regarding the formal banking system have been more rigorous than the agreed-on standards, putting China ahead of its international peers in several categories. For example, as early as 2012, China's capital adequacy was ahead of the Basel III level, and the minimum 3 percent leverage ratio under Basel III was scheduled to be phased in by the end of 2018. As it happened, China implemented a 4 percent leverage ratio and China's full compliance with Basel III occurred in 2016, two years before the global deadline. This has been "commended" by the IMF (2017, 2) in an assessment report on China's financial stability.

According to scholars such as Knaack (2017) and Walter (2019), there have been a range of reasons behind China's commitment regarding Basel III. First, the Basel standards are voluntary and allow for substantial domestic discretion in implementation. Second, China's membership in the Basel Committee allows scope for international policy influence and allows its regulators, through rule negotiation and peer learning, to gain a greater understanding of what is considered "best practice" by their international peers. Third, the tougher prudential framework has helped empower technocrats within the regulatory authorities against strong political pressures for easy credit. Nevertheless, the great spike in credit growth in 2009 rattled the nerves of the regulators, who felt overrun by the leadership and politicians, central and local, who had forced open the credit floodgates to what were often seen as uncreditworthy projects. Moreover, the regulatory authorities would have to directly shoulder any potential consequences from financial instability. Therefore, adopting an international prudential standard, and going beyond it, became not only a macroeconomic management framework but, more importantly, a tool for the technocrats to try and regain at least some control over banking and finance. As Walter (2019, 10) argues, "Actors who favor compliance with Basel standards may include pro-reform politicians and policy makers who prioritize measures to improve financial stability."

Fourth, from the banks' point of view, their adjustment costs for implementing Basel III have been relatively low. As we saw in chapter 6, most of the major banks had gone public by 2010, raising total equity of $74 billion on the stock market. As a result, Tier 1 capital as a proportion of risk-weighted assets for China's seventeen major banks reached 9.6 percent. Moreover, in 2010, the equity-to-asset ratio stood at an average of 6 percent, and loan-loss provisions at 218 percent, all of which exceeded the relevant Basel III standards (IMF 2011, 5). In addition, as the Chinese banks increasingly expand their businesses internationally, it has been essential to address their "credibility gap" regarding confidence and reputation in the world market in the absence of an international track record. Hence, overcompliance regarding the global regulatory standards, according to Knaack (2017, 61), "serves as a quality seal for Chinese banks," helping them to garner market confidence. Furthermore, for the banks, overcompliance with the stringent global regulatory standards has helped boost their capacity in fending off risks as debt grows and as financial products and markets become increasingly complex. As noted, compliance also helps signal their credibility in the often-difficult early stage of branching out into international markets.

On the other hand, compliance serves as another layer of regulation of the traditional business of intermediation and now sits atop a unique set of Chinese administrative rules and regulations, including restrictions on bank lending to industries featuring high pollution and high energy consumption, as well as those with overcapacity. For the SOEs and to a range of other borrowers, the extra regulation has simply become an extra burden, to circumvent if possible. Overall, the cocktail of financial repression, administrative controls, and regulatory compliance, combined with rising demands for credit and the pressures for profitability in the formal banking system, have formed fertile ground for banks to venture into "the shadows" through regulatory arbitrage.

Tacit Bureaucratic Support for the Shadow Sector

Given these pressures, there has been a degree of convergence of preferences among major government institutions toward supporting the shadow sector, albeit from different perspectives. First, institutions that traditionally had a negative view of informal and shadow banking, especially the National Development and Reform Commission (NDRC) and the Ministry of Finance, changed their positions. The NDRC can be traced ultimately to the once mighty State Planning Commission (dubbed "the little State Council"), which oversaw the drafting and implementation of state plans in the planned economy (Wang and Fewsmith 1995). Although the commission had undergone several rounds of institutional restructuring during the 1980s and 1990s, the NDRC remains the most powerful institution within the central government in terms of macroeconomic management. Institutionally, it is not involved directly in financial affairs, but given its key status in coordinating the national economy and the state's industrial policy, it is usually included in the general process of policymaking in financial regulation. As the direct heir of the planning apparatus, the NDRC has been negative toward, if not hostile to, anything that runs beyond the formal planned sector. For instance, in 1997 it was a major force behind the dissolution of the Rural Cooperative Foundation, a nonstate institution that provided rural finance (Zhou, Feng, and Dong 2016, 588). The NDRC pushed the PBC to crack down on the foundation's nationwide operation, as the latter was alleged to have been embroiled in several financial scandals (Huang 2008, 112).

However, the NDRC has not objected to state institutions gaining finance through informal channels after the GFC. The NDRC was in charge of drafting, implementing, and coordinating Beijing's stimulus package, becoming directly responsible for ensuring China's economic stability and recovery. As discussed in chapter 6, the program's massive scale ran beyond China's fiscal capacity, so much so that the gap had to be filled through credit expansion, facilitated by the growth of shadow banking. Therefore, although the NDRC held concerns about the informal or shadow sector, it had to rely on it to finance greatly expanded public investment.

Another key player has been the Ministry of Finance, with its stake in the banking system. The state-owned banks used to be controlled by the Finance Bureau of the MOF, with the MOF acting as the representative of state ownership in these banks. However, the PBC seized control of the SOBs during the 2002 round of recapitalization through Central Huijin, an investment vehicle of the PBC (Bell and Feng 2013, 263). Subsequently the MOF managed to acquire Huijin through the establishment in 2007 of the China Investment Corporation, China's sovereign wealth fund (Wang 2013). After that move, the MOF regained control of the SOBs (except the Bank of Communications).

As the nominal owner of the banks, the MOF would not have been content to allow nonbank financial institutions, particularly the shadow banks, to stage a credible challenge to the banks' core business—credit creation. After all, as we have seen, the shadow banking sector tends to lure both investors and borrowers away from the main banks through more attractive market-based returns. Our interviews suggest that the MOF raised the issue of the lack of transparency of "irregular financing activities" on several occasions in 2010 and 2011, even during a session of the PBC's Monetary Policy Committee, a venue designated mostly to the discussion of monetary policies, not bank regulation.[1]

However, the MOF's position changed markedly after 2011 as the banks increasingly became the major players in shadow banking. The banks started issuing wealth management products (WMPs), the Chinese version of asset securitization and a major source of fundraising for off-balance-sheet activities. This became a lucrative business for the banks as they scrambled to cope with a decline in profits in the face of competition from various nonbank financial institutions. At the same time, the MOF faced pressures from local governments. As both provincial and municipal governments were legally prevented from borrowing from the banks or issuing bonds, both found it imperative to finance their investment needs through informal channels, and the MOF's opposition to shadow credit was increasingly neutralized given these concerns and developments.

The PBC's Shadow Agenda

Perhaps the most supportive position toward shadow banking has been held by the PBC. From the 1990s, when Premier Zhu Rongji briefly took over the governorship, the senior management of the bank has been dominated by figures generally seen as liberal who prefer a more market-oriented framework for China's economic transition (Bell and Feng 2013, 112). This trend was further reinforced by the governorship of Zhou Xiaochuan from 2002, during which time the PBC strengthened its capacity in policymaking, masterminded banking restructuring, and spearheaded a range of financial reforms in areas such as exchange rates and bond issuance. In fact, the PBC has become a key liberal element within the Chinese state in macroeconomic management and a major force advocating liberal reforms (Bell and Feng 2013).

As we saw in chapter 5, the PBC, under the leadership of Zhou, led the previous round of banking reform from 2002, in which the banks were turned into shareholding entities, publicly listed in stock exchanges, and subjected to greater market scrutiny. But some of the key issues that haunted the banking system remained—namely, the directed credit system that favors the SOEs but encumbers the banks with bad loans, and the lack of competition among the banks, which were largely shielded under an administered interest rate regime that guarantees their margins. In this regard, shadow banking fits the PBC's agenda of further reforms of the banking system. It helps in channeling funds to the more efficient private sector and forces the banks to offer market-level returns to investors, thus helping drive interest rate liberalization and private consumption. Therefore, although shadow banking became a new focus of the PBC's reform agenda, Zhou and the PBC had to resort to persuasion, especially of the leadership, given the wariness of some of the other state institutions at the time.

First, the PBC was very careful in picking the "right" language in its external communications. Our interviews suggest that the senior management of the PBC convened at least two joint meetings with relevant staff from its Research Bureau on the strategy of naming "the thing." According to the participants in one of the meetings, a range of notions was proposed for discussion, including "private financing," "informal financing," "underground financing," "alternative financing," and "shadow lending." As one source explained,

> "Underground" financing was the first to be off the list because it refers to "illegal fundraising," and according to practice in China, it potentially carries capital punishment. We were not satisfied with other terms, such as "private," "informal," and "alternative," all of which imply a sense of grayness and lack of formal sanction. "Shadow" is more or less new, thus open for [our] interpretation, but the implications of the notion of "shadow" are unsatisfactory to us as it means lack of control, regulation, and full of uncertainty. There was no consensus from the meeting in the end. However, around that time, influential financial media outlets, especially *Caijing*, started using "shadow banking" [*yingzi yinhang*], which, as I know, was a direct translation from English. This practice was quickly followed by other domestic media and became popular. This forced us to use the term as well. It was not our preference, I tell you, not quite.[2]

Although the PBC reluctantly accepted the term, it tried to define it in the bank's terms. For instance, in a research paper by staff from the PBC's Research Bureau, Jin, Liu, and Zhou (2013, 2) argued that "due to the lack of development of asset securitization in China, shadow banking is itself representative of our national situation. The shadow banking system is in fact the product of the economic and financial system with Chinese characteristics, and the intermediary linking depositors, borrowers and money market. Intermediations by shadow banks and normal commercial banks are indeed mutually *complementary* and *conducive*" (emphasis added). Zhou (2013b) further maintains that "shadow banking is inevitable when banks are developing their business." As a result, the tacit acceptance for the informal credit system has been supported under the name of "supporting financial innovations" and "increasing the efficiency of financial resource allocation."

According to Davis (2011b), Zhou "tricked" the Chinese leadership in the push for the internationalization of the renminbi in 2009 when his real agenda was to liberalize China's capital controls and domestic financial markets. More precisely, Zhou employed a Trojan horse strategy using the language of economic nationalism, which sounded attractive to the leadership, while pushing for his own reform agenda, aligning this reform agenda with the "stability" imperative of the leadership. The same case can be made for the PBC's (and Zhou's) tactics in shadow banking. The narratives have been two pronged. On the one hand, it was argued that Beijing's anticrisis strategy in 2008–9, which is heavily reliant on finance, was necessary. In a press briefing in March 2009, Zhou said that "if we act slowly and less decisively, we are likely to see what happened in other countries, a slide in confidence. . . . We would rather be faster and heavy-handed if it can prevent confidence slumping during the financial crisis, and spur fast recovery of the economy amid the crisis" (Zhang 2009). At the same time, the undertone of the narrative, standing firmly on the side of the political leadership and the latter's stability priority, was that the urgency and necessity of a heavy-handed stimulus program would warrant unorthodox and unusual measures to be considered and implemented, including ways of financing a surge in investments. At least for the leadership, the PBC's expertise in finance gained their trust and confidence.

To be sure, the PBC did not blindly sanction unfettered growth of the shadow sector. Rather, it has been aware of the risks, which, as discussed earlier, led to the adoption of the Basel III capital standards. The PBC has also at times warned the market through active moves. One response was the credit crunch in 2013, especially in the interbank lending market, in which the PBC, by tightening liquidity in the market, sent a warning to cool down shadow banking activity reliant on the interbank markets (Elliott and Qiao 2015, 23). This surprised lenders and the banks, which stopped lending and soon saw interbank lending rates shoot up to between 20 and 30 percent. The market reaction surprised the PBC, which soon backed down. It was still the case, however, that Zhou, at least before 2015, had discounted the *systemic* risks associated with shadow banking in China in his articles and public speeches, in a bid to allay commonly held concerns. The emphasis of his campaign was that shadow banking was smaller and better regulated in China than in its counterparts among the more advanced economies, where elements of shadow banking, such as investment banks and hedge funds, had contributed to the inflation of the mortgage securitization bubble that ultimately led to the GFC (Rabinovitch 2013). Zhou argued that "based on references and lessons drawn from the international experience, it [the PBC] is exercising effective supervision over shadow banks" (Zhou 2013a). Moreover, for Zhou (2013b), shadow banking was useful because "China is working to improve the economy's resources allocation, and to ensure more resources flowing to the private sector, high-tech companies and the service sector." On an even more sanguine note, he added that "credit flows outside the banking system are a *healthy* development for China, so long as they are monitored and kept in check" (emphasis added).

As we have demonstrated in previous chapters, the statist growth model, underpinned by a financial system of directed credit, had been a persistent feature institutionally in the pre-GFC era. The system had enabled low borrowing costs for the SOEs, guaranteed fat margins for SOBs, and facilitated the state's industrial policies. The system also survived the challenge of external shocks, such as the Asian financial crisis in 1997, although that crisis prompted a limited round of banking restructuring in the early 2000s, as we saw in chapter 5 (see also Shih 2007). Against this backdrop, informal finance was not taken seriously because the formal sector served a range of interests, at least from the perspective of the leadership. Moreover, the informal sector had been a very small part of the overall credit market. However, the role of shadow banking, as we have seen, changed in a far more constructive manner in the post-GFC era, enhancing economic growth and the leadership's priority of stability. In the wake of the economic slowdown and potentially massive unemployment given the slump in external demand, the shadow banking sector helped stabilize the economy by providing finance for greatly expanded domestic investment. It also helped finance the state sector, particularly local governments, and the nonstate sector, which has been more dynamic in creating jobs and growth. This, coupled with the assurance by the financial technocrats in the bureaucracy that the risky side of shadow banking was largely in check, made the leadership mostly comfortable with the new arrangement, in which the informal, shadow sector was sanctioned to operate without much regulatory "harassment."

Conflicting Institutional Mandates

The initial light-touch regulatory approach was also aided institutionally by the fact that financial regulation in China has traditionally been marred by friction between major regulatory agencies under a scattered power structure. The PBC is in charge of overall financial stability, with (until April 2018) three prudential watchdogs supervising the banking (CBRC), securities (CSRC), and insurance (CIRC) sectors, respectively (Feng 2007a). Like other Chinese bureaucracies, the current system of financial regulation suffers from ambiguous boundaries of authority and often overlapping jurisdictions (Lieberthal and Oksenberg 1988, 35). At the same time, the rigid alignment of regulation to particular areas of business has seen regulatory blind spots, especially in relation to shadow banking, which itself is a result of regulatory arbitrage.

This is further exacerbated by the earlier limited communication and coordination among the major regulators. For example, a joint meeting system was initiated in 2000 to include key decision-makers from the PBC (then in charge of banking regulation), the CSRC, and the CIRC, aimed at enhancing cross-agency information exchange and policy coordination. But the first such meeting was not held until September 2003. Nor was the joint meeting institutionalized. In the eighteen months between March 2004 and October 2005, the heads of the regulators did not even bother to meet (Feng 2007a, 45). A cross-ministerial Financial Stability Council, chaired by the PBC, was finally established in August 2013 (Anderlini 2014a). However, the council was not able to meet, in part due to the CBRC's fears of the PBC's domination within the council.

Among the relevant agencies, the relationship between the PBC and the CBRC has often been strained. The CBRC is generally seen among China watchers as a liberal force, largely because its senior management often rotates with that of the PBC, a liberal stronghold in the Chinese bureaucracy. Nevertheless, the banking watchdog has been keeping a wary eye on the development of shadow banking, particularly in relation to the formal banking sector under its jurisdiction. On the one hand, it has recognized the need to liberalize China's interest rate regime (CBRC 2010, 1, 3; 2012, 3) and the need to increase the competitiveness of the banks through fostering genuinely competitive financial markets (CBRC 2012, 5). Therefore, it has stressed the positive effects of shadow banking in achieving these goals (CBRC 2010, 2012). On the other hand, it has had concerns about the increasing cooperation between banks and financial institutions, such as stock brokerages and insurance companies, in issuing shadow banking products, with the brokerages and insurance companies being beyond the CBRC's regulatory radar. This tends to create risks associated with regulatory arbitrage. The CBRC's position and regulatory ambitions were perhaps best summarized by Shang Fulin, a former chairman of the CBRC, in 2012: "Trust and financial products are currently regulated by the CBRC. As a next step, the CBRC will research the content, function, size, structure, and risk of shadow banking under present conditions. It will improve industry standards, crack down on illegal behavior, and strengthen regulation of certain aspects of shadow banking, such as leverage ratios and consolidated credit risk. At the same time, the CBRC will promote bank reform and innovation to provide better and safer financial services" (quoted in Yan and Li 2016, 124).

The CBRC took over the PBC's portfolio of bank regulation in 2003, but the PBC has been uneasy about this loss of supervisory authority. The CBRC, on the other hand, has been wary of the PBC's attempts at "power grabbing" (Anderlini 2014a). The PBC has accused the CBRC of having developed intimate relationships with the banks, so much so that the regulator has allegedly become unwilling or unable to control the banks' off-balance-sheet activities. According to Anderlini (2014a), "The PBC argues the regulator is not up to the task. . . . [T]he central bank, which has responsibility for overall financial stability in

China, has expressed frustration at the CBRC's unwillingness or inability to rein in the off-balance sheet activity of the state-controlled banking system." In turn, the CBRC blamed the PBC for being irresponsible in not managing the risks it had created through the PBC's "aggressive promotion of 'financial innovation'" (read shadow banking). "They argue," noted Anderlini (2014a), "that having forced the banks to carry the burden of the stimulus, the PBC then encouraged the creation of the vast shadow banking sector that it now blames the CBRC for not regulating properly."

Finance under Xi: From Liberal Reforms to Tougher Regulation

As discussed above, shadow banking's great leap forward after the GFC was fostered largely by tacit support from various elements within the Chinese state, from the leadership in general to key liberal institutions like the PBC. However, this largely conducive context has changed to one that has increasingly centered on risk aversion and tightened regulation under the Xi administration, especially since 2015, due to various developments that have changed the preferences of the leadership and the position and influence of key bureaucratic actors.

First, the priorities of the leadership—reform, development, and stability— have been redefined in a general context of a slowing economy. Back in 2002, Jiang (2002) proclaimed that "development requires that we always concentrate on economic growth." This was subsequently adjusted to Hu's (2007) agenda of pursuing "quality" growth. Ten years later, Xi (2017) stated that "our development must be sound development. We must pursue with firmness of purpose the vision of innovative, coordinated, green, and open development that is for everyone." This shift in emphasis from an economy of high growth to one of high quality implies that Beijing was willing to accept, and could afford, a slower growth rate.

At the same time, there have been increasing concerns at the top about financial risks and systemic stability. A flood of warnings from international institutions, media, and think tanks since around 2015 has increasingly pointed to the dangerously high level of debt (see chapter 10 for more detail) and made the leadership realize that the binge drinking of both formal and informal credit to keep the economy powering along is not sustainable. As Lardy (2017, 3) notes, "China's leadership has clearly elevated the priority of reducing financial risks relative to maximizing economic growth. They even seem prepared to accept somewhat slower growth and even some increase in financial stress as a price for more moderate credit growth." In May 2016, the party's official *People's Daily* published an interview with an "authoritative person," widely believed to be Liu He, Xi's top economic adviser. During the interview, the individual stressed that "high leverage will lead to high risk; if not well controlled, it will lead to systemic financial crisis and negative growth. . . . *China should put deleveraging ahead of short-term growth* and drop the 'fantasy' of stimulating the economy through monetary easing" (emphasis added) (An Authoritative Person 2016). This statement made it clear that financial risks and stability have become a key aspect of the leadership's view of more general stability.

At the same time, the financial system has suffered in various ways since 2015, from the stock market meltdown to subsequent capital flight and other outcomes, which is believed to be at least partially related to shadow banking—hence a change in the general attitude toward the latter. The most dramatic event in this regard, however, was the collapse of the stock market in the summer of 2015 and its wider consequences for the renminbi, China's balance of payments, and capital flows.

After a much-hyped rally, the stock market suffered a major meltdown between June and August 2015. A third of the value of A-shares was lost within one month on the Shanghai Stock Exchange. More than 1,400 companies, more than half those listed, had to halt trading to prevent further losses in July (Bradsher and Tsang 2016). Despite Beijing's heavy bailout, estimated to be around 3 trillion yuan, the benchmark Shanghai Composite Index eventually plunged over 40 percent by September 2015. It was believed that one of the major contributors to the crisis had been exuberant investors borrowing funds from shadow banking channels, such as stock brokerages, insurance companies, and online lending platforms (Wu 2015, 11).

The PBC took action and devalued the yuan almost 2 percent against the US dollar on August 12, 2016. For the PBC, this was an important part of reforming China's foreign exchange regime. According to its statement, "The reform of [yuan] exchange rate formation mechanism will continue to be pushed forward with a market orientation. [The market] will play a bigger role in exchange rate determination to facilitate the balancing of international payments" (Riley 2015). However, the sudden move caught the global market by surprise. Coupled with the economic slowdown and stock market crash, it triggered an acceleration of capital outflows that saw China's foreign reserves falling by more than $980 billion between its June 2014 peak and January 2017 (*South China Morning Post* 2017). The persistently high level of debt, a massive reduction in China's foreign reserves, and lackluster economic growth led major international credit ratings agencies to downgrade China's sovereign credit ratings. These included Moody's (in May 2017, for the first time since 1989) and Standard & Poor's (in September 2017, for the first time since 1999).

These events saw the Chinese leadership come to the view that financial changes had brought a series of financial risks, which increasingly threatened China's economic and social stability. Although China missed the worst of the AFC and the GFC, those crises nevertheless provided warnings as well as lessons to the leadership and the regulators about potential financial vulnerabilities. The stock market meltdown only reinforced this view and increased pressure to rein in wayward markets and the shadow banks. This has especially been the case as China has itself moved more and more toward a financial system with high leverage and increasingly complex and interlinked financial markets that were the sources of crystallizing systemic risk during the AFC and especially the GFC. Curbing financial risks has thus become one of Xi's top priorities, even at the expense of other reforms such as external opening. Reflecting this priority, since 2015 the PBC has had to resort to strengthened capital controls in curbing capital flight, thus dialing back some of its prior liberalization and market-opening measures. During the strategic five-yearly Central Finance Work Conference in 2017, Xi proclaimed that "guarding against systemic financial risks is the eternal theme of financial work and the government should take stronger initiatives to monitor, warn against and deal with risks in a timely manner." Xi insisted that China "will control local government debt growth, crack down upon financial irregularities and improve supervision on Internet finance" (*China Daily* 2017), all of which implicate shadow banking. Regulators are also on notice to have greater accountability, with the conference statement suggesting it would be a "dereliction of duty" if regulators failed to spot and dispose of risks in a timely manner, and that China should create an "austere regulatory atmosphere" (Feng 2017c). The new theme, which prioritizes stability and regulation, was reiterated in the subsequent CCP's Nineteenth Party Congress in October 2017 and the Central Economic Work Conference in January 2018.

The PBC's position on shadow banking has also changed from the prior tacit support to growing concerns regarding risks. First, for the PBC, shadow banking has largely fulfilled its historical role in fostering greater interest rate liberalization and a more competitively oriented banking system in China. As demonstrated in chapter 8, the rapid development of the informal shadow sector has had a significant impact on the formal banking system in terms of the latter's pricing, services, and greater marketization. The parallel and largely contrary development in recent years under the Xi regime, however, has been renewed politicization of the banking system, with directed lending to the SEOs in particular.

Second, from around 2015, sporadic default cases gradually spread from the real estate sector to sectors under distress, such as steel and coal mining (Hsu 2015). For stability reasons, these cases did not evolve into open default, as local governments invariably stepped in with bailouts, but the PBC and the CBRC took note. A series of high-profile scandals in online P2P platforms that erupted from 2016 have also called for more serious regulation of the sector (Feng 2017b). It is also the case that the shadow banking sector in China has a high reliance on short-term wholesale funding, which proved to be a source of weakness during the GFC in the West. Analyses by the IMF (2016c) and others suggest that as economic growth slows down and debt levels rise, borrower solvency is inevitably deteriorating in China, which, coupled with the more limited transparency of the shadow sector, tends to generate systemic risks.

This is also the reason behind the PBC's push to establish a macroprudential assessment framework that monitors key indicators across the entire financial system and to use various macroprudential tools, both administrative and market based, to achieve countercyclical effects. According to the PBC (2017, 100), the bank introduced a dynamic provisioning regime for commercial banks in 2011, and enhanced this into a stronger macroprudential assessment system that included "indicators for capital and leverage, asset and debt, liquidity, pricing, asset quality, risk of cross-border financing and the implementation of credit policy." Apparently, given the interconnectedness of the shadow sector and the formal credit system, one of the central targets of the assessment framework has been to contain and reduce potential systemic risks resulting from the spillover effects of shadow intermediations.

For the PBC, the rapid expansion of the shadow sector has also complicated its monetary policymaking and implementation. The PBC's efforts after 2009 to clamp down on the massive surge in credit growth were more or less hampered by the growth of shadow bank credit channels. The PBC used to take the lead in monetary policy by controlling money aggregates as well as administrative directives to the commercial banks (Bell and Feng 2013, 155). However, this policy framework and approach have increasingly been losing their effectiveness as the operation of the shadow sector has interfered with the formally closed circuit between the central bank and commercial banks. In particular, since 2015, the big SOBs have expanded lending to smaller banks in the interbank market to fund the latter's off-balance-sheet activities. Therefore, from the system's point of view, the big SOBs act effectively as shadow central banks in the sense that, although they do not create base money, they help to transfer liquidities obtained from the central bank and other sources to small and medium-sized banks (Feng 2017). The rapidly bulging interbank business has thus largely rendered the PBC's monetary policy ineffective and has resulted in increasing funds circulating within the financial system instead of serving demands from the real economy. As Naughton (2018, 506) puts it, the PBC's "quantitative controls just weren't working anymore, and the envisaged transition to interest rate-based policy became even more urgent." These factors have forced the PBC to attempt to better integrate China's financial system and to focus more squarely on banking regulatory issues.

The severe disruptions in financial markets, especially the stock market meltdown in 2015 and the increasing difficulty the PBC has faced in its policy arena, coupled with ever-rising debt levels across the sectors, have thus changed the PBC's attitude toward shadow banking, to one of growing concern regarding systemic risks. PBC governor Zhou highlighted a warning about the financial sector in 2017: "When there are too many pro-cyclical factors in an economy, cyclical fluctuations will be amplified. If we are too optimistic when things go smoothly, tensions build up, which could lead to a sharp correction, what we call a 'Minsky Moment'" (Feng 2017c).

The fact that both the leadership and the PBC increasingly look at the shadow banking sector from a risk perspective has resulted in an overall tightening of regulation and a reining in of the sector. Such regulatory initiatives have also been fostered by the general statist proclivities of the Xi Jinping regime. The institutional reforms in recent years have also promoted a more integrated approach in financial regulation. As discussed earlier, bureaucratic turf wars have caused confusion in the market and created room for regulatory arbitrage. The highly compartmentalized regime has thus prompted calls for a single, unified super-body to be established to deal with an increasingly integrated financial market. Many rounds of debate have occurred, and proposals have been floated among relevant authorities over the years but have failed to reach consensus. After several rounds of (sometimes heated) debate on this issue, a new cabinet-level coordination institution, called the Financial Stability and Development Committee (FSDC), was established under the State Council in 2017. The aim of the FSDC is to help improve the effectiveness of regulation as well as centralize regulatory authority to address challenges brought by the increasingly complex, cross-sectoral financial services sector. The new FSDC is seen as a compromise. Zhou Xiaochuan failed to achieve his desired outcome of a super central bank, but interviews with insiders reveal that the administrative office of the FSDC will be nested under the PBC. In China's bureaucratic settings, this effectively means the PBC has the strongest influence on its decision-making (Feng 2017a). In addition, the introduction of the macroprudential assessment framework under Zhou's personal auspices further cemented the PBC's leadership and its role in charge of overall financial stability.

Further moves have seen the CBRC and the CIRC merged into a single, more unified regulatory agency, the China Banking and Insurance Regulatory Commission (CBIRC), in March 2018. The securities regulator—the CSRC—remains a separate entity. This move has effectively reduced the number of institutional

TABLE 9.1 Regulatory measures on shadow banking, 2009–18

DATE	ISSUING INSTITUTION	TITLE OF REGULATORY DOCUMENT	TARGETED AREAS OF SHADOW BANKING
Dec. 2009	CBRC	Notice concerning Further Regulation of Business Cooperation between Banks and Trust Companies	Finance-purposed assets under wealth management by bank-trust cooperation shall not exceed 30 percent of total wealth management assets.
Aug. 13, 2010	CBRC	Notice concerning the Regulation of Bank-Trust Cooperation Business	Inclusion of the wealth management assets under bank-trust cooperation into bank's balance sheets.
Jan. 13, 2011	CBRC	Notice concerning Further Regulation of Bank-Trust Cooperation Business	Commercial banks must transfer off-sheet assets from bank-trust wealth management into their balance sheet; outstanding trust loans should be reduced by 25 percent each quarter.
March 25, 2013	CBRC	Notice concerning the Regulation of the Investment of Wealth Management by Commercial Banks	Outstanding nonstandard equity assets under wealth management investment must not exceed 35 percent of total wealth management product or 4 percent of total assets disclosed in previous year's audit, whichever is lower.
May 14, 2013	CSRC	Announcement on Further Regulation of Issues in Relation to Connected Transactions	Forbids connected transactions between any of the bond accounts of the same financial institution.
July 2, 2013	PBC	Announcement No. 8 2013	All bond-related transactions in the interbank market to be handled by the National Interbank Lending System. Offline transactions are forbidden.
April 8, 2014	CBRC	Guidelines on Risk Regulation for Trust Companies	Trust companies should not undertake businesses of shadow banking characters, such as asset pools for nonstandard wealth management.
May 8, 2014	CBRC	Notice on the Regulation of Interbank Businesses of Commercial Banks	Interbank business by commercial banks should be undertaken exclusively by bank-designated subordinates or branches; all other entities within the banks shall not open individual accounts in financial markets.

(continued)

TABLE 9.1 Continued

DATE	ISSUING INSTITUTION	TITLE OF REGULATORY DOCUMENT	TARGETED AREAS OF SHADOW BANKING
June 1, 2016	CIRC	Notice on the Regulation of the Channel Businesses by Insurance Asset Management Companies	Designated review of the channel businesses by insurance asset management companies.
June 13, 2016	CIRC	Notice on Tightened Regulation on Combination Products under Insurance Asset Management	Forbids the issuance of any financial products of an asset pool character and of "nested" structures by insurance companies.
July 14, 2016	CSRC	Temporary Administrative Rules on the Operation of Private Funds by Securities and Future Companies	Leverage ratios for shares and mixed wealth management shall not exceed 1; leverage for futures, fixed returns, and nonstandard asset management plans shall not exceed 3; leverage for all other types of asset management plans shall not exceed 2; total assets for integrated asset management plans shall not exceed 140 percent of total net assets.
July 27, 2016	CBRC	Measures on the Supervision and Regulation of Wealth Management Businesses by Commercial Banks (Draft for Comment)	The market value of all bonds issued by the same institution held by each wealth management product shall not exceed 10 percent of the total outstanding value of the WMP.
Oct. 27, 2016	PBC	Announcement No. 6 2016	Wealth management is to be included in the broad lending category of the PBC-led macroprudential assessment system.
Jan. 24, 2017	CIRC	Notice on Further Tightening of Regulation of Equity Investment by Insurance Funds	Tightening regulation on equity investment by insurance companies and insurance asset management companies; new restrictions on information disclosure and industrial sectors of the bid by insurance companies of listed companies.

DATE	ISSUING INSTITUTION	TITLE OF REGULATORY DOCUMENT	TARGETED AREAS OF SHADOW BANKING
March 28, 2017	CBRC	Notice on Designated Review of Irregular, Illegal and Noncompliant Practices by Commercial Banks	Strengthening compliance regulations of the banks through banks' self-checks and regulatory checks by the CBRC.
March 28, 2017	CBRC	Key Issues in the Designated Regulation of Regulatory Arbitrage, Financial Arbitrage and Connected Arbitrage	Curbing cross-sector and cross-market interbank business, investment, and wealth management businesses between banking institutions.
March 31, 2017	CSRC	Administrative Rules on Liquidity Risks of Investments by Public Securities Funds	Strengthening regulation on curbing liquidity risks of open funds.
April 6, 2017	CBRC	Notice on Designated Regulation against Inappropriate Innovations, Transactions, Incentives and Fees in the Banking Industry	Focusing on interbank businesses, wealth management, and trust lending that have outstanding values since the end of 2016.
April 7, 2017	CBRC	Notice on a Crackdown of Irregular Practices in the Banking Market	Crackdown on irregular practices by banks through self-check and regulation to avoid systemic risks.
April 10, 2017	CBRC	Notice on Effectively Covering the Supervision Shortness and Enhancing the Supervision Efficiency	Reinforcing shareholders' access and conduct, improving equity management, and reinforcing on-site and off-site supervision.
April 26, 2017	NDRC, PBC, MOF, CBRC, CSRC, Ministry of Justice	Notice on Further Regulation of the Financing by Local Governments	Establishing comprehensive finance mechanisms of local governments and cross-agency supervision and risk prevention mechanisms; clarifying policy perimeters and negative lists for local government financing.

(continued)

TABLE 9.1   Continued

DATE	ISSUING INSTITUTION	TITLE OF REGULATORY DOCUMENT	TARGETED AREAS OF SHADOW BANKING
April 27, 2018	PBC, CBIRC, CSRC, SAFE	Guiding Opinions on Standardizing the Asset Management Operations of Financial Institutions	Clarifying and strengthening regulations of cross-sector and cross-agency asset management business of financial institutions. These include elimination of implicit guarantees, regulatory arbitrage, and maturity mismatch.
Sept. 2018	CBIRC	Administrative Measures for the Supervision of Commercial Bank Wealth Management Operations	Clarifying that WMPs are separate from the proprietary assets of the manager and the custodian. In the event of liquidation of a manager or custodian as the result of disbandment according to law, cancellation according to law, or bankruptcy declaration according to law, the assets of wealth management products are not liquidated property and cannot undergo creditor rights offsetting.

Source: Author's collections.

players, thus facilitating a more coherent framework. Moreover, and perhaps more interestingly, the head of the CBIRC, Guo Shuqing, was also appointed the party secretary of the PBC. It is yet to be clear whether this dual appointment is institutionalized, or is a one-off move that intends to utilize Guo's expertise in finance and central banking to aid the transition of the PBC's governorship from Zhou Xiaochuan to Yi Gang, announced at the same time as the merger of the CBRC and the CIRC. Nevertheless, it was widely believed that Guo's dual position at the CBIRC and the PBC fostered better coordination between the central bank and the key watchdog.

The change in regulatory focus and the institutional reforms discussed above have seen a more integrated regulatory approach under the FSDC. Table 9.1 shows some of the details of the mounting levels of regulation of shadow banking since 2009, with an escalation in recent years. While the measures before 2017 had been mostly issued by sectoral regulators, major regulations since 2017 have been across the board, involving a range of relevant institutions. For example, the PBC, in conjunction with other financial regulators, issued joint regulatory measures in April 2017 on local government financing and in April 2018 on the wealth management industry, both of which have been key segments of the shadow banking market. There have also been moves to curb the "channel business," designed to hide bank loans as interbank or off-balance-sheet liabilities through NBFIs to evade regulation, and to increase the limits on leverage, interbank lending, and entrusted loans. Moreover, the authorities have jointly carried out a further clampdown on the P2P sector from around mid-2018 after a wave of reports on defaults.

The Regulatory Impact

As noted above, a key factor hindering regulatory cooperation and reach has been the scattered authority structure of regulation of an industry whose internal businesses are increasingly interconnected and mutually embedded. The earlier institutional structure of "one plus three" (the central bank, the PBC, and three prudential regulators, the CBCR, CSRC, and CIRC) tended to create problems with cooperation and coordination due to the different scope of the mandates of the regulatory institutions involved. The sectoral regulators tended to foster the development of, and attempted to prevent major risks in, their particular jurisdictions. This was in contrast to the broader institutional interest of the PBC, with its concerns for overall financial performance and stability rather than sectoral gains and losses. This resulted in a regulatory pattern in which the line regulators tended to promote sectoral development through deregulation. Banks would then increase their cooperation with the relevant sector through shadow lending, given the lowered regulatory scrutiny and costs for particular sectors. The sectoral regulator would then often envisage heightened risks within its jurisdiction. Although the PBC would be reluctant to weigh in, given its perception that systemic risk was low at the time, the sectoral regulator would partly reregulate the sector, curbing its involvement in shadow banking and often resorting to a knee-jerk, reactive approach to regulation. This pattern in turn resulted in a stop-go cycle among the different segments of the shadow banking industry. Thus, the evolution of shadow banking from a regulatory perspective can be divided into three phases since the GFC.

The first phase, between 2008 and 2010, featured cooperation between banks and trust companies in extending trust loans. The huge extra demand for credit due to the stimulus program could not be met by the formal banking system, which was constrained by stringent regulatory rules regarding on-sheet lending. At the same time, trust companies faced few constraints on lending, which made them a first choice for banks to help move the latter's credit off their books. Hence there was an explosive expansion of trust loans channeled by trust companies (other than banks) during this period, with their share in total trust loans rising from less than 9 percent in 2007 to a peak of 64 percent in 2010 (see figure 9.1). The CBRC, on the other hand, was worried that this segment of off-balance-sheet credit did not reflect the actual capital adequacy of the banks. Consequently, the CBRC stepped in to regulate the channeling with measures issued in December 2009, August and December 2010, and January 2011, ordering the banks to transfer the trust-related activities back onto their balance sheets by the end of 2011. As a result, the share of trust-channeled loans among total trust loans declined to 30 percent at the end of 2011 and has been at that level since.

As cooperation with trust firms declined, banks found a new channel to package credit in a second phase, between 2011 and 2012, through undiscounted bankers' acceptance bills. During this period, commercial banks, in cooperation

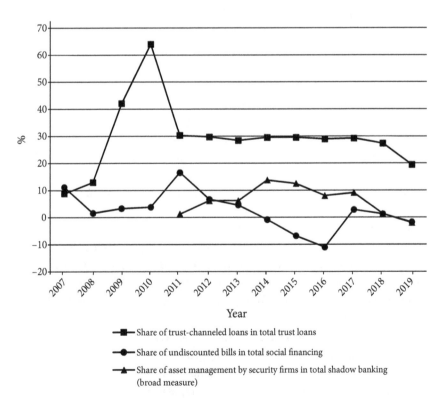

FIGURE 9.1. Selective channeling and sectoral regulation (%).

Sources: Almanac of China's Finance and Banking, various years; National Bureau of Statistics of China.

with rural financial institutions, expanded shadow credit by exploiting the transition in accounting regimes and converting undiscounted bankers' acceptance bills into nonstandard credit assets, which were largely beyond regulation at the time. Subsequently, the CBRC started tightening up the regulation in June 2011, and the scale of the acceptance bills has been on the decline since then (see figure 9.1).

In October 2012, the CSRC issued a decree granting a wider investment scope under asset management handled by security firms. This had effectively made asset management an ideal channel for the banks to transfer credit off their books. As a result, stock brokerages quickly replaced trust companies as the banks' major partners in shadow lending, which skyrocketed by over 60 percent within four months following the CSRC's policy relaxation (Ren 2017). The rapid growth in shadow credit using brokerage companies then ramped up concerns within the CSRC, forcing it to reregulate the asset management business in March 2013 by raising the minimum asset scale and asset adequacy ratio of the banks in cooperation with brokerage companies (Ren 2017). This gradually reduced the shadow business in this sector by 2016 (see figure 9.1).

The next sector that surged in this cat-and-mouse game with regulators was certificates of deposit (CDs), between 2015 and 2017, during which banks exploited the interbank sector through CDs. CDs were developed in the United States as a typical means of arbitrage, but were introduced into Japan and South Korea, in 1979 and 1984, respectively, as an important tool in fostering interest rate liberalization, since these instruments provided an alternative to market-oriented funding sources for banks (Li and Wang 2014). The PBC gave a green light to CDs in China in late 2013, which was followed by rapid development in this sector, as interbank CDs are not subject to stringent requirements on bank deposits. Banks, particularly the small and medium-sized banks, have increasingly relied on interbank CDs as funding sources since 2015, given the gradual contraction of WMPs from retail investors. This has also spurred a range of irregularities in the financial market because part of the funds raised in the interbank market were circulated mainly in the financial system, and not within the real economy. Subsequently, the PBC and the CBRC felt compelled to intervene in 2017, leading to a sharp decline of interbank CDs in 2018.

Overall, despite the growth in restrictive regulations just outlined, the shadow banking sector, both in broad and narrow (PBC) measures, continued to grow in size until the downturn from 2017, with the broad measure sitting at almost 50 trillion yuan in 2019.

Figure 9.2 shows how the composition of financing for the real economy in China has changed, with a declining contribution from shadow banks (based on the PBC's narrow measure of shadow banking in total social financing). The share of shadow credit was very little in the early 2000s, surged from 2008 until 2013, and has declined since then. Shadow credit entered into negative territory for the first time in 2018.

By the end of 2017, the growth of all measures of shadow banking—broad, intermediate (Moody's), and narrow (PBC)—fell below the growth rate of total renminbi credit, as depicted in figure 9.3. At the same time, traditional shadow banking activities, reflected by the PBC's narrow gauge, have fluctuated greatly since 2010, while the growth of our broader shadow credit has declined more steadily. This suggests that regulation has had more impact on the traditional sectors of loan packaging and channeling. The exception was the corporate bonds sector, which saw steady growth over the years until 2018. This was not much targeted by regulatory tightening given the perception that this sector is

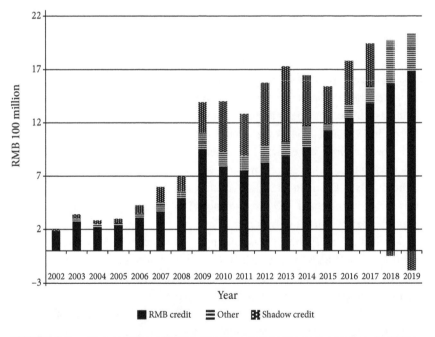

FIGURE 9.2. Composition of aggregate financing to the real economy in China (RMB 100 million). "Shadow credit" is based on the PBC's narrow measure of shadow banking, which includes entrusted loans, trust loans, and undiscounted bills. "Other" includes bank loans in foreign currencies and domestic equity finance. Since September 2018, special-purpose bonds issued by local governments have been included in the PBC's total social financing, which is reflected in the "Other" category here.

Source: National Bureau of Statistics of China.

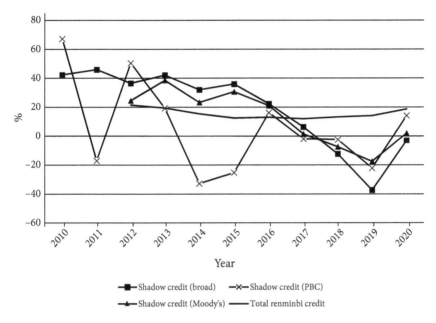

FIGURE 9.3. Growth rates of shadow credit and total renminbi credit (%, YoY).

Sources: The broad estimation is based on data from the PBC, the CBRC, the CSRC, the CIRC, and the China Securities Depository and Clearing Corporation; Moody's is according to its *Quarterly China Shadow Banking Monitor*, various issues; the PBC's is from its *Monetary Policy Implementation Reports*, various years.

less risky with more stable yields in China's context. Compared with the traditional sectors of shadow banking, the growth of new forms of shadow activities, such as asset management by NBFIs and interbank activities, declined more gradually.

Other specific sectors of shadow banking are also slowing in terms of their rate of growth. For example, assets under management in trust companies actually contracted by 4.85 percent in 2019, compared to 50 percent growth between 2010 and 2013 (*China Banking News* 2020). Other key sectors, such as the WMPs, have seen a significant slowdown in their rate of growth in recent years (except a mild increase in 2020 due to a relaxation in policy restrictions because of the COVID-19 pandemic) (see figure 9.4).

Regulators have also cracked down on financial risks in the P2P sector since 2015, spurred by the number of failed P2P lenders, which had increased steadily over the years.[3] Pressure further intensified in 2018 with a wave of reports on defaults of lenders that were not able to repay investors and were subject to police investigation, halted operations, or saw lenders flee with client funds (Bloomberg 2018). For a financial industry with 1.3 trillion yuan ($192 billion) in outstanding loans in 2018 and fifty million registered users, the potentially widespread risks,

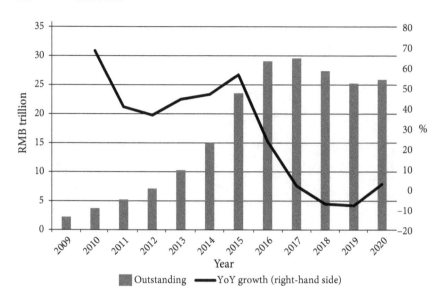

FIGURE 9.4. WMPs by banks, outstanding and growth.

Sources: China Securities Depository and Clearing Corporation, *Annual Report on WMPs by Banks*, various issues.

both financial and political, sparked a further bout of regulatory tightening in this sector since mid-2018, eventually leading to the whole sector ceasing operation by the end of 2020 (Tang 2020a).

The Ongoing Cat-and-Mouse Game of Regulatory Arbitrage

Despite the regulatory crackdowns just outlined, the recent history of regulatory advancement has nevertheless been met by ongoing attempts to escape the radar. Like squeezing a balloon, pressure at one point leads to expansion in another. Hence, regulators are attempting to play an endless game of catch-up with market developments, a pattern also found in the West prior to and since the GFC (Bell and Hindmoor 2014). Indeed, the mounting regulatory agenda and the banks' response strategy in selecting various shadow channels have resulted in high levels of change and volatility regarding the nature of transactions in subsectors of shadow banking.

In particular, banks have been utilizing more sophisticated mechanisms in packaging shadow credit via a myriad of "bridging parties," including financial institutions and enterprises (Ren 2017; see also figure 9.5). The bridging parties are employed to be the intermediate entities that help nonbanks disguise the flow of credit for transactional and accounting purposes.

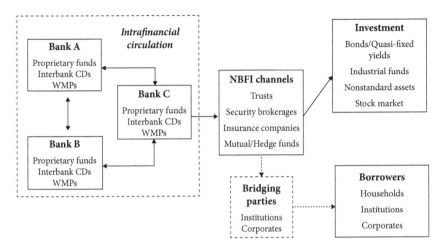

FIGURE 9.5. Recent business models of shadow banking. Note that the dashed arrows indicate that these transactions are in the gray zone in avoiding regulatory scrutiny, compared with other, more legitimate transactions shown with solid arrows.

A good example of increased shadow banking complexity and arbitrage due to regulatory tightening has been the evolution of business models for trust beneficiary rights (TBRs), a new form of structured shadow banking product. Typically it refers to an arrangement in which, as Li (2016, 5) describes it, "a bank transfers part of its loan book to a trust company but buys back the right to receive the income stream from the loans and retains all credit risks by serving as a guarantor." Such transactions are essentially credit intermediation between the bank and the borrowing party but are recorded as investment receivables on the bank's books.

In recent regulatory tightening, the CBIRC has prohibited banks from using WMP funds to invest in TBRs directly. Consequently, banks have developed new mechanisms for working around the rules by employing bridging parties in the chain of transactions. There are two models for this purpose, depending on whether banks use WMP funds or proprietary capital. In the first scenario, a bridging enterprise is deployed to purchase the TBRs from the trust company in the form of a trust loan, which is subsequently transferred to the bank in the form of WMP investment (see figure 9.6). By doing so, the bridging enterprise is not required to register the transfer of TBRs on the book of the trust company, and the bank can circumvent the CBIRC's relevant regulation.

An even more complicated model allows for bank repurchase operations using their proprietary funds in the interbank market (see figure 9.7). Compared with the funding arrangement in figure 9.6, this model involves another

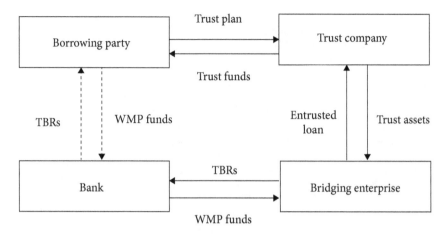

FIGURE 9.6. TBRs involving WMPs. Note that the solid arrows indicate transactions on the books, while the dashed arrows mean the actual/eventual flow of funds.

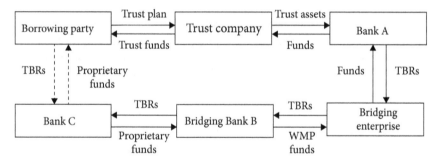

FIGURE 9.7. TBRs involving banks' proprietary funds. The solid arrows show transactions on the books, while the dashed arrows mean the actual/eventual flow of funds.

two banks, which help to transform a shadow loan between the actual lender and borrower. By packaging and repackaging the loan from a trust plan to TBRs and then to interbank investment by proprietary capital, the loan can be eventually recorded by the lender as an interbank investment, which is subject to lower regulatory requirements for risk provisions. This increased complexity in the structure of shadow lending, demonstrated in figure 9.7, has resulted in an expansion in the chain of credit, thus adding more risks to the entire financial system.

The Decline of Shadow Banking?

Regulation and earlier forms of financial repression encouraged the escape toward shadow banking in China, essentially a form of regulatory arbitrage by both the banks and shadow banking players. Increasingly, however, greater liberalization and marketization of the main banking sector and the relaxation of administered interest rates, together with greater regulation of the shadow banks, are leading to increased financial integration as the banks and shadow banking entities become ever more intertwined, producing greater complexity as well as greater opacity in financial markets. Although the shadow banking system has faced increasing challenges from regulatory authorities, spurring a decline in general growth rates in recent years and a contraction of the sector since 2018, this does not suggest the phaseout of an industry of more than RMB 100 trillion at its peak (in broad terms). Both shadow banks and shadow banking are already deeply intertwined with the formal financial system and have become an integral part of this wider system, with financial integration proceeding apace. The shadow banking system, rapidly evolving in complexity, is here to stay and is likely to develop in new forms, especially as the cat-and-mouse game of regulatory arbitrage continues.

Indeed, not only has the shadow banking sector become integral to the main banking system, but it has also been serving the political purposes of the leadership and liberal technocrats within the Chinese state. Just as the rise of shadow banking can be partially attributed to its contribution to the stabilization and recovery of the Chinese economy in the wake of the GFC, it will remain a handy tool for the leadership's imperatives. The Chinese economy faces dire challenges, at least in the short-to-medium term, at home and abroad. These include an economic slowdown as well as major trade tensions with the United States. In this context, shadow banking remains instrumental when Beijing needs to stimulate economic growth. In fact, in the wake of the COVID-19 pandemic, the Chinese government ramped up infrastructure investment, which saw the return of an increase of trust loans to local government financing vehicles. This led to an increase of shadow credit in the first quarter of 2020 (Moody's 2020).

The banks, too, are always ready to join the political game. For example, during industry consultation after the authorities issued the draft of new rules curtailing the WMP sector in November 2017, the China Banking Association, a national industrial body consisting of all the major banks, engaged in a campaign to soften the rules. In a circulated document, it warned that the rules would "reduce the strength of support for the real economy," directly appealing to Beijing's desire to maintain economic growth (Wildau and Jia 2017). Consequently, according to

Moody's, the authorities are now "taking a more gradualist approach in response to slower domestic credit growth," which includes a bumping-up of the banks' lending capacities, increased investment in corporate bonds, and "more lenient application of rules on asset management and wealth management products" (White 2018).

The definition of the leadership's strategic priorities in economic policy has been changing over time, in this case from the post-GFC imperative of economic growth to growing concerns about financial risks and stability. This dynamism has been exploited by senior bureaucrats, especially by the PBC in initially pursuing its liberal agenda and subsequently increasing regulation using the political language of stability. This has been complicated by a fragmented regulatory system that has encouraged regulatory arbitrage. The subsequent tightening of the shadow credit system is indeed a two-steps-forward, one-step-back process, in that both the leadership and the financial authorities need to address the risks created by off-balance-sheet activities that, if poorly managed, could derail the Chinese economy and reform. Therefore, a range of challenges remain. The Reserve Bank of Australia (2018, 12) notes that, "given the risks, maintaining stability in a large, complex and opaque financial system will be challenging." Much will depend on how increased supervision and regulation will be handled and implemented, as well as on the risks posed by increased regulation of credit allocation and economic growth. Given these trends in the shadow market and the dynamics of regulation, the next chapter will assess the overall risks of China's credit system.

10

MOUNTING DEBT AND LURKING RISKS

China's financial system has changed institutionally and has become riskier. The parallel rise of the shadow banking system and its omnipresent yet opaque interconnections with the main banks and other financial institutions have been one aspect of this. The complexity, opacity, and traditional patterns of light-touch regulation that are typical of shadow banking, as well as the sector's role in major financial crises such as the GFC, have all raised concerns by policymakers worldwide as well as in China. However, the relative immaturity of China's financial system means that the range of products and practices typically seen in modern financial engineering, such as securitization and derivatives that are popular in the West (especially prior to the GFC), have only begun to emerge in recent years in China. The business model of the shadow industry in China is still based mainly on regulatory arbitrage focused on relatively simple patterns of credit intermediation.

Nevertheless, China's state-directed credit surge following the GFC strengthened state direction over finance but also encouraged new channels of financial liberalization. Both changes supercharged credit growth, shifting the Chinese economy toward a high-debt growth path and away from the earlier pattern prior to the GFC of strong growth without excessive credit expansion. China is now a high-debt economy, accounting for about half of the expansion in global debt between 2005 and 2016 (Magnus 2018, 77). As we have seen, most of the supercharged credit growth has gone to the SOEs and local governments. Yet rapidly increasing debt is also spreading to the household sector. Households see property investment as an alternative to relatively low returns from bank deposits. Under soaring property prices, outstanding mortgage lending more than doubled between 2011 and 2016 (Magnus 2018, 78), leading to a pattern of increased reliance on the growth of income and wealth through rising property prices. A chorus of critics is predicting a looming financial collapse in China as its debt-to-GDP ratio continues to rise amid fears of a potential property bubble and worrying trends in unsustainable corporate debt. As Michael Pettis (2013, 9) points out, "Every country that has followed a consumption-repressing investment-driven growth model like China's has ended with an unsustainable debt burden caused by wasted debt-financed investment."

This chapter first deals with risks in the real estate market. We then review risks in China's rising level of debt across the government, corporate, and household sectors. Risks and especially systemic risks have increased, and the Chinese leadership is increasingly aware of the risks and is responding in a range of ways, including greater regulation and the reining in of the shadow banking sector (as we saw in chapter 9). There have also been attempts at reducing the overall rate of credit growth (deleveraging), although this has faced short-term challenges and setbacks as growth has slowed. We maintain that there are features of the Chinese financial system that suggest that some risks may be manageable. Nevertheless, we are learning from the experiences of large and complex financial systems that there can be few guarantees when it comes to financial stability. The increased reliance on debt and rising asset prices to underpin growth, as well as the role of the state in backstopping the financial system, poses particular risks. It is also the case, as we argue more fully in the next chapter, that without effective economic rebalancing, the financial and credit system will continue to be distorted in supporting prevailing unsustainable credit flows and will thus be rendered increasingly vulnerable.

A Property Bubble?

One source of financial risk potentially stems from the real estate sector. Real estate has been a "pillar industry" that has helped sustain China's rapid growth in the past decade and is of systemic importance for China's financial stability given the high exposure of the financial system to the real estate market. Indeed, a widely held concern regarding financial stability in China stems from a potential collapse in the highly leveraged real estate sector. Investment in the real estate sector almost quadrupled, from 4 to almost 15 percent of GDP, between 1997 and 2014, and almost doubled between 2011 and 2018.

Investment in residential property has been particularly high, accounting for about 73 percent of total real estate investment and almost 9.8 percent of

China's GDP in 2019, according to China's National Bureau of Statistics. The forces that have helped boost the demand for property have been negative real interest rates on bank deposits and capital control measures that prevent most households from investing abroad (Barboza 2012). As a pillar industry, real estate is also strongly connected to other sectors, both upstream and downstream (Liang, Gao, and He 2006), while the formal and informal credit systems have large exposures to the property sector. The share of bank credits to the property sector in total lending skyrocketed from around 20 percent in 2016 to 39 percent at the end of 2020 (Tang 2020b). Of the underlying assets of wealth management products, a key part of the shadow credit system, 27 percent were based in the construction and property sectors. Property is also extensively used as collateral for corporate borrowing.

Furthermore, the real estate sector has been a highly distorted market in China's political economy, with embedded political incentives that have inflated the market, including from spending from China's economic stimulus program after 2008. Moreover, land sales account for up to half of local government revenue, and therefore matching supply and demand in the normal market sense is often not the main consideration. In fact, local governments have been limiting the supply of land for development in order to maintain high land prices, which in turn translates into high property-sale prices, thus boosting local government revenues. This is particularly pronounced for tier 1 and tier 2 cities, where local governments often provide legitimate reasons for containing the growth of big cities despite net migrant inflow.

Moreover, and more importantly, financial repression in China has also led to major distortions in the real estate market by restricting investment opportunities. The main state banks for a long time offered only low deposit rates; the stock market has been a roller coaster, especially during the 2015 crash; and capital controls make it difficult for investors to invest overseas. Given the limited options, property became an attractive channel for profit-seeking investors, driven by both retail investors and SOEs, the latter having access to cheap funds from the banks. All of these have led to several cycles of property-price surges in 2012–13 and again in 2015–16, which saw year-on-year price rises of over 30 percent.

Given the gigantic size of the property market and its deep entanglement with the financial system, either upward asset-price inflation or a downward market correction will inevitably carry large risks of financial and social instability. According to a study by Deutsche Bank, 40 percent of winning bidders in land auctions will lose money if there is no increase in house prices (*Economist* 2016). Fitch Ratings (2016) estimates that Chinese banks' exposure to the property sector could be as much as 60 percent of overall credit, especially if off-balance-sheet lending and loans using real estate as collateral are included. According to a survey by BBVA, if Chinese property prices fell by 10 percent, this could lead to a 1 percent decline in China's GDP. A drop of 15 to 20 percent in property prices could lead to recession, and a drop of 30 percent would place a huge fiscal burden on local governments, lift the level of nonperforming loans, and cut an estimated 46.9 trillion yuan from household wealth (Lee 2018).

Wang Jianlin, one of China's top real estate developers, admitted in a public interview that the property market was the "biggest bubble in history" (Mullen and Stevens 2016). And Ma Jun, the PBC's chief economist, told the China Business Network (quoted in Tu 2016) that there was a property "bubble" that needed to be curbed. This was in the context of property prices rising over 60 percent in the city of Shenzhen in a single year. Widespread speculation regarding an emerging property bubble resulted in central and local governments rolling out harsh administrative restrictions on the financing and purchase of properties, leading to erratic behavior among buyers. For example, there have been several major buyer stampedes on property sales in major cities in recent years. In more extreme cases, limits on ownership for families in Shanghai led to a spike in local divorce rates as couples sought to evade the relevant restrictions (Fong, Qian, and Xie 2016).

Yet there are also factors in place that could prevent or ameliorate a property bubble. First, unlike the situation in the United States or Ireland, for example, where there was a massive oversupply of property and a subsequent crash, the situation in China, especially in tier 1 and 2 cities, is that there remain strong demands that support rising prices. Second, while there is an oversupply in smaller cities, the demand in the tier 1 and tier 2 market has been so strong that the authorities have had to resort to administrative measures in curbing such demand. The down payment required for mortgages is comparatively high, usually between 20 and 30 percent of purchase prices. In addition, the average loan-to-value ratio in China is also comparatively moderate at around 55 percent, reflecting the propensity of saving for down payments among property buyers in China (IMF 2016c, 22). This suggests that Chinese homeowners and banks have large buffers in the face of any market corrections.

Another factor is that the disposable incomes of Chinese households have grown substantially over the last decade or more. It is also likely that official data underestimate household incomes. According to the economist Andy Xie (2013), the scale of China's informal income is large, accounting for about 10 percent of GDP. Not surprisingly, a big portion of gray incomes goes to the real estate sector, which also contributes to the relatively lower leverage of property investment in China. This means the liquidity base of the property market in China is very large, suggesting that it is more capable of withstanding downward corrections in property prices.

More importantly, a crisis might be more likely to be averted, since the property market is widely perceived as being too important to fail and is clearly on the radar of policymakers and regulators, quite unlike the situation in the United States prior to the GFC, for example. Concerns about a potential crash in the property market and its systemic impact have been raised and examined by a wide range of players, including government officials and regulators, Chinese business leaders, and think tanks, as well as foreign analysts. Central officials from the NDRC, the MOF, the Ministry of Civil Affairs, and financial prudential regulators have met repeatedly since at least July 2016 to discuss how to stabilize prices without triggering a sharp downturn.[1] In a December 2020 article, CBIRC chairman Guo Shuqing (2020) noted that "among the 130 financial crises since the start of the 20th century, more than 100 of them are related to property markets," and admitted that banks' excessively high exposure to the real estate sector represents the "biggest gray rhino risk" that could jeopardize the stability of the financial system. Subsequently, Chinese banks were ordered to reduce their lending to the property sector to below 40 percent of their books (Tang 2020b). Moreover, Beijing has both market-based and administrative tools that could bring a soft landing in property prices. As the Reserve Bank of Australia (2018, 11) puts it, "Chinese authorities have avoided a sharp housing correction by using a range of policy tools to actively manage the housing cycle."

China's Rising Debt

One of the key features of China's development model is that growth is generated mainly by investment stemming from borrowing and therefore debt. Over time, this has led to an accumulation of debt in almost every economic sector. In an IMF report, Chen and Kang (2018, 8) warn that "international experience suggests that China's current credit trajectory is dangerous with increasing risks of a disruptive adjustment and/or a marked growth slowdown."

Public Debt

In contrast to China's general debt trend, total government debt is relatively low compared to many other industrial economies, with the major debt risks resting primarily with local governments. There are several explanations for the unusually high level of local government debt in China. First, since fiscal policy reforms in the 1990s, there has been a mismatch of revenue distribution and spending obligations between central and local governments. According to Gruber (2013), local governments account for around 52 percent of total fiscal revenue but 85 percent of expenditure. This imbalance was further exacerbated by the post-GFC spending on stimulus projects. As we have seen, local governments have been forced to finance much of their local infrastructure spending off-budget, through either land sales or borrowings through their local government financing vehicles (LGFVs), with the latter accounting for over 50 percent of local government debt since 2014 when Beijing started the formal auditing of local government debt.

To gain a clearer picture of China's government debt, the IMF included market borrowings of LGFVs in its measure of augmented government debt.[2] Doing so increased total government debt by the end of 2020 from 46 trillion yuan, or 45 percent of GDP, to 95 trillion yuan, or 92 percent of GDP (IMF 2021, 59). China's Ministry of Finance forbids local governments from paying the debt obligations (interest payment and principal) of their financing vehicles with taxpayers' funds, but many local governments continue to do so.[3] As a result, local spending has been leveraged with opaque linkages with shadow finance, with LGFV debt measuring more than 52 percent of total local government debt in 2020 (IMF 2021, 59; see also figure 10.1).

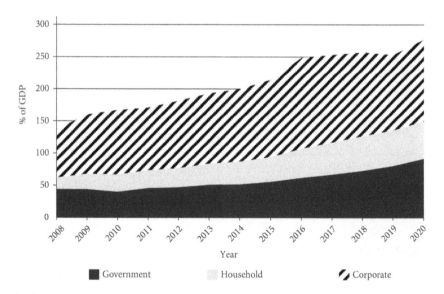

FIGURE 10.1. Sectoral breakdown of total non-financial-sector debt in China (% of GDP). Government debt includes general government debt, explicit local government debt (recognized by the Ministry of Finance and National People's Congress), local government financing vehicles, and government funds. Corporate debt does not include that of LGFVs.

Sources: Adapted from Chen and Kang 2018, IMF 2016b, 2019, 2021.

Beijing has been curbing excessive practices since 2015. The main priority for fiscal reform was to address the imbalance in revenue sharing and public obligations between central and local governments. In addition, Beijing has also taken steps to deal with local government debt through a more formal and transparent approach, by fostering the issuance of local government bonds (LGBs). Beijing revised its Budget Law in 2014 to allow local governments to issue bonds, albeit subject to more or less strict annual quotas set by the national legislature, the National People's Congress.

In essence, there are three types of LGBs in terms of their purposes. First, the central government implemented a three-year debt swap program starting in 2015 that enabled the LGFVs to swap their mostly opaque debt with LGBs worth about 15 trillion yuan. By swapping relatively short-term LGFV debt with longer-term bonds, this move also helps reduce interest costs to local governments (Lam and Wang 2018, 7). The other two types of LGBs are general bonds and special-purpose bonds. Revenues from issuing general bonds are used to pay for general government expenditures, while special-purpose bond issuances are used to finance specific infrastructure projects with reasonable cash flows and are also repaid from the revenues generated from these projects.[4] Of the 4.55 trillion yuan in new local government bonds in 2020, 950.6 billion yuan was general bonds and 3.6 trillion yuan was special bonds (Xinhua 2021). The LGB market has grown very rapidly since 2015, particularly since late 2018, becoming a major source for financing local government debt and public infrastructural investment. According to the Ministry of Finance, the LGBs' share of total local government debt increased from 7 percent in 2014 to around 90 percent in 2019. LGBs have also become the largest component of China's bond market, accounting for almost 40 percent of the market in 2020 (Ma 2021). Outstanding LGBs reached $4 trillion in 2018, making it the largest municipal bond market in the world (Holmes and Lancaster 2019).

There are several issues with the LGBs, however. First, although the LGBs help reduce the demand for shadow finance by local governments, the scale of LGB issuance has still been far short of local governments' financing demand for infrastructure projects. An LGFV official from Shanxi Province reportedly suggested that the RMB 10 billion allocation of special-purpose bonds for midsized cities is "like a drop in the bucket given that total fixed-asset investment could easily exceed Rmb100bn in a city" (Lockett and Sun 2019). Given the funding gap, the LGFVs, and therefore shadow financing, will continue to be in demand. Moreover, about 90 percent of cash raised from the special-purpose bonds, which is meant to support public projects, has been diverted into the real estate sector, prompting Beijing to clamp down on the practice in September 2019 (Lockett and Sun 2019).

There are emerging signs of debt stress on the part of local governments in repaying their debt obligations, which are estimated to amount to about 3.8 trillion yuan between 2019 and 2021. There were also several defaults by LGFVs on both renminbi and US-dollar-denominated bonds in 2019 (Weinland 2019). Overall, however, the level of government debt (including LGFV debt) appears manageable in China.

Corporate Debt

As in most developing countries, the corporate sector in China (both public and private) relies heavily on the banking system and far less so on direct finance through bonds and equities. For example, at the end of 2020, total capitalization of the equity market was 79 trillion yuan, while the bond market was around 100 trillion yuan and total outstanding RMB loans were almost 172 trillion yuan. A worrying sign is that corporate debt has been rising fast. It rose from less than 100 percent of GDP in 2008 to 165 percent of GDP in 2020 (of which 38 percent was LGFV debt), the second highest in the world next to Hong Kong (Somasundaram 2020; IMF 2021). Corporate debt (excluding LGFV debt) accounted for 127 percent of China's total nonfinancial debt in 2020 (figure 10.1), well above the 74.2 percent for the United States or 101.9 percent for Japan (Bloomberg 2020b).

Such high leverage has been caused largely by the high level of debt-funded corporate investment in the post-GFC era. At the same time, the "efficiency of credit" (measured by incremental GDP growth relative to incremental credit growth) has been declining during the same period. "Growth payoffs from additional capital spending," according to the IMF (2016b, 33), "have been falling despite the additional borrowing to finance balance sheet expansion." Over time, this has led to a rising corporate leverage ratio but at the same time a falling return-on-asset ratio (see figure 10.2).

As a result of such trends, firms find it increasingly difficult to service their debts in the face of increasing debt burdens and falling revenues. Lower revenues have seen the debt-to-earnings ratio more than double since 2010 (IMF 2016a, 13). The value of problem loans has also been rising. According to the IMF (2016a, 16–17), for example, corporate borrowings of $1.3 trillion, or 15.5 percent of commercial bank loans, were potentially at risk of not having sufficient income to meet even their interest obligations, which amount to between $567 billion and $756 billion, or between 5 and 7 percent of GDP.

Within the corporate sector, the debt of SOEs has been disproportionally high, especially for those in the real estate and related sectors, accounting for "more than half of corporate debt but less than 20 percent of industrial value added,"

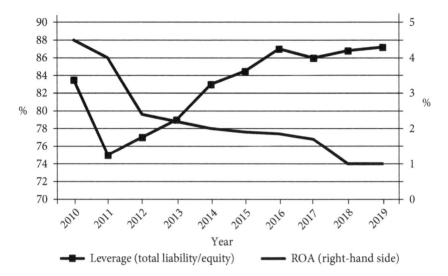

FIGURE 10.2. Increasing leverage and falling profits (listed nonfinancial companies, %).

Source: PBC website.

according to the IMF (2017, 15). By the end of 2019, SOE liabilities accounted for almost 40 percent of total liabilities of industrial firms (IMF 2021). By the end of 2020, SOE debt accounted for more than 85 percent of corporate debt in China (Yeung 2021). According to Zhang et al. (2018, 21), SOEs are able to ramp up borrowing because of implicit state support and lower borrowing costs. According to the IMF (2016b, 30), "Implicit guarantees translate to a 4–5 notches upgrade in credit ratings and appear to lower borrowing costs by about 1–2 percentage points. As borrowing costs are not commensurate with returns and risks, they distort the allocation of resources and promote inefficiency." An independent study by the Unirule Institute of Economics (2016) finds that the real average interest rate for SOEs between 2001 and 2013 was 1.6 percent, compared with 4.68 percent of the weighted average real interest rate (which can be deemed the market rate) for other types of corporate borrowers. If the SOEs were required to borrow at the market rate, the interest gap would have accounted for almost 48 percent of the total SOE profits during the same period.

The quality of bank loans has also been declining. Official NPL figures remain relatively low, running at under 2 percent since 2008 and standing at 1.9 percent in 2020. This figure is impressive, essentially in the same league as those in the developed economies, such as the UK, the United States, and Japan, and significantly below those in other emerging economies, such as Brazil and India. However, nonperforming corporate loans are rising. For instance, based on corporate data, the IMF (2016a, 16) suggests that "potential 'debt-at-risk' amounts to 15.5 percent of the total corporate loan portfolio, which could yield estimated potential losses of about 7 percent of GDP when applying a 60 percent loss ratio on these loans." Thus, without the speedy and proper management of risks, this could lead to much slower economic growth and/or troubles for the banks.

Commercial bank loans are not the only source of corporate finance. Firms have increasingly turned to the corporate bond market for funds, leading to a huge increase in bond issuance, which quadrupled from RMB 1.1 trillion in 2010 to RMB 4.45 trillion in 2020. However, given the increasingly high leverage of the corporate sector, defaults on corporate bonds have also been on the rise, exceeding RMB 100 billion each year between 2018 and 2020 (Ren and Paul 2020). In 2020, for example, Chinese state firms defaulted on 71.8 billion yuan worth of debt, accounting for 51 percent of all defaults, which is the largest default total for SOEs since China allowed such defaults in 2014 (Lee 2021). On the other hand, defaults remain a small percentage of total outstanding corporate bonds (5.3 percent in 2019). In nominal terms, SOEs tend to have lower risk of default than private firms, due to state support. Local governments have often stepped in to cover any missed payments, thus exposing themselves to further financial risk and moral hazard on the part of the borrowers.[5] However, as Fitch Ratings (2020) notes, "SOEs owned by state entities with limited capacity for support, along with those that are several layers of ownership away from their ultimate state parent, are also less likely to be bailed out in times of distress."

Household Debt

Another notable development has been the rise in household debt, whose growth rate has been even higher than that of corporate debt since 2016. As we have argued in chapter 1, the Chinese are strong savers, partly due to a culture of thrift and partly due to the need for high levels of precautionary savings given limited welfare provisions and the steep and ever-rising costs of health care and education. High savings have been a significant contributor to the pool of capital that has assisted China's economic development. However, the high savings rate is increasingly being offset by a rapid buildup of household debt (figures 10.1 and 10.3), accounting for more than 20 percent of total nonfinancial debt and almost 60 percent of GDP in 2020 (IMF 2021, 55). In addition, the growth rate of household debt has increased recently even as savings levels have decreased (figure 10.3). This is because rich families contribute most to the savings while the majority of other households tend to leverage up, particular given rising housing costs. Moreover, general household leverage, the ratio of household debt to household disposable income, has also been on the rise given the fact that the household-disposable-income-to-GDP ratio has been declining in recent years, from 61.1 percent in 2015 to 57.6 percent in 2020 (IMF 2021, 55). As a result, household leverage increased from 43 percent in 2008 to a peak of 115 percent in 2018, and stood at 101 percent in 2020 (IMF 2021, 55), a level comparable to that in the United States, the Euro area, Japan, and the OECD (Reserve Bank of Australia 2019).

The rapid increase in household debt is due partly to an increase in consumer loans, such as the rise in the issuance of credit cards by banks and a boom in non-bank lending, including activities by auto finance companies, consumer finance companies, and online lenders that provide easy access to credit for household borrowers (Li 2018). For example, according to an annual consumer credit report, online credit to household exploded four hundredfold, from RMB 20 billion in 2014 to RMB 7.8 trillion in 2018 (Guanghua School of Management and Du Xiaoman Financial 2019, 3). In 2020, total consumer credit reached 10.8 trillion yuan, or 18 percent of total household debt. However, as figure 10.4 shows, mortgage lending has made up more than half of China's household debt since 2018, accounting for 61 percent of household debt at the end of 2020 (IMF 2021, 55; PBC website).

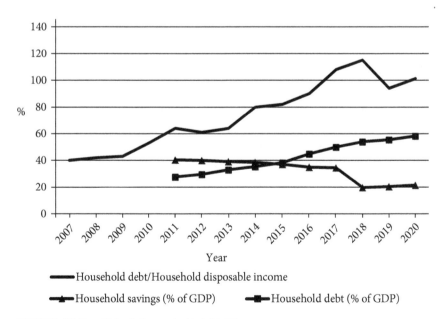

FIGURE 10.3.   China's household debt (%).

Sources: Bank of International Settlement; National Bureau of Statistics of China; IMF 2021.

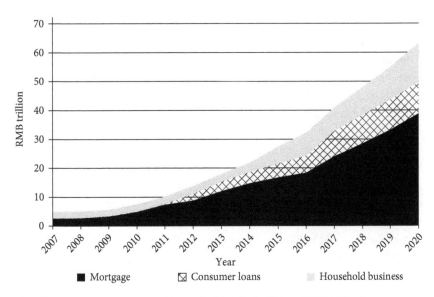

FIGURE 10.4.   Breakdown of household debt in China (RMB trillion).

Sources: PBC website, 2021; IMF 2021.

A study by China's Haitong Securities (2016) shows that total home loans made up 30 percent of China's GDP in 2016, up from less than 20 percent three years prior. That was higher than Japan's level during its property-bubble years in the late 1980s. As discussed earlier, surges in property prices have consequently forced the household sector to increase debt levels. Overall household debt levels increased from 18 percent of GDP in 2008 to almost 60 percent of GDP by the end of 2020 (PBC 2019, 10; IMF 2021, 55). This is high by developing-country standards, but it is below the 80 percent level for the United States, 85 percent for South Korea, and 66 percent for Japan. The investment bank Goldman Sachs (2016, 22) says it is not particularly concerned about a "foreclosure crisis" because Chinese lenders require down payments of at least 20 to 30 percent. Moreover, banks can also liquidate property to cover for loan losses if needed. However, as we will show in the next chapter, the ramping up of household debt is having an impact on the rebalancing of the Chinese economy as rising debt-servicing costs tend to have a negative impact on private consumption.

Foreign Debt

China's foreign debt at the end of 2020 stood at 15.3 percent of GDP (IMF 2021, 56), after having hit an all-time high of 17 percent of GDP at the end of 2014. Comparatively, this level is not particularly high. Furthermore, foreign-currency-denominated debt is relatively low, making up only about half of China's foreign debt, with the remainder denominated in RMB (IMF 2016b, 20). The size of this outstanding foreign debt is unlikely to be problematic for China's balance of payments and financial stability. At the end of 2014, only about 19 percent of listed nonfinancial firms on the mainland were net US dollar loan borrowers. Only a small number, or only 3 percent of listed nonfinancial firms, would be unable to cover their foreign exchange losses with their earnings before interest and taxes from a hypothetical 10 percent devaluation of the RMB. However, firms in excess-capacity sectors, making up more than 30 percent of net US dollar borrowers, would be particularly vulnerable.

Again, of greater concern here is that many of the firms that have problems with foreign debt are SOEs. For example, about 62 percent of the nonfinancial firms unable to service foreign-currency-denominated debt after a hypothetical 10 percent devaluation would be SOEs. In addition, some of China's globally branded corporations have been hit by a falling RMB. In 2015, for example, China's three state-owned airlines—China Eastern Airlines, China Southern Airlines, and Air China—suffered a combined $3.2 billion foreign exchange loss from RMB depreciation (Zhang 2016). The downward pressure on the RMB exchange rate, largely due to the escalation of US-China trade frictions since 2018, has seen the long-held psychological barrier of seven yuan per dollar broken in August 2019 (Feng 2019). This apparently worsened the debt-servicing positions of corporate China, but as the yuan reversed its trend against the dollar since the second half of 2020, a substantial part of the debt-servicing costs have been reduced. Overall, China's exposure to foreign liabilities has been quite limited, even taking into account the associated risks in a downward adjustment of the exchange rate.

Debt and Deleveraging with Chinese Characteristics

We have seen from the above that increasing debt is spreading across the economy in the post-GFC era. According to the IMF (2021, 55), total nonfinancial debt in China reached almost 280 percent of GDP in 2020, with rising public and household debt, although corporate debt growth has tapered mildly since 2016 (see figure 10.1). Combined with the debt of the financial sector, this brought China's total tally of debt to about 335 percent of GDP at the end of 2020 (Institute of International Finance 2021, 4). This places China's debt well above that of emerging economies and makes China comparable to advanced economies carrying high debt levels, such as Japan and the United States.

To be sure, China has successfully deleveraged before, especially after the rapid debt buildup following the Asian financial crisis. In the five years prior to 2008, the credit-to-GDP ratio fell substantially on the back of rapid GDP growth. It is possible, then, for the Chinese economy to deleverage without having an impact on economic growth. But this experience occurred under very favorable conditions, especially strong export growth. Moreover, in the current context, further factors that once were conducive to economic growth, such as the demographic structure and labor market dynamics, are now more likely to constitute a drag on growth.

The major challenge in maintaining economic stability is to reduce the buildup of debt and foster the more efficient use of debt. Figure 10.5 suggests that, despite a continuous increase in the nonfinancial sector's debt, Chinese GDP has been steadily decreasing over the last decade. Sahay et al. (2015) find that China has passed the point where increased credit growth maximizes the positive effect on GDP growth. Chen and Kang (2018, 4) argue that "over the last five years [between 2013 and 2018], the efficiency of this credit expansion has deteriorated, pointing to growing resource misallocation." In 2007–8, new credit of around RMB 6.5 trillion was required to increase nominal GDP by

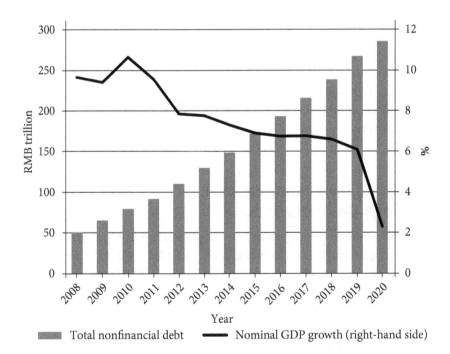

FIGURE 10.5.   Total nonfinancial debt and nominal GDP growth in China.

Sources: PBC and National Bureau of Statistics of China.

RMB 5 trillion per year. However, by 2015–16 it took an increase in debt of about RMB 20 trillion to achieve the same nominal increase in GDP (Chen and Kang 2018, 5). Debt is now roughly evenly distributed across the industrial and service sectors in China, yet by 2016, inefficiencies in the industrial sector's use of credit saw this sector contribute only about one-fifth of GDP. By contrast, two-thirds of GDP were contributed by the more efficient services sector (Chen and Kang 2018, 5).

Warning signs are therefore flashing, and have been acknowledged by the Chinese government. Considering the fact that SOE debt constitutes the majority of nonfinancial corporate debt, Xi Jinping has "criticized" his colleagues for not pushing sufficiently hard at reforming poorly performing SOEs and for relying on loose monetary policy to stimulate growth and support weak SOEs. Liu He, Xi's chief economic adviser, using the pen name "an authoritative person" (*quanwei renshi*) in the party's mouthpiece, *People's Daily*, has also commented that "as the marginal effect of monetary stimulus on economic growth diminishes, we should completely abandon the illusion that we can reduce leveraging by loosening monetary conditions to help accelerate economic growth" (An Authoritative Person 2016).

There are two distinctive features of China's deleveraging campaigns so far. First, weak or "zombie" firms in the state sector, including local government financing vehicles, pose serious problems in terms of their financial liabilities, accounting for over 70 percent of total corporate debt in China in 2018 (IMF 2019, 15). According to the Reserve Bank of Australia (2018, 10), "Excess capacity in parts of the industrial sector has resulted in some unprofitable companies that are highly leveraged and rely on loan forbearance to survive. Many of these are state-owned enterprises." The leadership is concerned, with Xi arguing that the government should "protect people, not firms, and have the courage to dispose of 'zombie firms'" (An Authoritative Person 2016). Premier Li Keqiang has also weighed in, arguing that "we need to avoid having zombie companies," yet in the same sentence he added, "We need to help them, to let them live and live well" (quoted in Lardy 2019, 78). Amid these mixed messages and despite occasional tough talk from the leadership, there are few signs or improvements in the more chronic sectors of SOE debt, although bank lending to the loss-making SOEs has halved in recent years, meaning that this aspect of credit efficiency has improved. Overall, however, zombie firms in the state sector are being kept afloat or bailed out by central and local governments, providing few incentives to improve performance. In 2019 the return on assets from state-owned industrial firms was 3.5 percent, compared with 6.3 percent from the private sector (IMF 2021, 55). Rising investment in the state electric power sector, despite falling demand, is indicative of the wider problem of state-sector capital misallocation and weak returns (Lardy 2019, 78).

A key problem is that SOE reforms have largely stalled since 2012, due to the rise of the more statist Xi Jinping administration and a lack of operational initiatives from the top. The latest approach in SOE reforms has been the so-called "mixed-ownership" reforms, which allow for private investment in SOEs (Han 2018). At this initial stage, and not surprisingly, private participation in SOEs remains limited. In addition, given the growing political interference in SOEs under the Xi administration, it is doubtful that the mixed-ownership model will bring any significant improvement in capital efficiency (Naughton 2018).

A second aspect of deleveraging, despite harsh rhetoric from the leadership, is that the deleveraging campaigns have been stop-and-go and half-hearted at best. As noted above, the SOEs have not been targeted for deleveraging; instead it has been private firms that have largely borne the brunt of deleveraging, with the leadership tightening the screws on shadow banking, a major funding source for the private sector. Moreover, while acknowledging the overall imperative of bringing down debt, even at the expense of faster growth, the political leadership clearly feels compelled to maintain its bottom-line growth targets and to go slow on deleveraging if needed to achieve its five-year plans, as well as short-term employment and social stability goals.

The political will on deleveraging is also susceptible to disruptive shocks in the economy that could jeopardize short-term stability and growth, with the leadership remaining ready to releverage through mini-bouts of stimulus to sustain economic growth. The growth slowdown in late 2018, for example, saw the leadership suspend deleveraging as infrastructure investment and credit were ramped up in response. This is a knee-jerk, albeit proven, approach, yet it is one that is increasingly inefficient and risky. The situation is not helped by the ongoing trade tensions with the United States since late 2017, which have generated downward pressure on the economy. The IMF (2019, 7) reported in its annual *Article IV Consultation with the People's Republic of China* that the policy easing in early 2019 had seen a "sharp increase in the pace of debt accumulation," with corporate lending "expanding strongly," favoring the SOEs, while lending to the private sector and small and medium-sized enterprises was curtailed. Hence, in March 2019, Premier Li announced policy moves aimed at "increasing credit supply and bringing down the cost of borrowing" (Wolf 2019), a clear sign that deleveraging had taken a step backward in the face of short-term growth ambitions. Stimulatory policies were rolled out, with the central bank loosening monetary policy. The deleveraging campaign was dealt another huge blow with the eruption of the COVID-19 pandemic in 2020. As will be detailed in the next chapter, Beijing resorted to debt-driven infrastructural investment again, which led to a releveraging across the public, corporate, and household sectors.

It is clear that the leadership knows that slowing down credit growth will slow the economy. Yet as Lardy (2016, 132) notes, even if GDP growth drops to around a little over 6 percent for the rest of the decade, China will still have doubled the size of its economy over the last decade, thus meeting one of the declared goals of the leadership. At present, however, the leadership seems caught in the dilemma between short-term growth imperatives and longer-term stabilization and rebalancing, without much in the way of resolution or forward momentum. Overall, as figure 10.5 indicates, the aggregate debt level as a share of GDP continues to rise, while GDP growth has been slowing down, indicating a rising trend of capital intensity.

China's Financial Risk Cushions?

Figure 10.6 provides a comparison of rapid credit growth across several countries that subsequently experienced a financial crisis.

Based on such comparative experiences, China could be the next country to experience a debt-fueled credit and banking crisis. Chen and Kang (2018, 8) have found that across forty-three cases where there was an increase in the credit-to-GDP ratio of over 30 percent, only five such cases did not end with a significant growth reduction or financial crisis. Moreover, in all cases, like China's, where

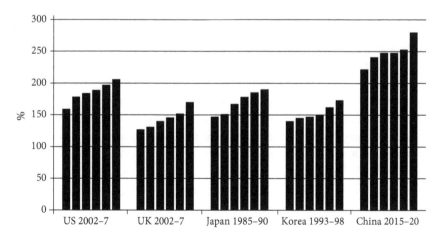

FIGURE 10.6. Trends in the ratio of pre-stress credit to GDP. Lending to the nonfinancial sector for Korea and China, and domestic credit to the private sector for all other countries.

Sources: Bank for International Settlements; World Bank Development Indicators; PBC.

the credit-to-GDP ratio exceeded 100 percent over a five-year period, the outcome was a financial crisis. Chen and Kang (2018, 9) also point to the exceptionally long duration of the current overall debt buildup, which dates from the early 1990s, as well as to the relatively small scale and duration of credit downturns or corrections along the way. They further note the very large buildup in the size of bank balance sheets, which, at 310 percent of GDP, now sees China with one of the biggest banking sectors in the world, one well above the advanced economy averages and over three times emerging market averages (Chen and Kang 2018, 10).

The financial risks therefore look threatening, yet China does have a range of cushioning or mitigating characteristics that might act as sources of stability, notwithstanding the growing complexity in its financial system and the large buildup in credit and risk.

First, one source of risk, according to Wright and Rosen (2018, 33), is that the stable, mainly deposit-based funding structure of banks and financial institutions has changed, with the growth of alternative, less stable sources of funding derived mainly from new shadow banking sources. "It is difficult," they write, "to overstate the changes that have taken place in China's financial system. . . . The funding base of the banking system has changed and is now less stable . . . [which is] a key reason for concern about a possible financial crisis" (34). Orlik (2020) observes that a typical banking crisis is driven by two ingredients: a pileup of bad loans and a subsequent drying up of the bank funding base as depositors and wholesale lenders flee. Chinese banks have a high exposure to bad or potentially bad debts, but thus far and in aggregate the funding base has remained solid, although this is less true for smaller and medium-sized banks that do have a higher exposure than the main banks to riskier forms of funding.

On the liability side, the main component of bank funding continues to be a relatively safe and stable deposit base, as opposed to more skittish forms of wholesale funding. To start with, China's debt is basically a domestic affair, and banks are supported by a large deposit base made possible by a very high national savings rate, accounting for over 40 percent of China's GDP (standing at 45 percent in 2020). Although the savings rate in China may gradually fall in the long run, it will remain higher than the global average, providing support for domestic debt servicing (IMF 2016b, 20). The relatively strong funding base for China's banks is also reflected in a low loan-to-deposit ratio, which was 81.3 percent in 2020. However, from the flow perspective, new deposits have been trailing the volume of new loans in recent years. While this dynamic is not sustainable in the long run, it is less likely to trigger sudden liquidity shocks to banks given the relatively small gap between the two. At the same time, the PBC has kept bank required reserve ratios very high at over 12 percent (despite consecutive reductions since 2018), a huge reservoir of liquidity for the banks.

Figure 10.7 shows that multiple new sources of bank funding have come onstream, including banks' bond and equity issuance, borrowings from the central bank, and shadow banking sources, including funding from other financial institutions and interbank funding, and from WMPs. Notably, however, as figure 10.8 suggests, these alternative sources peaked in 2015. It is true that while WMPs can be opaque given the way their collaterals are structured, these transactions are typically less dangerous because they are either unleveraged or leveraged on a level far lower than those prior to the GFC in the West (Zhang and Lin 2015, 83). Moreover, and importantly, the share of new deposits in new liabilities has risen from 41.7 percent in 2014 to 62.6 percent in 2019. In other words, deposits have remained the bedrock liability, especially for the main banks.

Figure 10.8 shows the evolution of the shares of deposits, WMPs, and interbank funding in China's new liabilities since 2010. There had been a general decline of deposits' share between 2010 and 2014, mainly due to an increase in alternative sources of liabilities, as just noted. However, and as noted above, the

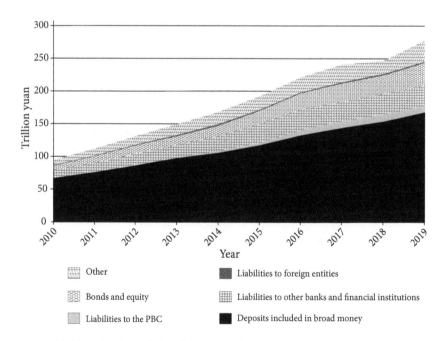

FIGURE 10.7. Bank liabilities (trillion yuan).

Source: National Bureau of Statistics of China.

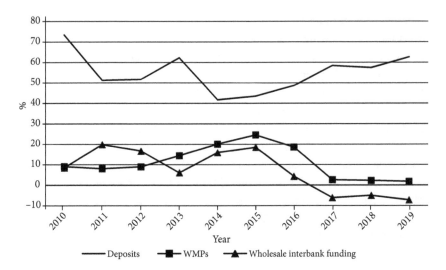

FIGURE 10.8.   Share of deposit growth in overall augmented banking liabilities (%).

Source: National Bureau of Statistics of China.

share of deposits has been increasing since 2014, standing at over 60 percent in 2019. At the same time, the shares of both WMPs and interbank funding have been reduced very substantially since 2015, with the share of interbank funding running into negative territory since 2017, reflecting regulatory efforts in reining in shadow banking activities.

Overall then, while there has been a diversification of banks' funding sources, there has not been a decline in the value of deposits over time. Moreover, the share of new sources of liabilities, especially from off-sheet channels, has seen a sharp recent decline, while there has been a rise in the share of new deposits in new liabilities. All of this suggests that Wright and Rosen's (2018, 1) argument about a "fundamentally different outlook" from deposits to riskier sources of funding, such as WMPs and interbank borrowing, is less convincing given the substantial crackdown on shadow banking since 2015.

The second characteristic that helps stabilize China's financial system is that, in relation to the property sector, bank exposure to this sector is cushioned somewhat because the average down payment on a property is around 30 percent of the purchase price, while urban Chinese households carry a debt of less than 50 percent of annual disposable income. This stands in stark contrast to the pre-crisis situation in the United States, for example, where down payments were minimal or often nonexistent and household debt soared to over 130 percent of disposable household income (Kroeber 2016, 134).

Third, China's debt problems are centered mainly on the state-owned banks lending to the SOEs, with often poor prospects for loan repayments and associated problems with the buildup of NPLs. However, unlike the situation in Western banks amid the GFC, where market forces determined the crystallization of risk in the shape of bad loans and shaky bank assets contributing to a banking crisis, the situation in China is different. SOEs and SOBs are essentially a part of the Chinese state. This means that the recognition and management of bad loans and bank assets in China is primarily a matter for the state, not the market, suggesting the possibility of a more stable process of unwinding risk and bad debts.

Fourth, the predominance of *domestic* bank liabilities and debt means that China's banks are not reliant on international wholesale funding or capital markets, which proved to be the major Achilles heel of many Western banks during the GFC as asset values soured and global wholesale funding froze (Bell and Hindmoor 2015). Indeed, China still has a positive external position, and has been a large net provider of credit for the rest of the world. In addition, as the surpluses from China's external accounts have declined in recent years, the central bank has at times boosted central bank funding, which peaked in 2016. The Chinese government is also actively managing its external accounts through capital controls in an attempt to insulate itself from the destabilizing capital flight that has afflicted other high-debt developing economies. Large capital outflows became a serious problem in 2015 amid the stock market troubles. This saw the depreciation of the yuan and threatened bank funding. Yet the slowdown in capital outflows in subsequent years after the tightening of capital controls shows that China's capital controls are still relatively effective, although there are no guarantees here if a truly substantial domestic financial crisis spurs strong incentives for capital outflows.

Fifth, like Japan's, China's debt is denominated mainly in domestic currency. Foreign currency debt accounts for less than 6 percent of overall domestic debt. In contrast, this figure for many other emerging market economies is four times the Chinese share (Lardy 2016, 135). It is still possible, however, that domestic funding pressures could mount, especially when balance sheets are reliant on short-term funding. Japan experienced this in its early 1990s financial meltdown, despite having a strong external position (Chen and Kang 2018, 11). Nevertheless, among a range of financial and institutional resources, the Chinese government has access to the country's foreign exchange reserves (standing at a little over $3 trillion in 2020), which have been used in the past to help support the government-owned banks and which might be used in any further debt or banking crisis. It is nevertheless true, however, that the level of China's foreign reserve holdings may not be able to cope with the potential magnitude of sudden shocks in the domestic financial markets, particularly when the figure of $3 trillion in reserves is set against the rapid increase in banking assets running into the tens of trillions of dollars over the last decade or more.

Sixth, debt levels in national economies are often measured by debt-to-GDP ratios. While this has the merit of analytical convenience, a more nuanced approach is needed when this is applied to varying political-economic settings across countries. In particular, the essence of the notion of "leverage" should be the ratio of debt to equity. In this regard, GDP is a measure of national income, a concept of flow, rather than "equity" as a concept of stock. This may not make much difference in the West, but it is quite a different story in China, where the government owns the bulk of productive assets and most of the land. Taking into account the equities owned by the government, an analysis by Li Yang (2018) from the Chinese Academy of Social Science suggests that the actual debt level for China was no higher than an equivalent of 70 percent of GDP by the end of 2015, less than a third of the level observed by other studies, which measure the level of debt as a debt-to-GDP ratio. It is true, however, that equities in productive assets or land are less liquid for short-term-crisis purposes. Liquidating assets or shares in SOEs would require policy changes, suggesting that (if effectively managed), the government (including local governments) potentially possesses substantial fiscal capacities, if needed, in dealing with shocks in the system. The government in China also carries relatively low debt, with general government debt (central government debt and explicit local government debt) at less than 45 percent of GDP and total debt at a little over 90 percent of GDP in 2020, suggesting considerable fiscal capacity to support the financial system if needed.

Risks in the Bigger Picture

Despite the various cushions and caveats outlined above, it is still the case that China's credit expansion now stands as the largest and longest in world history. Chen and Kang (2018, 16) warn that "historical precedents of 'safe' credit booms of such magnitude and speed are few and far from comforting." Some of the mitigating factors outlined above add a degree of stabilization or crisis management capacity. Yet we also know, especially with the experience of the GFC, that financial crises can begin and unfold in often unpredictable ways, especially in highly leveraged and increasingly complex, interlinked, and opaque financial systems—the direction in which China is headed. It is also the case that China's sources of financial stabilization, financial bailouts, and localized crisis management measures contain their own moral hazard: acting in a way that potentially extends current practices, postponing the day of reckoning, and making an eventual potential correction or crisis larger and more devastating. Chen and Kang (2018, 16) thus advise that "decisive policy action is needed to arrest the negative feedback loop between slowing growth, excessive credit provision, and worsening debt servicing capacity."

A further worrying factor is that Chinese households and investors increasingly rely on financial investments and rising asset prices as a route to income and wealth generation. This is one aspect of the wider phenomenon of "financialization" (Van der Zwan 2014), or the growing scale and scope of financial activity, creating a situation where new forms of mass financialization increase China's financial fragility, increase societal risk exposures, and also make financial reform more challenging. This also means that the Chinese leadership's traditional quest for growth and stability has moved beyond supporting macroeconomic growth and now extends into the heartland of financial markets on which so many Chinese increasingly depend. For Wright and Rosen (2018, 96), this represents a transformation of the traditional Chinese "banking bargain" (cf. Calomiris and Haber 2014) from the earlier financial repression of households and investors to the new game of greater financial liberalization and greater dependence on and exposure to asset markets, especially property. As Wright and Rosen (2018, 97) note, "Most improvements in living standards have been delivered through asset price growth returns on financial assets rather than wage growth." They point out that financial asset incomes have risen faster than wage growth in recent years, that property prices have risen at over twice the pace of real national income growth over the last ten years, and that household wealth is increasingly dependent on the inflated property sector, all suggesting that the party regime's political bargain with Chinese households is now more fragile and riskier.

This also means that the extent and indeed the manageability of financial risks, and the stability of the financial system, hinge increasingly on the actions and credibility of the Chinese government in stabilizing and supporting markets. The extension of financial activity into new terrains has increasingly seen the authorities backstop financial markets, providing stabilization where needed. For example, potential defaults on corporate loans and bonds rarely eventuate, as governments are likely to step in and organize refinancing and debt relief.[6] Nor was any bank ever allowed to fully default until November 2020, when Baoshang Bank, a regional lender, was allowed to go bankrupt. The bank was alleged to have engaged in malpractice, and its de facto controller, Xiao Jianhua, failed to stand on the right side of elite politics in China (Hong 2020). Periods of financial instability so far have been short lived. For example, there was the scarce liquidity culminating in the interbank credit crisis in mid-2013, which was prompted by the PBC's attempts to wind back the growth of WMPs and shadow banking. However, the PBC soon reversed course under pressure from the leadership and provided emergency liquidity to stabilize the market. The authorities were also eager to come to the rescue by pouring massive amounts of state funding into the equity market amid its meltdown in 2015. As Wright and Rosen (2018, 88) conclude, these bailouts "created a powerful signal to the market that the government would step in if there was any significant market instability, thereby reinforcing risk appetite throughout the financial system."

Such actions have radically increased the problem of moral hazard in Chinese banking and finance, a situation whereby state guarantees and support supercharge market expansion and risk taking, based on the belief that the state will ride to the rescue when and where needed. This widespread belief is based on the view that the Chinese leadership is particularly susceptible to concerns regarding economic and political instability, especially as growth slows. Government support and guarantees, however, lead to mispricing of risk and misallocation of resources. This includes financial institutions frequently honoring the liabilities of nonguaranteed products that they market, such as bank-sponsored WMPs, official statements and policies that bolster asset markets, and distortions in bond pricing, especially those issued by SOEs and LGFVs, as well as various forms of liquidity support by the central bank (Chen and Kang 2018, 32–33).

However, as Wright and Rosen (2018, 27) argue, "moral hazard was not a problem in China, it was part of the strategy." They maintain that the role of the Chinese state in this regard has amounted to a form of financial market "credibility" that has reassured investors and helped prevent credit or bank runs. This is one reason why China's massive credit and financial market expansion has not thus far ended in a major financial crisis, despite the fact that this expansion has now outstripped the levels found in a range of countries that have experienced such crises in the recent past (figure 10.6).

The main problem with China's strategy, however, is that it breeds a financial system that is increasingly large, risky, and fragile in its role in intermediating one of the highest national savings systems in the world. In turn, this trend could eventually deliver a financial crisis on a scale that could potentially be beyond the state's capacity to respond effectively or in a timely manner. For example, the stock market slide between 2015 and 2016 was far from a systemic crisis, but stabilizing the situation cost Beijing a quarter of its foreign reserves.

The authorities have, however, taken at least some steps. Shadow banking has been wound back, as we have seen, and bank asset growth has slowed, although attempts at deleveraging have been a stop-and-go process. A further key challenge going forward will be breaking the web of implicit and explicit financial guarantees and dialing these back. Such guarantees from the state not only support further financial expansion but lower productivity growth by distorting market pricing. Any scaling back of guarantees will, however, introduce greater uncertainty, itself generating financial and political risks. Therefore the state's attempts to provide emergency support to troubled markets directly contradict efforts at financial reform. If the state is to wind back such support, this will require careful spadework and an effective communications strategy. Any scaling back of guarantees will need to be done in a cautious and well-managed manner, as the market gets to learn how to anticipate and tolerate particular and well-articulated forms of defaults, credit events, and bankruptcies.

In fact, Beijing has been increasingly conscious of managing such risks. For example, when the failed Baoshang Bank was taken over in September 2019, the regulators chose not to guarantee all of the bank's deposits and investments during the liquidation process. Only personal and small-business accounts were fully guaranteed, while corporate and interbank customers suffered losses (Wang 2019). By doing so, the government issued warnings regarding counterparty risks to market actors and financial institutions without jeopardizing wider social stability. In addition, current moves by the leadership and the authorities to scale back growth ambitions and to increase financial regulation are all steps in the right direction. But of course, more needs to be done to scale back leverage and the inefficient use of credit by the state sector, and to accelerate current momentum toward rebalancing the economy.

As the Chinese economy loses its former gloss of double-digit growth, it increasingly attracts attention from international institutions and analysts who are concerned about a potential debt and financial crisis. It is true that the speed of the debt buildup has been unprecedented, even compared with advanced and other emerging economies. And even though earlier rapid growth has been scaled back, there are still worrying signs in the shadow credit sector in terms of capital, liquidity, and growing complexity. There are also concerns about household and corporate-sector leverage. All of these could translate into mounting bad debts, banking stress, and ultimately a systemic crisis.

Yet it is also the case that the Chinese government possesses the fiscal and, importantly, the policy and institutional capacity to rein in high-risk sectors such as real estate and the shadow banking system should it wish to. Indeed, the latter has already been reined in. Nevertheless, the leadership faces pressure in reducing debt in the SOE sector, suggesting the need for the leadership to somehow deal with powerful vested interests that, if not dealt with, could ultimately jeopardize regime survival. This, then, is essentially a matter of politics, of overcoming entrenched vested interests and dealing with the twin challenges of economic growth and deleveraging. In this regard, the failure to make much progress in recent years on the seemingly eternal issue of SOE reform and restructuring is not comforting. If this can be done, however, and if the leadership can develop further forward momentum on reform and deleveraging, then the various financial risks are perhaps "manageable," according to the IMF (2016a, 25; see also IMF 2014, 2016b). The point, however, has now been reached where the leadership must soon undertake further substantial reforms.

Certainly, wider economic rebalancing would help digest the debt issue. Progress here on external rebalancing has been encouraging, but internal rebalancing is more challenging, particularly in raising domestic consumption, lowering investment levels, and increasing the efficiency of capital investment. The turn toward intensified statism under the current Xi regime is not helping here. All of this will be discussed in the next chapter.

11

CHINA'S TROUBLED ROAD TO ECONOMIC REBALANCING

It is often agreed, including according to statements by the Chinese leadership, that economic rebalancing is essential for sustaining economic growth and for buttressing the Chinese Communist Party's rule. This is even truer today than it was in 2007, when Premier Wen famously called China's economy "unbalanced, unstable, uncoordinated, and unsustainable." Rebalancing is widely agreed to require bringing down China's extraordinarily high national savings. This will need to entail a transition from an expansive investment-led economy to an economy based more on a growing private business sector, on income redistribution that will help increase household consumption, and on service-sector growth, innovation-led productivity growth, and higher-value-added activities. For the IMF (2016c, 4), rebalancing entails "shifting from investment to consumption on the demand side, from industry to services on the supply side, reducing the credit intensity of output, and improving the efficiency of resource allocation."

This chapter examines the dynamic development of both the external and internal dimensions of China's economic structure. We argue that there have been emerging signs of external rebalancing, which reflects more mixed results than internal rebalancing. The restructuring of China's banking and credit system through a degree of liberalization and the rise of shadow banking initially promised to aid in economic rebalancing through making more credit available to households and the private sector. On the other hand, the desirable trend of lowering investment and increasing consumption has been much more limited.

As Naughton (2016, 55) argues, "Evidence of large-scale structural change is remarkably weak" in China, a product of "inconsistent and unsuccessful economic reform policymaking." The state sector remains dominant in key strategic sectors, increasingly so under the Xi Jinping regime, while the main banks, despite greater commercialization, nevertheless remain the servant of the state in intermediating China's excessive savings and providing ever more credit to the debt-laden state corporate sector. Moreover, the initial growth of credit to the private sector during the credit surge after the GFC has been reversed in recent years, and private-sector investment levels have declined. The growth of household consumption remains subdued relative to GDP. Overall, there are some signs of rebalancing in terms of a gradual reduction in the national savings rate, but robust, longer-term rebalancing largely remains elusive. However, Beijing's response to the outbreak of the COVID-19 pandemic in 2020 has largely reversed the trend and worsened the situation in rebalancing. This chapter outlines these developments and trends and concludes by exploring the political forces that have constrained economic rebalancing in China.

Savings Matter

To begin with, and as argued in chapter 1, a consistently high savings rate is at the heart of China's internal and external imbalances. While low savings are likely to constrain the financial resources needed for economic growth, high savings are likely to result in a distorted economic structure that limits growth. A pronounced, if not central, feature of China's macroeconomy is that it has one of the highest national savings rates in the world. National savings ran at a high level during the 1980s and 1990s, between 35 and 40 percent of GDP. Savings then surged to peak at 52 percent of GDP in 2008, and then declined gradually after the GFC, standing at about 45 percent of GDP in 2020. This is still well above the global average of 20 percent for advanced economies and 15 percent for emerging economies (Chen and Kang 2018, 8). In the following discussions, we will examine both the external and internal imbalances that the high savings rate have entailed, and their post-GFC trajectories in terms of rebalancing.

External Rebalancing

According to the well-known national income identity, any trade surplus (i.e., positive net exports) that is not consumed or invested will be saved. Before the GFC, China's high savings had been reflected in external imbalances.

This was due to the fact that domestic investment had been more or less restricted for fear of overcapacity (especially in import-substituting heavy industries) due to prior investment expansion (Yang 2012, 25). This resulted in the rapid increase in China's external imbalance, in the form of increasing current- and capital-account surpluses on the one hand, and increasing foreign reserves on the other.

In fact, a relatively large proportion of net exports was a feature of the old growth model. From the early 1990s, manufacturing exports in particular helped spur the economy. However, the global growth slowdown in the wake of the GFC, the rise of domestic wages (to be discussed later), and the more recent global resistance to trade imbalances have weakened global export markets and have had a heavy impact on China's external trade. Tepid external demand since the GFC has been especially pronounced in this regard, which highlights the fact that this aspect of the old growth model had run into diminishing returns, was highly vulnerable to external shocks, and also helped perpetuate unstable global imbalances. As Lardy (2019, 120) notes, "About half the slowdown in China's growth in 2009–2016 compared with 2005–2008 was the result of the necessary moderation of its trade surplus, compounded by the weak recovery of global trade." As a result, net exports (the difference between a country's exports and imports) have declined from a peak of 15 percent in 2006, but since 2010, this figure has been fluctuating around zero, ending in negative territory in 2018 before bouncing back in 2019 (see figure 11.1).

Annually since 1993, China has run a current-account surplus, which is the rough sum of its positive trade balance and net income from foreign investment. Nevertheless, a further breakdown of China's current-account balance after the GFC suggests that, on top of the reduction in China's trade in goods, an increase in trade in services, such as outbound tourism, investment, and entertainment, has also helped bring down China's current-account balance. Trade frictions with the United States, a major export market, are also expected to have at least a short-to-medium-term negative impact on China's current-account position. For instance, China recorded its first current-account deficit in seventeen years in the first quarter of 2018 (Bloomberg 2018). Overall, China's current-account balance has been reduced from almost 10 percent of GDP in 2008 to less than 2 percent in 2020.

From a global perspective, this puts China's external balance well below those of major creditors in the world, such as Japan, Europe (particularly Germany), and the oil exporters in the Middle East (Chen and Kang 2018, 13). This indicates a remarkable correction of China's external position, bringing it more in line with the desirable level. This led the State Administration of Foreign Exchange to express its confidence that "in recent years our nation's current-account balance

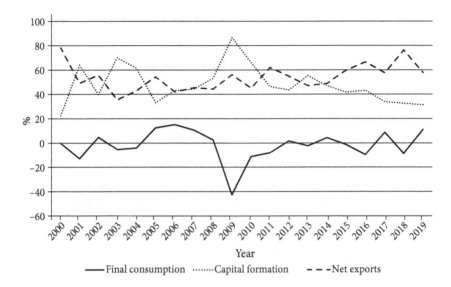

Year

——Final consumption   ········Capital formation   – – –Net exports

FIGURE 11.1. Demand-side contribution to GDP growth (%). "Final consumption" refers to consumptions of the household sector, the government (in the form of social transfers), and nongovernmental institutions serving the households; "capital formation" includes net fixed-asset investment, net increase in the value of inventories, and net lending to foreign countries.

Source: National Bureau of Statistics of China.

has entered an equilibrium range, and either a moderate surplus or moderate deficit indicates basic balance" (Moore 2018). Nevertheless, this trend was more or less disrupted after the COVID-19 pandemic, given the reduction in private consumption and strong exports growth, leading to almost a doubling of China's current-account surplus in 2020. It remains to be seen how the trend will be established in the post-COVID era.

Internal Rebalancing

Although China's external imbalances have been largely corrected, there remain substantial internal imbalances in terms of domestic investment and consumption. Thus, for China, and as noted, rebalancing from an internal perspective essentially means the need for a reduction in excessive and inefficient investment and increases in private consumption, as well as service-sector and innovation-led growth. Ultimately, this will require a reduction of China's national savings rate.

Investment

The Nobel laureate economist Arthur Lewis (1954, 155) argued that "the central problem in the theory of economic development is to understand the process by which a community which was previously saving and investing 4 or 5 percent of its national income or less, converts itself into an economy where saving and investment is running at about 12 or 15 percent of its national income or more . . . because the central fact of economic development is rapid capital accumulation (including knowledge and skills with capital)." China has been an extreme example of this argument: it achieved rapid economic growth on the back of high savings and investment rates.

The reduction in external surpluses suggests that high savings were funneled through the financial system, fueling credit-driven investment. As we have seen, high savings, credit growth, and investment in China are tightly linked and form a key component of the traditional statist growth model. The major arena of credit growth has been the state-owned corporate sector as well as local governments, using increasing debt to spur investment. Investment as a share of GDP had averaged around 30 percent in the 1980s but increased after that. By 2011, as the credit surge grew in the wake of the GFC, gross investment represented a massive 48 percent of GDP (figure 11.2).

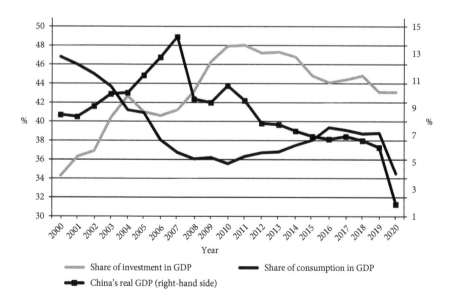

FIGURE 11.2.   Internal rebalancing: investment, consumption, and GDP.

Sources: IMF World Economic Outlook Database and CEIC.

A key goal, therefore, in terms of internal rebalancing is to reduce China's reliance on high savings and investment as shares of GDP, a growth strategy that has clearly run into mounting inefficiencies and diminishing returns. As figure 11.2 shows, the investment drive worked for a period from the early 2000s, with investment and GDP growth rising together. However, from around 2007, GDP growth slowed substantially while investment as a share of GDP continued to grow (until 2010). Since 2010, the investment share of GDP has been in slow decline, with an upsurge from around 2016. As investment declined for a period, consumption picked up slightly, suggesting at least a small degree of rebalancing, although the recent increase in the investment-to-GDP ratio has seen consumption flatten out. Despite the decline in investment from its peak in 2010–11, the average share of investment in GDP between 2008 and 2020 has been over 45 percent, higher than the pre-GFC average of 39 percent between 2000 and 2007. It is also well above the level found in a range of advanced economies and other major emerging economies.

Savings and credit have thus been absorbed by elevated investment, yet part of the reason for China's declining GDP growth, despite high investment, is that since the early 1990s the gross rate of return on investment has steadily declined. The incremental capital-output ratio, which serves as an indicator of capital efficiency by measuring the investment needed to generate a given level of output, started to increase (worsen) after 2007. Indeed, from 2007 to 2018, the incremental capital-output ratio more than doubled, meaning that more than twice the level of investment was needed in 2018 to generate the same level of output achieved a decade earlier, suggesting rapidly growing inefficiencies in investment and a clear sign of diminishing returns (Naughton 2018b, 384; Orsmond 2019, 4).

Income

As discussed in chapter 1, the dramatic rise in China's national savings before the GFC can be largely attributed to a declining share of household disposable income in national output, essentially a transfer of income from the consuming household sector to the investing nonhousehold (government and corporate) sector. As Wolf (2018) argues, "A surge in consumption sufficient to offset the impact on domestic demand of a big cut in investment spending would be impossible without a far bigger shift in incomes towards households." Therefore, a starting point in rebalancing the economy is to increase the household share of income in order to support increased private consumption.

Such a trend has emerged after the GFC, with household disposal income rising from 58 percent of GDP in 2008 to 61.6 percent in 2016. This has been at the expense of a decline in corporate income and stagnation in government income (IMF 2012, 23; 2015, 21; 2021, 55). Wages and, increasingly, asset income are the two major components of urban household income in China. The rising share of household disposable income, compared to falling corporate income after the GFC, reflects a broader trend of rising wage levels. On the one hand, the long-term impact of the one-child policy has continued to deliver a shrinkage of the working-age population. At the same time, surplus rural labor has been more fully absorbed by the urban manufacturing industries and, more importantly, the growth of the more employment-intensive services sector in China. This has led many to argue that China had arrived at the Lewis turning point in the early 2010s, which has resulted in an increase in wage bills that favor labor (Zhang, Yang, and Wang 2011; Loyalka 2012). In addition, there has been a rise in asset incomes as returns for retail depositors and asset investors improve under a degree of financial liberalization and rising asset prices.

However, this trend has reversed since 2017, as the share of household disposal income entered a steady decline that reversed back from 61.6 percent in 2016 to the pre-GFC level of 57.6 percent of GDP in 2020 (IMF 2021, 55). As of 2020, China's GDP per capita was 72,447 yuan, more than twice the amount of household disposable income per capita of 32,189 yuan (National Bureau of Statistics of China 2021). The gap between the two represents corporate and government income.

Consumption

One of the key consequences of the distributional imbalance between household and nonhousehold income has been a slow growth in private consumption. Although aggregate household consumption has risen strongly in absolute terms, as a share of GDP it has been in long-term decline in recent decades, falling from over 50 percent of GDP in the early 1980s to a low of around 35 percent of GDP by 2010. It has only recently started to climb, rising from its low in 2010 to almost 39 percent by 2020, although this trend flattened after 2016. When China's GDP per capita reached $10,000 in 2020, its consumption-to-GDP ratio of 38.8 percent was much lower than that in the United States (60.5 percent) and Japan (53.9 percent) when their GDP per capita went over $10,000 in 1978 and 1981, respectively (Wang 2021). China's figure was also well below that of emerging economies, such as Brazil and India, as well as the global average of 60 percent (IMF 2019, 24). Therefore, a key goal of internal rebalancing is to wean the economy off the old growth model of high savings and debt-fueled investment in order to spur the growth of private consumption, a major source of GDP growth in mature economies.

One of the major drivers of consumption repression before the GFC had been the weakness of the social welfare system and public goods provision, which had forced Chinese households to set aside funds for retirement, health care, and education (Liu 2004; Chamon and Prasad 2010). According to Roach (2009, 8), this was a system of "fear-driven precautionary saving that inhibit[ed] the development of a more dynamic consumer culture." Efforts have been made to address this situation, such as the development of a nationwide universalist pension system that provides coverage for both urban and rural retirees. There have also been reforms and somewhat improved access to the health care, health insurance, and education systems (Liu 2004; Burns and Liu 2017; Lardy 2019, 33–35). This has been reflected largely in increasing social transfers on the part of the government budget, from 40 percent of total government expenditures in 2008 to over 60 percent in 2019.

A very moderate decline in household savings has been accompanied by a moderate increase in household consumption since 2011. The latter is reflected in the growth of the household final consumption expenditure, a gauge of consumer spending that includes expenditures by resident households domestically and abroad (as outbound tourists). Given the rapid increase of outbound tourism among China's urban middle class in recent years, the household final consumption expenditure better captures the scale of real household consumption in China. The annual growth rate of private consumption peaked in 2011 before declining sharply since then, standing at 6.4 percent in 2019. Although it is still marginally above the growth of GDP, it nevertheless reflects the cautiousness of household spending in the face of China's ongoing economic slowdown.

There have been a number of factors that have continued to contain consumption in China. First, although the government has increased its social spending in providing public services, the coverage and the services provided by the emerging social security and welfare system, according to Liu and Sun (2016, 17), have been "incomplete," "inadequate," and "unaffordable," all of which continue to incentivize precautionary savings by families and households (see also Millar et al. 2016). As Naughton (2017, 22) argues, "China's relatively weak performance in achieving broadly redistributive policies, social fairness, and improved public goods provision appears to reflect the limits of responsiveness and the power of entrenched economic and political interests."

At the same time, as discussed in chapter 10, the household debt burden has become an increasingly important factor crowding out consumption. According to the PBC's (2019) *Financial Stability Report*, outstanding household loans have more than doubled, from 23.1 trillion yuan in 2014 to 47.9 trillion yuan in 2018. Indeed, household loans jumped 18.2 percent in 2018, compared with a 10.7 percent increase in disposable income, pushing the debt-to-disposable-income ratio (the indicator of household leverage) to almost 100 percent by the end of 2018.

Here, the role of household mortgages is particularly pronounced, accounting for more than half of total household loans. Rising housing expenditures on property down payments and mortgage-servicing costs thus tend to reduce consumption. On the one hand, there is a wealth effect as rising property prices and easier access to credit in a more liberalized financial system encourage greater consumption. On the other hand, there is a crowding-out effect as rising household debt and debt repayment tend to erode disposable income, and hence constrain consumption (Han et al. 2019). According to the IMF (2019, 22; 2021, 16), household debt in China doubled between 2011 and 2019. The majority of household debt in China is mortgage based, and the increase in mortgage debt is due mainly to rising property prices. In fact, Shanghai, Shenzhen, and Beijing are among the most expensive housing markets in the world, ranked at third, fifth, and ninth globally (Zhang 2019). The two effects above, relating to debt and consumption, exist at the same time, and the net impact on consumption depends on the level of debt relative to the level of income. In August 2018, for example, monthly mortgage repayments took more than half of monthly household disposable income in almost all tier 1 and 2 cities (except Chengdu). In three out of four tier 1 cities, average mortgage repayments exceeded monthly disposable income.[1] This means that mortgage repayments needed to rely on additional sources of repayment, such as savings or borrowed funds, often from wider family networks. Such disproportionally high housing costs have translated into the lackluster trend in private consumption.

In summary, a degree of internal rebalancing has occurred in China, as indicated by a slow and gradual reduction in the high national savings rate since around 2010 due to financial liberalization, rising incomes, and certain improvements in social security. And while lower household saving should help spur consumption, the robustness or sustainability of this shift is still in question given the recent decline in the rate of consumption growth, largely due to ongoing propensities for precautionary saving as well as high property prices and debt burdens. In addition, even with the limited improvements noted above, the share of investment remains higher and consumption lower than in the pre-2000 era. Overall, the continuing and comparatively high level of savings and investment in the context of declining GDP growth is not suggestive of robust rebalancing. As will be demonstrated later in this chapter, rebalancing is indeed very fragile in the time of the COVID-19 crisis, in which both household income and private consumption dived in 2020.

The Rise of the Services Sector

Another dimension of internal rebalancing involves development in the service/ tertiary sector. The employment share of agriculture has gone from 60 percent to below 30 percent since the 1990s, while the share held by industry and services rose from 22 percent and 27 percent in 2000 to 28 and 47 percent, respectively, in 2019. Tertiary employment exceeded that of agriculture for the first time in 2012. Moreover, according to the National Bureau of Statistics website, the contribution of the tertiary sector to GDP has exceeded that of the secondary sector since 2015.

However, internal rebalancing toward services as a share of GDP has stalled in recent years. In comparative terms, the share of services in GDP in China remains significantly lower than in other advanced economies, such as the United States and Japan. It is also lower than in emerging market economies, such as Brazil, and is comparable only with that of India. Moreover, as Naughton (2016, 57) notes, in the last half decade, most of the service-sector increase has been driven by price increases in that sector rather than by sectoral shifts in real growth rates. The IMF (2016c, 5) similarly observes that the falling nominal share of industry and the rise in services has been due largely to price effects and that changes in real share have been "much more muted."

It should also be noted that industrial productivity is about 1.3 times higher than services productivity in China (Wu 2018, 152). This means that, although there has been an expansion of the service sector at the expense of other industries, economic growth is likely to be moderated due to the lower level of service-sector productivity. In addition, despite poor returns, SOEs dominate investment in key service or tertiary industries, such as public administration, transport, utilities, and education (Bai and Zhang 2018). Unless the private sector is allowed a level playing field in market entry, this will also hinder the future development of the services sector.

Innovation and Productivity

Another key dimension of economic rebalancing entails the shift from expansive capital investment toward improving the efficiency of investment. China has made efforts to ameliorate this situation. For example, in terms of the share of research and development spending in GDP, China is catching up with advanced economies and is well ahead of several key developing countries, such as India and Brazil.

This trend is also demonstrated by the Global Innovation Index (Cornell University, INSEAD, and WIPO 2020), which "aims to capture the multi-dimensional facets of innovation" among 142 economies that account for almost

99 percent of the world's GDP. On this measure, China was ranked fourteenth in the world, ahead of traditionally advanced countries such as Japan and Canada, and well ahead of major developing countries like India and Brazil.

Another important gauge is the Mastercard Caixin BBD China New Economy Index, which measures labor, capital, and technology inputs in ten emerging industries, including key industries such as information technology, energy conservation, environmental protection, and advanced materials. The reading has been oscillating around 30 percent since 2017, indicating that the new economy accounted for about 30 percent of overall economic activity. However, there has been a general slowdown since early 2016 when the index was established.

Although it is generally assumed that technological innovations tend to increase productivity, development in China has been mixed. China has shown a capacity for innovation in areas such as e-commerce and internet businesses that are led mainly by the private sector. However, Naughton (2016, 60) finds that business income in new technology sectors, such as technology services, consulting, and cultural and related services, grew only marginally more in 2015 than the average incomes for all service-sector firms, suggesting that these new sectors "are not going to drive major structural change." In addition, as noted above, the Chinese economy has been shifting toward services, whose labor productivity tends to be lower than that of the industries. Moreover, the capital productivity of state-sector firms is about half that of private firms (Hsieh and Song 2015, 4), and, as noted above, many areas of the service sector in China are dominated by inefficient SOEs. There is currently a fourfold gap between China and the world leader, the United States, in terms of productivity (Orsmond 2019, 9). In addition, total factor productivity (value-added per unit of capital and labor), which stood at 2.25 percent in 2018, has declined by half compared to its average in the decade before the GFC (IMF 2019, 30). Overall, Beijing has put in enormous effort and deployed substantial resources in its attempts to reform the SOEs and drive creativity and productivity. Yet the impact on much-needed structural change has been limited, suggesting that policy reforms, as Naughton (2016, 64) puts it, "are not driving the kind of productivity improvement and creation of new growth drivers" that rebalancing would require.

The Xi Jinping Regime and the Politics of (Not) Rebalancing

Economic rebalancing entails nothing short of a transformation in China's growth model. The Chinese leadership has long agreed with the notion of rebalancing, but under the current Xi Jinping regime since 2012, it is also increasingly clear that politics and the entrenchments of the old statist growth model are standing in the way. Indeed, despite earlier endorsements of the need for rebalancing and boosting resource allocation through markets, the current leadership seemingly has no intention of jettisoning the old statist growth model. Instead the aim has been to try and revamp it. From the current leadership's perspective, despite its inefficiencies, diminishing returns, and financial risks, it is still the model that has delivered sufficient economic growth to sustain the party's legitimacy thus far, and that has formed part of the "resilience" of Chinese authoritarianism (Nathan 2003; Dickson 2008; Shambaugh 2008). It has also been the model of emergency force-fed growth that has pulled the Chinese economy out of two external shocks, the Asian financial crisis and the GFC. How long this strategy will prove viable is another question. Chen (2016, 237) argues that "at least so far, the old growth model can still generate the required output through policy stimuli." But this strategy is running into diminishing returns as growth slows and debt builds. There is also the absence of earlier tailwinds, such as favorable demographics and accommodating export markets in the West, while the challenges of trying to revitalize the state sector are immense.

The liberal and market reforms in banking and finance, as well as the growth of the shadow banking system in the wake of the GFC critical juncture, looked for a time to have marked a substantial departure, offering to assist with economic rebalancing. However, it now looks as though these liberalizing changes, along with the stock market meltdown in 2015, set the stage for the rise of a reactionary, revitalized set of statist ideas, with Xi's state "striking back" (Lardy 2019). Early signs of this were apparent. Despite endorsing market reforms, the Party Congress in 2013 also stated that the regime "must persist in the dominant position of the public sector, give full play to the leading role of the state sector, continuously increasing its vitality, controlling force and influence" (Central Committee of the CCP 2014b). It is this latter approach that has increasingly been a hallmark of the Xi regime, with Eaton (2016) arguing that a statist ideology and mindset have been central to the resurgent statism under Xi. Indeed, long-standing tensions between liberal and conservative elements within the Chinese state have (somewhat unusually) been resolved for now in favor of more conservative elements and ideas. The Xi regime's statism and conservatism has only been reinforced by growing worries within the leadership about the consequences of earlier liberalizing reforms. Indeed, between 2015 and 2017, the leadership and regulators had to deal with a stock market meltdown, exchange rate instability, a $1 trillion depletion of its foreign reserves, and capital flight, all stemming from exuberant and unstable financial markets. As Magnus (2018, 64) writes, "The array of measures taken at the time to stabilize financial markets, currency reserves, capital flows and the Renminbi, were a clear demonstration of China's limited tolerance for markets to work freely."

Earlier sanguine views about the liberalization of finance have thus been reversed. The Xi regime has also become concerned about the rise of the private sector and what this could potentially mean for party dominance. McGregor (2019, 69) argues that the aim has been "to ensure that the private sector, and individual entrepreneurs, do not become rival players in the political system in a way that threatens the single party state." An increasingly virulent statist mindset is thus taking hold. Indeed, there appears to be a growing belief that the state possesses the competence to control, intervene in, and guide the economy and thereby promote economic growth, with leaders possessing a sense of "national efficacy" with regard to growth and innovation (Kennedy 2012). The elevation of statism as well as economic nationalism and belief in the "China Model" is only being further entrenched by the current trade tensions and confrontation with the United States, and by China's relative success thus far in dealing with the COVID-19 crisis.

There also remain strong vested interests within the party-state and the state sector of the economy that are active rent seekers and major beneficiaries of the statist growth model. These interests, within parts of the leadership and central state, within the SOEs, and in local and provincial governments, are resistant to change, especially if it would weaken their grip on the state and its resources (Xie 2015). As Wu Jinglian (2009a) writes, a major constraint on liberal, more market-oriented reform "comes mainly from vested interests . . . state-owned monopolies and government departments," that see that further reform could "harm their interests." He goes on to note that "pushing reform of state-owned monopolies and that of the political system means the government will have to reform itself. Consequently, reform has entered a more difficult battle." Eaton (2016, 109) also writes about the influence of the state-owned enterprises in pushing a statist agenda, arguing that "particularistic interests opposed to liberalization and increased competition in the state sector have definitely shaped state sector policy." These interests have always been influential, but their fortunes have waxed and waned over time. The difference now, however, is that they have secured a very accommodating position within the statist ambitions of the Xi regime that aims to further boost the SOEs and the state sector.

Apart from the party leadership and those who directly gain from the state sector, another key stakeholder group in the investment- and debt-driven growth model has been local government leaders who have strong incentives to spur local growth and avoid social instability. These actors have become major players in China's infrastructure investment and major holders of public debt, and are increasingly active in controlling rural and regional banking (Lardy 2019,

115–16; see also chapters 7 and 10). A critical factor in the "business model" of local infrastructural investment has been that land prices, and thus property prices, are kept at high levels to help sustain the finance for such investment. This has been achieved in part by local governments controlling the supply of land. While such practices helped finance public spending, high property prices have significantly eroded private consumption, as noted above.

These interests form an intimate nexus of top political elites, state bureaucrats, and managers and personnel in the state and local public sectors. As we have argued, the high-savings- and investment-driven growth model has secured and mobilized key strategic productive and financial resources at the disposal of this elite. These resources are seen as central in maintaining the party's grip on power and in protecting key assets and resources. As a result, association with the state sector offers substantial political, career, and personal benefits and thus helps entrench such interests that have long been resistant to fundamental restructuring. The potential winners from rebalancing—households and the private sector—are far more numerous than the controlling elite, but they are far less powerful under an authoritarian state, a power imbalance that has only increased under Xi, whose regime works ceaselessly to further entrench its power, its statist ambitions, and its control over society.

Through coercion involving a popular nationwide anticorruption campaign and softer maneuverings around a program of cult-building propaganda emphasizing the leader's infallibility, Xi Jinping has also transformed Chinese politics by centralizing the CCP's decision-making power away from the collective leadership promoted by Deng and subsequent leaders into a form of one-man rule signified by the label of "core leader" (Zheng and Gore 2015; Hart 2016; Shirk 2018). Xi has taken control of key committees and leading small groups within the party hierarchy. As Magnus (2018, 61) writes, "Under Xi, the Communist Party has, in effect, usurped the machinery of government," with Leading Small Groups within the party playing a key role in policymaking. The State Council (China's cabinet) has also been weakened, and the role of the leadership's number two, the premier, has been downgraded to a point where Xi has usurped the key leadership role in economic policymaking, a function normally assumed by the premier (McGregor 2019, 25). Xi has also enshrined his philosophy—"Xi Jinping Thought on Socialism with Chinese Characteristics for a New Era"—within the party constitution, the first time this has happened since Mao.

Equally dramatic has been Xi's campaign to intensify the political grip of the party over the society and economy. Shambaugh (2000, 183) noted that "if one of the hallmarks of the Maoist state was the penetration of society, then the Dengist state was noticeable for its withdrawal. The organizational mechanisms of state penetration and manipulation were substantially reduced or dismantled altogether." This resulted in what Ding (1994, 300) calls a "gradual functional and organizational decay of the massive party-state machinery." However, this trend has been reversed under Xi's leadership, which now emphasizes the central and omnipresent role of the CCP. This degree of centralization is risky. An important problem with one-man rule and the cult of the infallible leader under Xi is that they stifle discussion and criticism within policymaking organs and increase the potential for large policy missteps. Pragmatism and flexibility used to be hallmarks of decision-making during the earlier reform era, but dogma and rigidity have become the new norm. As Economy (2018b, 22) argues, "Centralization of power and anti-corruption campaigns have slowed decision making at the top of the Chinese political system, which in turn has led to paralysis at local levels of governance and lower rates of economic growth." Undeterred, the party regime is further extending its reach and is seeking to control all domains of social and economic life. This includes repression of different views within and outside the party, crackdowns on the media and on internet access, and the tightening of social controls through a mass surveillance system backed by high technology. There is also a new "social credit system," in which a wide range of factors, from political loyalty to personal credit records, are measured to reward or punish individuals in terms of their access to social and financial services (Parton 2018; Shirk 2018).

The Public versus Private Sector under Xi

The changes discussed above have thus meant that China's much-heralded "market transition" (Lardy 2014) is being challenged and partly rolled back by the state. Xi reportedly remarked in 2015 that SOEs should form the backbone of the Chinese economy and that the government must "avoid the blindness of the market" (Reuters 2015). Earlier, there had been high expectations of more ambitious reforms at the beginning of the Xi administration. During its congress in 2013, the party declared it would "let the market play a more decisive role in resource allocation" (Central Committee of the CCP 2014b). Yet the rhetoric of a more decisive role for the market has not been matched by the reality so far. On the contrary, the role of the state and of the party in the economy is not being wound back but is being further enhanced. As Economy (2018a, 5) observes, "The leadership has embraced a process of institutional change that seeks to reverse many of the political, social and economic changes that emerged from thirty years of liberalizing reforms." This is evidenced in the march of the SOEs in major economic sectors, which is having a crowding-out effect on the private sector. State firms are also taking ownership stakes in many formerly private firms, leaving only about 20 to 30 percent of firms in the enterprise sector as purely private entities (Magnus 2018, 65). As Magnus (74) argues, "In Xi's China the private sector is going to succumb to much greater intrusion by the Party." Such encroachment reflects the leadership's "continued refusal to acknowledge a legitimate dividing line between state and society as well as a continuing distrust of the private sector," according to Fewsmith (2014, 157). The role of party leadership in the SOEs is being further entrenched and party committees are slated to sit in every Chinese firm, including private and foreign joint ventures. By 2016, almost 70 percent of nonstate enterprises and foreign companies had party cells (Tai 2018). Party officials carry advisory authority in operational management and the making of major decisions, thus blurring the line between political and commercial imperatives.

These are worrying developments. The private sector has been the central driver of China's economic expansion in recent decades. Lardy (2016, 48) notes that "a major source of China's growth in the reform era has been the increasing share of investment undertaken by private firms that have been able to generate a return on assets as much as three times that of state firms." China's private sector is dominated by small and medium-sized enterprises (SMEs), which account for around 98 percent of registered enterprises. SMEs contribute around 60 percent of national GDP, 50 percent of taxes, and around 80 percent of urban employment (ACFIC 2016, 6). However, the headwinds faced by the private sector under the Xi regime have been pronounced. The sector has suffered from reductions in heavy industry capacity, the decline in export opportunities, and credit restrictions from the clampdown on shadow banking. These and other pressures have seen the sector's return on assets declining since around 2011, as figure 11.3 shows. The return on assets of state firms, has, since 2007, also been declining. According to an independent report by the Unirule Institute of Economics (2016), when state subsidies and the discounts on their financing costs were factored into the SOEs' nominal income, the real return on equity of SOEs was in negative territory for most of the period between 2001 and 2014 (except for 2006 and 2007) (see figure 11.3).

As a result of the headwinds noted above, as well as weak property rights, the slowdown in GDP growth, and persistent barriers to entry for the private sector into key economic sectors, private entrepreneurs have increasingly been losing confidence, so much so that even Xi and other top leaders have felt compelled to reassure the private sector amid growing fears regarding an increasingly intrusive state. Xi met dozens of private entrepreneurs in November 2018, together with the ministers and bankers. During the meeting, Xi recognized the contribution of private enterprises to China's economic growth, and reiterated that Beijing's policy of "encouraging, supporting and guiding" the private economy "has not

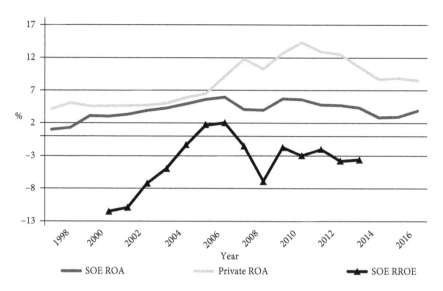

FIGURE 11.3. Profitability: SOEs vs. private companies.

Sources: National Bureau of Statistics of China; Unirule 2016; IMF 2019, 2021.

changed," and that major measures, such as tax cuts, would be rolled out in supporting the private sector (Zhou 2018). In his report to the National People's Congress in March 2019, Premier Li Keqiang endorsed Xi's line and stressed the need to "ease funding shortages faced by private enterprises," "encourage private actors to engage in innovation," and "attract more private capital into projects in key areas" (Xinhua 2019).

However, the seemingly strong political rhetoric and subsequent policies aimed at reducing financing costs for SMEs have so far had limited impact in altering the balance between SOEs and private enterprises. As Magnus (2018, 74) argues, "The irony is that many of China's prominent leaders understand fully the dynamic role that the private sector and more liberal markets play. Yet there is no chance that they will, given the prevailing political environment, be deployed to rebalance the role and function of the state vis-à-vis the private sector."

The SOEs have grown substantially over the last two decades. For example, the assets of state nonfinancial firms totaled around 20 trillion yuan in 2000, but by 2015 this figure had grown sixfold to 120 trillion yuan (Magnus 2018, 66). Over the same period, China's GDP growth rate shifted down from around 12 percent in 2008 to less than 7 percent in 2016. The rising prominence of the underperforming state sector has been a key driver of this growth slowdown (Lardy 2019, 78). Xi has reportedly said that SOEs were "the material and political foundation of socialism with Chinese characteristics" and "the key power and reliance for the

Communist Party's rule of China" (Lee 2018). In a visit to a major SOE, Xi also remarked that SOEs "should continue to become stronger, better and larger" and claimed that the view that the SOEs should wither was "wrong and one-sided" (Gan 2018).

China's SOEs suffer from a lack of a clear commercial focus, generous state subsidies that weaken profit search and encourage rent seeking, and weak accountability and in many cases outright corruption. Attempts to improve the economic performance of the moribund SOEs were first conducted in the late 1990s, with mass layoffs and SOE consolidation. Reform efforts faded somewhat from the mid-2000s. The Xi regime now wants to try once again to revamp the SOEs, to subject them to greater political oversight and make them key players in the regime's new developmental agenda (Naughton 2018). In contrast to the mass layoff of workers in the SOE reform push in the 1990s, the current reforms are in part aimed at protecting or reshuffling employment within the SOEs to support social stability. Instead of layoffs or bankruptcies, the focus instead has been on mergers and acquisitions (Economy 2018b, 109), with the consolidation of SOEs delivering increasingly bigger conglomerates that further weaken competition. The SOEs are thus being promoted to take on an even more prominent role in the national economy and are being favored in key national industrial policies, especially the *Made in China 2025* program, which aims to boost industrial development, innovation, and high-tech manufacturing (Fang and Walsh 2018).

The major move here was the release of an SOE reform roadmap in September 2015 entitled *Guiding Opinions of the Communist Party of China Central Committee and the State Council on Deepening the Reform of State-Owned Enterprises* (Xinhua 2015), which was followed by a series of accompanying policy documents. There are two key elements of the program. First, SOEs are to be divided and reconsolidated into two groups according to their functions, each with different strategic goals and performance standards. Those dedicated to the public sector and national security will prioritize their capacity to promote stability and other political goals over profitability, while those dedicated to commercial interests will have to be competitive in the market and deliver gains in innovation and corporate performance. Premier Li Keqiang also put forth the principle of "competitive neutrality" in his annual government report to the People's Congress in 2019, in which he stressed that "when it comes to access to factors of production, market access and licenses, business operations, government procurement, public biddings, and so on, enterprises under all forms of ownership will be treated on an equal footing" (Xinhua 2019).

There are several issues with the recent round of SOE reforms. Orsmond (2019, 8) writes that the *Made in China 2025* strategy lacks clarity about which companies will be involved, what goals are to be achieved, and how central funding will be allocated. It is also the case that the SOEs in the competitive sector have to fulfill certain political goals, such as maintaining social stability and advancing Xi's signature initiatives abroad (Leutert 2018). The latter is especially the case with the Belt and Road Initiative, which largely amounts to the offshoring of the domestic debt/investment growth model. In addition, the new programs also proclaim a critical role for the party in the SOEs, reflected in SOE charters and management structures (Leutert 2016). Naughton (2018b, 379) argues that these multiple SOE objectives, including the SOEs' role in technological leadership, in becoming national champions in world markets, in assisting with macroeconomic stability, and in offshore infrastructure programs such as the Belt and Road Initiative, will complicate and weaken management incentives and the SOEs' economic performance. "The pursuit of contradictory objectives," he writes, "has hobbled the recent program of SOE reforms and will continue to obstruct progress in the future."

Second, the *Guiding Opinions* document calls for a "mixed ownership" reform to the SOEs by allowing in nonstate investors as SOE shareholders. At the same time, it also allows state funds to take shares in private firms. However, given the disparity in political privileges between state and private companies, the mixed-ownership approach under its current design is likely to result in corruption, insider control, and unfair competition. Only the "lemons" of the SOEs—those struggling in terms of performance and finance—would welcome private investors without controlling stakes. On the other hand, competitive private firms would not dare to say no if the state sought partial ownership. A further twist in such state-private capital exchanges is that private firms are willing to risk a state takeover in a hybrid private-public ownership structure in order to exploit the state investor's political power and privileges in the market, thus leading to unfair competition (Ding 2018).

In summary, rather than acknowledging a key role for the more efficient and productive private sector, the current leadership clearly sees a central and continuing future for the SOEs, despite a lack of progress with what has now been several decades of on-and-off-again attempts to reform and modernize them. The record shows that China's private sector is the main innovator and driver of economic growth, yet the current regime is instead intent on trying to revive the largely moribund state sector.

The Xi regime's statism and the SOEs' renewed privileges have been reflected in changes in financial flows. As Lardy (2019, 105) shows, in 2011, 54 percent of new corporate lending in the formal credit system was allocated to the private sector, far outpacing the 28 percent that went to the SOEs. Since 2012 this has been reversed. By 2019, SOEs gained almost 75 percent of new credit, compared with just 18 percent for the private sector (see figure 11.4). The private sector has

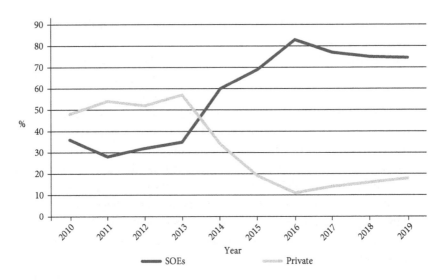

FIGURE 11.4. Destination of corporate loans by ownership type in formal sector (%).

Source: PBC.

also been forced to pay an interest rate premium. In 2016, for example, private firms were paying almost 10 percent interest on their loans, almost 6 percent higher than the rate paid by SOEs (Economy 2018b, 106). There was a 40 percent drop in loans to private firms between 2013 and 2018, although there has been a moderate rise since 2016. As Lardy (2019, 20) puts it, "In a stark reversal of the earlier trend, beginning in 2012, banks directed a larger share of credit to state firms, essentially crowding out the private sector." Private firms were able to access alternative credit from the shadow banks, but, as discussed in chapter 9, the crackdown on shadow banking has further reduced the flow of credit to private borrowers.

The weakness of the state sector also continues to corrupt the main banks, directed as they are to provide rising levels of misallocated credit to prop up state-sector firms. As Song and Xiong (2018, 270) observe, "The special mission of the financial system to support the SOEs has had profound impacts on both the efficiency and risks of the financial system. In particular, it made the financial system heavily exposed to the problems of the SOEs." Unswerving support from the leadership, soft-budget constraints, and implicit guarantees for the state sector have helped create a sector that often displays weak profit incentives, corrupt practices, and misallocated capital (Lardy 2019, 76). The SOEs dominate key sectors such as steel and coal that have long suffered from excess capacity as managers strive to invest retained earnings to boost short-term growth and employment levels in their firms. In steel in 2015, for example, there were 336 million tons of overcapacity, making up 46 percent of world steel overcapacity (Economy 2018b, 107). Before-tax profits of the core SOEs under the control of SASAC in 2017 were only 2.6 percent of gross capital, a substantial drop from the 6.7 percent figure achieved in 2007 (Naughton 2018b, 377). More than 40 percent of SOEs were losing money in 2016, while, according to Lardy (2019, 55), "the return on assets of state firms in industry and services fell by two-thirds and two-fifths respectively between 2007 and 2016."

The political nepotism and favored treatment meted out to the SOEs has coincided with a marked slowdown in private investment. The ratio of private-sector investment to GDP in China has been falling since the GFC, with only a slight increase more recently. It is also the case that private-sector investment has been increasingly skewed away from relatively productive forms of manufacturing investment and toward property development. Indeed, private-sector manufacturing investment fell from a peak of 45 percent of total private-sector investment in 2007 to only 23 percent by 2019, while the share of property investment rose from 8 percent of total private investment in 2000 to 38 percent by 2019.

From an economic performance perspective, the leadership appears to be backing the wrong horse, a point underlined by the Chinese liberal critic Prof. Zhang Weiying (2013):

> Over the past decade, our ideas have experienced a major setback. We have gone from believing more in the market to believing more in government, from believing in entrepreneurship to believing in the dominance of the SOEs. This has led to the 'advance of the state and the retreat of the private sector.' . . . We have seen the emergence of the China Model of guidance by the state and state sector. But I think the China Model is completely wrong. The reason China has made such big achievements was that the state was less and less and the scale of the SOEs smaller and smaller.

COVID-19 and the Setbacks to China's Rebalancing

The COVID-19 pandemic, which originated in January 2020 in Wuhan, in China's Hubei Province, brought on an episode of panic and disruption to the Chinese political economy. First-quarter GDP shrank by 6.8 percent from a year earlier, representing the first drop since 1992 when China started to publish quarterly data. Fixed-asset investment and retail sales contracted by 16.1 percent and 15.8 percent, respectively. A brokerage report, later withdrawn due to political pressures, estimated the unemployment rate to be as high as 20 percent (Bloomberg 2020a). The emergency measures for containing the health crisis, as well as expansionary policies for stimulating the economy, while conducive to short-term stability and recovery, have tended to more or less undo the limited structural rebalancing achieved in recent years.

To be sure, Beijing's strong measures have worked in containing the pandemic through swift lockdowns, effective contact tracing, and mass testing. Preventing a health crisis from developing into an economic crisis, however, is a more daunting task. Given the concerns about an already high level of public debt, Beijing this time avoided using a large, high-profile stimulus program. This has been in stark contrast both to its own post-GFC approach and to the current whatever-it-takes approach adopted by a range of countries around the world (Feng 2020). On the fiscal front, the government increased spending on infrastructure and the national health system, as well as in a range of more targeted areas. The latter included corporate tax relief; expansion of the social safety net, particularly the coverage of unemployment insurance; and the waiving of part of employers' social security contributions (IMF 2021, 1). The PBC also provided emergency support for the economy. This included pumping liquidity into the financial markets by slashing banks' reserve ratios; extending lending facilities to the real economy, particularly to SMEs, with lowered policy interest rates; relaxing NPL classifications for bank loans; and subsidizing banks' repayment moratoriums for SMEs and other firms in distress (PBC 2020, 12). As a result, credit expansion, as gauged by the PBC's total social financing measure, accelerated to 13.7 percent as of October 2020, compared with 10.7 percent at the end of 2019 (IMF 2021, 13). The fiscal and monetary measures, combined, have had a positive impact on the economy, at least in terms of short-term recovery. GDP has returned to positive territory, growing at 2.3 percent for 2020, something rarely seen by any other COVID-battered major economy in the world (Bloomberg 2021).

Although Beijing shied away from jump-starting the economy with heavy stimulation as it did in 2008, the approach was still akin to a state-driven investment boom aided by credit expansion. An obvious consequence of this has been releveraging across the government, corporate, and household sectors, after limited achievement in deleveraging since 2016. Restrictive policies on business, such as lockdowns and social distancing, have reduced business income, and hence government revenue. At the same time, Beijing increased infrastructure investment, partially funded by an issuance of special treasury bonds worth RMB 1 trillion in 2020 (Xinhua 2020). This, together with increases in local government borrowing, has seen government debt reach 91.7 percent of GDP in 2020, compared with 80.5 percent in 2019. At the same time, SOE-led corporate investment has seen an increase in corporate debt by 10 percent of GDP in 2020 compared with 2019. Tax relief and loan moratoriums helped to avoid bankruptcy, but this also means that insolvent firms are being kept afloat. SOE-dominated investment has also likely led to overcapacity. Household debt was also on the rise, reflecting weak disposable income (see figure 10.3). Overall, China's total nonfinancial debt reached 277 percent of GDP in 2020, compared with 253 percent in the previous year (IMF 2021, 60; see also figure 10.5).

Beijing's post-COVID recovery support has also had a profound impact on the banking and financial system. On the one hand, decreasing disposable income and increasing corporate and household debt reduced debt-servicing capacities, especially for those borrowers that had already been highly leveraged. On the other hand, relaxations in NPL recognition standards helped hide the bad loans on the banks' books. This has created big problems for the lenders, especially the small regional banks that tend to be thin in capital bases and liquidity but are burdened with NPLs. As of June 2020, there were four thousand regional banks operating with a quarter of total banking assets (Bloomberg 2020c). After isolated cases of bank failures in 2019, there were a string of restructurings and mergers of smaller banking institutions in 2020, as the latter were increasingly squeezed on both the funding and lending sides in the financial market. Given the fact that small and regional banks have been the main source for lending for SMEs, their increased financial vulnerability will be a further blow to the private sector, posing risks to the financial system.

Apart from rising debt levels, measured against China's structural imperative of economic rebalancing, this episode of disruption and recovery is likely to cause setbacks in the medium to longer term. Public investment, again, trumped private consumption as the main driver of growth. Although the national investment rate was steady in 2020, the increased infrastructure investment made up for the decrease in private investment. This is reflected in the augmented government debt, with LGFVs jumping almost 30 percent of GDP, compared with a growth of 10 percent of GDP for corporate debt, from 2019 to 2020.

At the same time, weak labor markets and a lack of government income support have seen a drop in the share of household disposable income in GDP. Given this drop in disposable income, especially that of low-income earners, and an increase in precautionary savings, private consumption has been lagging behind the rebound in investment led by government and the SOEs. In fact, using retail sales, which dropped 3.9 percent in 2020, as a proxy, private consumption will be likely to shrink on a similar scale for 2020 despite robust public investment and industrial outputs. This overinvestment trend was also reflected in China's external imbalance, with current account surpluses almost doubling, reaching 1.9 percent of GDP in 2020, compared to 1 percent in 2019 (see figure 11.5).

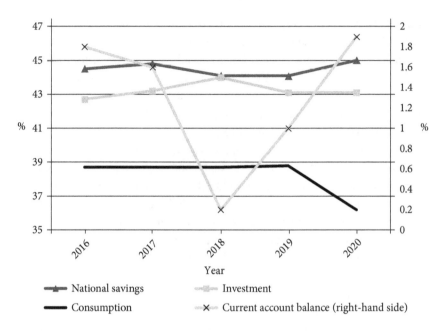

FIGURE 11.5.   COVID-19 and rebalancing.

Sources: National Bureau of Statistics of China; IMF 2021.

Beijing's similar responses to the GFC and COVID-19, centered on state-led, debt-driven infrastructure investment, are reflective of the statist mentality in China. However, this comes with a higher price tag for the years to come, in terms of the much-needed reforms to its growth model and economic rebalancing toward private consumption.

The general findings of this chapter echo those of Chen (2016, 237) at a Reserve Bank of Australia symposium, who noted that since the global financial crisis in 2008–9 and under the current party leadership, "little progress has been made" with rebalancing. Despite some positive movement on wages, consumption, and savings reductions, the momentum behind internal rebalancing is still too limited. In addition, the broader direction of favoring the state sector against the market and the private sector is threatening to further constrain what has been China's main engine of growth over recent decades. For a regime that has made many astute decisions regarding economic development over the last four decades, the current regime now poses major risks to China's future. China's authoritarian regime now seems incapable of making tough decisions about the economy, and especially decisions that reduce the role of the state or confront vested interests aligned with the state sector. Amid a secular decline in growth, the prevalence of short-term growth targets and fears that economic restructuring might drive up unemployment and lead to social unrest appear to have overwhelmed structural reform and economic rebalancing. As Naughton (2016, 75) puts it, "Fears about the growth rate have blocked effective implementation of critical reforms." Despite the earlier success with the market drive during the reform and opening era, there remains an entrenched statist ideology that animates the current political elite and a vast array of vested interests within the state, the bureaucracy, the SOEs, and local governments. Current arrangements suit these interests, which show few signs of commitment to fundamental reform.

For all the talk about markets and rebalancing, China remains stuck with two faltering growth models. The emergence of a new, consumption-driven growth model was originally facilitated by increased credit flows to the household and private sectors through the rise of shadow banking. For a time, it looked as though financial liberalization and the rise of the market sector were in the passing lane, but in recent years this sector has been eclipsed by a resurgent state sector. Xi's approach to macroeconomic management and the short-term growth imperative, together with an ongoing commitment to the statist project of debt-fueled investment, stands in the way of effective rebalancing. Current attempts to force-feed the old growth model with mounting debt and to stymie or retard the new growth model will most likely only further impede growth. Compared to mounting risks within the financial system, the current statist surge and the dead weight it imposes on the economy pose more serious threats to China. To maintain legitimacy and its grip on power, especially without democratic reforms, the party must deliver sustained economic growth and rising prosperity. Yet the challenges here are apparent. Growth has slowed substantially in recent years, from well below the 10-plus-percent-per-annum averages of prior decades to only around 6 percent or less now. There are also headwinds from an aging population, the decline in the labor force since 2016, and growing environmental constraints, as well as rising tensions with trading partners and the international community. The current statist trajectory is unlikely to bring high-productivity growth and investment returns, both of which have fallen over the last decade. Meanwhile, debt continues to mount. This fragile context would become much worse if a debt and banking crisis actually did occur.

CONCLUSION

One of Deng Xiaoping's original aims at the start of China's economic reform era had been to "turn our banks into genuine banks" (1993a, 193). One might have thought that, subsequently, the banking and financial system might have become the jewel in the crown of China's miraculous economic expansion. Yet in the last four decades, China's banking and financial system has instead evolved into a fragile juggernaut, largely subservient to the ongoing statist growth model. The major state-owned banks top the chart of the world's largest in terms of their balance sheets. They are also expanding into other corners of the world and are the major creditors supporting the state sector and China's SOEs, both domestically and now internationally, perhaps in the largest investment drive by a single country in world history. And yet China's banks are weak and troubled. Their lending is still politicized, and they have increasingly underpinned an unsustainable credit surge to support administratively set economic growth targets. Their major customers, which remain the SOEs, often make more losses than profits and regularly fail to pay back their loans. As we have seen, generations of policy elites have tried in various ways to reform the banking and financial sector, yet such efforts have invariably been embroiled in battles and heated debate across ideational lines and amid political and economic struggles involving entrenched vested interests within the party-state.

China's future depends on whether it can harness a properly functioning financial system to support a coherent and sustainable growth model. Thus far, this crucial nexus has not been achieved despite decades of financial and banking reforms and attempts to alter the growth model. Effective and productive political economies depend on the right combination of state activism and market forces. China has thus far failed to achieve the right combination. The first three decades of economic reform from the late 1970s appeared to be heading in roughly the right direction. Except for the setbacks and the brief freeze on reforms in the immediate aftermath of Tiananmen, liberal elements within the party-state had been more or less dominant and reform had seen an increasing role for markets and private or quasi-private businesses, albeit operating under the hierarchy of the state and the party regime.

This relatively liberal era had seen the incremental and judicious relaxation of state controls and greater liberalization of market forces, to a point where, from the beginning of the 2000s, markets and market-based businesses were clearly driving Chinese economic, employment, and productivity growth (Lardy 2014). In growth model terms, the traditional statist model based on the SOEs and seemingly endless infrastructure investment was being outperformed by the alternate market-based growth model. Nevertheless, the statist and credit-fueled growth model that was ramped up amid the GFC was not wound back after the emergency conditions but has continued to be further expanded under the Xi Jinping regime, with its pronounced reemphasis on statist economic development. The main banks and credit system have been deeply enmeshed in all this. Meanwhile, and despite the growth of the shadow banking sector, which was a further product of the GFC critical juncture, the private-business sector is once again being credit constrained and crowded out by the state sector, with the result that the private sector is losing confidence and is now seeing investment slide.

In terms of institutional change, what we have is a prevailing institutional path of statist economic development supported by powerful actors, with the main credit system still directed to serve statist needs. In many ways since the GFC, this path has only been reinforced. The prevailing theory of institutional analysis and change, historical institutionalism, currently offers two competing accounts: one that emphasizes the "sticky" and constraining nature of institutions and change, and another that gives a greater role to agency and incremental and more flexible patterns of institutional change over time (Bell 2011, 2017). Although usually presented as alternative and indeed competing accounts, both of these dynamics have occurred in the case we have been analyzing.

The continuing statist outcomes in all this reflect the sticky, constrained, conservative, and path-dependent theory of institutional change. Ultimately, however, it is agents who are both institutionally constrained and enabled to create and change institutions. The institutional path in question reflects a strengthening statist ideology among many within the leadership, a huge array of vested interests within the party and bureaucratic elite that benefit from the existing arrangements. This reflects a degree of path dependency whereby prior statist choices have shaped and helped entrench further choices and outcomes in this direction, and a steeply hierarchical Chinese state has been further reinforced by Xi's concentration of power under a one-man rule. In this latter sense in China, institutional change has been very much "power constrained" by key agents (Moe 2015, 297). Financial repression and bank subservience to the statist growth model thus persist despite the presence of market elements marked by efforts to change and modernize banking systems and to introduce at least some commercial criteria in banking operations. Yet there were clear limits or perimeters to such incremental reforms, and directed credit remains a key aspect of the prevailing system.

Nevertheless, for a time after the GFC, it appeared as if this sticky and seemingly entrenched path of institutional change might be challenged or at least altered by the role of those pushing for more liberalizing change among the leadership, and by several key agencies, as well as by those within the informal financial system marked by the rapid rise of shadow banking. Many state actors as well as market actors in businesses and households supported this change because it offered better access to credit and new financial opportunities. The regulatory authorities also pushed a liberalizing agenda and the growth of the shadow banking sector. As we have seen, this alternative path of institutional change was initially prompted by the GFC critical juncture and then further supported by liberalizing and market-oriented ideas and interests in pursuit of more effective market reforms and shifts in the growth model. This path was also supported by growing market momentum based on increasing returns and economic functionality in supporting the highly productive growth of private business and in boosting household consumption as part of helping to reorient the Chinese growth model. This informal and off-the-dominant-path shift was also supported by the fact that it did not constitute a direct attack on the main financial system but grew up in its shadow and became functional for it, especially through off-balance-sheet links back to the main banks. Instead of confronting powerful vested interests head-on, efforts were made to foster developments in sectors *alongside* the existing system. Such efforts to reduce confrontation reflect what Shirk (1993) calls "the political logic of economic reform" in China, with its attempts to produce win-win outcomes. Hence, reformers in the PBC and CBRC supported the expansion of the informal shadow sector that funneled funds into more dynamic sectors of the economy while offering better market-level returns to investors. Over time, as we have seen, this forced the main banks to engage with such competition, which led to greater convergence of practices and interest rates within the system. These changes even helped formally relax elements of China's interest rate regime and financial repression.

The shadow banking sector is now entrenched and remains a major feature of China's changed financial landscape. Nevertheless, much tighter regulation, partly aimed at financial stability, as well as the shift toward statism under the current leadership and the redirection of credit toward the state sector, has seen the growth rate of shadow banking greatly slow in the last few years and now halt. Despite better access to credit and a greater range of financial services, the banking and financial system has not been "commercialized" in any strong sense and in large part still remains at the service of the prevailing statist growth model.

Fundamental change has not been pursued or achieved, and the growth model is increasingly reliant on credit growth. The swing toward the state sector under the Xi regime and the slowing momentum of the private sector, within a general context of the current economic slowdown, are worrying. The debt-fueled trajectory of economic recovery from the COVID-19 pandemic makes it clear that state capitalism will stay rather than fade. If so, then it is unrealistic to expect the prevailing bank-SOE nexus to be wound back, a situation that highlights the question of how to deflate the debt incurred by the predominantly loss-making SOEs operating under the prevailing system of soft-budget constraints. Thus far, China's growth is increasingly debt driven, with continued bulging SOE debts. The debt issue, in both the local-government and corporate sectors, has been further exacerbated by a structural slowdown of the economy from double-digit growth to below 7 percent in recent years.

The fundamental problem thus relates to the limited progress in rebalancing the economy and altering the growth model. An important facet of this has been on the demand side of the economy, constrained by the limited gains in reducing savings. The high savings rate has placed big limits on household consumption growth relative to GDP, and remains a key problem inhibiting effective rebalancing. This failure to reduce savings and boost household consumption stems from the continuing pressure for discretionary saving, which in turn is driven by the low share of labor income in national output, weaknesses in welfare systems, and the high actual or potential costs of health care and education, as well as pressures to save for a deposit in the property market. The high level of savings means that monetary resources that are used less for consumption are funneled through the main banks that continue to fuel the credit needs of the statist growth model on the supply side of the economy. The state is central in shaping both the supply and demand sides of the economy in these terms. It sets the broader conditions that encourage or even force precautionary savings, and that set the limits on consumption growth, which then sees credit and activity ramped up in the state sector. The continuation of this strategy only delays or inhibits economic rebalancing, whereby household consumption takes on a much larger role in driving a more sustainable pattern of growth.

For now, for the current Chinese leadership, the Western model of market capitalism has lost much of the appeal it might have once had, especially after the instability of the GFC and the stock market troubles of 2015–16. Hence, a form of "Beijing Consensus," featuring a strong state directing resources and with the market playing only a complementary role, has more or less become the consensus at the top in the current era (Ramo 2004; Halper 2010). On the economic front, this has led to calls for strengthening the SOEs and the role of the party in the business decisions of the SOEs, as well as a series of strategic industrial policies, such as the *Rejuvenation Program for Ten Industries* and *Made in China 2025*. This has been further reinforced by the idea that the state-mobilized boom in infrastructure, production, and new technology has laid the foundation for long-term economic growth that has made the Chinese economy number two in the world. Given this cognitive turn and the newly found statist confidence in recent years, Beijing has been more assertive, reflected in the reinforcement of Xi Jinping's re-Leninization of the party-state.

All this means that China is encumbered with two faltering growth models. Attempts to make the statist growth model work through higher debt, through efforts to boost and reform the SOEs, through ambitious industrial policies, and through the expansion of domestic infrastructure investment offshore through the Belt and Road Initiative do not instill confidence that major efficiency or productivity gains will be achieved. The current and possibly irreconcilable tensions with the United States and other global players will not help either. The alternative growth model, based on boosting the private sector, the household sector, and the services sector, showed earlier promise, but the gains here have been too shallow and too fragile to withstand another crisis, which is COVID-19.

As for China's banking and financial system, it is becoming larger, even more opaque, and more prone to systemic risk. Debt levels keep growing despite several years of efforts at deleveraging. Indeed, China's financial system resembles a giant Ponzi scheme, with the state sitting atop the pyramid. According the US Securities and Exchange Commission (n.d.), "A Ponzi scheme is an investment fraud that involves the payment of purported returns to existing investors from funds contributed by new investors," with the "false appearance that investors are profiting from a legitimate business." An ordinary Ponzi scheme relies on continued inflows of funds from new investors and tends to collapse when it cannot lure new investors or when investors cash out en masse.

In China's situation, however, such a scheme does not even need to *lure* investors. Despite the options now available through shadow banking, financial repression in the form of capital controls and the continued dominance of state-owned banks still more or less *force* investors to participate in the game so that state fundraisers can pool funds through the banking system, which then discounts returns. New sources of funding vital for the working of the system have, however, partially shifted. True, China's massive savings levels fund much of the credit system, but other sources of credit have shifted somewhat, from trade and capital-account surpluses before the GFC to banking credit expansion and the central bank's credit facilities after the GFC (Shih 2019). In the meantime, the historical returns to this pool of funds have been dismal, if not negative, witnessed by bad debts on the part of the banks and the pileup of probably unsustainable debt in the wider sectors of the economy. So far, the pool of funds is large enough to have enabled the state to avoid any liquidity crises, with the hitherto perceived financial credibility of the state serving as the very foundation for the fraudulent system. However, such credibility is increasingly shaky as debt continues to grow while the economy loses steam and becomes more fragile.

The Chinese state faces a fundamental political dilemma in avoiding the day of reckoning and avoiding dangers in its financial system. The way out will be to reduce savings and the historical debt as well as to turn the financial system more into a legitimate business of commercially driven financial intermediation. As we have argued throughout this book, this will need to involve banking on the growth of private market activity, household consumption, and innovation instead of on the growth of the insatiable steroids of inefficient statism, credit, and debt.

At least in the short-to-medium term, such a move will entail hardship, with growth likely to slow, with a range of SOEs and even banks experiencing difficulties. In any transition period, unemployment is likely to go up and there will be a weakening of credibility and public confidence in the state as the overall guarantor of the economy and the financial system. Indeed, moving forward with serious reforms will be a dangerous enterprise, yet business as usual does not appear to be sustainable. China's road toward economic rebalancing needs sophisticated economic and political statecraft, treading a fine line between stability, reform, and development. China has succeeded here in the past, yet the future is uncertain, and the stakes could not be higher, more so than at any time in the reform era—and not just for China, but also for the wider world economy. Whether the leadership can engineer a soft landing from its mountain of debt and recreate the economy and fulfill Deng's dream of making the banks "genuine banks" will be *the* question for the new century.

Notes

INTRODUCTION

1. The comment was made at the National People's Congress in 2007.

2. Premier Zhu Rongji told US Federal Reserve chair Alan Greenspan in 1994 that "in China even perhaps a 10 percent increase [in interest rates] might not have a great effect because some enterprises have no intention of repaying the money and don't care what the interest rate is." Quoted in Wright and Rosen 2018, 15.

3. Moral hazard can exist when a party to a business or lending transaction is given an incentive to take unusual business risks because the party in question is unlikely to suffer damage, in this case because the state is willing to backstop the banking system for any bad debts.

4. The Financial Stability Board (2013, 1) defines shadow banking as "credit intermediation involving entities and activities (fully or partly) outside of the regular banking system."

5. The major components of bank assets in China are bank loans, investment (including shadow credits), and fixed assets. Another measure of debt used in this book is nonfinancial debt, which accounts for outstanding financing for nonfinancial institutions and includes bank loans, shadow credits, bonds, and equities.

6. Although the official NPL ratio of major banks currently stands at only around 1 percent, the market is skeptical and has already factored in the medium-to-long-term risk of mounting NPLs by shorting bank shares at home and abroad despite their strong profits. Moreover, the credit surge since the GFC is likely to see NPLs grow again.

7. China's strict prudential regulations, embodying the idea that "anything that is not specifically permitted is prohibited," may well be a practice that could be taken more seriously in the West. As the acting head of the general office of the CBRC has stated, China's banking regulations now make it "nearly impossible for exotic financial instruments, such as the ones blamed for the subprime crisis, to exist in China" (quoted in Anderlini 2006).

1. INTERACTIONS BETWEEN CHINA'S GROWTH MODEL AND THE FINANCIAL SYSTEM

1. Author's interview, September 7, 2012, Beijing.

2. "Absolute control" generally means majority ownership by the state, while "strong control" implies an ownership share of between 30 and 50 percent.

2. INTERESTS, IDEAS, INSTITUTIONS, AND THE POLITICS OF BANKING AND ECONOMIC REFORM IN CHINA

1. For example, both Zhou Xiaochuan (former PBC governor) and Guo Shuqing (chairman of the China Banking and Insurance Regulatory Commission) had served as chairman of the China Construction Bank. Liu Mingkang and Shang Fulin were chairman of the Bank of China and the Agricultural Bank of China, respectively, before taking over the CBRC.

2. Author's interview, August 2005, Beijing.

3. GROWTH MODEL REFORM AND THE BANKS AS THE STATE'S CASHIER, 1979–96

1. For example, in 1952, the PBC handled 92.8 percent of total savings and deposits and 90 percent of all financial transactions. In 1957, the PBC managed twenty thousand branches and one hundred thousand rural financial institutions (Miyashita 1966, 117).

2. Chen was also the first secretary of the Central Disciplinary Committee of the CCP between 1978 and 1987.

3. "Zhonghang luodi, Nonghang jin cheng, Gonghang jin cun, Jianhang jin chang."

4. Author's interview with a China Banking Regulatory Commission official, April 9, 2012, Beijing.

4. QUICK-FIX BANKING REFORMS AFTER THE ASIAN CRISIS, 1997–2002

1. Author's interview with a PBC official, July 26, 2006, Beijing.

2. Author's interview with a PBC official, July 26, 2006, Beijing.

3. Author's interview, September 14, 2015, Beijing.

5. FURTHER BANKING REFORMS, 2003–8

1. BOCOM is often seen as a nonlisted joint stock bank, but it had also been seen as a form of state bank, with the MOF as a major shareholder (owning about 30 percent of the capital). Moreover, the bank was also asked to provide loans in the same manner as the Big Four. In 2007, the CBRC defined BOCOM as a state-owned bank in the CBRC's published banking statistics.

2. Author's interview with a PBC official, October 12, 2010, Beijing.

3. For example, the number of staff in charge of financial regulation in a provincial-level center branch is set at twenty-five, compared to four hundred who deal with monetary policy issues (Liang 2006).

4. For an empirical discussion of the variety of supervisory models, see Arnone and Gambini (2007).

5. Author's interview with a PBC official, July 17, 2009, Beijing.

6. Author's interview with a PBC official, July 17, 2009, Beijing.

7. Author's interview with a PBC official, October 12, 2010, Beijing.

8. Author's interview with a PBC official, July 17, 2009, Beijing.

9. Author's interview with a PBC official, July 17, 2009, Beijing.

10. According to Article 9 of CBRC (2003), "Where the combined equity investment proportion of all overseas financial institutions in a nonlisted Chinese financial institution is equal to or exceeds 25 percent, the nonlisted Chinese financial institution shall be treated as a foreign-funded financial institution by the regulatory authority."

11. Author's interview with a former PBC and Huijin official, October 8, 2010, Beijing.

12. The MOF's "purchase" of foreign reserves from the PBC by issuing treasury bonds was intermediated by the ABC, as the PBC by law could not purchase treasury bonds directly after 1995.

13. Author's interview with a PBC official, July 26, 2006, Beijing.

6. THE GFC AND STATE CAPITALISM ON STEROIDS

1. Author's interview, May 5, 2014, Brisbane.

2. Author's interview, September 24, 2012, Beijing.

7. THE GFC CRITICAL JUNCTURE AND THE RISE OF SHADOW BANKING

1. The shadow banks involve nonbank financial institutions, mainly trust companies and stock brokerages, that help package loans with higher lending rates into wealth management products, which are in turn sold to retail and institutional investors with higher returns than administered deposit rates.

8. SHADOW BANKING AFTER THE GFC

1. Author's interviews with multiple officials from the PBC and the CBRC, September 21, 2011; September 24, 2011; September 25, 2013; September 21, 2014, Beijing.

2. Author's interview by telephone, April 11, 2016.

3. Author's interview, September 25, 2015, Beijing.

4. In a traditional credit card transaction, fees paid by merchants are usually split in half between banks and payment processors (card companies). However, for transactions on a third-party platform, banks receive much less in fees.

9. THE POLITICS OF BANKING REGULATION AND REFORM

1. Author's interviews with PBC and CBRC officials, September 2013 and September 2016, Beijing.

2. Author's interview, September 29, 2016, Beijing.

3. On July 18, 2015, the PBC, together with nine other ministries, issued its first major regulatory package in this sector, entitled *The Guiding Opinions on Promoting the Healthy Development of Internet Finance*. These guidelines, together with another set of draft rules released on July 31, 2015, introduced China's first regulatory regime for internet finance with a series of regulatory principles, such as establishing the online third-party depository and custodian system for customers' funds, as well as information disclosure, risk disclosure, and a qualified investor system. These measures aim to protect consumer rights and interests, and strengthen network and information security as well as statistical-monitoring and information-sharing mechanisms (Feng 2017c).

10. MOUNTING DEBT AND LURKING RISKS

1. Author's interviews, September 19, 2016, Beijing.

2. This excludes government assets and therefore measures only gross debt. It does not include the liabilities of SOEs and other state entities. See Zhang and Barnett (2014, 4) for an extensive explanation.

3. For example, in July 2017, the MOF discovered that in 2015, Zhumadian County in Henan Province used $120 million of taxpayers' funds to meet the debt obligations of one of its financing vehicles. It was the third local government caught in such a manner in the first half of 2017 (Tang 2017).

4. In accounting terms, debt-swapping bonds are part of the local government special bonds.

5. A good example is the case of Dongbei Special Steel, an SOE in Liaoning Province. Since March 2016, the steelmaker has defaulted on the repayment of seven bonds with a combined value of RMB 3.1 billion. Its largest shareholder, holding 46 percent of its shares, is the Liaoning provincial government. It presented a proposal whereby banks would swap 70 percent of the debt owed to them for equity while underwriters of the bonds would lend the steelmaker the remaining 30 percent to repay the outstanding bonds. Understandably this raised objections from bondholders, including from one of China's three policy banks—the China Development Bank, the lead underwriter for three of the bonds. In response, the bondholders called on the authorities to bar the Liaoning government

and all firms in the province from all forms of borrowing and called on all financial institutions not to purchase any bonds issued by them (Zhang 2016).

6. In 2012, Huaxia Bank issued the first WMP to default, though the investment was made good after intervention from an anonymous third party. Since then, a range of WMPs have defaulted, with retail investors generally being compensated (Chen and Kang 2018, 10).

11. CHINA'S TROUBLED ROAD TO ECONOMIC REBALANCING

1. Disposable-income data are from the statistics section of the National Bureau of Statistics website; mortgage-repayment data are from the mortgage calculation tool on Lianjia.com.

References

ACFIC (All-China Federation of Industry and Commerce). 2016. *Survey Report on the Development of Small and Medium-Sized Enterprises.*

Aligica, Paul, and Vlad Tarko. 2012. "State Capitalism and the Rent-Seeking Conjecture." *Constitutional Political Economy* 23 (4): 357–79.

Almanac of China's Finance and Banking 2004. 2004. Beijing: Zhongguo Jinrong Chubanshe.

Almanac of China's Finance and Banking 2009. 2009. Beijing: Zhongguo Jinrong Chubanshe.

An Authoritative Person [pseud.] [Liu He]. 2016. "Kaiju shouji wen dashi" [The prospect of the economy based on the first quarter]. *People's Daily*, May 9, 2016.

Anderlini, Jamil. 2006. "China Says West's Lack of Market Oversight Led to the Subprime Crisis." *Financial Times*, May 28, 2006.

——. 2010. "China Banks Resigned to Defaults." *Financial Times*, July 28, 2010.

——. 2014a. "China Bank Regulators Caught in Turf War." *Financial Times*, April 9, 2014.

——. 2014b. "Into the Shadows: Risky Business, Global Threat." *Financial Times*, June 15, 2014.

Ang, Andrew, Jennie Bai, and Hao Zhou. 2015. "The Great Wall of Debt: Real Estate, Political Risk, and Chinese Local Government Financing Cost." Georgetown McDonough School of Business Research Paper no. 2603022.

Archer, Margaret. 2000. "For Structure: Its Reality, Properties and Powers; A Reply to Antony King." *Sociological Review* 48:464–72.

Ariyoshi, Akira, Karl Habermeier, Bernard Laurens, Inci Otker-Robe, Jorge Ivan Canales-Kriljenko, and Andrei Kirilenko. 2000. "Capital Controls: Country Experiences with Their Use and Liberalization." Occasional Paper no. 190. International Monetary Fund.

Armstrong-Taylor, Paul. 2016. *Debt and Distortion: Risks and Reforms in the Chinese Financial System.* London: Palgrave Macmillan.

Arnone, Marco, and Andrew Gambini. 2007. "Architectures of Supervisory Authorities and Banking Supervision." In *Designing Financial Supervision Institutions: Independence, Accountability and Governance*, edited by Donato Masciandaro and Marc Quintyn, 93–110. Cheltenham: Edward Elgar.

Australian Treasury. 2012. "The Familiar Pattern of Chinese Consumption Growth." *Economic Roundup*, no. 4, December 12, 2012.

Baccaro, Lucio, and Jonas Pontussen. 2016. "Re-thinking Comparative Political Economy: The Growth Model Perspective." *Politics and Society* 44 (2): 175–207.

Bach, David, Abraham Newman, and Steven Weber. 2006. "The International Implications of China's Fledgling Regulatory State: From Product Maker to Rule Maker." *New Political Economy* 11 (4): 499–518.

Bai, Chong-En, and Qiong Zhang. 2018. "Is the People's Republic of China's Current Slowdown a Cyclical Downturn or a Long-Term Trend? A Productivity-Based Analysis." In *Slowdown in the People's Republic of China: Structural Factors and the Implications for Asia*, edited by Justin Yifu Lin, Peter J. Morgan, and Guanghua Wan, 181–219. Tokyo: Asian Development Bank Institute.

Banker. 2011. "Top 1000 World Banks 2011." June 30, 2011. https://www.thebanker. com/Top-1000-World-Banks/Top-1000-World-Banks-2011?ct=true.

——. 2020. "Top 1000 World Banks 2020." https://www.thebanker.com/Top-1000.

Barboza, David. 2012. "The Imbalances of China's Economy." *New York Times*, April 11, 2012.

Barnett, Steven, and Shaun Roache. 2014. "What's Lurking in the Shadows of China's Banks." *IMF Blog*, September 15, 2014. https://blogs.imf.org/2014/09/15/ whats-lurking-in-the-shadows-of-chinas-banks/.

BCBS (Basel Committee on Banking Supervision). 2010. "Group of Governors and Heads of Supervision Announces Higher Global Minimum Capital Standards." September 2010.

Bell, Stephen. 2011. "Do We Really Need a New 'Constructivist Institutionalism' to Explain Institutional Change? Defending an Agent-Centred Historical Institutionalism." *British Journal of Political Science* 41 (4): 883–906.

——. 2017. "Historical Institutionalism and New Dimensions of Agency: Bankers, Institutions and the 2008 Crisis." *Political Studies* 65:723–39.

Bell, Stephen, and Hui Feng. 2013. *The Rise of the People's Bank of China: The Politics of Institutional Change*. Cambridge, MA: Harvard University Press.

——. 2019. "Policy Diffusion as Empowerment: Domestic Agency and the Institutional Dynamics of Monetary Policy Diffusion in China." *Globalisations* 16 (6): 919–33.

Bell, Stephen, and Andrew Hindmoor. 2009. *Rethinking Governance: The Centrality of the State in Modern Society*. Cambridge: Cambridge University Press.

——. 2014. "The Ideational Shaping of State Power and Capacity: Winning Battles but Losing the War over Bank Reform in the UK and US." *Government and Opposition* 49:342–68.

——. 2015. *Masters of the Universe, Slaves of the Market*. Cambridge, MA: Harvard University Press.

Bell, Stephen, and Michael Keating. 2018. *Fair Shares: Competing Claims and Australia's Economic Future*. Carlton, Victoria: Melbourne University Press.

Berger, Laurence, George Nast, and Christian Raubach. 2002. "Fixing Asia's Bad-Debt Mess: A Banking Crisis Crippled Asia's Economies in 1997; A Bad Debt Crisis Threatens to Do So Again Unless Governments and Banks Crack Down on Nonperforming Loans." *McKinsey Quarterly* 12:139–45.

Bergera, Allen N., Iftekhar Hasan, and Mingming Zhou. 2009. "Bank Ownership and Efficiency in China: What Will Happen in the World's Largest Nation?" *Journal of Banking and Finance* 33 (1): 113–30.

Bernanke, Ben. 2005. "The Global Savings Glut and the US Current Account Deficit." Federal Reserve Board speeches, Sandridge Lecture, Richmond, Virginia, March 10, 2005. http://www.bis.org/review/r050318d.pdf.

Bisio, Virgilio. 2020. "China's Banking Sector Risks and Implications for the United States." Staff Research Report, US-China Economic and Security Review Commission, May 27, 2020.

Blaauw, Erin. 2013. *Outlook 2014—China: Balancing Reforms and Growth*. Economic Report, Rabobank Economic Research Department, November 13, 2013.

Blanchard, Raymond. 1997. "The Heart of Economic Reform." *China Business Review*, January–February 1997.

Bloomberg. 2014. "China Banks Drained by 'Vampire' Internet Funds." March 25, 2014.

——. 2018. "China's Peer-to-Peer Lenders Are Falling Like Dominoes as Panic Spreads." July 20, 2018.

——. 2020a. "China Brokerage Retracts Estimate That Real Jobless Level Is 20%." April 27, 2020.

——. 2020b. "China Corporate Deleveraging Push May Be on Hold for Years." March 29, 2020.

——. 2020c. "China's Failing Small Banks Are Becoming a Big Problem." October 28, 2020.

——. 2021. "China's Growth Beats Estimates as Economy Powers Out of Covid." January 18, 2021.

Blyth, Mark. 2002. *Great Transformations: Economic Ideas and Institutional Change in the Twentieth Century*. Cambridge: Cambridge University Press.

Borst, Nicholas. 2013. "China's Credit Boom: New Risks Require New Reforms." Peterson Institute for International Economics, *Policy Brief*, October 2013.

Bowman, Joel, Mark Hack, and Miles Waring. 2018. "Non-bank Financing in China." Reserve Bank of Australia, March 15, 2018.

Bradley, Bardner. 2011. "Monetary Controls and Bank Reform in China." *Economonitor*, April 12, 2011.

Bradsher, Keith, and Arnie Tsang. 2016. "Stock Markets Shudder after Chinese Stock Plunge Forces a Trading Halt." *New York Times*, January 7, 2016.

Bremmer, Ian. 2009. "State Capitalism Comes of Age: The End of the Free Market?" *Foreign Affairs* 88 (3): 40–55.

——. 2020. *The End of the Free Market: Who Wins the War between States and Corporations?* New York: Portfolio.

Breslin, Shaun. 2011. "China and the Crisis: Global Power, Domestic Caution and Local Initiative." *Contemporary Politics* 17:185–200.

Brink, Tobias. 2012. "Perspectives on the Development of the Private Business Sector in China." *China: An International Journal* 10 (3): 1–19.

Brugger, Bill, and David Kelly. 1991. *Chinese Marxism in Flux*. Stanford, CA: Stanford University Press.

Bucknall, Kevin B. 1989. *China and the Open Door Policy*. Sydney: Allen & Unwin.

Burns, Lawton Robert, and Gordon G. Liu. 2017. *China's Healthcare System and Reform*. Cambridge: Cambridge University Press.

Cai, Yongshun. 2005. "China's Moderate Middle Class: The Case of Homeowners' Resistance." *Asian Survey* 45 (5): 777–99.

Callahan, William A. 2004. "National Insecurities: Humiliation, Salvation, and Chinese Nationalism." *Alternatives* 29 (2): 199–218.

Calomiris, Charles W., and Stephen H. Haber. 2014. *Fragile by Design: The Political Origins of Banking Crises and Scarce Credit*. Princeton, NJ: Princeton University Press.

Campbell, John L. 2004. *Institutional Change and Globalization*. Princeton, NJ: Princeton University Press.

Campion, Mary K., and Rebecca M. Neumann. 2003. *Compositional Effects of Capital Controls—Theory and Evidence*. London: Blackwell.

Cao Fengqi, ed. 2006. *Zhongguo shangye yinhang gaige yu chuangxin* [China's commercial banks reform and innovation]. Beijing: Zhongguo Jinrong Chubanshe.

Capoccia, Giovanni, and R. Daniel Kelemen. 2007. "The Study of Critical Junctures: Theory, Narrative, and Counterfactuals in Historical Institutionalism." *World Politics* 59:341–69.

CBIRC (China Banking and Insurance Regulatory Commission). 2021a. "Banking Sector Assets and Liabilities in 2020 (Monthly)." January 28, 2021.

https://www.cbirc.gov.cn/cn/view/pages/ItemDetail.html?docId=963085&item
Id=954&generaltype=0.

——. 2021b. "Major Regulatory Indicators of Commercial Banks, 2020 (quarterly)."
https://www.cbirc.gov.cn/cn/view/pages/ItemDetail.html?docId=966727&item
Id=954&generaltype=0.

CBRC (China Banking Regulatory Commission). 2003. "Measures for the Administration of Equity Investment by Overseas Financial Institutions in Chinese-
Funded Financial Institutions." December 5, 2003. https://www.qidulp.com/
article/p/2990/.

——. 2007. "The Guidelines on the Implementation of the New Basel Accord by China's Banking Sector." November 14, 2007. http://www.cbrc.gov.cn/EngdocView.
do?docID=200703190C3356986BEDAB3AFF45DA32BF983500.

——. 2009. *Annual Report 2008*. Beijing: CBRC.

——. 2010. *Annual Report 2009*. Beijing: CBRC.

——. 2012. *Annual Report 2011*. Beijing: CBRC.

Central Committee of the Chinese Communist Party. 2011. *The 12th Five-Year
Plan for Economic and Social Development of the People's Republic of China,
2011–2015*.

——. 2014a. "Communiqué of the Third Plenary Session of the 18th Central Committee of the Communist Party of China." January 15, 2014. http://www.china.org.
cn/china/third_plenary_session/2014-01/15/content_31203056.htm.

——. 2014b. "Decision of the Central Committee of the Communist Party of China on
Some Major Issues concerning Comprehensively Deepening the Reform." January 16, 2014. http://www.china.org.cn/china/third_plenary_session/2014-01/16/
content_31212602.htm.

——. 2016. *The 13th Five-Year Plan for Economic and Social Development of the People's Republic of China, 2016–2020*.

Chamon, Marcos, and Eswar Prasad. 2008. "Why Are Saving Rates of Urban Households in China Rising?" IMF Working Paper no. 08/145, January 2008.

——. 2010. "Why Are Saving Rates of Urban Households in China Rising?" *American
Economic Journal: Macroeconomics* 2 (1): 93–130.

Chancellor, Edward. 2010. "China's Red Flags." GMO White Paper, March 2010. http://
georgiancapital.ca/gcpwp123/wp-content/uploads/2017/02/GMO_White_
Paper_Chinas_Red_Flags.pdf.

Chang, Gordon. 2002. *The Coming Collapse of China*. London: Arrow.

Chang, Xiao, Tongliang An, Pui Sun Tam, and Xinhua Gu. 2020. "National Savings
Rate and Sectoral Income Distribution: An Empirical Look at China." *China
Economic Review* 61:1–15. https://doi.org/10.1016/j.chieco.2019.01.002.

Chen Caihong. 1995. "Chengli zhengcexing yewude yinhang bushi zuihao de xuanze"
[Creating policy banks is not the best choice]. *Gaige* 2:28–33.

Chen, Feng. 1999. "An Unfinished Battle in China: The Leftist Criticism of the Reform
and the Third Thought Emancipation." *China Quarterly* 158 (June): 447–67.

Chen, Ke. 1998. "China's Economy Chief Plans to Speed Financial Reform—Zhu
Rongji Emerges as Leading Candidate to Take Prime Minister Post." *Wall Street
Journal*, March 1, 1998.

Chen, Sally, and Joong Shik Kang. 2018. "Credit Booms—Is China Different?" IMF
Working Paper no. 18/2, January 5, 2018.

Chen, Xindong. 2016. "Discussion." In *Structural Change in China: Implications for
Australia and the World*, edited by Iris Day and John Simon, 237–40. Sydney:
Reserve Bank of Australia.

Chen Yanpeng. 2013. "Guoziwei hanyuan: Bugui women guan" [SASAC claims wronged: Not in our control]. *Huaxia shibao*, January 11, 2013. http://www.chinatimes.cc/pages/126081/moreInfo.htm.

China Banking News. 2002. "Yinjianhui dansheng ji" [The lead-up to the establisment of the CBRC]. April 29, 2002.

——. 2020. "Assets under Management of China's 68 Trust Companies Drop 4.85% YoY in 2019." March 23, 2020. https://www.chinabankingnews.com/2020/03/23/assets-under-management-of-chinas-68-trust-companies-drop-4-85-yoy-in-2019/.

China Daily. 2013. "Market to Play 'Decisive' Role in Allocating Resources." November 12, 2013.

——. 2016. "China's Economy to Follow 'L-shaped' Trajectory for Foreseeable Future." May 9, 2016. http://www.chinadaily.com.cn/business/2016-05/09/content_2516 7774.htm.

——. 2017. "President Xi Urges Stronger Financial Regulation to Contain Risks." July 16, 2017.

——. 2020. "NBS: China's GDP Grows 4.9% in Q3." October 19, 2020.

——. 2021. "Chinese Banking Sector Assets Up 10.1% in 2020." January 25, 2021.

Chi Fulin. 2012. "Chi Fulin Talks about Consumption Dominating China's Big Transition Strategy." China.com.cn, March 6, 2012. http://fangtan.china.com.cn/2012-03/06/ content_24817744.htm.

Chong Min. 1995. "Zhiding yu pochan xiangpipei de caishui jinrong zhengce" [Making fiscal and financial policies compatible with bankruptcy]. *Caimao jingji*, no. 2, 25–30.

Chu, Tianshu, and Qiang Wen. 2017. "Can Income Inequality Explain China's Saving Puzzle?" *International Review of Economics and Finance* 52:222–35.

Clarke, Donald. 2003. "Corporatisation, Not Privatisation." *China Economic Quarterly* 7 (3): 27–30.

Clarke, Donald, and Fang Lu. 2017. "The Law of China's Local Government Debt: Local Government Financing Vehicles and Their Bonds." *American Journal of Comparative Law* 65 (4): 751–98.

Clarke, Simon, and Tim Pringle. 2009. "Can Party-Led Trade Unions Represent Their Members?" *Post-Communist Economies* 21 (1): 85–101.

Clennam, Arthur. 2012. "Sector Report: Chinese Banking." *Global Finance*, June 6, 2012.

Collier, Andrew. 2017. *Shadow Banking and the Rise of Capitalism in China*. London: Palgrave Macmillan.

Cong Xiangping. 1996. "Guanyu fei yinhang jinrong jigou xinyong kuozhang wenti de fenxi he zhengce jianyi" [The analysis of the credit expansion of nonbank financial institutions and policy proposals]. *Hongguan jingji yanjiu* 2:21–25.

Cookson, Robert. 2010. "China: Regulators' Turf War Helps Market Take Root." *Financial Times*, March 10, 2010.

Cornell University, Institut Européen d'Administration des Affaires, and World Intellectual Property Organization. 2020. *The Global Innovation Index 2020: Who Will Finance Innovation?* Geneva: World Intellectual Property Organization. https://www.wipo.int/edocs/pubdocs/en/wipo_pub_gii_2020.pdf.

Cortell, Andrew, and Susan Petersen. 1999. "Altered States: Explaining Domestic Institutional Change." *British Journal of Political Science* 29:177–203.

Courtis, Neil. 2006. *How Countries Supervise Their Banks, Insurers and Securities Markets*. London: Central Banking Publications.

Crouch, Colin, and Maarten Keune. 2005. "Changing Dominant Practice: Making Use of Institutional Diversity in Hungary and the United Kingdom." In *Beyond Continuity: Institutional Change in Advanced Political Economies*, edited by Wolfgang Streeck and Kathleen Thelen, 83–102. Oxford: Oxford University Press.

Dai Xianglong. 1994. "Jinrong tizhi gaige de jibeng shilu he nandian" [The basic approaches to and difficulties in reforming the financial system]. *Zhongyang dangxiao baogao xuan* 9:33–41.

——, ed. 2001. *Lingdao ganbu jinrong zhish duben* [Textbook on financial knowledge for leading cadres]. Beijing: Zhongguo Jinrong Chubanshe.

——. 2002. "Zhongguo jinrongye zai gaige zhong fazhan" [The development of the Chinese financial industry with reform]. China-embassy.org, October 11, 2002. http://ru.china-embassy.org/chn/xwdt/t73693.htm.

Davis, Bob. 2011a. "Political Overlords Shackle China's Monetary Mandarins." *Wall Street Journal*, April 15, 2011.

——. 2011b. "Were China's Leaders Conned?" *Wall Street Journal*, June 2, 2011.

DBS (Development Bank of Singapore). 2018. "China Banking Sector." *China/Hong Kong Industry Focus*, October 24, 2018.

Deng Xiaoping. 1993a. "Qiye gaige he jinrong gaige" [Enterprise reform and financial reform]. In *Selected Works of Deng Xiaoping*, vol. 3, 192–93. Beijing: Renmin Chubanshe.

——. 1993b. *Selected Works of Deng Xiaoping Volume 3*. Beijing: Renmin Chubanshe.

——. 1993c. "Shicha Shanghai shi de tanhua" [Speech during the tour of Shanghai]. In *Selected Works of Deng Xiaoping*, vol. 3, 366–67. Beijing: Renmin Chubanshe.

Dickson, Bruce. 2008. *Wealth into Power: The Communist Party's Embrace of the Private Sector*. Cambridge: Cambridge University Press.

Ding, X. L. 1994. "Institutional Amphibiousness and the Transition from Communism: The Case of China." *British Journal of Political Science* 24 (3): 293–318.

Ding Xiaoqiang. 2018. "Hunhe suoyouzhi gaige zenyang rang siying bumen fangxin" [How to make the private sector not worry about the mixed ownership reform]. *Zhongguo zhengquanbao*, November 11, 2018.

Dittmer, Lowell. 1992. "Patterns of Leadership in Reform China." In *State and Society in China: The Consequences of Reform*, edited by A. L. Rosenbaum, 13–30. Boulder, CO: Westview.

——. 1995. "Chinese Informal Politics." *China Journal* 34 (July): 1–34.

Dittmer, Lowell, and Yu-shan Wu. 1995. "The Modernization of Factionalism in Chinese Politics." *World Politics* 47 (July): 467–94.

Eaton, Sarah. 2016. *The Advance of the State in Contemporary China: State-Market Relations in the Reform Era*. Cambridge: Cambridge University Press.

Economist. 2012. "State Capitalism: The Visible Hand." January 21, 2012.

——. 2016. "When a Bubble Is Not a Bubble." October 15, 2016.

Economy, Elizabeth. 2018a. "China's New Revolution: The Reign of Xi Jinping." *Foreign Affairs*, May–June 2018.

——. 2018b. *The Third Revolution: Xi Jingping and the New Chinese State*. Oxford: Oxford University Press.

Elliott, Douglas, Arthur Kroeber, and Yu Qiao. 2015. *Shadow Banking in China: A Primer*. Economic Studies at Brookings. Washington DC: Brookings Institution.

Elliott, Douglas, and Yu Qiao. 2015. *Reforming Shadow Banking in China*. Brookings Institution, May 2015.

Er Jin, ed. 1999. *Guojia jinrong anquan baogao* [A report on the financial safety of the country]. Beijing: Zhongyang Dangxiao Chubanshe.

Eslake, Saul. 2020. "Is Time Running Out for the Chinese Economy?" *Inside Story*, August 17, 2020.

Fan Gang. 2010. "Getting Economic Recipe Right." *China Daily*, July 2, 2010.

Fan Jianping. 2009. "Guojia xinxi zhongxin jingji yuce bu zhuren: Kaiensi zhuyi nan jiushi" [Director of Economic Prediction Department at State Information Centre: Keynesianism cannot save the market]. 163.com, January 10, 2009. http://money.163.com/09/0110/09/4V9O1O3N00253529.html.

Fang, Jason, and Michael Walsh. 2018. "Made in China 2025: Beijing's Manufacturing Blueprint and Why the World Is Concerned." ABC News, April 28, 2018. https://www.abc.net.au/news/2018-04-29/why-is-made-in-china-2025-making-people-angry/9702374.

Feng, Hui. 2006a. "The Emergence of a Modern Payment Infrastructure in China." *Settlement, Payment, E-money and E-trading Development* 1 (2): 17–21.

——. 2006b. "How the People's Bank Is Shaping China's Financial Sector." *Central Banking* 17 (1): 35–41.

——. 2006c. *The Politics of China's Accession into the World Trade Organisation: The Deeragon Goes Global.* London: Routledge.

——. 2007a. "Broken China: Fixing a Fragile Regulatory Framework." *Financial Regulator* 12 (2): 43–48.

——. 2007b. "China's New Reserve Strategy." *Central Banking* 17 (3): 29–36.

——. 2009. "Beijing's Precarious Balancing Act." *Central Banking* 20 (2): 39–43.

——. 2011. "Beijing's Second Thought." *Central Banking* 22 (2): 64–68.

——. 2012. "The Beginning of the End." *Central Banking* 23 (1): 43–47.

——. 2017a. "Achieving the China Dream or Facing a Minsky Moment: China after the 19th Party Congress." CPI Analysis, October 2, 2017. https://cpianalysis.org/2017/10/27/achieving-the-china-dream-or-facing-a-minsky-moment-china-after-the-19th-party-congress/.

——. 2017b. "Internet Finance in China: Digital Disruption and Regulatory Dilemma." In *Digital Disruption: Impact on Business Models, Regulation and Financial Crime*, edited by David Chaikin and Derwent Coshott, 53–68. Sydney: Australian Scholarly Publisher.

——. 2017c. "Zhou Did Not Get What He Wanted, but Has Not Left Empty-Handed." Central Banking, August 8, 2017. https://www.centralbanking.com/central-banks/financial-stability/3279476/zhou-did-not-get-what-he-wanted-but-has-not-left-empty-handed.

——. 2019. "The China-Trump Trade War Has Spread to Australia: We're Now at Risk of Global Currency War." The Conversation, August 7, 2019. https://theconversation.com/the-china-trump-trade-war-has-spread-to-australia-were-now-at-risk-of-global-currency-war-121486.

——. 2020. "PBoC's Post-pandemic Policy Is Still Up in the Air." Central Banking, May 18, 2020. https://www.centralbanking.com/central-banks/monetary-policy/unconventional-monetary-policy/7546716/pbocs-post-pandemic-policy-is-still-up-in-the-air.

Feng Ximing. 2017. "Jiemi yingzi yanghang" [Revealing the "shadow central bank"]. *Caixin*, May 9, 2017.

Ferri, Giovanni, and Li-Gang Liu. 2010. "Honor Thy Creditors Beforan Thy Shareholders: Are the Profits of Chinese State-Owned Enterprises Real?" *Asian Economic Papers* 9 (3): 50–71.

Fewsmith, Joseph. 1994. *Dilemmas of Reform in China: Political Conflict and Ecoomic Debate.* Armonk, NY: M. E. Sharpe.

——. 1996. "Institutions, Informal Politics, and Political Transition in China." *Asian Survey* 36 (3): 230–46.

——. 1998. "Jiang Zemin Takes Command." *Current History*, September 1998.

——. 1999. "China and the WTO: The Politics behind the Agreement." *NBR Analysis* 10 (5): 23–39.

——. 2001a. *Elite Politics in Contemporary China*. Armonk, NY: M. E. Sharpe.

——. 2001b. "The Political and Social Implications of China's Accession to the WTO." *China Quarterly* 167:573–91.

——. 2013. *The Logic and Limits of Political Reform in China*. Cambridge: Cambridge University Press.

——. 2014. "Mao's Shadow." *China Leadership Monitor*, March 14, 2014.

Financial Stability Board. 2013. *Global Shadow Banking Monitoring Report 2013*.

——. 2017. *Global Shadow Banking Monitoring Report 2017*.

——. 2018. *Global Shadow Banking Monitoring Report 2018*.

Fitch Ratings. 2016. "Banks' Mainland China Exposure Remains a Key Risk." June 7, 2016.

——. 2020. "China's Corporate Bond-Market Stress May Persist in 2021." November 16, 2020.

Fong, Dominique, Junya Qian, and Yifan Xie. 2016. "In Shanghai, Couples Rush to Divorce to Buy Property Later." *Wall Street Journal*, August 29, 2016.

Forbes. 2019. "Alibaba's 11/11 Singles' Day by the Numbers: A Record $38 Billion Haul." November 11, 2019. https://www.forbes.com/sites/sergeiklebnikov/2019/11/11/alibabas-1111-singles-day-by-the-numbers-a-record-38-billion-haul/?sh=784708ef2772.

Frazier, Mark W. 2014. "State Schemes or Safety Nets? China's Push for Universal Coverage." *Daedalus* 143 (2): 69–80.

Gan, Nectar. 2018. "Xi Says It's Wrong to 'Bad Mouth' China's State Firms . . . but Country Needs Private Sector as Well." *South China Morning Post*, September 28, 2018.

Gao Xin, and He Pin. 1993. *Zhu Rongji zhuan: Cong fandang youpai dao Deng Xiaoping jichengren* [A biography of Zhu Rongji: From antiparty rightist to one of Deng Xiaoping's successors]. Taipei: Xin Xinwen Wenhua.

Gardner, Bradley. 2011. "Monetary Controls and Bank Reform in China." *Economonitor*, April 12, 2011.

Garnaut, Ross, and Yasheng Huang. 2005. "The Risks of Investment-Led Growth." In *The China Boom and Its Discontents*, edited by Ross Garnaut and Ligang Song, 1–19. Canberra: Asia Pacific Press.

Garrett, Banning. 2001. "China Faces, Debates, the Contradictions of Globalization." *Asian Survey* 41 (3): 409–27.

Geiger, Michael. 2008. "Instruments of Monetary Policy in China and Their Effectiveness: 1994–2006." Discussion Papers, United Nations Conference on Trade and Development.

Gerschenkron, Alexander. 1962. *Economic Backwardness in Historical Perspctive*. Cambridge, MA: Harvard University Press.

Gilley, Bruce. 2000. "Moment of Truth: China Opts to Tread Softly on Debt Recovery—but the Price of Preserving Stability May Be a Huge Bill Later." *Far Eastern Economic Review* 6 (15): 23–30.

Girardin, Eric. 1997. *Banking Sector Reform and Credit Control in China*. Paris: OECD Development Centres.

Goldman Sachs. 2016. *Walled In: China's Great Dilemma*. January 2016. https://www.goldmansachs.com/what-we-do/investment-management/private-wealth-management/intellectual-capital/isg-china-insight-2016.pdf.

Green, Stephen. 2003. "'Two-Thirds Privitisation': How China's Listed Companies Are—Finally—Privitising." Chatham House Briefing Note, December 2003.

———. 2005. "Making Monetary Policy Work in China: A Report from Money Market Front Line." Working Paper, Stanford Center for International Development, Stanford University.

Greenspan, Alan. 2007. *The Age of Turbulence*. New York: Penguin.

Gries, Peter Hays. 2001. "Tears of Rage: Chinese Nationalist Reactions to the Belgrade Embassy Bombing.'" *China Journal* 46 (July): 25–43.

Gruber, James. 2013. "China Prepares Big Bang Financial Reforms." *Forbes Asia*, September 26, 2013.

Guanghua School of Management and Du Xiaoman Financial. 2019. *2019 Report on Consumer Credits in China*. December 2019, Beijing.

Guangxi Daily. 2009. "Ma Biao: Qianfang baiji jiakuai 2000 yiyuan xinceng daikuan toufang jindu" [Ma Biao: Speed up the degree of disbursement of the 200 billion in new loans through every means possible]. March 1, 2009.

Guo Shuqing. 2020. "Wanshan xiandai jinrong jianguan tixi" [Improving a modern financial regulatory system]. Sina Finance, December 1, 2020. https://finance.sina.cn/bank/yhgd/2020-12-01/detail-iiznctke4230566.d.html.

Guo, Yong. 2002. *Banking Reforms and Monetary Policy in the People's Republic of China: Is the Chinese Central Banking System Ready for Joining the WTO?* Basingstoke, UK: Palgrave Macmillan.

Hacker, Jacob S. 2005. "Policy Drift: The Hidden Politics of US Welfare State Retrenchment." In *Beyond Continuity: Institutional Change in Advanced Political Economies*, edited by Wolfgang Streeck and Kathleen Thelen, 40–82. New York: Oxford University Press.

Haitong Securities. 2016. *Zhongguo jiating touzi yu xiaofei yanjiu* [Report on the investment and consumption of Chinese households]. August 2016.

Hall, Peter A., and David Soskice. 2001. "An Introduction to Varieties of Capitalism." In *Varieties of Capitalism: The Institutional Foundations of Comparative Advantage*, edited by Peter A. Hall and David Soskice, 1–13. Oxford: Oxford University Press.

Hall, Peter A., and Rosemary C. R. Taylor. 1996. "Political Science and the Three New Institutionalisms." *Political Studies* 44:936–57.

Halper, Stefan. 2010. *The Beijing Consensus: How China's Authoritarian Model Will Dominate the Twenty-First Century*. New York: Basic Books.

Halpern, Nina. 1992. "Information Flows and Policy Coordination in the Chinese Bureaucracy." In *Bureaucracy, Politics, and Decision Making in Post-Mao China*, edited by Kenneth Lieberthal and David M. Lampton, 125–50. Berkeley: University of California Press.

Hamrin, Carol Lee, and Suisheng Zhao. 1995. *Decision-Making in Deng's China: Perspectives from Insiders*. Armonk, NY: M. E. Sharpe.

Han, Fei, Emilia Jurzyk, Wei Guo, Yun He, and Nadia Rendak. 2019. "Assessing Macro-financial Risks of Household Debt in China." IMF Working Paper no. 19/258, November 2019.

Han, Miao. 2012. "The People's Bank of China during the Global Financial Crisis: Policy Responses and Beyond." *Journal of Chinese Economic and Business Studies* 10 (4): 361–90.

Han Mingshan. 2006. "Jingji minzu zhuyi yu minzu yinhang ye de weilai" [Economic nationalism and the future of national banking industry]. *Jingji guanli* 11:6–9.

Han Ruiyun. 2010. "Xiantian quexian yinfa difang zhaiwu zhiyou" [Structural deficiencies lead to worries about local government debt]. *21st Century Business Herald*, March 15, 2010.

Han Wei. 2018. "China Seeks Foreign and Private Help in SOE Reform." *Caixin*, November 7, 2018.

Hancock, Tom, and Wang Xueqiao. 2018. "China Millennials' Love of Credit Cards Raises Debt Fears." *Financial Times*, August 6, 2018.

Hart, Brian. 2016. "Creating the Cult of Xi Jinping: The Chinese Dream as a Leader Symbol." *Cornell International Affairs Review* 9 (2): 2–21.

He, Baogang, and Guo Yingjie. 2018. *Nationalism, National Identity and Democratization in China.* London: Routledge.

He Guoqian. 1998. "Zhongguo jingji shichanghua jincheng zhong de huobi zhengce gaige" [China's monetary policy reform in the process of economic liberalisation]. PhD diss., Peking University.

He Keng. 2013. "Kaiensi zhuyi yu zhongguo dangqian de jingji wenti" [Keynesianism and China's current economic problems]. Cnr.cn, July 17, 2013. http://finance.cnr.cn/txcj/201307/t20130717_513077557.shtml.

Heilmann, Sebastian. 2005. "Regulatory Innovation by Leninist Means: Communist Party Supervision in China's Financial Industry." *China Quarterly* 181:1–21.

Helleiner, Eric, and Hongying Wang. 2019. "The Richness of Financial Nationalism: The Case of China." *Pacific Affairs* 92 (2): 211–34.

Holmes, Alex, and David Lancaster. 2019. "China's Local Government Bond Market." *RBA Bulletin*, June 20, 2019.

Hong, Iris. 2020. "Baoshang, China's First Commercial Bank, to Go Bankrupt." *Asia Times Financial*, November 26, 2020.

Hope, David, and David Soskice. 2016. "Growth Models, Varieties of Capitalism, and Macroeconomics." *Politics and Society* 44 (2): 209–26.

Hsieh, Chang-Tai, and Zheng Michael Song. 2015. "Grasp the Large, Let Go of the Small: The Transformation of the State Sector in China." NBER Working Paper no. 21006, March 2015.

Hsu, Sara. 2015. "The Rise and Fall of Shadow Banking in China." *Diplomat*, November 19, 2015.

Hsueh, Roselyn. 2011. *China's Regulatory State: A New Strategy for Globalization.* Ithaca, NY: Cornell University Press.

Hu Angang, and Wang Shaoguang. 1994. *A Report on State Capacity in China.* [In Chinese.] Hong Kong: Oxford University Press.

Hu Jintao. 2007. "Full Text of Hu Jintao's Report at 17th Party Congress." Gov.cn, October 15, 2007. http://www.gov.cn/english/2007-10/24/content_785505.htm.

——. 2012. "Full Text of Hu Jintao's Report at 18th Party Congress." Embassy of the People's Republic of China in the United States of America, November 17, 2012. http://www.china-embassy.org/eng/zt/18th_CPC_National_Congress_Eng/t992917.htm.

Huang, Yasheng. 1996. *Inflation and Investment Controls in China: The Political Economy of Central-Local Relations during the Reform Era.* Cambridge: Cambridge University Press.

——. 2008. *Capitalism with Chinese Characteristics: Entrepreneurship and the State.* Cambridge: Cambridge University Press.

Huang Zhijie. 2009. "Qiangguo zhanlue yuannian: Shida chanye zhenxing guihua diaocha" [First year of national strengthening strategy: A survey of ten industrial stimulus plans]. *Liaowang*, March 17, 2009. http://news.sina.com.cn/c/2009-03-17/112917423857.shtml.

Huang, Zixuan, and Nicolas Lardy. 2016. "China's Rebalance Reflected in Rising Wage Share of GDP." *PIIE China Economic Watch*, October 13, 2016. https://www.piie.com/blogs/china-economic-watch/chinas-rebalance-reflected-rising-wage-share-gdp.

Huang, Yiping, and Xun Wang. 2011. "Does Financial Repression Inhibit or Facilitate Economic Growth? A Case Study of Chinese Economic Experience." *Oxford Bulletin of Economics & Statistics* 73 (6): 833–55.

Huber, John, and Charles R. Shipan. 2002. *Deliberate Discretion? The Institutional Foundations of Bureaucratic Authority.* Cambridge: Cambridge University Press.

Hughes, Christopher. 2006. *Chinese Nationalism in the Global Era.* London: Routledge.

Hung, Ho-fung. 2008. "Rise of China and the Global Overaccumulation Crisis." *Review of International Political Economy* 15 (2): 149–79.

Huo Kan, Wang Changyong, and Wang Jing. 2009. "Can Stimulus Light China's Consumer Fire?" *Caijing*, March 6, 2009. http://english.caijing.com.cn/2009-03-06/110114349.html.

Hurst, William. 2004. "Understanding Contentious Collective Action by Chinese Laid-Off Workers: The Importance of Regional Political Economy." *Studies in Comparative International Development* 39 (2): 94–120.

Ikenberry, John. 1988. "Conclusion: An Institutional Approach to American Foreign Economic Policy." *International Organization* 42 (1): 219–43.

IMF (International Monetary Fund). 2011. *People's Republic of China: Financial System Stability Assessment.* November 2011.

——. 2012. *Article IV Consultation with the People's Republic of China.* July 2012.

——. 2013. *Article IV Consultation with the People's Republic of China.* August 2013.

——. 2014. *Global Financial Stability Report 2014.* April 2014. Washington, DC: IMF Publication Services.

——. 2015. *Article IV Consultation with the People's Republic of China.* August 2015.

——. 2016a. *China: Financial System Stability Assessment 2016.*

——. 2016b. *Global Financial Stability Report.* April 2016.

——. 2016c. *The People's Republic of China: Selected Issues.* August 2016.

——. 2017. *Article IV Consultation with the People's Republic of China.* August 2017.

——. 2019. *Article IV Consultation with the People's Republic of China.*

——. 2021. *2020 Article IV Consultation with the People's Republic of China.* January 2021.

Institute of International Finance. 2021. *COVID Drives Debt Surge—Stabilization Ahead?* February 17, 2021.

International Labor Organization. 2018. *Global Wage Report 2018/19: What Lies behind Gender Pay Gaps.* https://www.ilo.org/wcmsp5/groups/public/---dgreports/---dcomm/---publ/documents/publication/wcms_650553.pdf.

Jia, Hao, and Zhimin Lin. 1994. Introduction to *Changing Central-Local Relations in China: Reform and State Capacity*, edited by Hao Jia and Zhimin Lin, 1–15. Boulder, CO: Westview.

Jiang, Yang. 2015. "Vulgarisation of Keynesianism in China's Response to the Global Financial Crisis." *Review of International Political Economy* 22:360–90.

Jiang Zemin. 2002. "Full Text of Jiang Zemin's Report at 15th Party Congress on Nov. 8, 2002." Ministry of Foreign Affairs, November 18, 2002. http://www.fmprc.gov.cn/mfa_eng/topics_665678/3698_665962/t18872.shtml.

Jin, Jing, and Heng-fu Zou. 2003. "Soft-Budget Constraint on Local Governments in China." In *Fiscal Decentralization and the Challenge of Hard Budget Constraints*, edited by Jonathan A. Rodden, Gunnar S. Eskeland, and Jennie Litvack, 289–324. Cambridge, MA: MIT Press.

Jin, Leroy. 1994. *Monetary Policy and the Design of Financial Institutions in China: 1978–1990*. New York: St. Martin's.

Jin, Luo, Chun Liu, and Yinghui Zhou. 2013. "The Banking System in the Shadow of Sun: To Measure the Scale and the Risk of the Shadow Banking System in China." Cicfconf.org. http://www.cicfconf.org/sites/default/files/paper_7.pdf.

Jing Xuecheng. 1997. "Woguo jinrongye fengxian de xianzhuang" [The status of risks in our country's financial sector]. *Gaige*, no. 1, 12–14.

Jingji cankaobao. 1996. "Guoqi gaige shinian lu" [Ten years of SOE reforms]. January 18, 1996.

Jingji daobao. 1996. "Guoyou yinhang yewu gaige sanbuzou" [Three-step reforms for state-owned banks]. September 2, 1996.

Jingji guancha bao. 2004. "With Xie Ping's Steering, the Central Huijin Company Turns to Be Solid." September 27, 2004.

Jingu, Takeshi. 2014. "Internet Finance Growing Rapidly in China." Nomura Research Institute, vol. 189, March 10, 2014.

Jinron shibao. 2006. "Zhongguo tong Guoji Qingsuan Yinhang hezuo de shinian" [Ten years' cooperation and development between China and BIS]. August 1, 2006.

Ke Dawei. 2018. "China's State Financial Assets Worth About Half of Global GDP." *Caixin*, October 25, 2018.

Kennedy, Andrew Bingham. 2012. *The International Ambitions of Mao and Nehru: National Efficacy Beliefs and the Making of Foreign Policy*. New York: Cambridge University Press.

Keohane, David. 2016. "Authoritative Person Authoritatively Admits China Can't Keep Going This Way." *Financial Times*, May 9, 2016.

Klien, Matthew. 2018. "China's Household Debt Problem." *Financial Times*, March 7, 2018.

Knaack, Peter. 2017. "An Unlikely Champion of Global Finance: Why Is China Exceeding International Banking Standards?" *Journal of Current Chinese Affairs* 46 (2): 41–79.

Koreh, Michal, and Michael Shalev. 2009. "Dialectics of Institutional Change: Transformation of Social Insurance Financing in Israel." *Socio-Economic Review* 7:553–84.

Kornai, Janos. 1986. "The Soft Budget Constraint." *Kyklos* 39 (1): 3–30.

Krasner, Stephen. 1984. "Approaches to the State: Alternative Conceptions and Historical Dynamics." *Comparative Politics* 16:223–46.

Krippner, Greta R. 2011. *Capitalizing on Crisis: The Political Origins of the Rise of Finance*. Cambridge, MA: Harvard University Press.

Kroeber, Arthur R. 2012. *The Chinese Economy*. Oxford: Oxford University Press.

——. 2013. *Xi Jinping's Ambitious Agenda for Economic Reform in China*. Washington, DC: Brookings Institution.

——. 2016. *China's Economy: What Everyone Needs to Know*. Oxford: Oxford University Press.

Kwong, Charles. 2011. "China's Banking Reform: The Remaining Agenda." *Global Economic Review* 40:161–78.

Lam, W. Raphael, and Jingsen Wang. 2018. "China's Local Government Bond Market." IMF Working Paper no. 18/219, September 2018.

Lampton, David, ed. 1987. *Policy Implementation in Post-Mao China*. Berkeley: University of California Press.

Lardy, Nicolas. 1998. *China's Unfinished Economic Revolution*. Washington, DC: Brookings Institution Press.

——. 2001. "China's Worsening Debts." *Financial Times*, June 22, 2001.

——. 2006. "China: Toward a Consumption-Driven Growth Path." Policy Briefs in International Economics. Washington, DC: Institute for International Economics.

——. 2008. "Financial Repression in China." Policy Brief. Washington, DC: Peterson Institute for International Economics.

——. 2011. *Sustaining China's Economic Growth after the Global Financial Crisis.* Washington, DC: Peterson Institute For International Economics.

——. 2012a. "Comments in 'Book Chat, Talking to Authors about Their Work' with David Barboza." *New York Times*, April 11, 2012.

——. 2012b. *Sustaining China's Economic Growth after the Global Financial Crisis.* Washington, DC: Peterson Institute for International Economics.

——. 2014. *Markets over Mao: The Rise of Private Business in China.* Washington, DC: Peterson Institute for International Economics.

——. 2016. *No Need to Panic, China's Banks Are in Pretty Good Shape.* Washington, DC: Peterson Institute for International Economics.

——. 2017. *Focus on Financial Risk Puts China on a More Stable Path.* Washington, DC: Peterson Institute for International Economics.

——. 2019. *The State Strikes Back: The End of Economic Reform in China?* Washington, DC: Peterson Institute for International Economics.

Laris, Michael. 1999. "Chinese Say Bank Insolvent." *Washington Post Foreign Service*, January 12, 1999.

Laudermilk, Baron. 2019. "Chinese Banks Enhancing Direct Banking Channels to Cater to Increased Demand." *Asian Banker*, May 22, 2019. http://www.theasian banker.com/research-notes/chinese-banks-enhancing-direct-banking-channels-to-cater-to-increased-demand.

Laurenceson, James, and Joseph Chai. 2003. *Financial Reform and Economic Development in China.* Cheltenham, UK: Edward Elgar.

Lee, Amanda. 2018. "Why China's Property Market Won't Crash for Now." *South China Morning Post*, May 28, 2018.

——. 2021. "Debt at China's State-Owned Firms in Spotlight as Credit Tightening Raises Default Pressure." *South China Morning Post*, January 14, 2021.

Lee, Il Houng, Murtaza H. Syed, and Liu Xueyan. 2012. "Is China Over-investing and Does It Matter?" IMF Working Paper no. 12/277, November 2012.

Leng, Sidney. 2019. "China's Birth Rate Falls Again, with 2018 Producing the Fewest Babies since 1961, Official Data Shows." *South China Morning Post*, January 21, 2019.

Leutert, Wendy. 2016. "Challenges Ahead in China's Reform of State-Owned Enterprises." *Asia Policy* 21 (January): 83–100.

——. 2018. "Firm Control: Covering the State-Owned Economy under Xi Jinping." *China Perspectives*, no. 1–2, 27–36.

Lewis, W. Arthur. 1954. "Economic Development with Unlimited Supplies of Labour." *Manchester School of Economic and Social Studies* 22 (2): 139–91.

Li Anlan, and Shen Conglin. 2014. *Difang zhili gailun* [General introduction to local governance]. Beijing: Zhongguo Jingji Chubanshe.

Li, Cindy. 2016. "The Changing Face of Shadow Banking in China." *Asia Focus*, Federal Reserve Bank of San Francisco, December 2016.

——. 2018. "China's Household Credit Boom." *Pacific Exchange Blog*, Federal Reserve Bank of San Francisco, January 29, 2018. https://www.frbsf.org/banking/asia-program/pacific-exchange-blog/china-household-credit-boom/.

Li Gang, and Wang Qing. 2014. "Tongye cundan tuidong lilu shichanghua de guoji jingyan" [International experiences of interest rate liberalization through certificate of deposit]. *Yinhangjia* 3:10–13.

Li Mingyang. 2011. "Guojiban chuangli de qianqian houhou" [The background of the establishment of the international board]. *Jinrong shibao*, December 11, 2011.

Li Tao. 2005. "Yingai yuannian 'jinzhi' diaocha" [First year of banking reform, a prudential investigation]. *Chanquan shichang* 1 (1): 21–25.

Li Tong. 2014. "Shadow Banking in China: Expanding Scale, Evolving Structure." *Journal of Financial Economic Policy* 6 (3): 198–211.

Li Weiling. 2006. "Sanjia zhengcexing yinhang gaige jinnian qidong Zhou Xiaochuan qinzi zhihui" [Reform of the three policy banks to be launched this year under personal leadership of Zhou Xiaochuan]. *Guoji jinrong bao*, February 27, 2006.

Li Yang. 2018. *Zhongguo guojia zichan fuzhaibiao 2018* [China's national balance sheet 2018]. Beijing: Zhongguo Shehui Kexue Chubanshe.

Li Yiping. 2009. "GDP yao sudu gengyao zhiliang" [GDP is in need of growth but more of quality]. *Zhonghua gongshang shibao*, July 27, 2009. http://finance.sina.com.cn/roll/20090727/00022971672.shtml.

Li Yizhong. 2013. "Renzhen zongjie yingdui guoji jinrong weiji de jingyan" [Learn from the experience of responding to the global financial crisis]. Sina.com, March 6, 2013. http://finance.sina.com.cn/china/20130306/221814742265.shtml.

Liang Li, Gao De, and He Xin. 2006. *Fang dichan yu Zhongguo hongguan jingji* [The real estate sector and China's macroeconomy]. Beijing: Shehui Kexue Chubanshe.

Liang Zhongde. 2006. "Zhongguo jinrong jianguan de jigou peizhi youhua" [Optimizing the institutional configuration of China's financial regulation]. *Zhongguo zhengquan bao*, May 11, 2006.

Liao Haiqing. 2009. "Siwanyi qiedangao de Henan yangben" [The Henan sample of the 4 trillion cake distribution]. *Nan feng chuang*, March 19, 2009. http://www.nfcmag.com/article/1432.html.

Liao, Min, Tao Sun, and Jingfan Zhang. 2016. "China's Financial Linkages and Implications for Inter-Agency Cooperation." IMF Working Paper no. 16/181, August 2016.

Liao, Rita. 2019. "Alibaba's Alternative to the App Store Reaches 230M Daily Users." TechCrunch, January 29, 2019. https://techcrunch.com/2019/01/29/alibaba-alipay-mini-programs-230m-users/.

Lieberman, Robert C. 2002. "Ideas, Institutions, and Political Order: Explaining Institutional Change." *American Political Science Review* 96:697–712.

Lieberthal, Kenneth, and Michel Oksenberg. 1988. *Policy Making in China: Leaders, Structures, and Processes*. Princeton, NJ: Princeton University Press.

Liew, Leong. 2005. "China's Engagement with Neo-liberalism: Path Dependency, Geography and Party Self-Reinvention." *Journal of Development Studies* 41 (2): 331–52.

Liew, Leong, and Wu, Harry X. 2007. *The Making of China's Exchange Rate Policy: From Plan to WTO Entry*. Cheltenham, UK: Edward Elgar.

Lin, Karen Jinrong, Xiaoyan Lu, Junsheng Zhang, and Ying Zheng. 2020. "State-Owned Enterprises in China: A Review of 40 Years of Research and Practice." *China Journal of Accounting Research* 13 (1): 31–55.

Lin, Li-Wen, and Curtis Milhaupt. 2017. "Bonded to the State: A Network Perspective on China's Corporate Debt Market." *Journal of Financial Regulation* 3 (1): 1–39.

Lin, Nan. 2011. "Capitalism in China: A Centrally Managed Capitalism (CMC) and Its Future." *Management and Organization Review* 7 (1): 63–96.

Ling Zhijun, Ma Ke, and Deng Ke. 2003. "Fu zongli shiqi: 'Zhu laoban' shi yige zhenzheng dong jingji de ren" [The vice premierhood: "Boss Zhu" is one that really knows about economy]. *Nanfang zhoumo*, March 8, 2003.

Liu Daneng. 1996. "Zhengcexing yinhang: Yunying zhongde wenti ji daojie" [Policy banks: Operational problems and solutions]. *Caijin kexue*, no. 2, 30–31.

Liu Liang. 2006. "Huijin: Jinrong hangmu chuhai" [Huijin: The financial aircraft carrier sets sail]. *Zhongguo jingji shibao*, June 8, 2006.

Liu Mingkang. 2004. "The State-Owned Banks in China: Reform, Corporate Governance and Prospect." Speech at the Beijing International Financial Forum, Beijing, May 20, 2004. http://finance.sina.com.cn/g/20040520/0926769542.shtml.

Liu, Tao, and Li Sun. 2016. "Pension Reform in China." *Journal of Aging & Social Policy* 28 (1): 15–28.

Liu Xiaowu. 2005. "Gonghang zhuzi fang'an pilu Caizhengbu Yanghang ge chi 50% guquan" [ICBC's recapitalisation plan revealed, MOF and the PBC both holding 50% equity]. *Zhongguo jingying bao*, April 25, 2005.

Liu Xin. 2009. "Ma Guangyuan: Guoqi zhi shangjiao 10% lirun shi bushi tai shao" [Ma Guangyuan: Is 10% dividends payment too little?]. *Nanfang renwu zhoukan*, May 27, 2009.

Liu Yanxun. 2010. "Minying ziben xiayibu" [Private capital's next step]. *Zhongguo xinwen zhoukan*, no. 10. Sina.com, June 3, 2010. http://news.sina.com.cn/c/sd/2010-06-03/103320403301_4.shtml.

Liu Yonghao. 2016. "Liu Yonghao pilu Minsheng yinhang chengli shimo, ceng gei Zhu Rongji zongli xiexin" [Liu Yonghao reveals the founding of the Minsheng Bank, wrote to Premier Zhu Rongji]. Sina.com, December 10, 2016. http://finance.sina.com.cn/meeting/2016-12-10/doc-ifxypipt0797355.shtml.

Lockett, Hudson, and Yu Sun. 2019. "China's Special-Purpose Bonds Fall Short of Beijing's Ambitions." *Financial Times*, November 26, 2019.

Loyalka, Michelle Dammon. 2012. "Chinese Labor, Cheap No More." *New York Times*, February 17, 2012.

Ma, Guonan, and James Laurenceson. 2019. "China's Debt Challenge: Stylized Facts, Drivers and Policy Implications." *Singapore Economic Review* 64 (4): 815–37.

Ma, Jingjing. 2021. "Local Govts Issue $264.5 Billion Bonds to Support Economy." *Global Times*, May 10, 2021.

Ma, Jun. 1997. *Intergovernmental Relations and Economic Management in China.* London: St. Martin's.

MacFarquhar, Roderick. 1981. *Origins of the Cultural Revolution.* Cambridge, MA: Oelgeschlager, Gunn & Hain.

Magnus, George. 2018. *Red Flags: Why Xi's China Is in Jeopardy.* New Haven, CT: Yale University Press.

Mahoney, James, and Kathleen Thelen. 2010. "A Theory of Gradual Institutional Change." In *Explaining Institutional Change: Ambiguity, Agency, and Power*, edited by James Mahoney and Kathleen Thelen, 1–37. Cambridge: Cambridge University Press.

Matacic, Catherine. 2014. "Economists: China Faces Rough Road to Reform in 2014." *China Business Review*, January 9, 2014.

Mattoo, Aaditya. 2004. "The Services Dimension of China's Accession to the WTO." In *China and the WTO: Accession, Policy Reform, and Poverty Reduction*, edited by Deepak Bhattasali, Shantong Li, and Will Martin, 117–40. Washington, DC: World Bank Group.

McGregor, Richard. 2019. *Xi Jingping: The Backlash*. Sydney: Penguin Books.

McKinnon, Ronald I. 1973. *Money and Capital in Economic Development*. Washington, DC: Brookings Institution.

McKinsey Global Institute. 2017. *Digital China: Powering the Economy to Global Competitiveness*. December 2017.

McMahon, Dinny. 2018. *China's Great Wall of Debt: Shadow Banks, Ghost Cities, Massive Loans, and the End of the Chinese Miracle*. Boston: Houghton Mifflin.

McNally, Christopher. 2012. "Sino-capitalism: China's Reemergence and the International Political Economy." *World Politics* 64 (4): 741–76.

Mei Xinyu. 2010. "Chaoyue baoba" [Beyond ensuring 8 percent]. *Nanfeng chuang*, no. 21, 37–39. http://wxt.1xuezhe.com/qk/art/443692?code=F13&pageIndex=0&pdcyear=2011&pdcno=01&dbcode=1&flag=1.

Meng Sishuo. 2011. "Guoqi lirun chuangxigao, huikui shehui husheng zaiqi" [SOE profits record high, calls again for returning to society]. *China Business News*, January 18, 2011. http://www.yicai.com/news/2011/01/657962.html.

Miao Yan, and Li Dandan. 2008. "Yanghang qiantou, jinrong xietiao jianguan yi buji lianxi huiyi chuchang" [The PBC taking the leading role, financial regulation takes the form of interministerial joint meeting]. *Shanghai zhengquan bao*, August 15, 2008.

Millar, Ross, Weiyan Jian, Russel Mannion, and Robin Miller. 2016. "Healthcare Reform in China: Making Sense of a Policy Experiment?" *Journal of Health Organization and Management* 30 (3): 324–30.

Ministry of Human Resources and Social Security. 2010. "Zhongguo jiuye yingdui guoji jinrong weiji fanglue xilie yanjiu baogao" [China's employment strategy in response to the global financial crisis series report]. *Zhongguo jiuye*, no. 1, 12–18. https://www.ixueshu.com/document/a0d7bb67273064f3eff7448b89565d2d318947a18e7f9386.html.

Minzner, Carl. 2018. *End of an Era: How China's Authoritarian Revival Is Undermining Its Rise*. Oxford: Oxford University Press.

Miyashita, Tadao. 1966. *The Currency and Financial System of Mainland China*. Translated by J. R. McEwen. Seattle: University of Washington Press.

Mo, YK. 1999. "A Review of Recent Banking Reform in China." Bank for International Settlements. https://www.bis.org/publ/plcy07d.pdf.

Modigliani, Franco, and Shi Larry Cao. 2004. "The Chinese Saving Puzzle and the Life Cycle Hypothesis." *Journal of Economic Literature* 42:145–70.

Moe, Terry M. 2015. "Vested Interests and Political Institutions." *Political Science Quarterly* 130 (2): 277–318.

Moody's. 2017. *China Shadow Banking Monitor*, quarter 4, November 6, 2017.

——. 2020. "Chinese Shadow Banking Activity Grows for First Time since 2017 as Economy-Wide Leverage rises." June 24, 2020.

Moore, Nicholas. 2018. "China Sees First 6-Month Current Account Deficit since 1998." CGTN, August 7, 2018.

Mullen, Jethro, and Andrew Stevens. 2016. "Billionaire: Chinese Real Estate Is 'Biggest Bubble in History.'" CNN, September 29, 2016. https://money.cnn.com/2016/09/28/investing/china-wang-jianlin-real-estate-bubble/.

Murphy, David. 2003. "Bank on Zhou." *Far Eastern Economic Review* 166 (1): 30.

Murtaza, Syed, and Xiaoling Shi. 2012. *Transforming China's Growth Model: The Urgency of Financial Reform*. Beijing: China Institute for Reform and Development.

Nabar, Malhar S. 2011. "Targets, Interest Rates, and Household Saving in Urban China." IMF Working Paper no. 11/223, October 1, 2011.

Nathan, Andrew J. 2003. "Authoritarian Resilience." *Journal of Democracy* 14 (1): 6–17.

Nathan, Andrew J., and Tianjian Shi. 1996. "Left and Right with Chinese Characteristics: Issues and Alignments in Deng Xiaoping's China." *World Politics* 48 (July): 522–50.

National Bureau of Statistics of China. 2021. "2020 nian jumin shouru he xiaofei zhichu qingkuang" [Residents' income and expenditure in 2020]. January 18, 2021. http://www.stats.gov.cn/tjsj/zxfb/202101/t20210118_1812425.html.

Naughton, Barry. 1992. "Hierarchy and the Bargaining Economy: Government and Enterprise in the Reform Process." In *Bureaucracy, Politics, and Decision Making in Post-Mao China*, edited by Kenneth Lieberthal and David M. Lampton, 245–82. Berkeley: University of California Press.

——. 1995. *Growing Out of the Plan: Chinese Economic Reform, 1978–1993*. New York: Cambridge University Press.

——. 2002. "Zhurongji: The Twilight of a Brilliant Career." *China Leadership Monitor*, no. 1.

——. 2004. "Hunkering Down: The Wen Jiabao Administration and Macroeconomic Recontrol." *China Leadership Monitor*, no. 11.

——. 2005a. "The New Common Economic Program: China's Eleventh Five Year Plan and What It Means." *China Leadership Monitor*, no. 16.

——. 2005b. "SASAC Rising." *China Leadership Monitor*, no. 15.

——. 2006. "Waves of Criticism: Debates over Bank Sales to Foreigners and Neo-liberal Economic Policy." *China Leadership Monitor*, no. 17.

——. 2009a. "China's Emergence from Economic Crisis." *China Leadership Monitor*, no. 29.

——. 2009b. "Understanding the Chinese Stimulus Package." *China Leadership Monitor*, no. 28.

——. 2016. "Restructuring and Reform: China 2016." In *Structural Change in China: Implications for Australia*, edited by Iris Day and John Simon, 55–78. Sydney: Reserve Bank of Australia.

——. 2017. "Is China Socialist?" *Journal of Economic Perspectives* 31:3–24.

——. 2018a. *The Chinese Economy: Adaptation and Growth*. 2nd ed. Cambridge, MA: MIT Press.

——. 2018b. "State Enterprise Reform Today." In *China's Forty Years of Reform and Development*, edited by Ross Garnaut, Liang Song, and Cai Fang, 375–94. Canberra: ANU Press.

NDRC (National Development and Reform Commission). 2008. "Mingque renwu zhua luoshi, kuoda neixu cucengzheng" [Clarify responsibility and grasp implementation; expand domestic demand and foster growth]. November 10, 2008. http://www.ndrc.gov.cn/xwfb/t20081110_245192.htm.

North, Douglas. 1990. *Institutions, Institutional Change and Economic Performance*. New York: Cambridge University Press.

O'Brien, Kevin J., and Yanhua Deng. 2017. "Preventing Protest One Person at a Time: Psychological Coercion and Relational Repression in China." *China Review* 17 (2): 179–201.

O'Donnell, Guillermo A. 1979. *Modernization and Bureaucratic-Authoritarianism: Studies in South American Politics*. Berkeley: Institute of International Studies, University of California.

OECD (Organisation for Economic Co-operation and Development). 2002. *China in the World Economy: The Domestic Policy Challenges*. Geneva: OECD.

——. 2005. *Economic Survey of China*. Geneva: OECD.

Oi, Jean C. 1999. *Rural China Takes Off: Institutional Foundations of Economic Reform.* Berkeley: University of California Press.

Okazaki, Kumiko. 2007. "Banking System Reform in China: The Challenges of Moving toward a Market-Oriented Economy." RAND Corporation. https://www.rand.org/pubs/occasional_papers/OP194.html.

Olsen, Johan P. 2009. "Change and Continuity: An Institutional Approach to Institutions of Democratic Government." *European Political Science Review* 1:3–32.

Orlik, Thomas. 2020. *China: The Bubble That Never Pops.* New York: Oxford University Press.

Orsmond, David. 2019. "China's Economic Choices." Lowy Institute, December 17, 2019.

Parton, Charles. 2018. "The Fourth Weapon: Social Credit Is Just One Part of the New State Control." *Spectator*, November 17, 2018.

Paulson, Henry M., Jr. 2009. "Wang Qishan." *Time*, April 30, 2009. http://content.time.com/time/specials/packages/article/0,28804,1894410_1893847_1893846,00.html.

PBC (People's Bank of China). 1996. "Zhuanzhi zhong de guoyou qiye yinhang zhaiquan wenti de diaocha baogao" [A research report on rights of banks as creditors in the transition of state-owned enterprises]. *Jingji yanjiu cankao* 63:17–22.

——. 2012. "Yingzi yinhang tixi de neihan yu waiyan" [The definition and scope of the shadow banking system]. *Jinrong fazhan pinglun*, no. 8, 50–56.

——. 2013. *Financial Stability Report 2013.*

——. 2014. *Report on Financial Regulation in China 2014.*

——. 2017. *Monetary Policy Implementation Report*, quarter 4.

——. 2019. *China Financial Stability Report 2019.* November 25, 2019.

——. 2020. *Monetary Policy Implementation Report*, quarter 3.

——. 2021. "Assets and Liabilities Statistics of Financial Institutions (for 2020)." http://www.pbc.gov.cn/diaochatongjisi/116219/116319/3959050/3959049/index.html.

Pearson, Margaret M. 2005. "The Business of Governing Business in China: Institutions and Norms of the Emerging Regulatory State." *World Politics* 57 (2): 296–322.

——. 2007. "Governing the Chinese Economy: Regulatory Reform in the Service of the State." *Public Administration Review* 67 (4): 718–30.

Pei, Minxin. 1998. "The Political Economy of Banking Reforms in China, 1993–1997." *Journal of Contemporary China* 7 (18): 321–50.

——. 2012. "China's Politics of the Economically Possible." *Project Syndicate*, March 16, 2012. https://www.project-syndicate.org/commentary/china-s-politics-of-the-economically-possible?barrier=accessreg.

People's Daily. 2009. "10 Major Industries to Become China's Economic Engines." February 27, 2009. http://en.people.cn/90001/90778/90857/90862/6602754.html.

Peters, B. Guy, Jon Pierrea, and Desmond S. King. 2005. "The Politics of Path Dependency: Political Conflict in Historical Institutionalism." *Journal of Politics* 67:1275–300.

Pettis, Michael. 2013. *Avoiding the Fall: China's Economic Restructuring.* Washington, DC: Carnegie Endowment for International Peace.

Pierson, Paul. 2000. "The Limits of Design: Explaining Institutional Origins and Design." *Governance* 13:475–99.

Plantin, Guillaume. 2015. "Shadow Banking and Bank Capital Regulation." *Review of Financial Studies* 28 (1): 146–75.

Prasad, Eswar S. 2007. *Is the Chinese Growth Miracle Built to Last?* Ithaca, NY: Cornell University Press.

PricewaterhouseCoopers. 2002. "Quanguo Jinrong Gongzuo Huiyi zai Jing zhaokai" [The National Financial Work Conference was held in Beijing]. *People's Daily*, February 8, 2002.

———. 2015. *Banking and Finance in China: The Outlook for 2015*.

———. 2017. *eCommerce in China—the Future Is Already Here*. https://www.pwccn. com/en/retail-and-consumer/publications/total-retail-2017-china/total-retail-survey-2017-china-cut.pdf.

Rabinovitch, Simon. 2013. "China Averts Local Government Defaults." *Financial Times*, January 29, 2013.

Rajan, Raghuram G. 2010. *Fault Lines: How Hidden Fractures Still Threaten the World Economy*. Princeton, NJ: Princeton University Press.

Ramo, Joshua Cooper. 2004. *The Beijing Consensus*. London: Foreign Policy Centre.

Rana, Shruti. 2012. "The Emergence of the New Chinese Banking System: Implications for Global Politics and the Future of Financial Reform." *Maryland Journal of International Law* 27:215–34.

Rauhala, Emily. 2016. "How a Huge Chinese 'Ponzi Scheme' Lured Investors." *Washington Post*, February 8, 2016.

Reinhart, Carmen M., Jacob F. Kirkegaard, and M. Belen Sbrancia. 2011. "Financial Repression Redux." *IMF Finance and Development* 48 (1): 22–26.

Ren, Daniel, and Ethan Paul. 2020. "China's Corporate Bonds Market Is Heading for Another Year of Record Defaults, Raises Concerns about Rise in Irregularities." *South China Morning Post*, December 3, 2020.

Ren Hongbing. 2017. "Zhongxiao qiye rongzi ran, jiujing nan zai nali?" [Difficulties in SME financing: What are the exact reasons?] *Zhongguo zhengquan bao*, March 20, 2017.

Reserve Bank of Australia. 2018. *Financial Stability Review*, April 2018.

———. 2019. "Household Sector Risks in China." *Financial Stability Review*, October 2019.

Reuters. 2015. "China's Xi Says State Industry the Backbone of Economy Amid Reforms." July 18, 2015.

Reuters. 2019. "China's Debt Tops 300% of GDP, Now 15% of Global Total: IIF." July 18, 2019.

Riley, Charles. 2015. "China Devalues Yuan in Shocking Move." CNN, August 11, 2015. https://money.cnn.com/2015/08/11/investing/china-pboc-yuan-devalue-currency/index.html.

Roach, Stephen S. 2009. "A Wake-Up Call for the US and China: Stress Testing a Symbiotic Relationship." Hearing on "China's Role in the Origins of and Response to the Global Recession." Presented before the US-China Economic and Security Review Commission of the US Congress, Washington, DC, February 17, 2009.

———. 2011. "Myths Debunked: Why China Will Have a Soft Landing." Economy Watch, October 5, 2011. http://www.economywatch.com/economy-business-and-finance-news/myths-debunked-why-china-will-have-a-soft-landing-stephen-s-roach.05–10.html?page=full.

———. 2014. "China's Growth Puzzle." Project Syndicate, February 27, 2014. https:// www.project-syndicate.org/commentary/stephen-s--roach-says-that-china-s-economic-slowdown--unlike-that-in-other-emerging-countries--should-be-welcomed.

Saez, Lawrence. 2003. *Banking Reform in India and China*. London: Palgrave Macmillan.

Sahay, Ratna, Martin Cihak, Papa N'Diaye, Adolfo Barajas, Ran Bi, Diana Ayala, Yuan Gao, Annette Kyobe, Lam Nguyen, Christian Saborowski, Katsiaryna

Svirydzenka, and Seyed Reza Yousefi. 2015. "Rethinking Financial Deepening: Stability and Growth in Emerging Markets." IMF Discussion Note, May 2015.

Saich, Tony. 2001. "The Blind Man and the Elephant: Analysing the Local State in China." In *East Asian Capitalism: Conflicts and the Roots of Growth and Crisis*, edited by Luigi Tomba, 75–99. Milan: Annali della Fondazione Giangiacomo Feltrinelli.

SASAC (State Assets Supervision and Administration Commission). 2006. "Guanyu tuijin guoyou zibe tiaozheng he guoyou qiye chongzu de zhidao yijian" [The guiding opinion on promoting the adjustment of state-owned capital and the reorganization of state-owned enterprises]. December 18, 2006. http://finance.sina.com.cn/g/20061218/11133173443.shtml.

Scharpf, Fritz. 1997. *Games Real Actors Play: Actor-Centered Institutionalism in Policy Research: Theoretical Lenses on Public Policy*. Boulder, CO: Westview.

Schmidt, Vivien. 2008. "Discursive Institutionalism: The Explanatory Power of Ideas and Discourse." *Annual Review of Political Science* 11 (1): 303–26.

Scissors, Derek. 2014. "For Chinese Reform, It's Private Banks or Bust, Rate Liberalization Cannot Occur until There Is More Privatization in Banking." *Wall Street Journal*, March 17, 2014.

Shambaugh, David. 2000. *The Modern Chinese State*. Cambridge: Cambridge University Press.

——. 2008. *China's Communist Party: Atrophy and Adaptation*. Berkeley: University of California Press.

Shang Ming. 2000. *Xin Zhongguo jinrong 50 nian* [Fifty years of finance in New China]. Beijing: Zhongguo Jinrong Chubanshe.

Shaw, Edward S. 1973. *Financial Deepening in Economic Development*. New York: Oxford University Press.

Sheng, Andrew, and Ng Chow Soon. 2016. *Shadow Banking in China: An Opportunity for Financial Reform*. Hoboken, NJ: Wiley.

Shenzhen tequ bao. 2016. "Yu'ebao Users Exceed 260 Million." January 27, 2016.

Shi Chaoge. 2005. "Zhou Xiaochuan chonggou Zhongguo jinrong bantu, zhengjiu quanshang shuxie ziben shichang" [Zhou Xiaochuan reframes China's financial landscape, bailing out stock brokerages and infusing the capital market]. *Shanghai zhengquan bao*, November 5, 2005.

Shih, Victor. 2004. "Dealing with Non-performing Loans: Political Constraints and Financial Policies in China." *China Quarterly* 180:922–44.

——. 2007. "Partial Reform Equilibrium, Chinese Style: Political Incentives and Reform Stagnation in Chinese Financial Policies." *Comparative Political Studies* 40 (10): 1238–62.

——. 2008. *Factions and Finance in China: Elite Conflict and Inflation*. Cambridge: Cambridge University Press.

——. 2011. "'Goldilocks' Liberalization: The Uneven Path toward Interest Rate Reform in China." *Journal of East Asian Studies* 11 (3): 437–65.

——. 2019. "China's Credit Conundrum." *New Left Review* 115 (January/February): 59–74.

Shimek, Luke M., and Yi Wen. 2008. "Why Do Chinese Households Save So Much?" Federal Reserve Bank of St. Louis, *Economic Synopses*, no. 19. https://files.stlouisfed.org/files/htdocs/publications/es/08/ES0819.pdf.

Shirk, Susan. 1985. "The Politics of Industrial Reform," In *The Political Economy of Reform in Post-Mao China*, edited by Elizabeth J. Perry and Christine Wong, 195–222. Cambridge, MA: Harvard University Press.

——. 1992. "The Chinese Political System and the Political Strategy of Economic Reform." In *Bureaucracy, Politics, and Decision Making in Post-Mao China*, edited by Kenneth Lieberthal and David M. Lampton, 59–91. Berkeley: University of California Press.

——. 1993. *The Political Logic of Economic Reform in China*. Berkeley: University of California Press.

——. 1994. *How China Opened Its Door: The Political Success of the PRC's Foreign Trade and Investment Reforms*. Washington, DC: Brookings Institution.

——. 2017. "Trump and China: Getting to Yes with Beijing." *Foreign Affairs*, March/April 2017.

——. 2018. "China in Xi's 'New Era': The Return to Personalistic Rule." *Journal of Democracy* 29 (2): 22–36.

Simeon, Richard. 1976. "Studying Public Policy." *Canadian Journal of Political Science* 9 (4): 548–80.

Slater, Dan, and Erica Simmons. 2010. "Informative Regress: Critical Antecedents in Comparative Politics." *Comparative Political Studies* 43:886–917.

Soifer, Hillel David. 2012. "The Causal Logic of Critical Junctures." *Comparative Political Studies* 45:1572–97.

Somasundaram, Narayanan. 2020. "China Debt Fears Grow amid Wave of Corporate Defaults." *Nikkei Asia*, December 23, 2020.

Song, Zheng, and Wei Xiong. 2018. "Risks in China's Financial System." *Annual Review of Financial Economics* 10:261–86.

South China Morning Post. 2017. "Being Xi Jinping: The Difficult Art of Juggling Growth and Control after China's Communist Party Congress." October 10, 2017.

Southern Weekend. 2011. "Huan yige jiaodu kan jinnian xiabannian de jiuye wenti" [Employment in the latter half of the year from another perspective]. May 27, 2011.

State Council. 2008. "Zhongguo renmin yinhang zhuyao zhise, neishe jigou he renyuan bianzhi guiding" [Provisions of the PBC's major responsibilities, internal institutions and personnel scale]. August 14, 2008. http://www.gov.cn/gzdt/2008-08/14/content_1072077.htm.

——. 2015. "China Unveils Internet Plus Action Plan to Fuel Growth." July 4, 2015. http://english.gov.cn/policies/latest_releases/2015/07/04/content_281475140 165588.htm.

Steinmo, Sven, and Kathleen Thelen. 1992. "Historical Institutionalism in Comparative Politics." In *Structuring Politics: Historical Institutionalism in Comparative Analysis*, edited by Kathleen Thelen, Sven Steinmo, and Frank Longstreth, 1–33. Cambridge: Cambridge University Press.

Stiglitz, Joseph. 2010. *Free Fall: America, Free Markets, and the Sinking of the World Economy*. New York: W. W. Norton.

Stockhammer, Engelbert. 2015. "Rising Inequality as a Cause of the Present Crisis." *Cambridge Journal of Economics* 39:935–58.

Streeck, Wolfgang, and Kathleen Thelen. 2005. *Beyond Continuity: Institutional Change in Advanced Political Economies*. Oxford: Oxford University Press.

Su Manli. 2012. "Zhou Xiaochuan: Lilu shichanghua gaige daikuan xianxing" [Zhou Xiaochuan: Interest rate marketization should give priority to lending rates]. *Xin jing bao*, April 24, 2012.

Sun Jianfang, and Si Xi. 2009. "Jigou diaoyan xianshi 4 wanyi xindai zijin zheng liuru channeng guosheng hangye" [Institutional investigation suggests 4 trillion credits flowing into industries of overcapacities]. *Jingji guancha bao*, April 24, 2009.

Sun Shuangrui. 1996a. "Dui zhuanye yinhang shangyehua gaige ruogan wenti de tantao" [Issues concerning the commercialization of the specialized banks]. *Jingrong yanjiu*, no. 2, 22–25.

——. 1996b. "Dui zhuanye yinhang shangyehua gaige ruogan wenti de tantao" [Issues concerning the commercialization of the specialized banks]. *Caimao jingji*, no. 3, 8–9.

Szamosszegi, Andrew, and Cole Kyle. 2011. *An Analysis of State-Owned Enterprises and State Capitalism in China*. U.S.-China Economic and Security Review Commission.

Tai, Catherine. 2018. "China's Private Sector Is under Siege." *Diplomat*, December 22, 2018.

Tam, On-Kit. 1986. "Reform of China's Banking System." *World Economy* 9 (4): 427–40.

Tang, Frank. 2018. "China's Ailing Rust Belt Struggles to Shake Off Reliance on State Support." *South China Morning Post*, August 30, 2018.

Tang Gaohuai. 1996. "Dui woguo guoyou shangye yinhang jingying zhichan shouyi de fengxi" [An analysis of the return on assets in our country's state banks]. *Jingji yanjiu cankao* 16:11–13.

Tang Lin. 2017. "Difang zhengfu rongzi luanxiang mianmian guan" [The irregularities in local government financing]. *Zhongguo zhengquan bao*, July 20, 2017.

Tang Shengzhi. 2003. "Jinrong jianguan: Fen bi bufen yao hao" [Financial regulation: Split better than nonsplit]. *Jinrong shibao*, May 5, 2003.

——. 2020a. "China's P2P Purge Leaves Millions of Victims Out in the Cold, with Losses in the Billions, as Concerns of Social Unrest Swirl." *South China Morning Post*, December 29, 2020.

——. 2020b. "Is China Ripe for a Subprime Crisis? Regulator Sees Bank Property Loans as 'Biggest Grey Rhino Risk' for Financial System." *South China Morning Post*, December 1, 2020.

Tang Yuankai. 2003. "Central Bank to Focus on Policy." *Beijing Review* 46 (17): 32–37.

Teiwes, Frederick C. 1995. "The Paradoxical Post-Mao Transition: From Obeying the Leader to 'Normal Politics.'" *China Journal* 34:55–94.

Thelen, Kathleen. 2004. *How Institutions Evolve: The Political Economy of Skills in Germany, Britain, the United States and Japan*. Cambridge: Cambridge University Press.

Thelen, Kathleen, and James Conran. 2015. "Institutional Change." In *The Oxford Handbook of Historical Institutionalism*, edited by Orfeo Fioretos, Tulia G. Falleti, and Adam Sheingate, 51–71. Oxford: Oxford University Press.

Thomas, Stephen, and Chen Li. 2006. "Banking on Reform." *China Business Review*, May–June 2006.

Thun, Eric. 2004. "Industrial Policy, Chinese-Style: FDI, Regulation and Dreams of National Champions." *Journal of East Asian Studies* 4 (3): 453–89.

Thurbon, Elizabeth. 2016. *Developmental Mindset: The Revival of Financial Activism in South Korea*. Ithaca, NY: Cornell University Press.

Tobin, Damian. 2012. "The Anglo-Saxon Paradox: Corporate Governance Best Practice and the Reform Deficit in China's Banking Sector." *Journal of Chinese Economic and Business Studies* 10:147–68.

Tong, Pin, and Zhi-suo Ding. 2001. "The Commercial Banks' Liquidity Management in China." *China and World Economy* 9 (1): 22–36.

Tsai, Kellee S. 2002. *Back-Alley Banking: Private Entrepreneurs in China*. Ithaca, NY: Cornell University Press.

———. 2004. "Imperfect Substitutes: The Local Political Economy of Informal Finance and Microfinance in Rural China and India." *World Development* 32 (9): 1487–507.

———. 2006. "Adaptive Informal Institutions and Endogenous Institutional Change in China." *World Politics* 59:116–41.

———. 2007. *Capitalism without Democracy: The Private Sector in Contemporary China.* Ithaca, NY: Cornell University Press.

———. 2015. "The Political Economy of State Capitalism and Shadow Banking in China." *Issues and Studies* 51 (1): 55–97.

———. 2017. "When Shadow Banking Can Be Productive: Financing Small and Medium Enterprises in China." *Journal of Development Studies* 53 (12): 2005–28.

Tsai, Kellee S., and Barry Naughton, eds. 2015. *State Capitalism, Institutional Adaptation, and the Chinese Miracle.* New York: Cambridge University Press.

Tu, Lianting. 2016. "China Property Bubble Could Cause $600 Billion in Bad Debts." Bloomberg, October 7, 2016.

Tudor, Alison. 2010. "Agricultural Bank of China IPO Raises $US19.21bn." *Wall Street Journal*, July 7, 2010.

Turner, Adair, and Susan Lund. 2015. "The Debt Dilemma." *Project Syndicate*, April 17, 2015.

21st Century Business Herald. 2006. "Gonghang caiwu chongzu luomo" [ICBC's financial restructuring finished]. October 29, 2006.

Unger, Jonathan. 1996. *Chinese Nationalism.* London: Routledge.

———, ed. 2002. *The Nature of Chinese Politics: From Mao to Jiang.* New York: M. E. Sharpe.

Unirule Institute of Economics. 2016. *Guoyou qiye de xingzhi, biaoxian yu gaige baogao gengxin* [Update on the report of the nature, performance and reform of the SOEs]. Beijing, January 5, 2016. http://unirule.cloud/index.php?c=article&id=4017.

US Securities and Exchange Commission. n.d. "Ponzi Schemes." Accessed November 11, 2019. https://www.investor.gov/introduction-investing/investing-basics/glossary/ponzi-schemes.

Van der Zwan, Natascha. 2014. "Making Sense of Financialization." *Socio-Economic Review* 12 (1): 99–129.

Vermeiren, Mattias. 2012. "Challenging Global Neoliberalism? The Global Political Economy of China's Capital Controls." *Third World Quarterly* 33 (9): 1647–68.

———. 2013. "Foreign Exchange Accumulation and the Entrapment of Chinese Monetary Power: Towards a Balanced Growth Regime?" *New Political Economy* 18:680–714.

Wall Street Journal. 2015. "PBOC Official: Banks Should Hold Reserves on Yu'ebao Deposits." May 5, 2015.

Walter, Andrew. 2008. *Governing Finance: East Asia's Adoption of International Financial Standards.* Ithaca, NY: Cornell University Press.

———. 2019. *Emerging Countries in Global Financial Standard Setting: Explaining Relative Resilience and Its Implications.* Waterloo, ON: Centre for International Governance Innovation.

Walter, Carl E., and Fraser J. T. Howie. 2003. *Privatizing China: The Stock Markets and Their Role in Corporate Reform.* Singapore: Wiley.

———. 2011. *Red Capitalism: The Fragile Financial Foundation of China's Extraordinary Rise.* Singapore: Wiley.

Wang Baoan. 2013. "Shenhua jinrong tizhi gaige, wanshan gongsi zhili jiegou— Huijin gongsi chengli shizhounian huigu" [Deepening reform of financial system and improving corporate governance—a retrospect of Huijin's ten-year anniversary]. Ministry of Finance of the People's Republic of China, December 24, 2013. http://www.mof.gov.cn/zhengwuxinxi/caizhengxinwen/201312/t20131224_1028304.html.

Wang Fenglin. 1995. "Woguo jinrong tizhi gaige de fangxiang, nandian yu duice" [The direction, obstacles, and policy options in reforming our country's financial system]. *Jingji yanjiu cankao* 82 (4): 9–11.

Wang Huaqing. 2004. "Shangye yinhang fengxian kongzhi he yewu fazhan" [Risk control and business development of commercial banks]. *Jinrong yanjiu*, no. 3, 15–20.

Wang, Lixin, and Joseph Fewsmith. 1995. "Bulwark of the Planned Economy: The Structure and Role of the State Planning Commission." In *Decision Making in Deng's China: Perspectives from Insiders*, edited by Carol Lee Hamrin and Suisheng Zhao, 51–65. Armonk, NY: M. E. Sharpe.

Wang Ning. 2005. "Yinhangye jigou zongzichan yu zongfuzhai zengzhang yue 19%" [The growth of total assets and liabilities in the banking sector grows by approximately 19%]. *Zhongguo zhengquan bao*, October 26, 2005.

Wang, Orange. 2019. "Is China Losing Control over Its Economy after Baoshang Bank Failure?" *South China Morning Post*, July 31, 2019.

Wang Shuguang. 2003. "Zhongguo jingji zhuangui jincheng zhong de jinrong ziyouhua" [Financial liberalization in the process of economic transition in China]. *Jingji kexue* 3:3–5.

Wang, Tao, Donna Kwok, Harrison Hu, and Ning Zhang. 2014. "Why China Is Not Facing a Lehman Moment." *UBS Global Research—China Weekly Economic Focus*, March 2014.

Wang Tianyu. 2021. "PKU Economist: Increasing Household Income Key to Boosting China's Consumption." CGTN, March 23, 2021.

Ward, Benjamin. 1980. "The Chinese Approach to Economic Development." In *China's Development Experience in Comparative Perspective*, edited by Robert Dernberger, 91–119. Cambridge, MA: Harvard University Press.

Weinland, Don. 2017. "China's 'Bad Banks' Thrive as Alternative Lenders." *Financial Times*, April 4, 2017.

——. 2019. "China Local Governments Sound Alarm on Debt Obligations." *Financial Times*, September 5, 2019.

Weyland, Kurt. 2008. "Toward a New Theory of Institutional Change." *World Politics* 60 (2): 281–314.

Wheatley, Alan. 2008. "Turf Wars Hobble China's Financial Markets." Reuters, April 28, 2008.

White, Edward. 2018. "Chinese Shadow Banking Contraction Due to Moderate—Moody's." *Financial Times*, August 20, 2018.

Wildau, Gabriel. 2015. "Tencent Launches China's First Online-Only Bank." *Financial Times*, January 5, 2015.

——. 2018. "China Easing Threatens to Derail Debt-Cutting Efforts." *Financial Times*, August 1, 2018.

Wildau, Gabriel, and Yizhen Jia. 2017. "Chinese Lenders Lobby to Soften Shadow Bank Rules." *Financial Times*, December 14, 2017.

——. 2018. "China's State Enterprises Cut Debt as Private Groups Lever Up." *Financial Times*, June 7, 2018.

Wills, Ken. 2018. "Seeking Balance: China Strives to Adapt Social Protection to the Needs of a Market Economy." *IMF Finance and Development* 55 (4): 20–23.

Wolf, Martin. 2018. "The Chinese Economy Is Rebalancing, at Last." *Financial Times*, April 4, 2018.

——. 2019. "The Chinese Economy Is Stabilising." *Financial Times*, April 3, 2019.

Wong, Christine. 1991. "Central-Local Relations in an Era of Fiscal Decline." *China Quarterly* 128:691–715.

Wong, John. 2014. *China's Economy 2014/15: Reform and Rebalancing to Sustain Growth under the "New Normal."* EAI Background Brief. Singapore: East Asian Institute, National University of Singapore.

World Bank. 1996. *The Chinese Economy: Fighting Inflation, Deepening Reform.* Washington, DC: World Bank Group.

Worthley, John Abbort, and King K. Tsao. 1999. "Reinventing Governance in China: A Comparative Analysis." *Administration and Society* 31 (5): 571–87.

Wright, Logan, and Daniel Rosen. 2018. *Credit and Credibility: Risks to China's Economic Resilience.* Washington, DC: Center for Strategic and International Studies.

Wu, Harry X. 2018. "On the Sustainability of the People's Republic of China's Growth Model—a Productivity Perspective." In *Slowdown in the People's Republic of China: Structural Factors and the Implications for Asia*, edited by Justin Yifu Lin, Peter J. Morgan, and Guanghua Wan, 143–80. Tokyo: Asian Development Bank Institute.

Wu Jinglian. 1993. "Shichang jingji xingcheng de dangqian qingkuang he zhongqi qianjing" [The current situation of the formation of a market economy and medium-term prospects]. *Zhongyang dangxiao baogao xuan* 9:54–59.

——. 2009a. "Zhongguo jingji 60 nian" [The Chinese economy at 60]. *Caijing*, September 28, 2009.

——. 2009b. "Zhongguo jiujingji guangyou Kaiensi zhuyi duanqi tiaojie bugou" [Saving China's economy needs more than short-term Keynesian adjustment]. February 10, 2009. http://finance.ifeng.com/news/opinion/jjsp/20090210/ 361627. shtml.

Wu Jinglian, and Zhou Xiaochuan. 1999. *Gongsi zhili jiegou, zhaiwu chongzu he puochan chengxu: Chongwen 1994 nian Jinglun huiyi* [Corporate governance, debt restructure and bankruptcy procedures: Revisiting the 1994 Jinglun conference]. Beijing: Zhongyang Bianyi Chubanshe.

Wu Xia. 1995. "Guoyou yinhang kunjing fengxi" [An analysis of the difficulties of state banks]. *Jingji yanjiu cankao* 82:51–54.

Wu Xiaoling. 1992. *Zhongguo de jinrong shenhua yu jinrong gaige* [Financial deepening and reform in China]. Tianjin: Tianjin Renmin Chubanshe.

——. 1997. "Zhongguo jinrong tizhi gaige genzong yanjiu" [Tracking China's financial system reform]. *Gaige* 4:4–7.

——. 2015. *Zhongguo A gu shichang yichang bodong baogao* [Report on the abnormal fluctuations on China's A share market]. Beijing: Tsinghua PBC School of Finance.

Xi Jinping. 2017. "Full Text of Xi Jinping's Report at 19th CPC National Congress." Xinhuanet.com, October 18, 2017. http://news.xinhuanet.com/english/special/ 2017-11/03/c_136725942.htm.

Xia Ming. 2003. *Jinrong jianguan de lilun yu chuangxin* [Theories and innovation in financial regulation]. Beijing: Zhongguo Jinrong Chubanshe.

Xiao Fengjuan, and Donald Kimball. 2006. "Effectiveness and Effects of China's Capital Controls." In *WTO, China and the Asian Economies IV*, http://www.karyiu wong.com/confer/beijing06/papers/xiao-kimball.pdf.

Xie, Andy. 2013. "When the China Tide Goes Out." MarketWatch, June 27, 2013. https://www.marketwatch.com/story/when-the-china-tide-goes-out-andy-xie-2013-06-27.

Xie Changping. 2015. "Waixiangxing maoyi de liyi jiegou yu fazhan dongle" [The interest structure and dynamics of the externally oriented trade]. *Zhongguo qiyejia* 8 (4): 23–25.

Xie Ping. 2006. *Shangye yinhang yinjin zhanlue touzizhe fenxi* [Analysis on inviting strategic investors into commercial banks]. Beijing: China Society for Finance and Banking.

Xie Wei. 1994. "Woguo jinrong shichang de xianzhuang, wenti, duice" [The current situation and problems of China's financial markets and their solutions]. *Jingji lilun yu jingji guanli* 1:10–12.

Xing Shaowen. 2009. "2000 yi difangzhai yinren guanzhu: Xuduo difang zhengfu yi zhaitai gaozhu" [200 billion local debt attracts concerns: Many local governments are heavily indebted]. *Nan feng chuang*, March 17, 2009.

Xinhua. 2015. "China Issues Guideline to Deepen SOE Reforms." September 13, 2015.

——. 2019. "China to Expand Infrastructure Investment in 2019." March 5, 2019.

——. 2020. "China Utilizes over 500 Bln Yuan of Anti-virus Treasury Bonds by July-End: Minister." August 6, 2020.

——. 2021. "China Issues 4.55 Trln Yuan in Local Gov't Bonds in 2020." January 30, 2021.

Xu Ming. 2010. "Yangqi zhuye jizhongdu pingjun da 87.79 per cent" [Central SOEs' main business concentration reaches 87.79 percent]. Sina.com, August 13, 2010. http://finance.sina.com.cn/roll/20100813/13418477949.shtml.

Xu Xiaonian. 2010. "Kaiensi zhuyi haile Zhongguo" [Keynesianism harmed China]. 163.com, June 1, 2010. http://money.163.com/10/0601/15/683PGP5200254IFG.html.

Yan, Qingmin, and Jianhua Li. 2016. *Regulating China's Shadow Banks*. London: Routledge.

Yang, Dali. 2004. *Remaking the Chinese Leviathan: Market Transition and the Politics of Governance in China*. Stanford, CA: Stanford University Press.

Yang Fan, ed. 2001. *Yi min wei ben, guanzhu minsheng: Zhongguo xinshiji de qiantu yu xuanze* [Orientation of people and their welfare: China's future and choice in the new century]. Beijing: Shiyou Gongye Chubanshe.

Yang Jun. 2012. *Zhongguo waimao xinlun* [New introduction to China's foreign trade]. Xi'an: Shaanxi Renmin Chubanshe.

Yang Yi. 2009. "Guanyu Zhongguo nongye yinhang yinjin zhanlue touzizhe wenti de sikao" [Some thoughts on the issue of inviting strategic investors for the Agricultural Bank of China]. *Shidai jinrong* 386:29–31.

Yao, Kevin, and Koh Gui Qing. 2012. "China to Reform, Grow Economy, IMF Eyes Freer Yuan." Reuters, March 18, 2012.

Yao, Kevin, and Lusha Zhang. 2019. "China Slashes Banks' Reserve Requirements Again as Growth Slows." Reuters, January 4, 2019.

Ye Tan. 2009. *Na shenma zhengjiu Zhongguo jingji* [How to salvage the Chinese economy]. Beijing: CITIC.

Ye Yanfei. 2003. *The Way of Dealing with Non-Performing Loans and Its Effects on Macro-statistics in China*. Beijing: National Bureau of Statistics.

Yeung, Godfrey. 2009. "How Banks in China Make Lending Decisions." *Journal of Contemporary China* 18 (59): 285–302.

Yeung, Karen. 2021. "China Debt: Highly-Leveraged State Firms Could Threaten 'Efficient Growth,' Private Investment Post-pandemic." *South China Morning Post*, February 8, 2021.

Yu, Jie. 2018. "The Belt and Road Initiative: Domestic Interests, Bureaucratic Politics and the EU-China Relations." *Asia Europe Journal* 16:223–36.

Zhan Xiangyang. 2000. *Lun zhongguo buliang zhaiquan zhaiwu de huajie* [On the dissolution of bad bonds and bad debt obligations in China]. Beijing: Zhongguo Jinrong Chubanshe.

Zhang, Beidi. 2014. "Carl Walter on the Fragility in the Chinese Banking System." Cheung Kong Graduate School of Business, *Knowledge Newsletter*, April 15, 2014.

Zhang, Cathy. 2016. "Yuan Ends 2016 with Biggest Annual Loss since 1994." *South China Morning Post*, December 30, 2016.

Zhang Fucai, and Gao Lin. 2015. *Yingzi yinhang yu xiandai jinrong* [Shadow banks and modern finance]. Beijing: Shehui Kexue Chubanshe.

Zhang Jie. 2019. "HK Most-Expensive Housing Market in the World." *China Daily*, April 17, 2019.

Zhang, Joe. 2013. *Inside China's Shadow Banking: The Next Subprime Crisis*. Singapore: Enrich Professional.

Zhang, Longei, Ray Brooks, Ding Ding, Haiyan Ding, Hui He, Jing Lu, and Rui Mano. 2018. "China's High Savings: Drivers, Prospects and Policies." IMF Working Paper no. 18/277, December 11, 2018.

Zhang Ran. 2009. "Monetary Policy Should Be Fast and Heavy-Handed." *China Daily*, March 6, 2009.

Zhang Ruifan. 2003. "Caizheng zhengce zai yingdui yazhou jinrong weiji Zhong de hexin zuoyong" [The central role of fiscal policy in coping with the Asian Financial Crisis]. *Zhongguo zhengquan bao*, June 5, 2003.

Zhang Weiying. 2010. "Zhongguo buneng zai renyou Kaiensi zhuyi huyou le" [China should not be bamboozled by Keynesianism anymore]. Eeo.com.cn, November 30, 2010. http://www.eeo.com.cn/observer/gcj/2010/11/30/187760.shtml.

——. 2013. "Xiangxin guoqi daozhi guojin mintui" [Believing in the SOEs resulted in the advance of the state and retreat of the private sector]. ifeng.com, June 20, 2013. http://sd.ifeng.com/cj/jinrongjie/detail_2013_06/20/915187_0.shtml.

Zhang, Xiaobo, Jin Yang, and Shenglin Wang. 2011. "China Has Reached the Lewis Turning Point." *China Economic Review* 22 (4): 542–54.

Zhang, Yuan, Jianqi Chen, and Prins Wong. 2011. "Effect of Trade Unions on Industrial Labor Income in China." *Asian Politics & Policy* 3 (1): 95–114.

Zhang, Yuanyan, and Steven Barnett. 2014. "Fiscal Vulnerabilities and Risks from Local Government Finance in China." IMF Working Paper no. 14/4, January 2014.

Zhang Yuhe. 2016. "Chinese Banks to Pay Much Smaller Fees to Apple Pay Than US Counterparts." *Caixin*, February 22, 2016. http://english.caixin.com/2016-02-22/100911334.html.

Zhao Dingxin. 2002. "An Angle on Nationalism in China Today: Attitudes among Beijing Students after Belgrade 1999." *China Quarterly* 172:885–905.

Zhao, Suisheng. 1995. "The Structure of Authority and Decision-Making: A Theoretical Framework." In *Decision-Making in Deng's China: Perspectives from Insiders*, edited by Carol Lee Hamrin and Suisheng Zhao, 233–45. Armonk, NY: M. E. Sharpe.

——. 2004. *A Nation-State by Construction: Dynamics of Modern Chinese Nationalism*. Stanford, CA: Stanford University Press.

Zheng Yangpeng. 2019. "In a First, China Has More Companies on Fortune Global 500 List Than the US." *South China Morning Post*, July 22, 2019.

Zheng Yongnian, and Lance Gore. 2015. *China Entering the Xi Jinping Era*. London: Routledge.

Zhongguo zhengquan bao. 2005. "You zhuanjia dui guoyou yinhang xiyin waizi moshi biaoshi danyou" [Experts expressing concern of foreign participation in state-owned banks]. September 23, 2005.

Zhou Dongtao. 2010. "Basic Experience of China's Economic System Reform." In *Reforming China: Experiences and Lessions*, edited by Dongtao Zhou, 1–12. Beijing: Waiwen Chubanshe.

Zhou, Li, Hui Feng, and Xuan Dong. 2016. "From State Predation to Market Extraction: The Political Economy of China's Rural Finance, 1979–2012." *Modern China* 42 (6): 571–606.

Zhou Xiaochuan, ed. 1999. *Chongjian yu zaisheng: Huajie yinhang buliang zichan de guoji jingyan* [Restructuring and rejuvenating: International experiences of reducing nonperforming loans]. Beijing: Zhongguo Jinrong Chubanshe.

——. 2013a. "Roadmap for Financial Reform." *China Daily*, December 18, 2013.

——. 2013b. "Zhuanfang yanghang hangzhang Zhou Xiaochuan: Jieyi shihuo M2" [Exclusive interview with central bank governor Zhou Xiaochuan: Explaining M2]. Sohu.com, March 8, 2013. http://business.sohu.com/20130308/n368127293.shtml.

Zhou Xin. 2018. "Xi Jinping Tries to Give Private Business a 'Confidence Boost' as Economic Slowdown Bites." *South China Morning Post*, November 1, 2018.

Zhu Ciyun. 2017. "Zhongguo yingzi yinhang: Xingqi, benzhi, zhili yu jianguan chuangxin" [Shadow banking in China: Origin, nature, governance and regulatory innovation]. *Tsinghua faxue*, no. 6, 4–10.

Zhu Rongji. 1998. "Shenhua jinrong gaige; fangfan jinrong fengxian; kaichuang jinrong gongzuo xin jumian" [Deepening financial reform; prevent financial risks; create a new phase for financial work]. In *Xin shiqi jingji tizhi gaige zhongyao wenxian xuanbian* [A selection of important documents for economic structural reform in the new period], edited by the Document Research Center of the Chinese Communist Party Central Committee, 1468–86. Beijing: Zhongyang Wenxiang Chubanshe.

Zou Hengfu. 2009. "Zhang Weiying gaoxiao, kuanghou chedi maizang Kaiensi zhuyi" [Zhang Weiying joking, wildly calling for totally burying Keynesianism]. *Sina Blog*, February 24, 2009. http://blog.sina.com.cn/s/blog_4d6fb0f60100d1d8.html.

Zweig, David. 1998. *The Entrepreneurial State in China: Real Estate and Commerce Departments in Reform Era Tianjin*. New York: Routledge.

——. 2001. "China's Stalled 'Fifth Wave.'" *Asian Survey* 41 (2): 231–47.

Index

Page numbers followed by *fig* or *t* refer to figures and tables.

Lightning Source UK Ltd.
Milton Keynes UK
UKHW010150070722
405473UK00003B/70/J